D1046833

EMPIRE
BOOKS

MAILER
A BIOGRAPHY

by
Hilary Mills

EMPIRE BOOKS
NEW YORK

Published by EMPIRE BOOKS
527 Madison Avenue, New York, New York 10022

Distributed by Harper & Row Publishers, Inc.
Designed by Helen Barrow
Manufactured in the United States of America
Printed by R. R. Donnelley & Sons Company
Bound by R. R. Donnelley & Sons Company

FIRST EDITION

Library of Congress Cataloging in Publication Data

Mills, Hilary.
Mailer: a biography
Includes index.

1. Mailer, Norman—Biography. 2. Authors, American—20th century-Biography. I. Title.
PS3525.A4152Z78 1982 813'.52 [B] 82-70940
ISBN 0-88015-002-5

For Bob and for my family

Acknowledgments

I would like to thank Norman Mailer for agreeing to be interviewed by me for the *Saturday Review* in 1980, one of the factors that lead to the creation of this book.

In addition, I am grateful to the following people for their cooperation: Jack Henry Abbott, Anna Lou Aldrich, John W. Aldridge, Jay Presson Allen, Lewis Allen, Larry Alson, Louis Auchincloss, Theodore Amussen, James Baldwin, Richard Baron, Marvin Barrett, Anne Barry, John Morton Blum, Leo Braudy, Jimmy Breslin, Seymour Breslow, Bowden Broadwater, Chandler Brossard, Vance Bourjaily, Tina Bourjaily, Hortense Calisher, Saul Chaplin, Charles Conrad, Jr., John Crockett, Hope Hale Davis, Robert Gorham Davis, Midge Decter, Roger Donald, Roger Donoghue, E. L. Doctorow, Anne Edwards, Jason Epstein, Cynthia Fagen, Edwin Fancher, Buzz Farbar, Judy Feiffer, Clay Felker, Donald Fine, Joe Flaherty, Dudley Frasier, Stanley Geist, George Goethals, Dr. Robert Gilruth, Ralph Graves, Edward de Grazia, Germaine Greer, Thomas Griffith, Robert Gutwillig, Mrs. Francis Irby Gwaltney, Norman A. Hall, Pete Hamill, Thomas Hanrahan, Harold Hayes, Lillian Hellman, Rust Hills, Abbie Hoffman, Irving Howe, H. L. Humes, Peter Israel, Gloria Jones, Robert Joy, Howard Kaminsky, Harold Katz, Elaine Kaufman, Gene Kelly, Mickey Knox, William A. Koshland, Seymour Krim, Christopher Lehmann-Haupt, John Leonard, Robert Loomis, Henrique Lopez, Adeline Lubell, Peter Maas, Dwight Macdonald, Erroll McDonald, Robert Markel, Jean Malaquais, John Marquand, Jr., Sam Marx, Shelley Mason, Scott Meredith, Helen Meyer, Arthur Miller, Kate Millett, Walter Minton, Paul Montgomery, Willie Morris, Theodore Morrison, Frederic Morton, Jack Newfield, Tom O'Horgan, Jan Olympitis, Manoli Olympitis, Mike Pearl, D. A. Pennebaker, George Plimpton, Norman Podhoretz, Dotson Rader, Rosalind Roose, Barney Rosset, Norman Rosten, Katy Rothacker, Jerry Rubin, Tobias Schneebaum, Arthur Schlesinger, Jr., Charles Scribner, Jr., Irwin Shaw, Dr. Beatrice Silverman, Jonathan Silverman, William Sladen, Harriet Sohmers, Lyle Stuart, Rose Styron, William Styron, Horace Sutton, Jerry

Tallmer, Joseph B. Thomas, José Torres, Anthony Tuttle, Gore Vidal, Bill Ward, Richard Weinberg, Hannah Weinstein, Larry Weiss, Michael Weller, Leslie Aldridge Westoff, John Wilcock, Calder Willingham, Daniel Wolf.

I would also like to thank my researcher, Sarah Bahm, for her excellent work in the New York Public Library. And I would like to thank Cynthia Cook, Meredith Davis, Rosemary Ford, Jill Silberman and Cary Ryan for work beyond the call of duty.

Finally, and most important, I would like to thank my publisher and editor, Martin L. Gross. I will be forever grateful for his belief in me, his enduring patience, and his labors, without all of which this book would have been impossible.

Contents

MAILER
A BIOGRAPHY

• I •

THE PARADOX OF NORMAN MAILER

On the afternoon of Monday, January 18, 1982, two weeks before his fifty-ninth birthday, Norman Kingsley Mailer forged his way through a crowd of over one hundred reporters and spectators lining the corridor outside the thirteenth-floor courtroom in the Criminal Courts Building in downtown Manhattan. As television cameras and paparazzi pressed in on him, court officers cut a path through the insistent mob. Everyone wanted to question or at least steal a glimpse of the famed author.

Under his trench coat and dark-blue three-piece suit Mailer's girth was larger than it had been in recent years. He was no longer jogging every morning and had even discontinued his Saturday boxing ritual at the gym of his good friend, ex-light heavyweight champion José Torres. Mailer had just started drinking again after an abstinence of two years, and the extra pounds sat heavily on his short bull-like frame. His familiar Afro of unruly dark curls was now completely white and cut short. He looked more like a senior banker than the aging enfant terrible of American letters.

The inevitable entourage trailed behind Mailer as he made his way through the igniting flashbulbs into the packed courtroom. Among them was his sixth wife, thirty-three-year-old Norris Church, a statuesque auburn-haired beauty who carried herself with the wary pride of a lioness protecting her mate, and Jean Malaquais, the iconoclastic seventy-four-year-old French Marxist writer and teacher who had been Mailer's political mentor in the late forties and was now one of his oldest friends.

Mailer had come to testify on behalf of Jack Henry Abbott, the convict whom he had helped release from the Utah State Prison the previous June and who had subsequently stabbed and killed a young waiter, Richard Adan, on July 18, 1981. Abbott had begun writing to Mailer about prison violence in 1977 when he heard that the author was starting a book, *The Executioner's Song*, about Gary Gilmore, the first murderer to be executed in America in many years.

The letters so intrigued Mailer that he eventually showed them to his friend, Robert Silvers, editor of *The New York Review of Books*, who published a selection of them in the June 26, 1980, issue. Random House then offered to publish the letters in book form, and in early July 1981 *In the Belly of the Beast* was released to extraordinary critical acclaim. On the day that Abbott stabbed Richard Adan to death, Terrence Des Pres, in *The New York Times Book Review*, wrote that "out of nowhere comes an exceptional man with an exceptional literary gift."

By January the Abbott case had been headlined nationally and had led to intense speculation about Mailer's fascination with violence as well as public concern about the literary establishment's lionizing of a dangerous convict. Since the killing Mailer had remained silent except to say, "It's a tragedy all around." He had even avoided commenting the previous Friday, when Adan's father-in-law, Henry Howard, was ejected from the courtroom screaming, "You scum, Abbott, you useless scum . . ."

Mailer had been at the morning session of the trial, and by midday recess reporters were clamoring for word from him. He told them he would not comment until after his testimony that afternoon and left for lunch with his wife, Malaquais, photographer Jill Krementz, and actors Christopher Walken and Susan Sarandon, whom he had brought to the trial that morning.

When Mailer returned to the courtroom in the early afternoon, he took the stand and was sworn in at 3:50 P.M. His testimony was short, controlled, and to the point. Under questioning by Abbott's lawyer, Ivan S. Fisher, he recalled the start of his correspondence with the convict. "I received a letter from him, from a prisoner, and I receive many letters from prisoners, but this one caught my attention," Mailer told the court. "What it said was, 'Mr. Mailer, I hear you are writing a book about Gary Gilmore and violence. And I want to tell you that very few people know anything at all about violence in prisons. In fact, I would go so far as to say that even people who have been in jail for five years don't really understand the nature of the conditions of violence in prisons. So I don't know if you are interested or not in what I have to tell you about this. But if you are, I'd like to correspond with you.' So I wrote back and said, 'Well, it's true, I don't think I know a great deal about violence in prisons. . . .' "

Despite numerous objections by the prosecution, Mailer went on to testify that he met Abbott for the first time in 1979, when he visited Marion Federal Penitentiary to present the convict with one of the first printed copies of *The Executioner's Song*, a book Mailer characterized as a "true life novel" and which subsequently won the 1980 Pulitzer Prize for fiction. The guards at Marion would not let Abbott have the book, Mailer told the full courtroom.

The day Abbott was released from prison in Utah, June 5, 1981, Mailer picked him up at JFK Airport and brought him back to his home in Brooklyn Heights, where Abbott stayed briefly before going on to a halfway house on the Bowery. From then until July, when Mailer and his family left for Provincetown, Massachusetts, for the summer, he saw Abbott on the average of two to three times a week. Mailer told the court that Abbott had also come up to Provincetown in early July for a three-day visit, and when questioned, added that five of his eight children were there at the time: two of his daughters, one twenty-two and the other nineteen, and his three sons, aged seventeen, fifteen and three and a half.

Mailer admitted there had been some discussion in Provincetown of Abbott's emotional state. "He hated the halfway house," Mailer told the court. "He hated being situated on the Bowery because he felt it was full of provocation and humiliation and tension for him. It was violence all the time. . . . I might almost say he had a dream, of being able to live somewhere in the country in a quiet place far from everything. And naturally we began to talk more and more about Maine, which I know fairly well. . . . He might be able to cool out there." After a few more questions Mailer was dismissed.

When the afternoon session broke up at 4:30 P.M., thirty-five reporters were waiting for Mailer in the corridor. Someone suggested that an impromptu news conference was in order; it could be staged in the ground-floor newsroom rather than in the hallway. Surrounded by demanding journalists, Mailer made his way to the elevator and down to the newsroom. The moment he crossed the threshold, several microphones were thrust in his face. As questions were thrown at him at a furious pace, Mailer gravitated to a corner of the small back room, where he was surrounded by reporters standing and kneeling on desks. With his wife seated at his side and the lights of the television cameras assaulting his eyes, which were still recovering from a retina operation, what Mailer has called his "slumbering Beast" rose from beneath the conservative suit to do battle with the press.

"It was like an accident waiting to happen," says Thomas Hanrahan of the New York *Daily News*. "The press was a surrogate for the public, whose feelings about Mailer's role in the case were highly negative and suspicious and curious. Everyone's back was up right away."

"I've been working in the city for twenty-five years," says Paul Montgomery of *The New York Times*, "and that was the worst New York press gang bang I'd ever seen. Everybody went crazy at once, pushing forward."

As the hostile questions continued, Mailer's transformation from wordly author to aroused combatant was complete. Shifting from foot to foot like a boxer against the ropes, he began answering in the mean southern accent he had adopted in the army during World War II, a voice reminiscent of Rod Steiger's sheriff in *In the Heat of the Night*. As in the past, the emergence of his southern inflection presaged an explosion of the Mailer temper.

"I certainly have the strongest feelings and hopes that Abbott will not get the maximum sentence," Mailer began edgily. "Abbott is a very complex man with great gifts. He kept those gifts together under the most difficult circumstances. Prison tends to flatten artists. . . . Paranoia is an unhealthy stimulus for a writer. . . . It's far too easy to send him away forever."

Mailer began to talk about the law-and-order mood in the country, projecting his own sense of immediate oppression by the press into a larger framework, moving from his own subjective attitude to the universal, a technique he has successfully used throughout his life. "It's too easy for people to say they ought to put this guy in jail and throw away the key," Mailer told the reporters. "Jack Abbott didn't benefit from this. The only people who have gotten anything out of this whole mess are the ones who are calling for more law and order, and more law and order means moving this country toward a fascist state."

Mailer's use of the word *fascist* heated up the situation rapidly. In response to a question about his own culpability Mailer barked, "If you want my blood, you can't have it—but you can have my psychic blood if you want it. It's obviously something Abbott's friends are going to have to live with for the rest of their lives." Mailer went on to talk about the "hideous prison system" in this country and reiterated that while he thought Abbott should go to jail, he hoped that he did not get a major sentence "because it would destroy him. Adan has already been destroyed. At least let Abbott become a writer. . . . Something like a middle sentence of ten years or so."

At the suggestion of leniency the press pounced on Mailer. "What about the retribution of the family?"

"The family of the victim," Mailer railed back at them, "doesn't have the right to demand blood atonement of a criminal."

The atmosphere was now tense, and Mailer's "antitotalitarian" antennae were alerted. When one reporter yelled, "Wasn't it a gamble letting Abbott out?" Mailer compared gambling with Abbott's freedom to the larger threat of a nuclear war, flailing around desperately for a larger ideological underpinning for his argument. "To save this nation's honor, we say we are willing to gamble with nuclear weapons. I'm willing to gamble with a portion of society to save this man's talent," he angrily burst out. "I am saying that culture is worth a little risk. That's what I've been saying over and over for thirty years."

Sensing that Mailer was putting writers—and specifically himself—above the law, the press reacted strongly. Mike Pearl of the *New York Post* asked him who he was willing to see sacrificed. Waiters? Cubans?

"That's when the lever flipped," says reporter Thomas Hanrahan. Mailer began losing control and attacked his assailant directly. "What are you all feeling so righteous about, may I ask?" he yelled at Pearl.

Communication had all but deteriorated when Mailer tried to bring the discussion back on track. "One way or another, and I don't know how, I should have been doing more with Abbott," he answered another reporter, his southern voice still coming fast, loud, and angry. "I didn't realize the depth of the problem. It's not like I didn't know anything about prisons or prisoners. I knew I had a tough scene on my hands. I didn't read Abbott well enough when he got out, in the sense that he was such a gentleman and we got along so well that I didn't pay attention to the little warnings he gave me in a quiet little voice about how that halfway house was gettin' him ready to blow . . . . You could throw fifty psychiatrists at Jack Abbott and it wouldn't do any good at all. Jack Abbott and I are cousins in that respect."

Cynthia Fagen of the *New York Post* asked him if the killing hadn't shaken his belief in Abbott. Mailer wheeled around to his left to face her where she was kneeling on a desk. "If it hadn't shaken my belief, I'd be a little nuts," he fumed. Then he added: "Look at the hate in your eyes!" and asked her who she was. When she told him she worked for the *New York Post*, Mailer accused the paper of publishing "lying headlines," citing a crime story the paper had recently run. He then attacked the *Post* for practicing "scumbag journalism." Fagan asked him if he was calling her a scumbag. According to *Times* reporter Paul Montgomery, Mailer repeated the phrase "scumbag journalism."

Hanrahan then lost his temper and called out that what Mailer was doing was neo-Nixonian. "You don't want to answer her question, so you attack her," he yelled at Mailer. "And I believe in law and order, and I don't think Abbott should get off so he can kill somebody else. And I'm not a Nazi. You are full of shit."

Mailer yelled back at him. "*You* are full of shit. Fuck off. No more questions." The press conference was called to an abrupt halt.

The following day, in a story by Cynthia Fagen and Mike Pearl, the *New York Post* claimed that Mailer had called a female reporter a "scumbag." The story's headline read, "Mailer: I Would Risk Freeing Killer!" then continued: "Mailer stunned reporters by saying he had little sympathy for victims' families demanding an eye for an eye." Finally the paper said: "There was some speculation that Walken might be considered for a part if a movie were ever made and Mailer ever wrote the script."

Two days later Mailer announced his intention to sue the *Post* for defamation, demanding $2,000,000 in compensatory damages and $5,000,000 in punitive damages. His complaint focused on the Pearl-Fagen story plus a follow-up article and letters based on the original piece. He claimed that he had never stated that Abbott should go free; that he never called a female reporter a scumbag; that the wrong inference was drawn from his comment on blood atonement; and that he had vehemently denied to the *Post* reporters that he had any plans to write about Abbott's life.

On the evening of January 18, the television network news shows carried Mailer's combative image across the country. "He wasn't very proud of himself," says Jean Malaquais, who had witnessed the event, "because he lost his temper and let himself be manipulated by the media. They go after him because he is—though not now so much as he used to be—the battling kind. He trades punches, and they just love it, because it's a show. That's his idiosyncrasy. In the old days he used to like this kind of clashing swords with the press."

"Norman can't leave the camera," adds Jason Epstein, editorial director of Random House and publisher of Abbott's prison letters. "There are other ways to express your solidarity: by visiting Abbott in jail or whatever. But Norman likes to be where that kind of action is. He likes to be on stage. He's a personage, always attracting attention. Somehow that's his natural state. You wouldn't say a herring likes to be in the water, that's where he is. The stage is where Mailer is."

❦

In the thirty-five years since the publication of *The Naked and the Dead*, Mailer's exploits have placed him in the center of many a drama. He was, in fact, expected on another stage that evening, shortly after his news conference. This time it was at the Young Men's Hebrew Association on Ninety-second Street in Manhattan, where he was scheduled to read from his work in progress, the long-awaited Egyptian novel.

At 7:45 P.M. Mailer arrived in the backstage greenroom after having stopped off at the Irish Embassy to say goodbye to two friends leaving for Ireland. If Mailer's angry southern accent had dominated the stormy press conference, there would now be traces of his Irish brogue. By the time Mailer appeared at the Y, it was a packed house; some nine hundred people had found seats in the auditorium.

The spectators had arrived at the arena for blood sport, just as twenty-one years earlier a similar-sized crowd had jammed the same auditorium to witness Mailer's behavior at a reading while he was involved in yet another trial at the Criminal Courts Building. In that one he was the defendant, on trial for the stabbing of his second wife, Adele. That evening Mailer had given the spectators their anticipated show. The curtain had been rung down halfway through his performance because the author had recited an obscene poem. This night would be different.

New York Times critic John Leonard, who was to introduce Mailer, was in the greenroom when the author arrived in the same dark three-piece suit he had worn that afternoon. Leonard had not yet learned of the press conference, but Mailer brought it up himself, claiming it had been "rough." "I had no details on the press conference until I read the papers the following morning," Leonard recalls. "Considering that, Mailer was remarkably under control that night at the Y. He's a good performer, and his manner didn't seem peculiar. He was even offered a drink and refused it." At 8:00 P.M. Leonard introduced Mailer on stage, joking that he had been waiting for Mailer's Egyptian novel since "Trotsky was axed by the maligned dwarfs." The critic added: "I expect him to put together Marx and Freud and Dostoyevsky, and I wish him a bundle of petro dollars." There was laughter.

Many in the audience knew how apt his comments were, for ever since 1959, after the critical failures of his second and third novels, *Barbary Shore* and *The Deer Park*, Mailer has been promising his readers a big novel, one, he boasted, which "Dostoyevsky and Marx; Joyce and Freud; Stendhal, Tolstoy, Proust and Spengler; Faulkner, and even old moldering Hemingway might come to read, for it would carry what they had to tell another part of the way."

Now, twenty-five books after he was heralded as the major young novelist of the postwar generation for his World War II work, *The Naked and the Dead*, Mailer's ambition to find an enduring place in the pantheon of novelists is still burning. His admirers say he has long since done so with his fourth novel, *An American Dream*, his fifth novel, *Why Are We in Vietnam?*, and his Pulitzer Prize-winning book, *The Executioner's Song*. But his critics—and even some of his most ardent followers—insist he has yet to produce a great novel commensurate with his talent.

Mailer believes the Egyptian novel, entitled *Ancient Evenings*, is that book. He plans the novel as the first 360,000-word volume of a massive trilogy; the second part will take place in the future and the third part in the present, unless Mailer decides to change the sequence. Set during the decadent reign of Ramses IX in 1130 B.C., the story is told mainly from the viewpoint of Menenhetet I, who has been reincarnated in four lives. The novel is also narrated, in part, by his great-grandson, a brilliant six-year-old boy, Menenhetet II, who, as Mailer has said, "has the sensibility of Marcel Proust at age thirteen. I wouldn't claim for him more than that, but that much sensibility he has."

Mailer worked on *Ancient Evenings* on and off for over ten years until he completed it in the summer of 1982. "I have given up the Egyptian novel a number of times," Mailer explained during the writing of his manuscript. "I have written *Marilyn;* I have written *The Fight;* I did a book on Henry Miller, *Genius and Lust;* and I did *The Executioner's Song* during this period, plus a number of short stories, and the new book on Marilyn. So there have been six or eight interruptions to the writing of it. But this Egyptian novel is nicer to me than any of my wives have been. I leave it for two years and I come back and it says: 'Oh, you look tired. You've been away. Let me wash your feet.' I have been able to go back to it without trouble every time so far. But the novel is very much like that mythological creature, a good woman. You can't abuse her forever."

Mailer says the three parts of the trilogy will come to a total of close to one million words, and adds: "I've got a terribly tricky way of tying them up." The Egyptian background, he explains, stems from an original concept in which he planned one chapter on the Egypt of antiquity, another on ancient Greece, and still another on Rome. "I wanted to show how marvelously talented I was to be able to do all these things," Mailer says. "So I dipped into Egypt and I never got out." The completion of the trilogy will probably span much of Mailer's remaining active career. "To win a bet, I could write all three books in four or five years," he says. "But I know now that if they are going to get written, they are going to get written because I grow into the task. What I am attempting is a good reach beyond anything I have done before."

When it was announced in 1974 that Little, Brown and Company had taken over the rights to the proposed novel from New American Library for one million dollars, sight unseen, literary headlines declared it the largest sum ever paid for an unwritten book. Mailer felt compelled to explain that the million dollars was to be paid out only as he wrote 500,000 to 700,000 words, what Mailer called the equivalent of five novels. "If his candles had been burning low in the literary cathedral these last few years," he said of himself in his common third-person stance, "the news story went its way to hasten their extinction. He knew that his much-publicized novel (still nine tenths to be written) would now have to be twice as good as before to overcome such financial news. Good literary men were not supposed to pick up *sums.*"

But sums for the new book have been coming in. In 1974, Warner Brothers bought the movie rights to the book for a reported minimum of $250,000, with escalator clauses that could bring the price to over one million dollars. In September 1980, the 1-million-dollar deal with Little, Brown was increased to 4 million dollars for the trilogy and one other small novel. Mailer was to receive $30,000 each month against the advance.

By the end of 1981 half a dozen European publishers had bought rights to the book, sight unseen, some for near record-breaking sums. Julian Ashby, head of Macmillan in London, who had not read one word of the manuscript, offered a preemptive bid of $120,000, one of the largest blind English-rights sales ever. "The interest had been building up for years," said Jonathan Silverman, foreign rights director for Scott Meredith, Mailer's agent. "I told Ashby this was going to be an important book here and in the English language in general, and at the time I was selling it, I had only read a small portion. We really sold it on the basis of Norman's name."

The name clearly has drawing power. By the fall of 1981 Robert Laffont, Mailer's longtime French publisher, made another preemptive blind bid for $75,000; Swedish rights went for $100,000, Spanish market rights for $50,000. Italy and Finland have also bought. Little, Brown set a Spring 1983 publication date and was confident of the book's success. "I think it's going to be the most important book published in 1983 and probably for a number of years previous and thereafter," says Roger Donald, Mailer's editor. "He's written something that's totally different from anything he's written before. There are terrible risks in doing that. From a commercial publisher's point of view if you have a success, you want to repeat it, but this is a guy who never repeats himself. Each time he comes to it fresh. He's a gigantic risk taker. A pretty good comparison could be made between Mailer and Picasso in terms of their range, their refusal to age or to lose energy."

❦

On the evening of Mailer's reading at the YMHA 1600 pages of *Ancient Evenings* had been completed; there were only 250 more to go. Mailer told the audience that this last part was the most difficult because the novel was not "writing itself" as some books do. "A small example of that would be *The Executioner's Song*," he said. "If I had passed away before the final fifty pages, I could have turned it over to any of my contemporaries without a backward look, even Gore Vidal." The audience burst into conspiratorial laughter, acknowledging Mailer's ten-year-old feud with Vidal, which had reached its zenith four years earlier, when Mailer threw a drink in Vidal's face at a party.

Unlike his performance at the Abbott conference, Mailer's carefully modulated snipe at Vidal that evening showed his control of the audience as he tossed them portions of his legend in well-proportioned doses. "It is always said by my detractors," he went on, "that, well, Norman has a few flashes of talent, but finally he is a journalist, and I always say to myself, 'Bless them. They are going to find a way to talk about this book of Egypt as a piece of journalism.' No, truthfully, I chose this period of 1130 B.C., the twentieth dynasty, reign of Ramses IX, because very little is known about it, and therefore I would not have to be subservient to plot, another man's plot. I could try to find my own."

Mailer's reputation as a journalist has been a thorn in the side of Mailer-the-Novelist for two decades. Even though he was one of the first to transform objective reporting into a literary movement known as the New Journalism, culminating in his Pulitzer Prize-winning nonfiction work *Armies of the Night*, Mailer has hungered to join Hemingway, Faulkner, and Fitzgerald as one of the great modern American novelists. The enormous success of *The Executioner's Song* in 1979 has brought the man who sees himself as the literary "champ" closer in the public's mind to its image of a novelist. But the "true life novel" which won Mailer his second Pulitzer Prize was still considered by many to be nonfiction; it did not test whether Mailer possessed the fictional imagination which would grant him the immortality he seeks.

If the audience at the YMHA had come prepared for a Maileresque spectacle equal to the Abbott news conference, they were in for a disappointment. Not even provocative questions after the reading could ruffle Mailer's stance as the serious novelist. "Perhaps they wanted sparks," reflects Shelley Mason, managing director of the Y, "but what they got was the Egyptian novel."

Why, one woman in the audience asked Mailer, was he so preoccupied with the sadism of the battlefield? Mailer had just read aloud a powerful recreation of the Battle of Kadesh from *Ancient Evenings*, and there was a stern, controlled edge to his voice as he deflected the obvious query about his attraction to violence. "Those periods are known as barbaric," he said. "One of the reasons I was drawn to this era is that we close our minds to large periods of history by using words like *barbaric* or *sadism*. *'Nihil humanum mihi alienum est.'* It is the most demanding single remark ever posed to humans. To say that nothing human is alien to me is to say more than you may be willing to back with your deeds."

Another woman brushed aside the novel and asked what was on the mind of many in the audience: "What about the Abbott press conference?" The audience tensed for the notorious Mailer rage, but it refused to emerge. Mailer delicately admitted he had had a press conference "where I fear I lost my temper," but went on in a tone more of wonderment than anger. "Reporters are the most self-righteous bastards I've ever encountered in my life." The audience, as one, exploded into applause, and for the rest of the night they were his. Moving from the depths of rejection to the summit of appreciation in one day has not been unusual in the life of Norman Mailer.

❦

Mailer—novelist, cofounder of *The Village Voice*, two-time Pulitzer Prize winner, member of the American Academy and Institute of Arts and Letters, winner of the National Book Award, wife stabber, husband to six, father of eight, definer of hip, anti-Vietnam War activist, candidate for mayor of New York, women's liberation adversary, film maker, boxer, Hollywood screen actor, and fantasy lover of Marilyn Monroe—lives today in a brownstone at 142 Columbia Heights in Brooklyn, a home he first moved into in 1962 with his third wife, Lady Jeanne Campbell.

Few who have grown up in Brooklyn, as Mailer did, have willingly returned to the borough after tasting the seductions of Manhattan, but Mailer has created his own cultural outpost on the eastern edge of New York's harbor in Brooklyn Heights. Over the years hundreds of the famous have made the trek across the Brooklyn Bridge and mounted the four flights to Mailer's living room, where a spectacular view of Manhattan's skyline and the Statue of Liberty awaits them.

It is a celebrated room. It was here that Mailer hosted a large party for his friend José Torres on the night he won the light-heavyweight championship of the world in 1965. Truman Capote was there, as were James Baldwin, Reggie Jackson, Mitch Miller, and Gay Talese, the usual eclectic assemblage of friends and luminaries that have made Mailer's many parties a social theater not unlike his life. A fund-raising rally for the striking Columbia University students was held here in 1968, culminating in a fistfight between Mailer and author Bruce Jay Friedman. It was also in this room that Mailer, along with Jimmy Breslin, Gloria Steinem, Peter Maas, Jack Newfield, Pete Hamill, Jerry Rubin, and others first talked of a Mailer-Breslin campaign for mayor of New York City in the spring of 1969. Writers Richard Goodwin and Doris Kearns were given a wedding anniversary party here in 1976, which the Schlesingers, the Javitses, the Cavetts, and even Jackie Kennedy attended.

Four wives have made 142 Columbia Heights their home since 1962. They have taken over various rooms on other floors as nurseries and living quarters when the two bedrooms on the fourth floor no longer sufficed. Since 1975 Mailer has been living there with Norris, a beautiful former high-school art teacher, whom he met in Russellville, Arkansas, through his old war buddy, the late author Francis Irby Gwaltney. Within six weeks of their meeting in 1975 twenty-six-year-old Barbara Norris, who subsequently changed her name to Norris Church, decided to leave her small town and join Mailer in New York, complicating an already messy domestic situation.

Mailer was still legally married to his fourth wife, Beverly Bentley, even though the couple had been separated since 1969. In 1970 he had begun living with nightclub singer Carol Stevens, who bore him his seventh child in 1971. By the time he met Norris in 1975, he was involved with yet another young woman, who was putting pressure on him to marry her. But Norris was to be number six. Shortly after he met her, Mailer excitedly showed José Torres her picture. "I knew it was the end of Carol," the boxer recalls.

Mailer's recent game of matrimonial musical chairs has astounded many. When his divorce from Beverly Bentley became final in September 1979, the author was free to remarry. Marry he did, twice. First he married Carol Stevens, in November 1980, to legitimize their child, followed a few days later by an instant Haitian divorce. He then married Norris Church, who had given birth to Mailer's eighth child, John Buffalo, two years earlier. Once again Mailer's exploits provided stimulating material for headlines.

Mailer's domestic life has been the subject of endless speculation ever since he stabbed his second wife, Adele, in 1960. By 1970 his four battling marriages coupled with his swaggering macho image brought the wrath of the feminists down on him. Yet Norris says she has never experienced the acute tension that seemed to dominate his five previous marriages. "I guess he might have matured from the angry young man he once was," she said. "It happens."

Mailer's friends suggest that Norris herself is partly responsible for the change. "A southern type girl is much better for Norman," says Jan Cushing Olympitis, a close friend of the Mailers' and godmother to John Buffalo. "They have a way of convincing you that everything you're doing is your idea, and half the time it's their idea, but they're so smart about it. Eastern women can't do it very well. They compete." Journalist Pete Hamill, who has known Mailer for twenty years, adds; "Norris is sweet, Norman is nice, they're civilized. The boy who went to Harvard is now the man who went to Harvard."

Mailer's friends concur that until the *affaire* Abbott a new mellowness had come over the writer, one at dramatic odds with his mercurial bellicosity of the past. Historian Arthur Schlesinger, Jr., who is a friend of Mailer's, says of the author's evolving personality: "Before, Norman was like a bomb that might explode at any moment. He had so many facets of possible development that he moved off in all sorts of directions. But as you grow older, you begin to realize more and more what works for you and what doesn't, and you begin to see what roles are really comfortable as against those you assume, and after a while aren't, for better or worse, working. I think that's all that's happened. He's settled into himself and simplified his life by realizing these aren't right for him." Part of the change, Schlesinger suggests, is due to Mailer's two-year abstinence from alcohol.

Mailer's past exploits—whether butting heads with Jimmy Breslin at Arthur Schlesinger's home or with Gregory Hemingway, son of the author, at George Plimpton's; telling an embarassingly dirty joke at his fiftieth birthday party at the Four Seasons; insulting his campaign workers at the Village Gate during his mayoral bid; or spewing obscenities at a group of six hundred antiwar activist students before the march on the Pentagon—made him something of a social liability. It was impossible to predict when his hidden combustibility—often fueled by liquor—would explode into public outrage. But his recent social image has been more that of a literary elder statesman. Just as the Mailer name has been associated with every radical cause in the past, it is now as often identified with the chic New York society pages. By 1981 he had been rated as the fourth most "outstanding celebrity" by Earl Blackwell, following only Ronald Reagan, Frank Sinatra, and Luciano Pavarotti.

"If I have any entree at all," Mailer explained, "it's because society is always fascinated with mavericks. Till the point where they'll become bored with me, and then, boom, I'm out. But on the other hand, even as a maverick there are certain rules that I have to obey. If you start obeying those rules past the point where you want to go along with them as part of the game, then you are injuring yourself."

One rule of the game is decorous behavior. "At cocktail parties he's always incredibly polite," says Manoli Olympitis, a venture capitalist who met Mailer for the first time in November 1979, when Mailer and Norris joined the newlywed Olympitises on their honeymoon in England. "I've seen people make remarks at parties that could be misinterpreted, and he's gone out of his way not to misinterpret them. He will always make an effort to be charming and will discuss anything with anyone."

Mailer's close friends are an eclectic group but they include few writers except Schlesinger and Kurt Vonnegut, mainly because Mailer is wary of the New York literary community. "I don't socialize much with other writers," Mailer explains. "I didn't begin as a literary man; I began as an engineer. My distrust of the literary world is not too dissimilar to the distrust that a red-neck who starts to write would have. Which is: 'There are all those fancy, double-talking phonies up there in New York.' My view is somewhat more sophisticated, but I think that the literary world is a very dangerous place to be in if you want to do an awful lot of writing. I tend to stay away from it and pick friends for other reasons."

Dining at the homes of the Kennedy inner circle, Pat Lawford, the Schlesingers, or the Stephen Smiths, is common for the Mailers; the author was very active in Senator Edward Kennedy's 1980 bid for the presidency. There is irony in the recent embrace of the Kennedy clan, for Mailer was long the outsider, hoping for an intimacy with their power which, until recently, never materialized. The longtime maverick has finally been accepted into the royal court. "The Kennedys are all rather fascinated with Norman, which is disarming," says Schlesinger.

Mailer's friends also include a male entourage made up of boxer José Torres and Bernard ("Buzz") Farbar, who is both an editor and an ex-Golden Gloves boxer, and former actor Mickey Knox, who now visits from Rome. In the past the group also included another ex-boxer, Roger Donoghue. Collectively they provide the image of a royal court, one which troubles *Commentary* editor Norman Podhoretz, who was close to Mailer in the 1960s. "The problem with being Norman's friend was that he was always surrounded by a court of hangers on that I was much too proud to get mixed up in," says Podhoretz. "But it's not uncommon. I find that many successful writers tend to attract crowds of sycophants. In the case of Mailer—and this is one of his virtues—he's very loyal to his friends and courtiers and has a kind of paternal relation to them. He takes care of them and looks after them. He's willing to accept that responsibility."

Some perceive Mailer's entourage as a phalanx of bodyguards, protecting the author from unwanted intrusions by those who would like to take on the self-proclaimed "champ" of American letters. Mailer, who is himself an amateur boxer and friend to boxers, fits that image. "Norman has an immense ego, as fighters do," says José Torres, who until recently hosted Mailer's boxing workouts every Saturday at his gym, The Raging Jews. ("Mailer was the main rage," he says.) "We are all basically a bunch of narcissists. Norman doesn't want people to be too comfortable when he's around. Because of his ego he likes to intimidate. He has a real complicated head."

Over the last few years Mailer's fighting instinct had become muted, or had at least seemed to, until it was aroused by the Abbott controversy. As you get older," he told *The New York Times* in June 1982, "you realize that what's important is to do one's work and do one's best work and be serious about it. It's not that you're retreating completely—you're just saying, 'It's too much, I abdicate, I resign, I will cultivate my own garden.' "

❦

With age has also come a preoccupation with family life. Mailer has always been a concerned father to his large, disparate brood, an attachment that has recently grown stronger. "I think he's fascinated that he's produced totally different children," says Jan Olympitis. "He wants to get to know them all as individuals. He adores it. He's the Godfather in his family. He's Marlon Brando."

Mailer has certainly emerged as a supreme Jewish patriarch, ruling over his eight children with gentle authority. His oldest child, Susan, by his first wife, Beatrice Silverman, is now thirty-three and living in Chile with her husband. Mailer has two beautiful dark-haired daughters by Adele Morales, an attractive Spanish-Peruvian woman who is an artist. Adele's oldest daughter by Mailer, Danielle, or "Dandy," twenty-five, also paints and teaches art part time. Elizabeth Anne, or "Betsy," age twenty-three, graduated from Princeton in 1981 and has been living in California. Mailer's daughter by Lady Jeanne Campbell, Kate, is twenty and interested in acting.

Mailer has two tall sons by his blond fourth wife, actress Beverly Bentley. Michael Burks Mailer, eighteen, attended Andover and has become a proficient amateur boxer, while Stephen McLeod Mailer, sixteen, is at school in New York. He lives with his mother in Brooklyn, not far from the Mailer home at 142 Columbia Heights. Beverly, the only wife with whom Mailer is no longer friendly, hopes to resume her acting career. Maggie, twelve, lives with her mother, Carol Stevens, in Stockbridge, Massachusetts, where Mailer once resided for four years. His youngest son, John Buffalo, four, lives with Mailer and Norris at 142 Columbia Heights, as does Norris's ten-year-old son, Matthew, by another marriage. The older children have begun to lead their own lives, but a few are usually at 142 Columbia Heights or, in the summer, with Mailer and Norris in Provincetown or Maine.

As the patriarch of his large clan Mailer has become a living incarnation of what Diana Trilling refers to as his "call . . . to a Hebraic world," one that is molded "in the image of the stern father." The achievement is not slight, for Mailer has mainly overcome, in both his work and his life, the sometimes overcivilizing influences of Jewish matriarchy. In fact Mailer sees these influences as the basic flaw in his personality.

In 1968 he said of himself: "he had a fatal taint, a last remaining speck of the one personality he found absolutely insupportable—the nice Jewish boy from Brooklyn. Something in his adenoids gave it away—he had the softness of a man early accustomed to mother-love."

The irony of Mailer's long creative flight from the nice-Jewish-boy image is that throughout it he has remained profoundly tied to his mother, Fanny Schneider Mailer, the rock on which his ego is based. "I'm sure when Fanny conceived him she was convinced she was carrying a genius," says Mailer's first wife, Beatrice Silverman. "And I think she made him one, at least made him believe that he was one. She was the matriarch, but always with the hand in the velvet glove."

Fanny Mailer, who is now in her middle eighties, has been a constant presence in Mailer's life. She lives only a block away from her son in Brooklyn Heights, as she has for twenty years. "I keep kidding him about his mother," says Milton Greene, who collaborated with Mailer on the Marilyn Monroe pseudo-autobiography, *Of Women and Their Elegance*. "He's always worried about her. He looks after his mother like a baby. Every party at his house there's his mother, and she always has to get the last word in. If Norman tries, she beats him."

Fanny's proximity to her son has unnerved some of Mailer's wives, who cannot reconcile his sometimes exaggerated masculine image with that of the solicitous and dutiful son. "Here I married this great and powerful writer," Lady Jeanne Campbell once joked to Midge Decter, Mailer's former editor at *Harper's* magazine, "and all we ever did was to go to dinner with his mother." The relationship also invites a certain competitiveness between his wives and his mother. "His mother is the *only* Mrs. Norman Mailer," Beverly Bentley has said.

Until recently Mailer would have breakfast with Fanny virtually every morning. That mother-son ritual tapered off as he began his final effort on the Egyptian novel. By 1982 Mailer had been working regularly on the Egyptian novel in his telephoneless studio down the block from the Brooklyn Heights house. After spending June and July in Provincetown doing little else but cutting *Ancient Evenings* down to workable size, Mailer delivered the manuscript to Little, Brown, on August 1, 1982. Thirty-five years earlier, in August, 1947, he had handed in the manuscript of *The Naked and the Dead* to Rinehart and soon after left for Paris with Beatrice, on the G.I. Bill of Rights. No one then knew that the twenty-four-year-old was to become one of the most outspoken, controversial, and prolific of American writers.

And his output has been prodigious: At sixty Mailer has demonstrated his endurance. He has outlived many of his critics and continued to produce work with the urgent sense that only his writing can protect him from the excesses of his own life-style. He is, in the parlance of the boxing trade, a man who can go fifteen rounds.

The last few years have been particularly fruitful. One week after he completed *The Executioner's Song* in 1978 Mailer had begun work on the text for Milton Greene's album of photographs, *Of Women and Their Elegance*. In the midst of completing *Ancient Evenings*, Mailer found the energy and hours to organize a collection of his writings and interviews from the 1970s, entitled *Pieces and Pontifications*, brought out by Little, Brown in June 1982. Shortly before that he wrote a television screenplay of *The Executioner's Song* and a play based on *Of Women and Their Elegance*. Since 1980 Mailer has also been involved in a whirlwind of subsidiary activities, a testament of his curiosity. He has protested to Leonid Brezhnev about the treatment of Russian dissident Andrei Sakharov; boycotted the bookseller-sponsored American Book Awards, which replaced the National Book Awards; disagreed with Reagan on his decision to provide arms to Saudi Arabia; appealed to Lillian Hellman and Mary McCarthy to settle their bitter feud; held a fund raiser for Abbie Hoffman and attended the former Yippie's trial on cocaine charges. Mailer also acted in his first Hollywood film; he played the role of architect Stanford White in Milos Forman's movie *Ragtime*, and has since informed his agent at William Morris that he would be interested in other screen acting roles.

❦

For a period of several years everything had been harmonious in Mailer's life. His marriage was working; his long-promised novel was nearing completion. He had not been drinking and his reputation as an elder statesman of American letters was gradually replacing his combative image as a literary rogue. As Pete Hamill says, "I think people were slightly pissed at him because he'd become so respectable. They wanted Norman around making a fool of himself. They liked feeling superior to a guy who's really their superior. Well, he wasn't being arrested, he wasn't throwing up on his shoes, and he hadn't done some outrageous Peck's Bad Boy thing. He was working."

Mailer's calm and productive existence was suddenly shattered by the Jack Abbott case, which evoked Mailer's own violent past and his romantic, perhaps obsessive, fascination with the outlaw in American society. During the fall of 1981 article after article pointed an accusing finger, not at Abbott, the convict, but at Mailer. "For Mailer," wrote James Atlas in *The New Republic*, "it has always been the criminal who . . . by giving into impulses the more timid writer can only hope to enact in his work, is the true artist. For decades now he has been pushing the idea that violence is existential, hip, heroic. It would require a certain amount of 'courage,' he claimed in 'The White

Negro,' for 'two strong 18-year-old hoodlums to beat in the brains of a candy-store keeper,' for it meant 'daring the unknown.' "

Mailer's own violent past, specifically his stabbing of Adele in 1960, was implicit in the uproar. As Mailer's friend George Plimpton says, "I think the controversy was especially hard for him because of the thing with Adele. It must have kept crossing his mind. The sudden flash of rage that got Abbott into trouble almost put him away too."

What few knew was that Mailer was having his own doubts about Abbott's character before the murder. Shortly after Abbott was released from prison in June 1981, Mailer received a letter from an inmate at Marion Federal Penitentiary, Garrett Trapnell, who indicated that Abbott had snitched on his fellow inmates in order to obtain his parole. This was the same Abbott who in *The Belly of the Beast* had written, "To be a punk is surpassed in contempt only by being a snitch."

"I know Norman was very disturbed by the letter," says Jean Malaquais. "He came to me and told me, 'Do you know he snitched?' I just couldn't believe it, but for Mailer it was probably a very bitter experience. However, Abbott protested with all his might that he never snitched on anybody and that the only names he gave were those of some lawyers."

Jack Henry Abbott, radical, killer, convict, now sees Mailer as an enemy, as a voice of the established rulers who are indifferent to those beneath them. "What bothered me," Jack Abbott says from the Missouri prison where he is now incarcerated, "is that when Norman got this letter he acted surprised. I said, 'So what, you act surprised.' That's when I began to see that it was so far away from his experience that he couldn't understand it. It's a social class drift. Where I come from people are always beefing with the police, but Mailer isn't aware of any of this. He doesn't want to believe it. I would say that ultimately Norman and I are enemies, we're class enemies. Norman's is a society that sets the standards and rules of this government and country. He doesn't know this other world. He always wants to, but he always wants to do it in such a way that he pulls them into his world. In existential terms Norman is a philistine."

Mailer has lived the ideological life of a radical, but Abbott is convinced that he is still ignorant of proletarian realities, especially so far as his views of violence and the police are concerned. "Norman has gone off to where he identifies the working man with the police," says

Abbott from prison. "That has really been a blow to me. He's so naïve about the police it's incredible. He's with them. They might arrest someone like Norman for tearing up a bar, but then they would take him and pat him on the back and let him out on his own recognizance because of the class he belongs to. Norman doesn't realize the privilege he enjoys. The police are there to protect his class and his class interests and property, and its natural that he would see in them a macho image.

"Also the idea of violence that Norman and his class have is of a couple of men in a very polite argument. They think it's a Donnybrook type of thing where you step outside and roll up your shirt sleeves and punch each other out, then shake hands. He doesn't know that's not what happens. It's not a romantic view of it, it's an innocent view."

Abbott's personal and Marxist attack on the man who helped secure his freedom is startling, but it may be partially the result of a conversation they held shortly after Abbott killed Adan. Abbott called Mailer at his home in Brooklyn Heights. "Norman had a theory that I felt so bad because I was a snitch in prison that I took a knife and had to take it out on somebody, so I killed the first person who looked sideways at me," Abbott relates. "I said, 'Norman, that isn't true.' He said, 'Try to convince the jury of that.' I said, 'Listen, Norman, keep your theories to yourself, because you could get me into trouble. You're saying I committed premeditated murder.' "

José Torres was sitting in Mailer's living room when the author received the call from Abbott. "They made a deal," Torres recalls. "Abbott wouldn't mention Norman for anything in the future, and Mailer wouldn't mention Abbott. Then the trial came, and I was shocked."

Few knew of Mailer's conflicting feelings about Abbott both before and after the killing. Abbott confides that on January 13, six days after the trail began, he called Mailer again at his home in Brooklyn. Abbott told him that from the testimony of a witness he had just learned the reason for Richard Adan's behavior. The stabbing had taken place in the alley of a restaurant in the East Village where Abbott was eating. Abbott had asked to use the washroom and was apparently refused by the waiter, Richard Adan. To Abbott this was a provocation, answered in the language of the convict jungle with a kitchen knife. Now Abbott was telling Mailer on the phone that he had since found out from court testimony that it was all a misunderstanding. The bathroom, Abbott had apparently learned, was for employees only, and Adan had taken him outside so that he could urinate.

"I was so dumbstruck," says Abbott from prison, "that I couldn't stop crying. I haven't cried since I was a kid. I was reinterpreting the whole event. So I told Norman that I had found out what happened, that there was no restroom and why Adan took me out there. After we talked for a while, Norman hung up. The next day he was at the trial and he's been with me ever since. But he still thinks I purposely murdered the guy, and it really tears me up too."

Four days later Mailer not only testified on Abbott's behalf but defended him to a hostile press. "I told Norman that he was out of his mind," says Jean Malaquais, "that he was absolutely foolish for the kind of pseudo-Christian culpability he takes upon himself. It's absolutely ridiculous, but Norman dabbles in all sorts of karmas."

Abbie Hoffman, whom Mailer helped by serving as head of his defense fund when he surfaced after years as a fugitive from a cocaine charge, agrees with Malaquais that Mailer is taking excessive blame for Abbott's crime. "In January 1982 we had a big anti-heroin rally at Studio 54, and Norman was supposed to be one of the sponsors," Hoffman relates. "He called me up and said he was afraid to come, afraid he would hurt anything he touched. I told him he was not responsible for what Abbott did, and I didn't believe any of that nonsense about his having blood on his hands. I told him, 'Norman, you're taking the blame for society for not having rehabilitation centers for exiting convicts. Also you're taking the credit for getting Abbott out of prison when, in fact, it was only because he was a squealer that he was released.' "

Mailer's friend and former mayoralty running mate, Jimmy Breslin, believes Mailer is being naïve about Abbott. "Whenever you get anybody out of jail, and in my lifetime I've gotten several people out, they always disappoint you, and you've got to expect it," says Breslin. "You've got to take chances, but I've been burned so many times that I knew what was coming. I tried to say, 'Take the burn, but don't make it a first degree burn,' which I think Norman did."

Staking his reputation on the passionate defense of a man he was not sure about is typical of Mailer's sometimes misguided sense of heroism. "I think Norman believes the universe is evil," says his friend, author Dotson Rader, "and that it's only through great heroic effort that man is able to temper that essential evil and survive. I think that's one of the reasons Norman is so fascinated with Abbott and Gilmore and violence. He's like a Richter scale. He senses rumblings that could be the making of an earthquake, shocks he senses that no one else senses. These people that grab his interest are like small eruptions heralding the final cataclysm. Norman believes that if he can understand the nature of a Gilmore or an Abbott, he will have commanded an understanding of the essential nature of man."

In trying to explain to a hostile press at the explosive conference that nothing human was alien to him, Mailer lost his way and wound up paying tribute to Abbott's talents as a writer with his famous "Culture is worth a little risk" line.

When José Torres read about the news conference the following day, he immediately called Mailer. Norris answered the phone.

"Can I ask you a personal question?" he said. "What the hell is wrong with Norman?"

"José," Norris replied, "I'm glad you feel that way, because I'm packing. I'm going to Arkansas. I'll have Norman call you." Norris did not go to Arkansas, but as Abbie Hoffman explains, the Abbott affair "really strained the marriage." Hoffman also feels that since the marriage held together during this crisis, it "leads one to believe that this is Norman's last."

Four hours after Torres spoke with Norris, Mailer called him back. "I don't know what you're doing," Torres told him, "but the halls of the court belong to the devil, you should know that. You're going into the devil's camp, and it's fucking you up."

"What do you mean?" Mailer asked, surprised.

"People think that you think it's okay to kill if you are a writer—if you belong to that special elite class, you can kill and go free," Torres answered. "That's what people are saying."

Mailer told his friend that he would immediately arrange another press conference to defend his true intent. Two days later he held one in the offices of his agent, Scott Meredith, where he was under control, even amiable. Thomas Hanrahan, the reporter from the *Daily News* who had blown up at Mailer during the January 18 press conference, says of the later one: "He was much more calm and talked in more substantial terms and attempted successfully to iron out misconceptions. It was a working press conference where there was communication."

Dick Cavett then called Mailer and asked if he would like to explain himself further on his television show. On February 24 and

25, 1982, Mailer dressed again in a conservative dark-blue suit, restrained himself remarkably while Cavett prodded him with provocative questions. "You've been accused," Cavett said, "of romanticizing violence. You may remember that on this show Gore Vidal said, 'I'll tell you what I loathe about you, Norman, since you press me: your love of violence, your romanticizing of murder, your saying that sex is violent."

Mailer refused to respond to the charges Vidal had made in 1972. He simply answered, "I'm not here to reply to Gore Vidal."

Cavett continued: "My point is, has it made you rethink any of that romanticizing of violence you've been attracted to?"

"I do not romanticize violence," Mailer replied in his rapid, staccato diction. "I know a fair amount about it, and I don't like it much. All this comes from something I said many years ago. I said there are two kinds of violence: individual violence and the violence of the state. The violence of the state is not just wars, it's also concentration camps. . . . There can be violence in total censorship. Anything that cuts off expectations from people, possibilities from people, anything that compresses people by external government force is the violence of the state. . . . Individual violence is very often the natural answer of people to the collective violence of the state."

❦

The Abbott case has disturbed Norman Mailer and his admirers, particularly at this important point in his career, a time when his radical past seemed to be overshadowed by his increased acceptance. "He was taken over by the Establishment after the sixties and tamed," says mentor Jean Malaquais. "He told me once himself that he's just a businessman and lives like a bourgeois." Perhaps the ultimate irony in this view of Mailer as a cultural conservative is that while the world was startled by Mailer's defense of Jack Abbott, his convict protégé now sees him as a philistine, a member of the ruling class with a gentleman's view of violence and the police.

It is obvious that there is much about Mailer that is paradoxical: his radicalism and his essential bourgeois nature; his pugnacity and his gentility; his divorces and his patriarchal tendencies; his criticism of establishment power and his desire to share in it; his outrageous stance as a public performer and his serious demeanor as a novelist. In the years since the publication of his antiwar novel, *The Naked and the Dead*, Mailer has gained a worldwide reputation by representing both sides of his complicated personality, the angry rebel and the Harvard literary gentleman, as the *authentic* Mailer.

Today it would seem that the "psychic outlaw," as he once called himself, has been replaced by the mellowing writer of stature. But it is also evident that the mercurial Mailer is still capable of stimulating the public imagination with his attacks on contemporary culture, his bellicosity, his excessive self-promotion, his theatrical life-style, his prophetic insights into the underside of modern existence. It is even possible that the angry, provocative side of Mailer—his living affront to the ideas and mores of a conventional society—is the basis of his appeal. Literary critic John Aldridge, author of *After the Lost Generation*, has looked at the paradox of Norman Mailer and concludes that his credo is a "private paranoid revision of Descartes: 'I offend; therefore, I am.' "

The evolution of Mailer's personality, or personalities, and the impact of his work on the postwar world are the makings of an extraordinary life.

• II •

YOUNG MAILER AT HARVARD

The young man who entered Harvard University at the age of sixteen in September 1939 was a different Norman Mailer from the provocative figure who would later capture the world's imagination. There was little about him that seemed distinguished to his freshmen peers that fall. Younger than most, Mailer was also physically underdeveloped, a short, scrawny youth, only five feet seven, with ears that stuck out awkwardly from a small, narrow triangular face. The halo of curls that would become so familiar in later life was clipped in short, wiry waves. "He had none of the manner of the grand seigneur that he has now," says Bowden Broadwater, a fellow member of the Harvard class of '43.

When Mailer arrived at the second-floor suite, number 11-12 in Grays Hall, a freshman dorm in Harvard Yard, his two roommates had already installed themselves in one of the two bedrooms joined by a bath. As Mailer moved into his room and made his introductions to Richard Weinberg from Tennessee and Maxwell Kaufer from Pennsylvania, they saw no hint of future greatness in him. To Weinberg he was just "a little boy from Brooklyn, soft-spoken and rather shy."

The braggadocio and macho bearing that are now Mailer trademarks were absent. "He was genial and very laid back," remembers

Weinberg, "and you never got the feeling of him coming on strong." Mailer spoke with a Brooklyn accent, which only later became the now-classic Mailer voice, a provincial New York diction glossed over with a cultivated Harvard tone and sometimes edged with southern and Irish inflections. He had a tendency to talk fast even then, but there was little sign of the later aggressive, machine-gun speech. To his new friends his entire demeanor was unobtrusive.

Mailer's Brooklyn public school background, his small stature, and his shyness were obvious handicaps in the socially status-conscious Harvard of 1939. But Mailer had another disadvantage: He had chosen the least glamorous of undergraduate majors, aeronautical engineering. Some of his classmates still find it hard to believe that engineering was taught at Harvard, or that Mailer studied it. Engineering simply was not what one went to this academy of history, literature, politics, and economics to learn. Registration figures that year showed that the majority of the class of 1943 planned to be doctors, lawyers, or teachers, not the designers of America's future airplanes.

But Mailer had not come from a liberal arts background, and his only abiding interest as a boy was the painstaking assembly of model airplanes. It was not writing but constructing replicas of World War I fighter planes that occupied his agile mind. At Boys High School in Brooklyn, his skill in math and physics wedded to his love of airplanes made aeronautical engineering a practical choice for the only son of a second-generation immigrant family seeking to raise himself a notch above the Brooklyn lower-middle class.

Mailer's first choice in colleges had not been Harvard, but the engineering Mecca, the Massachusetts Institute of Technology. M.I.T. had accepted Mailer but insisted that he spend an additional year at secondary school because he was only sixteen. Rather than waste the year Mailer settled on Harvard, his second choice. Mailer would later joke that he had decided on Harvard only after becoming interested in girls. "I thought I would go to Harvard and come back with a pipe in my mouth and have all the girls I wanted," he told writer Frederick Christian. Whatever the truth of his quip, had M.I.T. accepted him without reservations, Mailer might today be an unknown builder of space vehicles instead of the author of *Of a Fire on the Moon*.

The man who was to marry six women and symbolize male chauvinism seemed a model of sexual innocence as a Harvard freshman. Mailer's two freshman roommates remember that Mailer socialized very little with women that year, spending his time at his desk studying diligently. To excuse his lack of dates, he told them he had a girl friend back in Brooklyn, which was true, but the only evidence of Mailer's later legendary sexual curiosity was the collage of Betty Grable and other Hollywood pinup girls nailed to the wall above his typewriter. "He was younger than we were, which makes a difference socially at that age," says Weinberg.

There was also no early clue to Mailer's later expansive life-style. He never joined his roommates for late-night snacks at the Eliot House grill, or indulged in the popular twenty-cent chocolate frappes at Mike's Club on Mt. Auburn Street. Twenty cents was not an insubstantial sum for a teenager in 1939, and Mailer was plagued during his college years by a perpetual lack of pocket money. Although not on scholarship and spared working at odd jobs, he never had the feel of extra dollars, a luxury that made Harvard gentlemen a class apart. His mother, Fanny Mailer, had saved enough from her one-truck oil-delivery business to send her son to Harvard, and his rich uncle, David Kessler, helped subsidize him all the way through college. But there was never more than just enough.

Weinberg and Kaufer were on restricted budgets as well, but they could afford occasional trips to Wellesley on weekends, while Mailer seldom left campus. However, they were as innocent as he about the goings-on of their social superiors. All three roommates would watch in amazement as the wealthier prep-school freshmen donned tuxedos on Friday nights to go out. "Those of us on the outside didn't even know where they were going," Weinberg recalls.

Most public-school Jews at Harvard, Mailer included, were painfully aware that freshman year of being outside the existing social order. The subtle distinctions of dress, manner, lineage, and wealth that made up a Harvard "gentleman" eluded them, while the boys from Groton, St. Paul's, or Milton, who considered Harvard a continuation of their privileged prep school days, instinctively knew how the system worked and which activities to join.

In 1939 Jews were a substantial presence at Harvard, making up approximately one fifth of the entire freshman class. Yet Mailer's Jewish classmates distinctly recall feeling part of a specific if invisible quota system. At Harvard in 1939 it was standard practice not only to isolate incoming Jewish freshmen by assigning them rooms together but to group the prep-school graduates as well, making it difficult for newcomers like Mailer to absorb the intricacies of the Harvard establishment, especially the club and house systems.

Mailer and his roommates discussed the painful subject of being outside the Harvard mainstream and their need to break in. "I'm sure Norman was as bewildered as I was," recalls Weinberg, "because he didn't perceive how you're supposed to dress or act or what the social distinctions were between prep school and private school and public school. Nobody really explained it to you if you were an outsider." Kaufer was the most socially mobile of the three, but Weinberg was lucky enough to have a friend in Lowell House who was a "club" man. Before long Weinberg too was invited to fashionable parties and began to understand the nuances that made up the inner workings of the Harvard social scene.

Mailer was less successful socially than his roommates. He gravitated toward the security of a fellow Brooklynite, Martin Lubin, an intensely bright science major who had been valedictorian of Mailer's class at Boys High School and is now a professor at Dartmouth. The two had not known each other well in high school, but they formed a friendship that lasted through the four years at Harvard. Lubin's freshman roommate, Harold Katz, a philosophy and math major from Indiana, soon joined their small circle, as did Seymour "Sy" Breslow, a premedical student.

It was this threesome that formed the nucleus of Mailer's social life at Harvard, and all would room together at various times over the next three years. As Breslow says: "We were just dumped together. Whoever was in one dorm became friendliest with the kids in that dorm, and that's how we met." A tight Jewish peer group was also a workable defense against an entrenched upper-class Anglo-Saxon world.

❦

The fall of 1939 was not the best of times for the three hundred and first freshman class to be entering Harvard. On September 1 Germany invaded Poland, only nine days after a shocked world had stood by as Stalin signed a nonaggression pact with Hitler. As pro- and antiwar debates swept the campus, the prospect of American involvement frightened many of the new freshmen, including Mailer, who found himself embroiled in an argument about the war at the end of his very first week.

Poet Archibald MacLeish, who later became the Librarian of

Congress, had been invited to address the freshmen after orientation week. MacLeish gravely warned the students that few would graduate before going into the armed services. "Your class has a prototype, the class of 1918," MacLeish predicted. "That generation, my generation, believed that the future was war, and there was no future after the war. . . . Now we do not see the war as a finality. The last war was not an end but a beginning."

Young Mailer, who was now launched on the first significant adventure of his life, did not appreciate the thought of a new war. In the midst of MacLeish's speech he jotted down a facetious reaction which would characterize his viewpoint on the war for the next two years. The note, which he later called "the shortest story I've ever written," read as follows:

> We were going through the barbed-wire when a machine gun started. I kept walking until I saw my head lying on the ground.
>
> "My God, I'm dead," my head said.
>
> And my body fell over.

One of Mailer's classmates, John Crockett, who later worked with Mailer on Harvard's literary magazine, the *Advocate*, remembers arguing with Mailer after MacLeish's speech. Mailer thought it a lot of "crap." There wasn't going to be any war, the young Brooklynite insisted, but Crockett vehemently disagreed. "I was annoyed," remembers Crockett, "that Norman, a Jewish boy from Brooklyn, was on the wrong side."

Mailer was not alone in dismissing MacLeish's warning of war; most of the freshman class booed the poet off the podium. *The Harvard Crimson* printed an editorial that set the newspaper's isolationist tone for the next two years: "We must convince ourselves now that no war is a holy war, that we might be heading for another great double-cross. . . ." By November 1939 three quarters of the undergraduates voted in favor of nonintervention, although the figure would drop by the end of the year.

Few American students, most of whom had been schooled by isolationist teachers who had seen the disastrous results of World War I, wanted to go to war in 1939. But opinion about the war raging in Europe varied greatly, and the campus became a furnace of political factions: leftists against liberals, liberals against conservatives. The leftists had been strongly anti-Nazi, but with the signing of the pact between Nazi Germany and Communist Russia on August 23, 1939, the leftist branch of the Harvard Teachers Union, led by literature professor F. O. Matthiessen, dramatically swung about-face and came out for neutrality, calling the Allied war ambitions "imperialist." The liberals, including Harvard president James Conant, remained anti-Nazi and interventionist, rallying around the Committee to Defend America by Aiding the Allies. They wanted to repeal the Neutrality Acts and speed up aid to Britain, as did President Franklin Roosevelt.

In this internal Harvard battle many on the right joined the left in their isolationism, and in June 1940 the right-wing America First Committee, or "America Firsters," led by Charles Lindbergh and Eddie Rickenbacker, insisted that no help should be given to our allies. America should instead prepare to defend itself against any foreign enemies. Not until the summer of 1941, when Germany suddenly invaded Russia, did most of the students realize the full threat of Nazism.

It seems impossible that anyone could remain indifferent to the political contretemps raging on the Harvard campus that fall of 1939, but the sixteen-year-old aeronautical-engineering major simply was not interested in politics or the war. Most of his classmates agree that until Pearl Harbor Norman Mailer did not want to hear about the conflict that would eventually become his lever to fame, as World War I was for Hemingway.

Mailer's early indifference to politics at Harvard may have been fortunate, for it allowed him to concentrate on what, by December of his freshman year, was becoming an all-consuming passion: modern American literature. Mailer had entered Harvard with little literary interest or knowledge. "My idea of a good novel was *Silas Marner*," said Mailer of the book that was taught routinely in New York City junior high schools. John Dos Passos and William Faulkner were names he barely knew existed, and when asked by Harvard to prepare a list of books he was reading, the young engineering student faked a bibliography he thought was impressive, from *The Americanization of Edward Bok* to *The Rise of Silas Lapham* by William Dean Howells.

That fall of 1939 was a critical period in Mailer's life, a time of personal transformation from a young man absorbed in the sciences to someone becoming insatiably curious about novels, particularly those written by contemporary Americans. The change came in his freshman English class, where Mailer and the others assembled for joint lectures in the basic course, English A, then divided into fifty seminars of twenty students each to learn the rudiments of good writing. An impressive roster of Harvard instructors, including writers Wallace Stegner, Delmore Schwartz, Mark Schorer, and Howard Nemerov, surrounded Mailer, and stimulated by this heady literary company, he began to take his assignments seriously.

During the months of December 1939 and January 1940, when the heaviest snowfall in thirty years blanketed the Harvard campus, Mailer read and reread *U.S.A.*, by John Dos Passos, *The Grapes of Wrath*, by John Steinbeck, and the works of Hemingway, Fitzgerald, Thomas Wolfe, and William Faulkner. But one book, *Studs Lonigan*, by James T. Farrell, worked literary magic on the sixteen-year-old. "Farrell demonstrated to me that everything in life is worth writing about," Mailer recalled. "I was fascinated by his books—*Studs Lonigan*, the Danny O'Neill series. The characters were in an economic group just one notch below mine, and it was thrilling to see how they lived." The reading of that one book, *Studs Lonigan*, turned Mailer's head and made him want to become a writer.

Novels of social realism like *Studs Lonigan* were in vogue in 1939. Mailer was clearly impressed by their concern for working-class people rather than for the bourgeoisie, and by his sophomore year he was passionately defending what he called the "proletarian" novel. The young student had little patience with the more precious belles lettres stylists, a radical literary attitude that matched that of the Harvard English Department, which by 1939 had an active American Studies Program developed by leftist scholar F. O. Matthiessen and his colleague Perry Miller.

Begun at Harvard eight years earlier, and already gaining acceptance at other universities, the program emphasized that literature should not be considered in isolation but be studied as part of the country's political and economic history. The program was born early in the Depression and was strongly dependent on the new Marxist view of literature, if not as narrow or dogmatic. Matthiessen's approach was creating a leftist intellectual environment at Harvard, and Mailer, developing his first sense of himself as a writer, eagerly absorbed it.

In early February of his freshman year, Mailer wrote his first short story, "The Lady Wears a Smile," and was soon spending many of his study hours in Grays Hall creating fiction. By the following September, when he had already written at least fourteen more stories, engineering had clearly been superseded by literature. This new allegiance was reflected in Mailer's attitude toward two of his final freshman exams in the late spring of 1940.

English A students had been asked to write a novella as their final test, and Mailer stunned his classmates by receiving an A+. That grade was not liberally granted at Harvard, and when it became known, Mailer was suddenly a freshman presence. His roommate Richard Weinberg believes Mailer owes a debt of gratitude to the teacher who gave it to him. "It really launched him on his career," he says, "and made him feel he had talent. When those grades came in, we all became aware of Norman."

Conversely when Mailer walked out of his physics exam, he commented that it wasn't a bad test. Someone asked him how he did on the rotation question, and Mailer glibly replied, "What rotation question?" His friend Sy Breslow remembers that he kept right on walking.

Despite Mailer's evolving interest in writing, he remained an engineering student and eventually received his degree in engineering sciences, cum laude. It was done partially to please his mother, Fanny, who, like so many Depression parents, believed that her son should study for a practical profession so that he could get a good job after graduation. Writing could be done on the side. Although there was great respect for scholarship in the Jewish community, writing was considered an impractical profession, the activity of the Yiddish intelligentsia whose life-style was painfully penurious.

Mailer was officially an engineering major throughout his Harvard career, but he would show only routine interest in that subject, while giving serious attention to writing and literature. Mailer's attitude toward engineering has convinced Beatrice Silverman that one should never hire a Harvard engineer. "When Norman had to take a course in stresses, he'd walk by a building and say, 'When you build a building, you just calculate the stresses and then multiply it by a hundred to make sure it won't fall.' " Bea Silverman adds, "I don't think he ever had the potential to become an engineer."

❦

By his sophomore year, writing had become Mailer's consuming concern. It would be an important year for the young author, one in which his literary talent would be acknowledged both on and off campus. He would be admitted into the inner sanctums of both

Harvard's literary magazine, the *Advocate*, and the exclusive literary and political club, Signet Society. He would also write his first novel, and win a national short-story competition.

In the fall of 1940, with Martin Lubin and Sy Breslow as roommates, Mailer moved into 24 Claverly Hall, on Mt. Auburn Street, a way station for the three friends before they were admitted into the house system. Since Claverly had no dining room, they would eat at small, inexpensive cafeterias around Harvard Square, but later in the year Mailer began taking most of his meals at Dunster House, his future home.

Their Claverly Hall suite was composed of three bedrooms joined by a common living room. Next door were the rooms of a transfer student from Northwestern, Larry Weiss, who was a class ahead of the three friends and as obsessed with literature as Mailer. Weiss stresses that they were not a very advanced group socially. Breslow had an artificial leg and lacked confidence in dealing with women. He loved classical music and played in the Harvard orchestra and did occasionally date a girl, Eunice Alberts, who later became a celebrated contralto. Martin Lubin was the "smart" one. Small, dark, and intense, he studied diligently and consistently received A's. During the year he began dating a girl whom he later married.

Mailer brought his Brooklyn girl friend, Phyllis, up to Harvard twice that year, but most of his sexual energy was directed at trying to have an affair with a Cambridge "townie," an adventure his friends believe was fruitless. The roommates never met the girl, and as Larry Weiss recalls: "It was all very surreptitious, something he did on the sly. On the one hand he was proud of it, and on the other hand he didn't consider it a very exalted experience."

Money was scarce, and the real weekend amusement were the home football games. Afterwards, the students would stream onto the field and tear down the goalposts, something Mailer did with particular zeal. Occasionally they would visit the local burlesque house, the Old Howard, on Scollay Square. For superior weekend meals they would go to Durgin Park in Boston, where one could get a steak dinner for $1.15. The group also frequented McBride's or the Beer Garden on the Square for beer-drinking sessions.

That year Mailer met George Goethals, a New England WASP from Phillips Academy, when they both were "heeling" for the *Advocate*. Goethals, who was to become the class poet, remembers that Mailer seldom went to such local stomping grounds as the

Raymore Playmore Ballroom, where you could pick up girls and listen to great swing combos. Had Mailer joined Goethals, he might have seen Frank Sinatra make his first major public appearance with Harry James, who had just splintered off from Benny Goodman to form his own band with Sinatra as soloist.

Goethals, now a Harvard professor of psychology, saw Mailer as a sexually naïve young man. "Norman's view on women and sex, as far as I'm concerned, was largely between his ears. I did not, by any standards, see him as sexually precocious, except in his fantasy life. There, my God, yes." Both Goethals and Mailer later attended a writing class in which Mailer wrote five daring short essays inspired by a ride on the Boston subway. He had seen a man grab a woman's private parts, and imagining what the woman felt like, Mailer wrote a series about sexual solicitation in public places. "He certainly didn't do any fieldwork on it," Goethals insists.

Serious dating did not start for any of them until their junior year; that sophomore year Mailer and his friends were more concerned with their studies and intellectual interests. Weiss started a small literary salon in his room, and each week a handful of Harvard men and people from the Cambridge community would take tea while they read samples of their own work or discussed literature. Mailer joined the group but soon became impatient with what he considered its pretentiousness. There was a phoniness about all literary groups, he complained, and he dropped out after a few sessions.

Weiss admits that his literary taste was "fancier" than Mailer's at the time, particularly since Norman was becoming adamant about the proletarian novel, scorning any romantic inclinations in writing. During one discussion in Mailer's room in Claverly to which Mailer had invited one of his English instructors, Herb Barrows, Mailer started an argument about the importance of describing bowel movements in literature. Weiss insisted that he had no objection to bowel movements per se; he just objected to describing people's bowel movements and calling it literature. Mailer later introduced Weiss to Joyce's *Ulysses* by picking out the sex passages and reading them aloud.

Weiss's tastes were more traditional than Mailer's, but Professor Robert Gorham Davis, whose English course Mailer had elected to take, was impressed by the young author's ideas and work. It was a rare meeting of teacher and student, one that was to launch Mailer as a published writer while he was still at college. Davis was a young leftist teacher, who was later to go to Smith College, where he taught Sylvia Plath. A member of the Teacher's Union, he was in full sympathy with F. O. Matthiessen's approach to literature and put great emphasis on the use of personal experience in writing.

Davis's class was composed of at least fifty students, which was relatively large for an elective. He would occasionally read from the works of well-known authors, but mostly he discussed the students' work, after which the class would criticize. Mailer was pleased by the experience but later compared it to being a "novice in the Golden Gloves" and having one's psyche bruised.

Mailer's psyche received even more battering when Davis read passages from John Dos Passos and Ernest Hemingway and compared the masters' prose style with the work of the students. The writing of Dos Passos, particularly his controversial novel *U.S.A.*, which had been published in 1937, held a special place in Davis's course. "I was very much aware of Dos Passos. He had been a great friend of my teacher of writing, Robert Hillyer, who is a character in *U.S.A.*," explains the critic and former Harvard professor.

Hillyer would also teach Mailer in his senior year, adding to the impact Dos Passos's work made on the impressionable young writer. Davis suggests that Dos Passos's *Three Soldiers* was a strong influence on the evolving Mailer. Although some critics later compared parts of *The Naked and the Dead* to *U.S.A.*, Davis believes that *Three Soldiers*, with its contrasting social types and its negative attitude toward the war machine, was the more important influence.

❦

But it was Ernest Hemingway, the living symbol of literary masculinity, and not Dos Passos, whom Mailer tried to emulate that sophomore year. He became obsessed wtih Hemingway, mesmerized by the famed author's work and life-style. Soon, in his own unsophisticated way, Mailer began to imitate the author of *A Farewell to Arms*. With bemused tolerance, Mailer's roommates watched him assume the role of the macho writer as if watching a baby take its first hesitant steps. "Hemingway was his idol," Sy Breslow recalls, "and if Hemingway drank gin while he was writing, Norman had to drink gin while he was writing."

It was all a magnificent fantasy for the emerging young writer, who saw in Hemingway everything he was not. Hemingway came from a "good" gentile American family from the idyllic midwestern community of Oak Park, Illinois, where Hemingway's father was a physician. Mailer came from a middle-class Jewish home where his mother was the dominant partner and his father less than successful. Hemingway was tall and brawny, Mailer was short and thin. Hemingway was supremely macho, even to the point of caricature: writing and living as sportsman, boxer, hunter, drinker, womanizer. Hemingway exuded virility as did his fictional characters. He lived with a swagger and was easy to provoke into bellicosity by an edgy phrase or a direct challenge.

Mailer's imitation of Hemingway even extended to a physical pugnacity, one which seemed ridiculous in the slightly built teenager. One night George Goethals was standing outside his dorm, Leverett House, with his two roommates when he saw Mailer approaching. Mailer was drunk. "It was not," Goethals says, "because Norman was a heavy drinker, but simply because he could not hold his liquor."

Mailer tottered up to them grinning and said, "I'm Rocky Graziano and I'm going to knock the shit out of you." Goethals, then some half-a-head taller than Mailer, put his hand on Norman's right shoulder and held him patiently at arm's length while the drunken young author unsuccessfully tried to throw a few punches. After a few minutes, Mailer just laughed and sauntered away.

By the end of his sophomore year Mailer had adopted his Hemingwayesque pose with enthusiasm. The stance was to become even more pronounced in later years, but at the age of seventeen Mailer had already conceived of himself in a heroic mold. He had actively begun to sculpt an aggressive image of himself, in both writing and life, that was at odds with that of the gentle and unathletic Jewish boy from Brooklyn. The discrepancy between his macho style and his natural gentleness would grow as time went on, and today it is difficult to tell which parts of Mailer's makeup are inherent and which have been adopted from Hemingway and others as literary coloration.

Sports were also becoming an important symbol for young Mailer. He had come to Harvard with little athletic interest except in the traditional two-sewer stickball game of the Brooklyn streets. Beatrice Silverman says that as one of the youngest and least physically developed in his class at Boys High School, Mailer even had difficulty jumping the "horse" in gym. But now he was embarking on a major masculine goal: playing football.

In his sophomore year Mailer tried out for the class football team along with Larry Weiss. Weiss dropped out, but Mailer made it and soon threw himself into the role of a jock. He kept a small football in his room, where his indoor forward passes disturbed the dorm proctor, who lived next door. Weiss also recalls that Mailer developed a chronic habit of applying football blocks to anyone he might be walking with in the Harvard halls. His roommate Martin Lubin became the target of most of these antics. "Norman was full of animal spirits. Football and blocking people seemed to release some kind of energy that he had to get out," Weiss believes.

Mailer even started playing squash that year, generally with Sy Breslow. Despite Breslow's wooden leg, he was a good player, who characterizes Mailer's game as being "about equal to mine." The fact that Mailer played squash at all is interesting, for the sport was then an upper-class one for which he had announced his disdain. John Crockett remembers meeting Mailer while he was carrying a squash racket. "Don't tell me you play squash," Mailer said, almost scornfully. When Crockett replied that he was giving lessons to the son of the president of Panama, Mailer made it clear he did not approve.

Mailer's Harvard friends recall with amusement his first attempts at playing the macho writer, but primarily they remember him for his other, more sensitive side: the warm, generous young man. Half the Faulkner books that George Goethals now owns were presents from Mailer at Harvard, and when Goethals tried to join the Signet Society in his senior year, it was Mailer, already a member, who helped him get in. The day Goethals was admitted, he found a note at his dorm alongside a copy of Faulkner's *Dr. Martino and Other Stories*. The note read, "Dear Doc, you made it. Congratulations. Norman."

Mailer's kindness was not self-advertised like his Hemingway pose. One example involved a boy in Claverly Hall who was extremely unpopular with his classmates and obviously lonely. Mailer made a point of befriending him when no one else would. Mailer's generosity later extended to Harvard itself. Goethals recalls that five years after Mailer graduated, when *The Naked and the Dead* was published, he sent a check for a thousand dollars to Harvard with a telegram that read, "I hit it out of the ballpark and I owe it to you guys." Out of a class that included scions of the wealthiest families in America, Mailer was one of the first to make a sizeable contribution to his alma mater.

The warmth in Mailer's personality was noticed by Hope Hale Davis, the wife of Professor Robert Gorham Davis, but she has since been disappointed by its virtual absence in his work. After arriving at

Harvard the Davises entertained Norman at their house during his sophomore year. "At Harvard," Robert Davis remembers, "we invited comparatively few students to the house, and it's notable that we asked Norman."

"Mailer came by himself for dinner one night," Mrs. Davis adds. "His eyes were beautiful, and he was just as sweet as his eyes were beautiful. He was eager but not too eager, and he was gently thoughtful and completely open to experience. There was a sweetness about him that I've noticed ever since, although it always struck us that this niceness, this sweetness, got so little into his writing generally. There's almost no love or affection expressed for people in his writing, but a great deal of cruelty. He's naturally a nice boy, but he has always felt he has to fight that." George Goethals noticed that same internal struggle within Mailer, one that has grown to mythic proportions over the years. "There is such a good self there that he is afraid of," Goethals says.

In retrospect Robert Gorham Davis agrees with his wife about Mailer's failings, but that sophomore year Mailer impressed him enormously. Davis thought so highly of a short story that Mailer wrote for his class that he suggested Norman send it to *Story* magazine's annual college contest. It was no routine suggestion: In his many years at Harvard Davis recommended only two other students for that competition.

Story magazine, then managed by Whit Burnett and his wife Hallie, was one of the nation's major forums for short-story writers. James T. Farrell, John Cheever, J. D. Salinger, Carson McCullers, Erskine Caldwell, and William Saroyan were first published in its pages. "*Story* was its own legend," Mailer later recalled, "and young writers in the late thirties and the years of the Second World War used to dream of appearing in its pages."

The short story Mailer sent in was "The Greatest Thing in the World," a fast-paced Hemingwayesque piece about three pool sharks who pick up a young man on the road and then try to hustle him in a few games of pool by letting him win at first. The young man eventually fools the sharks, escaping with the money by jumping out of a car. It won *Story's* first prize in June 1941, an impressive coup for a sophomore.

Prior to that Harvard's own literary elite had already acknowledged Mailer by publishing "The Greatest Thing in the World" in the April issue of the *Advocate* and appointing Mailer to its literary board as an associate editor. This was no small honor for the *Advocate*—even if it did not have the social rank of *The Harvard Lampoon* or the influence of *The Harvard Crimson*—was a predominantly Brahmin institution of considerable prestige. Competition to get on the *Advocate* was strong, and Jews were seldom admitted to the board. As the then-president of the *Advocate*, Marvin Barrett, now at the Columbia Graduate School of Journalism, acknowledges, "Between Walter Lippmann and Norman Mailer there were very few Jews on the *Advocate*. I think Norman was one of the first of a new dispensation."

In the Harvard literary world of 1941 what one wore and how one spoke were almost as important as what one wrote. And despite the "new dispensation," neither Mailer's social image nor his prose fit the *Advocate* mold. "Mailer just didn't wear the right clothes," remembers John Crockett, who was then an associate on the board. "He wasn't the right kind of person to come on the *Advocate*. He was Jewish; he came from Brooklyn. He didn't wear the tweed jacket that everybody wore at the time. He even wore sneakers. Bowden Broadwater and I thought 'The Greatest Thing in the World' was just dreadful, but also interesting."

Broadwater, who was considered by some on the *Advocate* to be the writer of the future, today is the registrar of St. Bernard's School in New York. In retrospect, he views Mailer's story more favorably. " 'The Greatest Thing in the World' was different from the usual pretentious nonsense we printed," he says. "It was such a relief from all the carefully well-made schoolboy stories. It was the real stuff. But it seemed awfully sort of childish in a way as well."

"The bow-tied, velvet-slippered, three-piece-suit types that made up the *Advocate* found Norman hard to take," says George Goethals, who was appointed to the board along with Mailer and was the only *Advocate* staffer fully on Mailer's side that year. Although Goethals was also a socially prominent Boston Brahmin, he had an eye for talent. He characterized the Harvard caste system as one based on "money and lineage" but believed that money and talent rarely went together. Mailer obviously didn't have the money, but he clearly had the talent, Goethals felt.

Mailer scorned the foppery of the board, but he was having qualms about the quality of his prose, a fear that Goethals understood. "Norman always told me I was a better writer, that he could write 'shit,' but I could really write. He said his aspiration in life—which was to be accomplished in a particular way—was to write a million words of shit and get bad writing out of his system and then get a job at five hundred dollars a week writing screenplays in Hollywood and screwing a different woman every night. He wanted to be a professional writer, not a great novelist. He said if he could ever get a novel going and make enough money at it and keep it coming, he'd much prefer to do that than be a professional hack. But if the choice came between being a professional hack and not writing, he'd be a professional hack."

Mailer may have been worried about his work that sophomore year, but his social status was improving rapidly. In addition to the *Advocate*, he was elected to Signet Society, an elite club which selected the leading campus intellectuals, writers, and politicians. This was a considerable achievement, for many Harvard clubs chose their members mainly on the basis of social status or lineage. This was especially true of such "final" clubs as Porcellian, Phoenix SK, and the Fly Club, to which FDR had belonged. Other clubs, such as Hasty Pudding, to which Alan Jay Lerner was admitted, were centered around the performing arts. Signet's aim was to offer the fellowship of a club to students with distinction in literary and extracurricular fields.

It was usual for the editors of the *Crimson*, the *Advocate*, and the *Lampoon* to be admitted into Signet's ranks, but only twenty-eight students a year from one class, chosen in groups of seven, were admitted to the club. Although Signet was more liberal than most, it was noteworthy when a Jew—or any minority member—was taken in. The year Mailer joined, there was a raging battle over the admittance of the first black in Signet's history, Drue King.

All new members of Signet were required to give an original speech to veteran members, after which they were bombarded with nasty questions. If they survived that harassment with poise, they were given a rose, which they were supposed to return along with a copy of their first work when it was published. Signet member John Morton Blum, now professor of history at Yale, recalls that when Mailer was called on to give his maiden speech, it was so awful that the members were stunned.

The talks were intended to be humorous, but Mailer, whose public attempts at humor are still often disastrous, settled for a hoary Irish joke which he delivered to an embarrassed audience. Blum remembers that Mailer's "speech" went something like this: Two New York Irishmen were standing on a street corner outside a bar. A woman drives up in a large Cadillac to park in a tiny space. One

Irishman says to the other, "If that babe parks that car, I'll kiss your ass." The woman backs successfully into the space. The Irishman turns to his friend and says, "What a driver!"

Mailer shone brighter at the passionate literary discussions that took place at Signet's daily lunch. There was both a literary table and a political table, but Mailer ignored the political table, where Elliot L. Richardson, class of 1941, and other future government leaders would expound. Instead he held forth courageously at the literary table against the phalanxes of Brahmins, defending the new proletarian novel.

By the end of his sophomore year Mailer was no longer an outsider. He had been elected to Signet, his literary talents had been recognized both on and off the campus, and he had made the class football team. There was only one more test for the shy boy from Brooklyn: women.

In the summer of 1941 Mailer went on a hitchhiking tour of the South in an attempt to imitate the nomadic life of John Dos Passos. It was during that trip that Mailer lost his virginity at the age of eighteen in a whorehouse somewhere in Virginia. Earlier in the year there had been another brothel escapade which Mailer recounted to his roommates, but no one can confirm his actual loss of virginity. The conclusive deflowering in Virginia was described by Mailer to George Goethals, who received a number of letters from him that summer, one of which included a graphic account of the whorehouse incident. The young man who was to become the notorious champion of the orgasm had begun his sexual odyssey.

During this same summer holiday Mailer wrote his first novel, appropriately about a boy breaking away from his parents. Mailer would later say that this 488-page unpublished tome, *No Percentage*, was about a rich boy who was trying to establish his independence from his family, but Larry Weiss, who read it the following year, describes the family as middle-class Jewish and not dissimilar to Mailer's own. "As I remember, it was about parents who thought they had a child prodigy and were suffocating him with attention," he says.

No Percentage was probably an outgrowth of Mailer's relationship with his strong-willed mother, Fanny Schneider Mailer. Throughout his life Fanny influenced her son more profoundly than any other person, and she has remained the only one to whom Mailer willingly defers. Although at Harvard Mailer was actively engaged in growing beyond his nice-Jewish-boy-from-Brooklyn image, and even though his novel pilloried suffocating parents, he would never break his ties with Fanny.

❦

Mailer was the firstborn and the only son in a family that was dominated by the matriarchal figure of Fanny. Mailer's father, Isaac Barnett "Barney" Mailer, was a good-looking but rather weak man of Russian-Jewish extraction who, says his former daughter-in-law Bea Silverman, had a penchant for gin and a good time. He had served in the British Army as a supply officer during World War I and had emigrated to America from South Africa via London shortly after the war.

Barney and Fanny were married, and on January 31, 1923, Norman Kingsley Mailer was born in Long Branch, New Jersey, where Fanny's family had a small hotel business. Four years later the Mailers moved to the Crown Heights section of Brooklyn, a neighborhood of trees and two-family homes, where Norman had a quiet and uneventful childhood.

Mailer was an excellent student at the local school, P.S. 161, and spent much of his leisure time building model airplanes, balsa wood and glue monsters powered by large rubber-band motors. He took the compulsory music lessons, saxophone and clarinet, but showed little talent for music. He also took a typically boyish interest in reading *Spicy Detective* and the adventure novels of Rafael Sabatini, particularly *Captain Blood.* There was little sign of the enormous ego Mailer would later display except for a hint in his bar mitzvah speech at the age of thirteen. Young Mailer told the assembly of friends and relatives that he hoped to follow in the footsteps of "great Jews like Moses Maimonides and Karl Marx."

Mailer was usually a dutiful son, but one time he shed his conventional young demeanor. He decided he would sleep on the Bowery all night. His mother objected, but he defied Fanny and stayed overnight with the derelicts. When he came home, Fanny wouldn't let him into the house until he agreed to take off all his clothes, which she quickly burned in the incinerator.

Grade school was not taxing for him, and as Fanny has said, "Norman always had the highest marks." He continued his excellent school record at Boys High in Brooklyn, where he was elected to Arista, an honor society for the highest-ranking students. He was intrigued by the sciences and math and during his years at Boys High,

1936–39, young Mailer served as honorary president of the Aviation Club and as editor of a student publication, *Physical Scientist*. His only literary output in high school was his first published piece: a tome on the building of model airplanes.

The family was poor during the depths of the Depression, then somewhat middle-class during the late 1930s, but Mailer's home environment was always a loving, nourishing one. Bea Silverman describes the relationship between Fanny, Norman, and his sister, Barbara, as very close. "Norman would delight in teasing Fanny like a lover," Bea says. Larry Alson, who married Barbara Mailer in 1950, recalls that this habit continued into adulthood. Norman would playfully try to agitate Fanny. "Fanny hated cursing, so Norman would shout out, 'Fuck, shit, piss,' " Alson recounts. "Fanny would call out, 'Norman, Norman,' as if to make him stop, and then she would giggle. It was like he was tickling her."

Barney Mailer was not a strong figure in the Mailer home. "Fanny and Barney should never have married," Bea says. "I think one of the reasons she married him is because he was handsome." But in spite of what Bea sees as a weak union, she stresses that Norman was always encouraged as a child. "What intelligence and talent Norman was born with certainly were not unaided by the people in his environment," says Mailer's first wife. "He had tremendous support. Fanny had a lot of sisters. His cousin, Charles Rembar, was the son of Fanny's oldest sister, Aunt Rosie. There was also an Aunt Jenny, and Charles had a sister, Marjorie. All the women in the family thought that Norman was the 'cat's meow.' "

Mailer was surrounded by adoring women, but his mother was, and is, the core of his strength. His father, who spoke with a Cockney-Yiddish accent, worked indifferently as an accountant, but Fanny was the economic backbone of the family. With the income from her small oil-delivery business Fanny was able to send Norman and Barbara to good schools. Later, with her son's assistance, she bought and ran a thriving nursing and housekeeping service. Fanny was the intellectual mentor of the family as well. She gave Mailer his first writing notebooks at the age of nine, which he dutifully filled with a two-hundred-and-fifty-page story about an invasion from Mars, writing a chapter a day. Mailer was reading the Tarzan novels of Edgar Rice Burroughs, and these fanciful adventures inspired his tale, "The Martian Invasion."

It was Fanny who convinced Norman that he would be a special person. Although Fanny's family, the Schneiders, had worked in the hotel business, there was an intellectual strain in Fanny's father which she would cultivate in her son. When Mailer's father was asked where Norman's genius had come from, he replied, "From his maternal grandfather, a Talmudic scholar." The union of the strong, practical mother and the weak, intellectual father was not an uncommon one among immigrant Jewish families, but in Mailer's case Fanny clearly provided nurture in both areas, the practical and the inspirational.

"I have always thought of Fanny as a lioness," says Larry Alson. "She looked like a lioness, and she protected her cubs the way a lioness should. When Norman, for instance, was in fourth or fifth grade, a teacher gave him a C. Fanny went to the school, saw the teacher, and said, 'You've got to change this grade. Norman is my child, and my child is incapable of doing mediocre work. Something is wrong with your evaluation.' She made the teacher change the grade. Norman is partially the result of a woman consumed with love for her son."

Of his six wives only his first, Beatrice, was cast somewhat in his mother's mold. But soon after she met him at Harvard, Bea recalls, Mailer made it clear to her that he really wanted to "lay *shiksas.*" It took ten more years for his desire for a gentile wife to come to fruition, but the seeds of revolt against his background had been clearly planted in Mailer's mind, and Harvard was to accelerate that rebellion.

❦

When Mailer returned to Harvard from Brooklyn for his junior year in the fall of 1941, he and Martin Lubin moved into Dunster House, a beautiful old red-brick dormitory near the Charles River. It was to be another momentous year for young Mailer. His short story "The Greatest Thing in the World" would appear in the November-December issue of *Story* magazine. A New York book editor would voice interest in any novels he might write. America would be drawn into the war, and Mailer would meet his first wife.

The political mood of the campus had altered that fall after Hitler's invasion of Russia. In his opening address to the undergraduate body President James Conant spoke not of the scholar's duties in a peacetime society but of his duties in wartime. A few days later, as the news columns of the *Crimson* reported that Harvard men had offered the girls at Mt. Holyoke College the use of their showers during the water shortage, an editorial confirmed a complete shift in the paper's war policy. Almost solidly noninterventionist the previous spring, the editors now thought differently: "Either we must believe that Hitler has to be defeated, or we must believe that America can live alone and like it. We believe the former."

The leftist Student Union, which only a year before had vigorously protested President Roosevelt's aid to the Allies, had adopted a different line now that Russia had been invaded by the Nazis: "The goal of all persons wishing to preserve democracy . . . must be the military defeat of Hitler." The shift toward prowar sentiment would not be universal until a few months later, but in the fall of 1941, students began to be concerned about their immediate futures. As the *Lampoon* put it, they were torn between "Scylla the Dean and Charybdis the Draft."

Mailer did not fully ignore the new prowar sentiment, but his immediate concern was Theodore Morrison's advanced composition course, A3, which he took that fall. Morrison, a gentlemanly New England WASP, was a breed apart from young Mailer. Although he found Mailer an impressive student and worthy of the A-minus grade he gave him, Morrison was not, and still is not, in full sympathy with the uses to which Mailer put his talent.

Morrison allowed the students to write what they wished as long as they produced three thousand words a week. Mailer, as George Goethals recalls, made it a personal rule to write three thousand words *a day;* this was in addition to his full load of engineering courses. The professionalism that would later enable him to meet grueling deadlines from magazine and book publishers was beginning to show.

George Goethals clearly remembers Mailer's early professionalism. "He was incredibly self-disciplined, but I never knew a more unenchanted writer in the making. To him it was work. He used to say, 'George, this business of inspiration is shit.' He would take a theme and sculpt it five or six different ways. He was going to be a writer, dammit." John Crockett recalls much the same industriousness: "Norman was very ambitious and very restless. He kept writing and writing. He wrote things over and over on the very same subject."

Mailer's best short story that junior year was "Maybe Next Year," a haunting piece about a young rural boy learning the cruelty of the world from his embattled parents during the Depression. Mailer had just read *The Sound and the Fury*, and his short story, he acknowledges, was derivative of Faulkner. That fall Mailer also met Whit

Burnett, the editor of *Story* magazine. A modest man with a white goatee, Burnett invited Mailer to lunch about the time that "The Greatest Thing in the World" appeared in *Story*. Mailer, who was still only eighteen, was embarrassed during the luncheon. He couldn't think of anything interesting to say, and Burnett was equally uncomfortable because he could not draw the young writer out. Burnett eventually asked him if he knew anything about chamber music groups, and Mailer admitted he was an "ignoramus" about such things. The two kept eating through longer and longer silences.

During his junior year Mailer also began a correspondence with another New York editor, Theodore Amussen of Rinehart & Co., the man who was eventually to publish *The Naked and the Dead*. Amussen relates the story of how he learned of Mailer. In the late fall of 1941 Amussen attended the seventy-fifth anniversary dinner of the *Advocate*, where he sat next to the late Roy E. Larsen, who was then president of Time, Inc. Larsen had just read Mailer's "The Greatest Thing in the World" in *Story* and was impressed. He told Amussen he really should contact Mailer about a possible novel, and by the end of the dinner Amussen had assured him he would get in touch with the young writer. Larsen, who liked *The Naked and the Dead*, was not enthusiastic about any of Mailer's later work, and by 1963 he was no longer reading Mailer at all. But the *Time* executive's role in establishing Norman Mailer was crucial.

Those final months of 1941 were not the best of times for an editor to be thinking about any undergraduate's future work, but almost no one foresaw the disastrous event that would take place on December 7. Few Americans viewed Japan as a real threat—although the first issue of the *Crimson* in December 1941 carried a prophetic editorial that turned into bloody reality only a few days later: "Though Secretary Hull's stand leaves the next move up to Japan, and though that next move might very conceivably mean war, comparatively little attention is paid to Japan by the American public; and if war does come, it will undoubtedly take us by surprise."

On December 3, while J. P. Marquand was presenting Harvard with the movie script of *H. M. Pulham, Esquire*, in Widener Library, President Roosevelt was demanding an explanation of Japan's recent aggression in Thailand. The following Sunday afternoon, while Mailer was playing football on a Harvard lot and George Goethals was having lunch with his father in Boston, Larry Weiss and Sy Breslow were in Breslow's room about to listen to the New York

Philharmonic on the radio. Like millions of other Americans who turned on the CBS broadcast at 3 P.M., they heard the fateful announcement, "The Japanese have today attacked Pearl Harbor." By nightfall the Harvard campus was in turmoil.

"Everybody congregated that night and wanted to talk about it," remembers Breslow. "The next morning there was a convocation for the entire student body. The dean got up and said, 'Look, fellows, keep living. Things are going to happen soon enough.' It was far and away the most traumatic thing that had happened to any of us up to that point."

That day Mailer and Larry Weiss went for a drive along the Worcester Turnpike and talked about the war. They stopped by a pond, and Weiss began violently throwing logs into the water. Weiss had been a pacifist, and it was now clear to him that "all kinds of militaristic things were going to come over the country." As Weiss fumed, he realized that Mailer thought he was being histrionic; Norman did not feel as strongly against the war as he did. At the beginning of the ride Mailer had voiced some anger that the war had come, but by the time Weiss had finished his rantings, Mailer was no longer as upset. "He thought it was foolish to be spouting like that," recalls Weiss.

Although Mailer had begun to accept the inevitability of war, the young man who was to write the first great World War II novel then viewed the conflict primarily as dramatic input for his work-to-be. As Sy Breslow puts it: "Rather than thinking about the horror of war or the fact that he might get killed, he looked at it as an experience which would feed the novel he wanted to write afterward. He was desperately searching for experience at the time, because he came to the realization that you can't write if you don't experience."

By early 1942 Mailer's ambitious eye was already envisioning the book he would later write, but his more immediate concern was finding a publisher for his novel *No Percentage*. Since Amussen had already gotten in touch with him, Mailer decided to submit *No Percentage* to him. Amussen read the book but rejected it. Soon after that Mailer brought the manuscript over to George Goethals's room and asked him if he would take a look at it. Goethals was too busy to read the whole manuscript, but after skimming it he told Mailer he thought it "looked good." Mailer replied, "Well, I just wanted you to get the feel of it. I don't know whether to push for it. With the war coming I don't think I will."

Mailer did try at least one more publisher, Whit Burnett, who ran a small trade-book line, Story Press, along with his *Story* magazine. Mailer wrote Burnett that he would like to come see him in New York during spring vacation to discuss the novel. As it happened, they missed each other, and nothing came of the idea.

❦

That year, his third at Harvard, Mailer became embroiled in his first literary controversy, one of the many that would erupt over the years. The *Advocate* had changed hands that fall, and Bruce Barton, Jr., was elected president, while John Crockett became Pegasus, or literary editor. Barton and Crockett had different views about what type of magazine they would publish. It created a conflict in which Mailer sided with Barton and which the author made famous in a 1977 *Esquire* story, "Our Man at Harvard." What Mailer did not make clear in the article was the significance of his own loyalty in the literary battle.

Mailer had become close friends with the socially prominent Barton, one of his first direct crossings of the Harvard social barrier. Many were surprised, but it was another strong move by Mailer away from the confines of his bourgeois Brooklyn background to a more socially mobile Harvard life. Barton, a chubby blond youth who was considered to be nice if not very talented, was still the ultimate Harvard WASP. His father, Bruce Barton, Sr., was an advertising giant, one of the founders of Batten, Barton, Durstine and Osborn, and famous for his best-selling book about Jesus, *The Man Nobody Knows*. Young Barton had attended the prestigious Deerfield Academy and had grown up surrounded by wealth.

According to Mailer, Barton's aim was to have a "benign, well-financed, and agreeable administration." Barton's first issue, to the staff's delight, was to be devoted to their own stories. Since Crockett was responsible for printing the magazine, he presumably took the carefully assembled issue with all the staff members' stories to the magazine's printer in Vermont that fall. But by February no issue had arrived, and the *Advocate* staff was becoming increasingly chafed. Crockett kept reassuring them but warned that nobody should disturb the printer with anxious telephone calls. Nobody did.

In March the printer finally delivered the finished magazine, but it bore no resemblance to the one the staff had prepared five months before. Instead, it was Crockett's own product, one which he had secretly put together over the past year as a seventy-fifth-anniversary issue containing the works of such illustrious writers as Wallace

Stevens, Marianne Moore, Djuna Barnes, Robert Hillyer, and John Malcolm Brinin. Crockett had printed his own poem in the issue, but no one else on the staff was so honored. An angry Mailer later termed Crockett's ruse "a mammoth virtuoso critico-literary crypto-CIA affair."

Barton immediately addressed the staff and chastised himself for not watching over the magazine more carefully. He would not fire Crockett, he said, if he could expect his future cooperation. Crockett nodded assent and then made an announcement that delighted the staff. Crockett had heard that novelist Somerset Maugham would be in Boston in April, and he had invited him to an *Advocate* party in his honor. Maugham had accepted, Crockett told the staff. "Nothing in four years at Harvard," rhapsodized Mailer, "not Dunkirk, Pearl Harbor, or the blitz . . . could have lit Harvard up more. Not to be invited to that party was equal to signifying that one had mismanaged one's life."

On the night of the Maugham party four hundred people were amassed in the five-room suite of *Advocate* offices. It was so crowded that when rumors rippled through the room that Maugham had arrived, no one could be sure they were true. After half an hour, more rumors made their way through the crowd. Maugham was leaving. Maugham had left. The next day, after lengthy cross-checking, it was woefully confirmed that Maugham had never set foot in the *Advocate* offices the previous night. When confronted, says Mailer, Crockett admitted that he had known for weeks that Maugham was not coming. According to Mailer's account Crockett had received a telegram from Maugham answering his original invitation. It read, "Certainly not."

John Crockett tells the story of the special issue and the Maugham affair differently, implicating Mailer as a dupe of the Brahmin establishment, if not worse. In Crockett's view, he had to publish the seventy-fifth-anniversary issue surreptitiously if he was to produce an international literary magazine of quality rather than the "smart-alecky undergraduate juvenalia" that he feels Barton and Mailer were intent on publishing.

The literary editors at Yale and the University of Chicago were now making the same transition toward professional journals. There were several impressive literary magazines edited by undergraduates, such as *Furioso*, first issued at Yale in 1939 by James Jesus Angleton, later the CIA's counterespionage chief, and Reed Whittmore. In 1942,

Dunstan Thompson and Harry Brown published *Vice Versa* in New York City.

"It was inconceivable for me not to want to do a magazine like these," says Crockett. "For anybody who wanted to be a writer at Harvard at this time to have chosen the route that Bruce Barton and Norman Mailer did showed that they had no taste." Six *Advocate* staff members, including the business manager, Dick Johnson, had met secretly in Crockett's room that fall to put the issue together. Barton and Mailer knew something was going on but did not have enough information to confront him, Crockett says.

Crockett felt he had to devote himself fully to the *Advocate* if he was to prevail over Barton, and he insists he used his own funds to buy several of the stories in the issue, money he earned working in a Hungarian restaurant. "Barton had literary pretensions, but we all agreed that he was no writer," Crockett says. "We were willing to sacrifice our own poems and short stories if we could keep Bruce's out. Barton and Mailer didn't know how complete the revolution was. When the magazine came out, it had tremendous critical acclaim." The *Crimson*, in fact, criticized the issue for containing "the worst things of the best people," but agreed that the issue had been a significant one.

Crockett's view of the Maugham party also differs markedly from Mailer's. It was not until the last minute that he discovered that Maugham was not coming. By then, Crockett says, it was too late to stop the party. At the party he decided not to say anything because everyone was having such a good time. Despite Mailer's claim, there never was a telegram from Maugham declining his invitation, Crockett swears.

What disturbs Crockett the most about the *Advocate* affair is his belief that the talented young Mailer had sided with the talentless Barton. "Norman was always devoted to Bruce Barton, but I don't think Barton was as devoted to Norman," says Crockett. "I think he regarded him as a bit of a deficit. Barton himself was very Deerfield and very snobbish with white suede shoes and pink shirts. But he had no literary talent or taste. I was absolutely furious that Norman, who had the talent and who wasn't a rich clubby type, would side with Barton rather than me. It seemed to be opportunism.

"I also thought he was betraying his social background. He wasn't as left-wing as he should have been. He was going off with a conservative right-winger, and I felt very strongly that the kind of material I was publishing and the kinds of ideas I was espousing were libertarian ideologies."

Mailer's friendship with Barton may have been opportunistic, but it was less a betrayal of his social background than a step beyond it. At Harvard, Mailer continued to characterize himself as a third-generation Jew from Brooklyn. In fact, George Goethals remembers that he was the most outspoken member of the class about being Jewish. "Norman was blatantly and abrasively Jewish," Goethals says.

Mailer's ethnic chauvinism was no doubt convincing to gentile acquaintances, who did not see it for what it probably was, a sign of defensive pride. But to a practicing Jew, it was obvious that Mailer had little interest in Judaism, either ethnically or theologically. Harold Katz, who was to room with Mailer the following year, came from a rabbinical family in Indiana. He explains: "Norman was not then an assimilationist, but neither was he a hard-core Jew. There were Zionist organizations at Harvard which he never became involved in. His activities were not specifically Jewish."

Some of Mailer's friends at Harvard saw the gradual shift in his social demeanor as evidence of Mailer's desire to belong. Although he was still vocally "Jewish," they believe that Harvard eventually got to him. They are convinced that Mailer began to take on the ethos of the seductive new environment, that he wanted to *be* Harvard. Sy Breslow thinks that, coming from such humble beginnings, Mailer was awed by the trappings of the Ivy League school. Richard Weinberg even believes that "Harvard became his new identity."

Beatrice Silverman witnessed the internal battles Mailer fought with his Jewishness in that upper-class Christian atmosphere. "Some of the guys Norman went around with were wealthy and upper-class, and it was kind of hard for a little boy from Brooklyn," she recalls. "He never felt like he fitted in." It was common for Jews of their generation to be ambivalent about being Jewish, Bea adds, and while Mailer was never "ashamed" of his Jewishness, he wanted to "lay down the burden," as she calls it, at least for a while.

Although Mailer would never renounce his Jewish heritage, he would stress it less and less as he grew older, and would transcend it to become an ultimate American writer. Like the country, Mailer was going through an assimilative process, one that would eventually make him a sounding board for Irish, black, Latin, WASP, and Jewish sensibilities, while always perceiving their distinctly individual and poetic contours. For him this assimilative stance was paradoxically the perfect defense against anti-Semitism. Few other Jewish writers of his generation would venture as far as he into the indigenous American culture.

After the Barton-Crockett contretemps subsided that spring, the staff's stories were published in the May issue of the *Advocate.* Mailer's was called "Right Shoe on Left Foot," the story of a black man in the rural South who comes to believe that passive resistance is the best way to evoke white guilt in sadistic southerners. The following month, "Maybe Next Year," the story about growing up during the Depression that Mailer had written for Theodore Morrison's class, was also published in the *Advocate.* It was the third and last of Mailer's stories to appear there.

John Marquand, Jr., the son of the famous writer John P. Marquand, remembers meeting Mailer for the first time during this same month. His account of their run-in illuminates Mailer's ambivalence about the powerful Harvard WASP establishment he was learning to deal with. Marquand was entering Harvard that June as a freshman on the accelerated war program. At that time all freshmen were required to stand in line to register at Memorial Hall, where it was standard practice for them to be approached by members of Harvard social, literary, and athletic organizations for recruiting. Because of his father's reputation young Marquand's name was headlined in *The Harvard Crimson*—along with that of Thomas Lamont, the grandson of J. P. Morgan—as a significant entering freshman. He was embarrassed by the publicity, but members of the *Advocate* had duly taken note: Marquand, Sr., was a venerable alumnus of the *Advocate.*

While Marquand was waiting in line, he had an uncomfortable encounter with an *Advocate* recruiter. "A guy appeared from the *Advocate* and kind of hovered over me, looking at me," Marquand recalls. "He said, 'I suppose you're going to want to come out for the *Advocate.*' His attitude was 'So you think you're a big shot with your name in the paper.' I just recoiled and said, 'No, not at all.' Years later, when *The Naked and the Dead* came out, I saw the author's photograph. I realized the man who approached me must have been Norman Mailer."

❦

If Mailer's *Advocate* days were winding down by the spring of 1942, his junior year, his love life was picking up. He had brought a "special" girl with him to the Somerset Maugham party. They had met several months before at a concert, which was surprising since Mailer had almost no interest in music. He had decided to join Larry Weiss and other Harvard friends at a "rush" concert given by the Boston Symphony in December. It was called "rush" because one waited in line for a fifty-cent ticket, then "rushed" upstairs to get a seat. While he was sitting on the tile floor in the lobby waiting for tickets, Mailer met Beatrice Silverman, an attractive Boston University music major from Chelsea, Massachusetts.

Beatrice had gone out with a friend of Larry Weiss's roommate, and a number of the boys there knew her. After Mailer and Beatrice talked for a few moments, she realized that "he didn't know his ass from his elbow about music," and they decided they would skip the concert. They spent the rest of the afternoon back at his room in Dunster House, beginning a relationship that would last ten years.

Mailer made it immediately clear to Bea, as he would call her, that he was a writer of no small ambition, displaying a bravado which impressed her. Bea was not the only college girl who had noticed the emerging writer; a number of other local coeds were already taken by Mailer's obvious talent. Larry Weiss remembers a trip to Radcliffe with Mailer to visit Norman's sister, Barbara, shortly after "The Greatest Thing in the World" appeared in *Story*. The young author was lionized by several of his sister's friends.

Bea did not go unnoticed herself. Ten months older than Mailer, she was intensely outspoken about both politics and sex and now admits she was "forty years ahead" of her time. When Bea met Mailer, she was adamant about America's getting into the war against Hitler. Staunchly Jewish, she had been sensitive to German anti-Semitism as early as 1939 and was bitingly intolerant of anyone who did not share her viewpoint. Although never part of a political group, she had been involved in such prowar activities as Bundles for Britain. Mailer appealed to her in part because of what she sensed was an intuitive, if uneducated, radicalism which he was beginning to articulate for the first time. "I remember our discussing politics a lot with his friends and arguing with them, too. I used to spend a great deal of time over at Harvard," Bea says.

Meeting Bea Silverman was to change Mailer's political consciousness. Growing up in Brooklyn during the Depression, Mailer had been in the center of the street socialism of the working-class Brooklyn Jewish community but had never become as involved as other boys his age, many of whom had been attracted to the Young

Communist League, or even the tamer Young People's Socialist League. In Boston, Bea guided Mailer toward political sophistication and a better understanding of radicalism.

Bea was a sexual mentor for Mailer as well. Unlike the girls he had met until then, Bea had no qualms about sleeping with him. In 1942, when probably more than half of the women at Boston University were still virgins, it was a stunning success for him. Just turned nineteen, Mailer felt victorious to have found a girl willing to have sex with him regularly. "I think he just liked me because I went to bed with him," Bea says. "In those days it was very hard to find someone to do that."

Nor was Bea bashful about letting everyone know about their affair. "All my friends were liberal about sex, and we would argue with other people about it," she recounts. "I used to get up on my soapbox and talk about it all over Harvard. I was a big loudmouth." Mailer found himself up on the same soapbox with Bea, expounding on their sexual affair with great candor. It was an avant-garde attitude for 1942, but at least one of Mailer's friends, Harold Katz, thought their stance of sexual openness was pretentious.

Neither Mailer nor Bea worried about breaking the 6:00 P.M. curfew for women at Dunster House. Today sleeping together in dorm rooms is commonplace among undergraduates, but in 1942 Mailer was seen as accomplishing a feat of legendary proportions. It was the beginning of a personal myth of sexuality which he has been willing to encourage ever since.

Mailer and Bea were a provocative pair for the relatively staid Boston of 1942. Larry Weiss remembers that the couple would dine at teahouses in Cambridge and purposely shock the old New England ladies with their loud, dirty talk. They were together constantly, their time often spent listening to Billie Holiday records in Mailer's room. Sy Breslow began dating Bea's roommate that year, and the foursome would often go to the movies on Saturday night, have a couple of beers, or have dinner together at Durgin Park in Boston.

Mailer's uncle, Dave Kessler, gave him an old black Chevrolet convertible that year, and Norman and Bea delighted in it. Kessler, who was married to Barney Mailer's sister, was the only member of the family who was rich. At the age of eighteen he had rented an opera house in South Africa and had managed to make a small fortune by bringing in international talent. In this country he started the Sphinx Chocolate Corporation in Brooklyn and grew wealthy with his invention, the chocolate-covered cherry. The Kesslers had no children of their own, and they doted on Norman, taking him to expensive restaurants and subsidizing him until his first novel was a success. Larry Alson believes that Kessler's generosity inspired Mailer's own generous impulses, especially toward younger writers.

As soon as Mailer got the convertible from Uncle Dave, he promptly made it over for dual use. He stripped the trunk and put in a mattress, making the car perfect for intimate dates with Bea as well as for transporting masses of friends around Cambridge and Boston. The convertible soon became a collective enterprise, with Breslow, Lubin, and Katz helping Mailer to support the car. The four would draw lots to see who would get to use it.

Breslow remembers that the convertible kept them perpetually broke. They had to pay for parking places, and all four would chip in when something went wrong with the car, which was often. But Breslow also recalls having a good time with the convertible, particularly one circuslike routine. "I remember one time when we pulled the black convertible up in front of a hotel. The four of us got out, and the doorman asked us if that was all. We said no. We opened the trunk, whereupon a lot of other people got out of the car." Mailer eventually took the car back to New York after graduation, where it died a quiet death on Canal Street.

Mailer's social life at Harvard also included drinking, but it was mainly a stag affair and Bea never saw him drink excessively, which he sometimes did. "We would go out on Saturday night with the kids, but no one had any money," she points out. "We'd have two beers or a bottle back in the room, but I never saw Norman drunk. Perhaps he got drunk with the boys when they went down to the Beer Garden on Harvard Square, but never with me."

In fact, Bea never saw another side of Mailer, the macho image he was so painstakingly cultivating. Nor, Bea makes it clear, would she have tolerated his posturing anyway. "We had an honest and good relationship. He never put on an act with me because I would have put him down." She was, however, sensitive to his need for a masculine show of strength, knowing the shortcomings he had to overcome from childhood. "Norman was a guy with tremendous insecurities from his childhood," Bea says. "He was always the youngest and smallest in his class, and he did not develop physically until later. Even at Harvard he was young, short, and skinny. I believe that's why this business of boxing and being tough came out later on in life."

Although Bea was providing much of the stimulation the awakened Mailer required, he decided that he still needed to gain new experience for his fictional mill. In the summer of 1942 he began working at a state mental institution outside Boston. In those days there were no medications to control psychotics, and Mailer was quickly exposed to insanity at its most naked. He remembers that experience: "I was assigned to the most violent ward. The place was unbelievably understaffed. . . . Two of us took care of sixty patients. The other hack told me the way to handle fights was to wait until one guy beat the other guy up, and then both jump the guy who won.

"After about four days the big thing blew. A colored kid went ape, a kid I knew, in another ward. He'd broken a table, and he had the two legs in each hand for clubs. The attendants were moving in on him with mattresses, trying to smother him back into a corner. But he broke through, and I tackled him. Then they closed in on him and took turns beating him until they knocked him unconscious, which took a while because he was tough. I didn't hit him, but I knew I was perhaps three months away from that kind of thing."

After four days at the hospital Mailer decided he had had enough. Bea remembers that he showed up unexpectedly that night at her father's house in Chelsea, bedraggled and rain-soaked. He told her that he had just run away from the hospital and described its horrors. He was not going back, he added. Although the experience had lasted less than a week, it would fuel his second novel, *A Transit to Narcissus*, which he started in the spring of 1943, his senior year, and finished eight months later. It would also provide the inspiration for a play Mailer wrote during the summer between his junior and senior years. The name of that unproduced play about mental illness was *The Naked and the Dead*, a title he was later to revive.

❦

In September 1942, when Mailer returned to Dunster House for his senior year, with Harold Katz as a roommate, the Harvard campus had been transformed. The day after Pearl Harbor President James Conant had pledged the resources of the university to the prosecution of the war. By now laboratories had been turned over to war research, and members of the faculty had joined the armed forces or accepted civilian posts in government agencies. Increasingly the army and the navy occupied dormitories and classrooms for the Army Specialized Training Program (ASTP). By the fall of 1942 those Harvard students who had been accepted in the Navy V-7 and V-12 officer training programs were required to attend school in full uniform. The Harvard professional schools—business, law, and medicine—were predominantly occupied by the military and attended by only a few remaining civilian students.

The college curriculum had been altered to allow rapid acceleration for those who wanted to finish school early and join the services. Many of Mailer's classmates, including George Goethals and Richard Weinberg, had accepted the challenge and had graduated the previous June. Goethals had tried to enlist in the army but was turned down for an athletic disability. Despite that, he was eventually sent to the Pacific in 1944. Weinberg had also accelerated, and upon graduation he joined the Harvard Business School as a reserve officer in the navy.

Larry Weiss graduated that June of 1942 as well but was classified 4F due to a bad knee and went to work as a reporter on the *Boston Herald*. Breslow, who had only one leg, was also classified 4F. Martin Lubin held a wartime medical school deferment. Mailer did not accelerate and continued at Harvard with a deferment as an aeronautical engineering major. As the campus emptied of his friends, Mailer continued his studies until he graduated in June 1943. "That's about as long as anybody in our class stayed around that I know about," says Richard Weinberg.

As uniformed men began marching in formation across Harvard Yard that fall, Mailer was intent on becoming a serious writer. He was accepted into the most advanced writing course Harvard offered, English A5, taught by the Pulitzer Prize-winning poet Robert Hillyer, then Harvard's distinguished Boylston Professor of Rhetoric. The undergraduate and graduate students Hillyer chose for his class were considered Harvard's finest literary talents; one had to know Hillyer to get in.

The elite group of aspiring Harvard writers was necessarily small since they met in Hillyer's living room at Adams House to read their works. John Crockett, who was in the class with Mailer that first semester, remembers how painful it was to be criticized by some of the graduate students. The primary assignment in Hillyer's course was to write the beginning of a novel, and Mailer wrote an entire novella called *A Calculus at Heaven*, in many ways a precursor to *The Naked and the Dead*. *A Calculus at Heaven* was the most ambitious piece he wrote at Harvard. He finished it in time for his twentieth birthday, in late January 1943.

Inspired by André Malraux's *Man's Fate*, the novella was an attempt to imagine what war in the Pacific might be like. Mailer thought it would be easier to write about the Pacific because it did not require a feeling for the impact of American upon European culture, which Mailer knew he lacked. Malraux and Hemingway were then being read avidly by the Harvard students, who were now intent on winning the war against fascism. These authors had become fashionable mainly because they represented a transition from pacifism to a belief in fighting the war.

As Mailer's class yearbook said, "[Malraux and Hemingway] presented something quite different from the 'warmongering' of 1939; they demonstrated unmistakingly that very literally there were forces of evil at work in the world and that it was the duty of men of good will to combat them." These lessons were not lost on Mailer, although in *A Calculus at Heaven*, the evil at work in the world is perceived as being primarily in our own backyard, in America. *A Calculus at Heaven* employs the same flashbacks and the same interweaving of contrasting social types that Mailer would later use in *The Naked and the Dead*. But without any war experience of his own, Mailer focused primarily on the inequities of American life.

❦

The liberal literary influence of the Harvard establishment on young Norman Mailer had been potent. At graduation that June of 1943, as he stood beside his classmates in cap and gown with Fanny, Barney, his sister, Barbara, and Bea looking on, Mailer had reason to appreciate the university. He had received a B.S. in engineering sciences, cum laude, but more than that Harvard had succeeded in honing the sensibilities that would one day make him a writer of stature and a prophet of more than occasional honor. A dozen years later, Mailer acknowledged the power of those four years: "I have often thought that the peculiar juxtaposition of a Brooklyn culture and a Harvard culture have had the most external importance I could name in making me wish to write."

In retrospect Mailer's accolade to Harvard may have been an understatement. Removed from his provincial Brooklyn background,

Mailer had been thrown into the three-hundred-year-old nucleus of American liberal Congregationalism. But he had not arrived naked. Mailer had come from a background of Talmudic philosophy and the modern street socialism of the 1930s with its dreams of a better tomorrow. Harvard had fused it all into the beginnings of a new Norman Mailer, a young man still too naïve to articulate what was happening but who knew that he had crossed over into a broader realm of American experience.

• III •

THE NAKED AND THE DEAD

After graduating from Harvard in June 1943 Mailer returned home to his mother's apartment at 102 Pierrepont Street in Brooklyn Heights and occupied himself with three concerns: his obsession with becoming a famous novelist, his relationship with his girl friend, Bea Silverman, and his impending entry into the United States Army.

In the months after graduation Mailer continued to work on his six-hundred-page novel, *A Transit to Narcissus*, based on his experience in the Boston mental hospital the previous summer. It was, said Mailer, a "romantic, morbid, twisted, and heavily tortured work." Mailer was then living with his mother, but he rented a small room a couple of blocks away in an industrial building near the Navy Yard in order to write *Narcissus*. It was the first of the many studios Mailer was to have throughout his life. "He always had to go away to write, and he had a propensity for wanting to be in the strangest places when he wrote," Bea recalls.

All through the summer of 1943 Mailer worked on *Narcissus*, aware that at any moment he might be drafted into the army yet surprised that he had not been. "The only explanation I can find for such delay is that my draft card must have fallen into the back of the file," he later recalled. "I worked on the book because I was out of college and my friends were at war and there was no sense in looking for a job if I would also be a soldier soon. . . . I was as lonely as I have ever been . . . a little frightened of going to war, and a great deal ashamed of not going to war, and terrified of my audacity in writing so ambitious a novel."

That fall the novella Mailer wrote at Harvard, *A Calculus at Heaven*, came to the attention of Edwin Seaver, a novelist and critic who was compiling an anthology of unpublished work by promising writers. In June 1943 Seaver had written various editors, and by November he had received a thousand manuscripts, including Mailer's *A Calculus at Heaven*. The novella was chosen by Seaver and his reader, Marjorie Stengel, as one of the fifty-one selections in *Cross Section*, published in 1944 by McClelland and Stewart.

The aspiring writer was not as lucky with *A Transit to Narcissus*. One editor who read the novel was Theodore Amussen of Rinehart, a man who was to play an important role in Mailer's life. Amussen had remained in contact with Mailer even after rejecting *No Percentage* and was still anxious to see anything he might write. But *A Transit to Narcissus* was not to be Mailer's first published novel; it, too, was rejected after several readings. Amussen thought parts of it were good, but he did not think it could be put into proper shape. Amussen now believes that his rejection of both *No Percentage* and *A Transit to Narcissus* must have soured Mailer on him. After the war Mailer did not bring *The Naked and the Dead* directly to Rinehart. Amussen had to hear about the book elsewhere, then voice his interest.

Bea was the most manageable of Mailer's concerns. She was six months behind him at college and not scheduled to graduate from Boston University until January 1944. During the last half of 1943 they met regularly in both Brooklyn and Boston, and their love affair progressed toward maturity.

Before Amussen rejected *Narcissus*, Mailer very sheepishly came to the editor's office with a pretty young woman whom he introduced as Beatrice Silverman. Nothing was said about the reason for the visit, but it was clear to Amussen that Mailer was indirectly asking his blessings for marriage. "He was very embarrassed, and he was very sweet," remembers Amussen. "I almost had tears in my eyes. He introduced us feeling very happy and proud, and they were obviously in love with each other. I remember kissing her in glee. I thought she was marvelous."

In February 1944, one month after Mailer's twenty-first birthday, he and Bea were married in a civil ceremony in Yonkers, New York, with a twenty-five-cent Mexican silver ring which Mailer had bought at a five-and-dime store. It was Mailer who had pushed for the marriage, Bea reveals, because he had received his draft notice and felt he needed an anchor on the home front. Bea wasn't sure she wanted to get married, but in 1944 there was great social pressure on women to be linked securely in matrimony. The war tipped the scales even further: It was common for women to marry their sweethearts quickly before they were sent overseas.

But theirs was not a typical wartime marriage. Because of the threat of Fanny's disapproval, Mailer and Bea eloped. Mailer had gauged his mother's sentiments correctly. It was not that Fanny objected to Bea; she didn't know the bright young woman that well. It was any woman, Bea believes. "Fanny just didn't want her little genius to be married," Bea says.

Within a few weeks Fanny discovered the secret marriage and, according to Bea, wanted to have it annulled. Bea's own mother was equally disturbed by the match. She had hoped her daughter would marry a doctor, not a ne'er-do-well writer who would not be able to make a decent living. Bea tried to explain to her mother that marrying a doctor would be too "prosaic." At that time no one entertained the thought that Bea could study to become a doctor herself, as she would do immediately after divorcing Mailer in 1951. In 1944, nice girls *married* into professions.

The two mothers gradually reconciled themselves to the match, but they insisted that the couple go through a traditional Jewish wedding ceremony. In early March, with members of the family looking on, Norman and Bea were married again by a rabbi under a *chuppah* at Bea's home in Chelsea, Massachussets. Only a few weeks later Mailer entered the army as a private, and soon after Bea joined the WAVES, the women's navy corps, as a lieutenant. Private Mailer later joked to his former roommate that he was one of the first men in World War II who had to salute before having intercourse with his wife.

❦

Mailer had purposely enlisted as a private. As he told Bea before he left for the army, he was determined to write the great war novel and didn't want the responsibility of rank. "As a Harvard graduate,"

Bea reflects, "Norman could have become an officer, but he preferred to go in as a private because he felt that if he was made an officer, he would be put behind a desk and never see combat." As it turned out, Bea says, "He didn't really see much combat anyway."

In late March, Mailer was called up by the army and sent to Fort Bragg, North Carolina, for basic training. When Bea visited him, she was shocked to see the toll the army was taking on her young husband. "Norman was down to a hundred and twenty-five pounds. He looked like a skeleton with his big ears sticking out," she recounts. "I asked him why he was so skinny. He said he had diarrhea, and besides, the army didn't give them any food. I said, 'What do you mean, no food?' He said, 'When the chickens come in, the cook steals the thighs and breasts and leaves us the wings.' He felt that if they were training men to become soldiers, they should feed them properly."

The first week Mailer was in the army, his novel *A Transit to Narcissus* was submitted to Robert Linscott, an editor at Random House, by Mailer's agent, Berta Kaslow of William Morris. Linscott liked it but found no in-house support. The editor rejected the book with a sympathetic letter which Kaslow sent Mailer and which he carried throughout the war. Kaslow tried approximately twenty other publishers after that, and as each one rejected it, she would send the news off to Mailer in the army. The novel was not published until thirty-five years later when a special edition of five hundred copies was issued at a hundred dollars each.

While Mailer was undergoing his basic training at Fort Bragg, the war on the Western front was moving rapidly. On June 4, 1944, only two months after he arrived in North Carolina, the U.S. Army liberated Rome, and two days later American soldiers waded onto the beaches at Normandy. But the war was not going as smoothly on the Pacific front. Franklin Roosevelt was forced to cut short an appearance at the Democratic National Convention in July and fly to Hawaii to meet with Admiral Nimitz and General MacArthur.

Nimitz, who was in charge of the Central Pacific with Admiral King, was suggesting that U.S. forces bypass the Philippines. MacArthur was furious and warned Roosevelt that if he agreed, "the American people would be so aroused they would register most complete resentment against you at the polls this fall." Luckily for Mailer's writing career FDR capitulated to MacArthur and authorized the recapture of the Philippines. As a result Private Mailer was able to join the general's crusade to liberate the islands.

In October four American divisions moved onto the beaches at Leyte Gulf in the Philippines, but it was not until January of 1945, at the tail end of the Philippine campaign, that Mailer was sent to Leyte to join the 112th Armored Cavalry Regiment from San Antonio, Texas. The young writer arrived just after one of the great naval battles of the war. Four separate Japanese task forces had sailed against Admiral Halsey's main U.S. fleet, which was protecting the invading forces on Leyte. In the ensuing sea battle the Japanese lost three battleships, four carriers, and twenty other warships, marking the end of Japan's sea power.

Although trained as an artillery surveyor, the Harvard graduate was immediately assigned to the Intelligence section of the 112th. But his stay in Leyte was short. The day after Mailer arrived there, January 16, 1945, the 112th embarked on the USS *Monrovia* and sailed in convoy to the main Philippine island of Luzon. Three weeks before, four American divisions had made an almost unopposed landing at Luzon's Lingayen Gulf, but there would still be significant action before the island was completely taken.

After four years at Harvard and nine months as a civilian before being called up, Mailer had finally arrived on the stage that would lead him to fame. But it would still be months before he saw action. He was initially assigned a desk job behind the lines at the combat team headquarters, typing reports in quintuplicate. When he proved to be of little use as a typist, he was sent farther behind the lines to interpret aerial photographs. His experience thus far had not matched the aspiring novelist's hopes, but, as he later said, it at least gave him a "general's-eye view" of the war. He also expanded his knowledge of strategy and tactics by reading *Infantry Journal*.

Military journals were not all Mailer was reading. He carried a four-volume set of Spengler's *Decline of the West* all the way through the Philippines in his duffel bag, where it became increasingly mildewed. In his off moments he read Dashiell Hammett and Raymond Chandler, and on his way home he finished *Anna Karenina*. But reading other authors was secondary to his dream of writing the great novel of World War II. Convinced that if he continued to sit behind a desk his book would remain a dream, Mailer requested a transfer to front-line duty with an Intelligence and Reconnaissance (I&R) unit, one similar to the platoon that appears in *The Naked and the Dead*.

He was finally assigned duty as a rifleman in an I&R platoon protecting a division that was fighting its way toward Manila. It was not a fierce combat compaign. As Mailer said three years later, he only took part in "a couple of firefights and skirmishes." His wife Bea describes it as even less frightening: "He took a few potshots, but I don't remember worrying every day that Norman would get killed. It wasn't that kind of fighting anymore."

In Luzon, Mailer wrote Bea four or five letters a week, and in each he jotted down pages of notes describing his war experiences. As he told the now defunct newspaper, *The New York Star*, "I kept my diary writing to Bea. . . . We were moving around so much there just was no way of keeping it otherwise." These letters would eventually form the basis of *The Naked and the Dead*.

Describing the members of the 112th reconnaissance platoon to Bea was hardly a cheerful task. These soldiers were a world apart from the upper-class literary gentlemen he had come to know at Harvard. The 112th was a division of the Texas National Guard, and Mailer's platoon was made up predominantly of "good old" southern boys who were less than friendly to Jews, let alone northern intellectual Jews. "We can't all be poets," snapped a disgruntled lieutenant to Mailer one day. Not surprisingly anti-Semitism would play a role in *The Naked and the Dead*, although only through two minor characters, Goldstein and Roth.

One of Mailer's defenses against the anti-Semitism of the Texans was his uncanny ability to integrate their culture, not only into his work but into his own personality. Just as Mailer had absorbed the culture of the Harvard WASPs by adding their more cultivated tones to his Brooklyn accent, Mailer adopted a new voice in the army, an officious southern one. It would later surface from time to time, particularly when he felt unsure of himself or threatened. By seeming to become one of them, Mailer was shielding himself from the enemy.

About a month after Mailer was assigned to the platoon, he heard of a man in the same regimental combat team who was strongly outspoken about army conditions. During the fighting they were placed in the same circle of foxholes, and Mailer decided to approach him. His name was Francis Irby Gwaltney. "I spent the first day griping as hard and loud as I could," Gwaltney, who died in 1980, recalled after the war. "Norman heard about it and looked me up."

Mailer discovered that Gwaltney, a redhead from Arkansas, was not a red-neck but an aspiring novelist. "We stayed up all night talking," Gwaltney remembered. "What impressed me was his wisdom more than his intelligence. I didn't discover till later that he was a Harvard graduate." Gwaltney took quick note of Mailer's personality, observing that even though Norman had to go out on patrol the next morning, he got little sleep that night. "Already Norman was burning up his inexhaustible nervous energy around the clock," he said. "But . . . he was very gentle, shy, quiet, not at all aggressive. It must be a burden to him to be aggressive. He has to work hard to be that way." Gwaltney and Mailer became lifetime friends as well as army buddies. When Gwaltney later tried to publish his own war novel, *The Day the Century Ended*, Mailer, who was a successful writer by then, helped him. After the war Mailer sent Gwaltney numerous letters using the back of his manuscript paper from *The Naked and the Dead* as stationery.

Gwaltney frequently saw Mailer in combat and distinctly remembers the young writer's lack of military skills. "He was a brave soldier but not a good one," Gwaltney said. "He couldn't see worth a damn. Nearsighted. He wore GI glasses when he read, but not otherwise, and he couldn't hit anything with a rifle. It's a miracle Mailer lived through the war."

By now Mailer had witnessed combat and had also absorbed the rudiments of army planning. It would all be used in his novel, but characters and plot had to be thought through as well. As an exercise Mailer and Gwaltney would spend time back at camp describing various officers to each other for future use in the novels they intended to write.

Mailer was also quickly learning the dark ways of the Philippine jungle and how it drained any desire for adventure or combat. He was afraid that the ordeal would kill his desire to write the war novel. "At a certain point you get awfully tired as an infantryman—not because you're in combat all the time, but just because it's a tough life: it's like being a dishwasher," he later said. "Your horizons come down and down and down, until you don't much care whether you remain alive or not. So I really did give up the idea that I'd ever come back and be a writer."

Mailer then heard about a three-day patrol behind enemy lines that had taken place before he joined the platoon. With imaginative embellishment this became the basis of the trek to Mount Anaka taken by his fictional platoon in *The Naked and the Dead.*

The war in the Pacific ended on V-J Day, August 14, 1945, and by the time the 112th Regiment left Batangas Bay for Japan on August 24, Mailer had absorbed enough of the Philippines to fill his novel with vivid detail. The Japanese surrender aboard the *Missouri* on

September 2, which marked the official end of World War II, occurred one day before the 112th Regiment landed at Tatiyama Naval Base and began its occupation duty in Japan. Mailer had spent only seven months in the war, but he would remain in the army another eight months, until the following May 1946. Ironically it was during this peacetime period that Mailer underwent a pivotal military experience which laid the philosophical groundwork for *The Naked and the Dead*.

To avoid more onerous duties, including drilling, Mailer had decided to become a cook in Japan and rose to sergeant fourth grade, or T/4, a first cook. The fact that he received stripes for this duty amused his friend Gwaltney, who had followed the regiment to the Tatiyama Base. "He was the worst cook who ever lived," recalls Gwaltney. "I mean, he was awful. Never did learn to separate the yellows from the whites of the eggs."

One day Mailer told his top sergeant off. As Mailer recounts the incident in his Harvard twenty-fifth annual class report: "The occupation [of cook] inspired me with shame . . . Harvard snobbery being subtler than one expects, so I picked a contretemps one day." The sergeant reported Mailer to the captain. "The Captain ordered me to apologize," recalls Mailer. "It was a week before I was going home. So I crawfished—the way Hearn did in the book."

In *The Naked and the Dead* Lieutenant Hearn is a liberal Harvard man who has an ambivalent fascination for the fascist ideology and sadism of General Cummings. Cummings demands that Hearn pick up a cigarette butt which the lieutenant has thrown on the general's immaculate floor in an act of rebellion. Hearn picks it up, an obsequious gesture which Mailer clearly abhorred for its moral cowardice.

When Mailer found himself "crawfishing" before his own superior officer, he felt the same self-loathing that Hearn does in the book. But unlike Hearn, Mailer sought to regain his self-respect. "The next morning, I went to the Captain and said I wanted to give the stripes back. But, because he was the kind of man he was, he said, 'You're not giving them back. I'm *taking* them back!' That," says Mailer, "was when the keel was laid for *The Naked and the Dead*." Mailer left the army as a private with an acute loathing for all officers.

Like all GI's, Mailer simply wanted to go home. He had experienced enough war, and now he wanted to write about it. Since the month after V-J Day the army had been discharging almost a million men a month, cutting a soldier's point requirement first to fifty, then to thirty-eight. Points were received for, among other things, the amount of time served, and it was expected that veteran soldiers would return home first. In certain cases, however, the army decided it needed to keep some experienced veterans and let the inexperienced ones return home first, which caused dissension. The GI's and their families felt that demobilization was too slow, and by early 1946 protest reached a crescendo. In Manila and Luzon 18,000 GI's wrote their congressmen that they wanted to be discharged.

On the home front a number of people, including Beatrice Mailer, were also writing letters to their congressmen urging them to bring the boys back. Since Mailer had joined the war late, he had few seniority points, which caused Bea consternation. She was living with Fanny at the time in Brooklyn and wanted to set up her own home. But massive congressional pressure eventually forced the army to speed up demobilization, and, on what Mailer called "a magic day," May 2, 1946, he was released. By June he was in a bungalow outside Provincetown on Cape Cod writing the beginning of *The Naked and the Dead.*

❦

The bungalow was set on the narrow neck of beach and dunes just outside Provincetown known as North Truro. Today North Truro is a neon strip of tacky motels and summer rentals, but in 1946 it was still a relatively deserted expanse of beach with breathing space between bungalows. The house Norman and Bea rented was a small one-bedroom cottage directly on the water.

Ever since World War I this fishing port, once populated by Portuguese fishermen, had attracted artists and writers. But its cultural heritage was not what lured the young Mailers. As Bea recalls, "We liked it because it was beautiful and very romantic." To them it was simply a serene span of broad, white beaches, a setting in which to escape tension and to write. For the next three decades Mailer would continually return to Provincetown, in both summer and winter, to write, recoup his losses, or relax. Inevitably he would become a part of the town's cultural heritage.

That summer in Provincetown, Mailer worked on his war novel every day, often retreating into the small bedroom with his typewriter and closing the door behind him. "He always liked to be enclosed in a small space while he was writing," remembers Bea. There was never a question of waiting for the muse to descend. "Norman was a very obsessive type of writer, not inspired," she says. "Everything was worked through: how many chapters, what would happen in each chapter." Mailer would chart this information on three-by-five cards, and as the novel progressed, he would shuffle the cards if he needed to alter the structure.

Each character's history was carefully recorded on these cards: age, height, family, place of birth, childhood education, idiosyncrasies. If a new idea came to him, it would be added. By the time a description was complete, Mailer would know as much about that character as anyone possibly could. This professional thoroughness was rare for a twenty-three-year-old writer, but Harvard had taught him well.

Mailer set *The Naked and the Dead* on the fictional island of Anopopei in the Philippines, where 6,000 American soldiers have landed to take the island back from the Japanese. The narrative focuses on a small Intelligence and Reconnaissance platoon of a dozen men who have come from various strata of American society. Mailer's microcosm includes Wilson, a hard-drinking southern red-neck; Goldstein, an intellectual Brooklyn Jew; Red Valsen, a rebellious migrant from a Montana mining town; Gallagher, an anti-Semitic Boston Irishman; and Martinez, a poor Mexican-American whose fierce pride is overcome by fear. Using intermittent "time machine" flashbacks to illuminate their pasts, Mailer shows how their personalities flourish or fold under the pressures of war.

The three central characters of the novel are not rank-and-file soldiers but authority figures: General Cummings, who is in charge of the Anopopei campaign, Lieutenant Hearn, and Sergeant Croft. Cummings is an intellectual career soldier with fascist tendencies. He is hypnotized by power and believes in the "fear ladder" which gives him control over his men. Barren of any sensitivity, he plans a militaristic future for America after an inevitable war with Russia. As he puts it, "This is going to be the reactionary's century." In Mailer's view this sadistic if brilliant taskmaster is more the victim of America's war machine than its hero.

Lieutenant Hearn is the renegade son of a well-to-do midwestern family. A graduate of Harvard, he is at once fascinated and appalled by Cummings. Despite Hearn's intellectual, even radical leanings, he is aware of a deep impulse in himself to control men, much like Cummings, a conflict that leaves him devoid of idealism. Cummings senses that Hearn can be converted to his own views, and he plays a subtle game with the lieutenant until Hearn rebels and disdainfully throws a cigarette butt on Cummings's floor. After humiliating the lieutenant by forcing him to "crawfish" and pick up the butt, Cummings assigns him to a grueling patrol with the I & R platoon. Their mission is to reach the base of Mt. Anaka, the highest mountain on the island, and make their way through a pass to scout the Japanese rear.

The sergeant of the I & R platoon, Croft, is the personification of Cummings's new reactionary order. He is driven by a lust for power and a sadistic will to push his men to victory whatever the cost. Throughout the patrol he despises Hearn for stepping out of the military hierarchy and siding with the men. Croft eventually tricks the lieutenant into exposing himself to enemy fire at the base of Mt. Anaka, where he dies. With Hearn dead and the pass cut off by Japanese troops, Croft relentlessly drives his men up the mountain, retreating only when he steps on a hive of angry hornets and is driven back down. But despite Cummings's elaborate military strategy and Croft's iron will, the Mt. Anaka mission is futile. On their return the platoon learns that during their six-day trek the Japanese have been virtually defeated.

The letters Mailer had written to Bea during the war became invaluable to him in writing *The Naked and the Dead.* Not unlike a war journal, they invoked the immediacy of the experience. In fact, many of the characters in *The Naked and the Dead* were drawn from real people in Mailer's platoon. When Francis Irby Gwaltney was later asked if he recognized any of the detail in the novel, he replied, "I recognized *all* of it. Some characters, he didn't even bother to change their names." Soon after the book's publication Mailer admitted that at least half its characters were based on the men with whom he had soldiered. When asked how he had come to know the officers, he answered, "Oh, you always get to know them. Working for them—there's no other kind of knowledge that can substitute for it. You generally operate on hate, and hate is the best aid to analysis."

❦

Mailer's analysis of power and authority in *The Naked and the Dead* would continue to evolve as he wrote the novel. During the fifteen months it took him, he was being affected by developments on the international scene which would help to shape the antiwar stance of the book.

Two months before Mailer returned home from the army, Winston Churchill, speaking with President Truman at Westminster

College in Fulton, Missouri, made a frightening pronouncement: "From Stettin in the Baltic," he intoned, "to Trieste in the Adriatic, an Iron Curtain has descended across the Continent." In March 1946 few Americans had Churchill's insight into Russian motives. As early as March 1945 Churchill had witnessed the breakdown of the Yalta accords to which he, FDR, and Stalin had agreed only a month before in return for Russian help in fighting against the Japanese. Stalin's promises at Yalta to set up democratic governments with free elections in Austria, Hungary, Czechoslovakia, Bulgaria, and Romania were never kept.

Truman had been warned of this earlier by Averell Harriman, the American ambassador in Moscow, but it was not until the Potsdam Conference on July 17, 1945, that Truman became convinced that the Soviets could not be trusted. He left the conference believing "force is the only thing the Russians understand" and that they were "planning world conquest." The Cold War would begin only months after the hot war had ended.

By 1946 the only member of Truman's administration who retained any idealism about the Russians was former Vice President, then Secretary of Commerce, Henry Wallace. He began to view Truman's disaffection with the Russians as warmongering, and when Churchill made his famous Iron Curtain speech, Wallace delivered an angry rebuttal. In September 1946, five months after Mailer arrived home from Japan, Wallace delivered a speech at a U.S.-Soviet friendship rally at Madison Square Garden in which he decried U.S. intervention in Eastern Europe. That year the Progressive Citizens of America, an organization which backed the Wallace movement, was formed.

Bea, whose radical-left opinions strongly influenced Mailer, remembers that period very clearly. "The whole year that Norman was writing *The Naked and the Dead* was a scary year," she recalls. "We were afraid war was going to break out between Russia and the U.S. It was that bad. We wanted better relations with Russia. We wanted to stop the Cold War." Mailer not only joined the Progressive Citizens that year, but he conceived the philosophic design of *The Naked and the Dead*. He feared that he had returned home only to face the prospect of another war, this time with Russia.

"I never thought of its being an antiwar book, at the beginning," Mailer said of *The Naked and the Dead* two years later. "But every time I turned on the radio and looked in the newspapers, there was this growing hysteria, this talk of going to war again, and it made me start looking for the trend of what was happening. It seemed to me that you *could* get men to fight again. They came out of the war frustrated, filled with bitterness and anger and with no place to focus their anger. They would begin thinking, 'I don't give a goddam. I'll go into it, at least it'll be a change!' "

Although Mailer's antiwar stance in *The Naked and the Dead* evolved partly from his fear of another war, there were other influences working on the young writer. One was the literary tradition of the post-World War I writers whom Mailer had been weaned on at Harvard. Dos Passos's hatred of the war machine in *Three Soldiers* influenced Mailer's own view of war, just as Dos Passos's technique, the use of flashbacks showing the sociological past of each character, helped shape Mailer's style.

An equally profound influence on Mailer's view of war was his own Jewish heritage. It was common for immigrant Jews who had been persecuted by nationalistic groups to perceive armies as semifascist organizations which tolerated, perhaps even encouraged, anti-Semitism. Mailer incorporated some of this feeling in his novel. The young Jewish soldier Goldstein ruminates about bigotry in the army: "They were just a bunch of Anti-Semiten, he told himself. That was all the goyim knew, to run around with loose women, and get drunk like pigs. Deeply buried was his envy that he had never had many women and did not know the easy loud companionship of drink. He was tired of hoping to make friends with them; they didn't want to get along with him, they hated him. Goldstein smacked his fist against his palm in exasperation . . . 'they're a bunch of *grobe jungen*. . . . It's hard to remember all the fine ideals. Sometimes even with the Jews in Europe I don't know why we're fighting.' "

Mailer's true genius in *The Naked and the Dead*, however, was that he was able to transcend both his literary and his Jewish heritage to create the universal voice of a new, radically changed generation.

In 1945 the military was generally held in high honor. The Allied armies had just won a great war against fascism, and leaders like General Eisenhower presented an image of beneficent democratic leadership. The pacifism of a generation fed on antiwar novels such as *All Quiet on the Western Front* seemed to have been wiped out by the brilliant victory over Hitler and fascism. But in *The Naked and the Dead* Mailer articulated an antiwar philosophy which would become the intellectual, even political, bedrock of a generation born during the war or in the postwar era. Unlike the novelists of World War I, he was linking the authoritarianism of the army with society itself and demonstrating a new loss of faith in individual possibility.

At the same time that he was expressing this antimilitary voice, Mailer seemed curiously entranced by that authority and its violence. Just as he had been fascinated with the WASP elite of Harvard, so he was drawn to military power. His portrayal of General Cummings, while one of an evil character, is intricately and vividly cast. But it is Sergeant Croft, equally fanatical in his will to drive his soldiers to the heights of Mt. Anaka for a selfish vision, who truly reflects Mailer's ambivalence toward power.

At the end of the novel Mailer has shifted the focus from the liberal Lieutenant Hearn, who dies at Croft's hands, to Croft himself. Ineffectual liberalism is dead. Pure authority remains evil, but Croft, a reactionary with a will to conquer at all costs, triumphs as a kind of romantic hero, whom Mailer later compared to Ahab in *Moby Dick*. In Croft, just as in Hearn, lies the secret of the ambivalence that continues to dog Mailer. It is a seemingly contradictory fascination with both violence and justice, both individuality and authority, an early sign of the growing paradox of Norman Mailer.

❦

By September 1946, just four months after his discharge from the army, Mailer had completed approximately a hundred and eighty-four pages of a rough first draft of his novel. He and Bea decided to move from Provincetown back to Brooklyn, where Mailer would complete the book. There was still a severe housing shortage facing the millions of ex-GI's, and many Brooklyn apartments had been cut up into one- or two-room flats to accommodate the veterans. He and Bea eventually found a two-room apartment for seventy-five dollars a month at 49 Remsen Street in Brooklyn Heights, around the corner from Fanny and Barney's apartment building.

The Remsen Street apartment was small but serviceable. The entranceway was a four-foot-wide kitchen jammed tight with a stove, sink, icebox, and a dish rack. The bathroom was farther in on the right, while straight ahead was a medium-sized room which served as a bed-living-dining room. There was an additional long, narrow room to the left of the living room, but Mailer converted this into a darkroom. His work as an interpreter of aerial photographs during the war had stimulated an interest in photography.

Another avocation which Mailer brought home from the war, and one which delighted his wife, was cooking, specifically baking. In spite of Gwaltney's chiding, Mailer had apparently become a skilled cook in Japan and now pridefully turned out scores of pies and breads for an admiring Bea. His commanding role as sergeant, first cook, was not easily abandoned in civilian life: One day he blew up at Bea because the pans in the kitchen were not spotlessly clean.

But Mailer's consuming passion was writing his war novel. He decided he could not work in the cramped two-room apartment and rented a garret under the eaves of a rooming house down the street at 20 Remsen. The room was only a few dollars a month, which was all they could afford. Bea had saved two thousand dollars from her pay as a WAVE officer, and Mailer had saved some from his fifty-dollars-a-month army pay. Both were in the 52-20 Club, which allowed returning veterans twenty dollars a week unemployment benefits for a year as part of the GI Bill. The two veterans would travel to the unemployment office each week to pick up a total of forty dollars in cash, which permitted them a secure if frugal existence.

Mailer's choice of a humble garret in which to write *The Naked and the Dead* was an economic necessity in 1946, but Bea believes it also reflected Mailer's artistic pretentiousness. "Norman always had this affectation about poverty, even though in those days we couldn't have afforded much else," she says. "But he carried on the affectation even when it was no longer necessary. When he made some money, he still had to have a garret."

From the fall of 1946 until the following summer Mailer would leave the Remsen Street apartment each morning at 10:00 A.M. and retreat to his garret, where he would write until the late afternoon. He averaged about twenty-five pages of first draft a week. "I doubt if ever again I will have a book which is so easy to write," he would later say.

Bea found her husband's routine immensely helpful, since she had begun to write a novel herself, a story about women in the navy. After Mailer left for his garret in the morning, she would clear off the card table on which they ate, take out her typewriter, and shuffle her own three-by-five cards. Bea admits that she was never highly motivated; in fact she often found writing distasteful. The youthful Mrs. Mailer was writing her own novel mainly because she had begun to identify strongly with her husband.

The independent, outspoken undergraduate who had shocked

the boys at Harvard with her liberated ways was beginning to suffer a regression common to many married women at the time. As she now says, "It was a lack of confidence in myself which all women have, especially of my generation." The stronger her husband's public image later became, the more Bea withdrew into a passive, yet in many ways competitive, state, one which would eventually lead to a severe depression and divorce.

In 1946, however, Bea was still happy to play the supportive wife to her "genius" husband. The original Mrs. Mailer, Norman's mother, was also a bulwark of support for him. Many evenings Mailer read sections of the manuscript aloud to either Bea or Fanny. Listening to the crude army talk, Fanny would occasionally interject, "But, Norman! The language! The language!" Not surprisingly, the book is dedicated to both of them. "Norman had a tremendous desire to be famous," Bea says, "and he was very fortunate because he had two people who believed in him—his mother and me."

Another important figure in Mailer's life during those fifteen months in Brooklyn was Charles Devlin, who lived in the rooming house where Mailer had his studio. A "black Irishman" who had his own aspirations as a writer, Devlin became close friends with Mailer while he was writing *The Naked and the Dead*, and the author trusted his literary opinion enough to let Devlin help cut and shape the book. Devlin, the author of two novels which had never found publishers, was very bright, a good critic, and unafraid to tell Mailer when something did not work.

When Mailer first showed him the manuscript, Devlin said, "It's a better book than I thought it would be, but you have no gift for metaphor. Metaphor reveals a man's character, and his true grasp of life. To the degree you have no metaphor, you are an impoverished writer and have lived no life." Mailer never forgot the lecture. Devlin was so valuable to Mailer in editing *The Naked and the Dead* that he received an acknowledgment in the novel.

Larry Alson recalls Devlin vividly. "Devlin was a marvelous Irishman," Alson says. "He had a nasal quality to his voice, and he was sharp as a razor. He was very witty and ideologically sound. He would pounce if you said the wrong thing and force you to buttress it with facts. He was Norman's greatest fan, and he was the one who forced Norman to rewrite the opening of *The Naked and the Dead*, the scene in which none of the soldiers could sleep on the ship because of the prospect of battle."

Devlin was the first intellectual Irishman that Mailer had met, and he would have a significant influence on the author. Although Mailer had been deeply impressed in his studies at Harvard by the characters in James Farrell's *Studs Lonigan* and by the works of James Joyce, Devlin helped solidify Mailer's attraction to the Irish consciousness. Over the years, as Mailer's life became increasingly uprooted, he would develop an Irish alter ego that was at odds with his Jewish middle-class roots. By his third novel, *The Deer Park*, this fantasy, in the form of a blond, swaggering, macho Irishman, would be in full bloom.

Devlin had been introduced to Mailer by another Brooklyn Heights writer, poet Norman Rosten, whom Mailer had met shortly before going into the army. Rosten, in turn, had been introduced to Mailer by playwright Arthur Miller, who was then living in the same apartment building as Fanny. The friendship between Rosten, Miller, and Mailer was casual. Not much socializing went on among them since Mailer was still perceived by these two already published authors as "a young upstart," according to Rosten.

But there was some psychic kinship among the three Brooklyn writers, and all would eventually become involved with the ultimate American fantasy girl, Marilyn Monroe. Miller, of course, married Monroe. Rosten and Mailer wrote books about her. Rosten's was a memoir and Mailer's a biography, but both were published at the same time in 1973. Arthur Miller also worked with Mailer in the Henry Wallace presidential campaign of 1948, but as Miller now says, "We saw each other only remotely."

Rosten played a more significant role in Mailer's career, particularly in the publication of *The Naked and the Dead.* That fall, after Mailer returned from Provincetown, he and Rosten ran into each other on a street in Brooklyn Heights. As they walked, Mailer told Rosten that he was having problems with a publisher, Little, Brown and Company, who had asked to see the first draft he had completed over the summer.

The twenty-one-year-old editor at Little, Brown who had asked for the manuscript, Adeline Lubell, had been the best friend of Mailer's sister Barbara at Radcliffe and she had also roomed with Bea's younger sister Phyllis. Even though she had never met him, Lubell had written to Mailer while he was in the army. "Norman's letters were marvelous," she remembers. She did meet Mailer briefly in Boston after the war just as he and Bea were heading up to Provincetown. "To tell the truth, I was disappointed by Norman," Lubell now recalls. "Despite that flash and verbal voracity, he was so thin and subdued. And both of us were shy."

As the summer moved into fall, Lubell heard from Barbara Mailer that the war novel was progressing. She wrote Mailer asking to see it, and that September she received the 184-page manuscript, which she read immediately. The same day, in the "white heat" of reading, she wrote a one-paragraph report which, in effect, said that the book would be the greatest novel to come out of World War II. Little, Brown, she felt, had to publish it. Lubell also filled out a blue card with estimated sales, price, and advertising budget, something she rarely did for a book that was not contracted for. She now thinks she estimated the book would sell 7300 copies, but it is also possible that she estimated only 3700. As of 1981 *The Naked and the Dead* had sold 250,000 copies in 23 hard-cover printings and 3 million in paperback.

With her report in hand Lubell showed the manuscript to her Little, Brown mentor and fellow editor, Angus Cameron. Cameron agreed about the worth of the novel but was worried about the "dirty words" Mailer had put in to document the explicit language of the GI's in the Anapopei campaign. Cameron showed the manuscript to Little, Brown's executive vice president, Ray Everitt. "He was less than wild about the book," Lubell remembers, "but agreed to go along with our enthusiasm provided the language was cleaned up."

Cameron and Everitt's attitude was understandable in 1946. The explicit language of Mailer's soldiers was revolutionary at the time. No previous novelist had dared to regularly use such obscenities as *fuck*, *shit*, *motherfucking*, and *son of a bitch*. Although the dialogue was undeniably real and portrayed the hellishness of the GI's war, Little, Brown was reluctant to publish it. Traditional literary attitudes were not easily overcome, and at the time obscenity charges could be leveled against the company. The use of such language was still risky despite the successful importation of James Joyce's *Ulysses* from France by Bennett Cerf.

A series of letters went back and forth between Mailer and Little, Brown. As Lubell characterizes the exchange: "Snotty letters flew between Miss Little, Brown and the lowly but intransigent Mailer about the boon LB was bestowing on him by potentially offering an option contract." Mailer was less than pleased by Little, Brown's "boon," but things got worse when Alfred McIntyre, Little, Brown's president, saw the manuscript. He was furious at the language and refused to publish the book unless what he considered obscenities were removed from it.

The publishing house was now in a stalemate over the book. Cameron finally asked Lubell if she would agree to let the decision be made on the basis of an outside reading by someone she approved of. Bernard De Voto was suggested, and she agreed. "De Voto was then the literary guru of greater Cambridge and alleged to be a foul-mouthed conversationalist," she points out, explaining her confidence that he would support her in backing Mailer's book.

A week after the manuscript was sent to De Voto, a six-page double-spaced critique arrived back. "All other considerations which this book presents are subsidiary to the problem posed by the profanity and obscenity of its dialogue," De Voto wrote. "In my opinion it is barely publishable. . . ." Lubell could do nothing further to preserve Mailer's original text. She wrote to Mailer urging him to purge his manuscript of excessive profanity and to consider an option contract with Little, Brown for a "munificent" advance of three hundred dollars.

As Lubell now reflects, Mailer had by now simply become disgusted with Little, Brown's equivocations. "He didn't sit around in a gentleman's fashion as authors are supposed to do," she recalls. In fact by this time Mailer had clearly begun to feel antagonistic toward publishers in general. Little, Brown was not responsible for the first disappointment in his postwar career. Soon after his release from the army the previous spring he had gone to see an editor at Random House to outline his plans for *The Naked and the Dead.* The editor, intending to be kind, he said, "Oh, Lord, don't write a war novel! None of us wants it." He did not consider war novels marketable at the time, which to Mailer seemed like an idiotic viewpoint.

When Mailer ran into Norman Rosten on the street during the Little, Brown debacle that fall of 1946, he was very upset. Rosten commiserated with him. "As young writers, we were very confident," Rosten remembers. "Our attitude was 'How dare they do that to us? We're too good for them.' " At this time Rosten was already a recognized poet, with two Rinehart books behind him. He was on good terms with his publisher and suggested introducing Mailer to his editor, who happened to be Theodore Amussen. Mailer never told Rosten that Amussen had already turned down two of his previous novels, *No Percentage* and *A Transit to Narcissus.* He merely asked

Rosten if he would go to see Amussen with him, and Rosten said he would be delighted.

On the appointed day Rosten and Mailer boarded the subway for a five-cent ride to Manhattan with the partially completed manuscript of *The Naked and the Dead.* "It was a nice pilgrimage," Rosten reflects. When they arrived at the Rinehart offices, which were then at 232 Madison Avenue, at the corner of Thirty-Seventh Street, Mailer already knew Amussen, but Rosten introduced him anyway with the comment, "This is a friend of mine who is a good writer, and you ought to read him." Rosten also mentioned Little, Brown's involvement in the project and their delay. Mailer, armed with Adeline Lubell's report and clearly feeling defensive about Amussen's two previous rejections, belligerently blurted out, "If you give me a contract, you can have it."

During the next few days Amussen read the manuscript of *The Naked and the Dead* with increasing excitement. He knew he wanted to publish it. To gain additional in-house support, he gave the manuscript to another young Rinehart editor, William Rainey, who was equally enthusiastic after reading it. But the editor-in-chief at the time was a man named John Selby, who Amussen now characterizes as "a terrible writer." Selby did not like Mailer's manuscript and instructed Amussen to turn the book down and to send it back to Mailer. Instead Amussen went over Selby's head, and one morning, as he describes it, he "went crashing into Stanley Rinehart's office."

Rinehart, then president and cofounder of the firm, was the son of author Mary Roberts Rinehart. He and John Farrar, who went on to found Farrar, Straus & Giroux, had started the company in 1929, when both of them had left Doubleday & Company. By 1947 they had built Rinehart & Company into a top New York publishing house, although the firm didn't have much available cash. Rinehart was a formidable figure, and young Amussen was being bold to barge in on him so abruptly. With a show of courage the editor blurted out, "You've got to read this because I want to publish it."

Rinehart, visibly upset by this breakdown in protocol, asked if it had been cleared by Selby. Amussen said, "No, he doesn't like it," then quickly added, "but I do, and you'll be a damned fool if you don't sign it up. So read it." Rinehart read it, and Mailer was subsequently offered a $1250 advance, which the publisher felt was exorbitant for a first novel.

At Little, Brown, Adeline Lubell had no way of knowing that

during the De Voto controversy Mailer had taken her complimentary one-paragraph report to Rinehart & Company and parlayed it into a contract. On November 14, 1946, Lubell was forced to write the following note to Angus Cameron: "I received a letter today from Norman Mailer, informing me that he has a contract with Rinehart for *The Naked and the Dead* with a $1250 advance. He stresses the point that they took only a week and that it was read by only two people."

Despite Rinehart's enthusiasm, the book contract was not offered free and clear. Before the novel was even accepted, Mailer had to attend a conference to discuss the problem of the book's profanity. As Mailer explained in 1948, "We agreed that I would cut it to what I thought was the irreducible minimum." To Mailer this meant taking out about one fifth of the profane language in the original manuscript, which he did not feel was sacrificing too much.

But another problem soon arose. Stanley Rinehart was bothered by Mailer's consistent use of the word *fuck*. As Theodore Amussen recalls, Rinehart was horrified at the thought of what his mother, Mary Roberts Rinehart, would think. Since Mrs. Rinehart was on the board of the company, the problem had to be dealt with.

Mailer and Amussen put their heads together, and as they were ruminating, Mailer came up with the now-famous replacement, *fug*. Since Stanley Rinehart didn't seem to object to any other obscene word, sentences would often read, "Fug the sonofabitch mud." Or, "Fug you. Fug the goddam gun." Or, "You're all a bunch of fuggin' whores." Words such as *bitch*, *goddam*, and *shit* were all permissible in Rinehart's lexicon, but not the unholy word *fuck*. Mailer had created a clever euphemism, but as Amussen now says, having to invent the word *fug* was just plain "silly."

After the initial profanity conference Amussen does not remember working extensively with the author on that problem. He does recall working on character definition and structural problems with Mailer at the Rinehart offices, but most of these changes were minor. Mailer apparently took editorial advice well but always stated his mind. "He was a brilliant talker," says Amussen. "Here was this kid who was far more articulate than I was."

It was not long after the book's acceptance that Amussen got an offer from Reynal & Hitchcock, a now defunct publishing company, and left Rinehart. The manuscript was turned over to William Rainey, since deceased, who did most of the editing on the book and saw it through publication. Both editors are cited by Mailer on the acknowledgments page, along with Charles Devlin, for their "aid and encouragement."

Before Amussen left for his new company, he also read Bea's manuscript, which Mailer had told him "wasn't bad." Amussen apparently suggested some changes, but Bea never got around to making them. "I didn't want to bother," she says. "I really didn't want to be a writer. I found out how hard it was." Shortly afterward Amussen left Rinehart and the matter was dropped.

❦

By August 1947 the writing and editing of the 721-page novel was completed, but Mailer did not want to wait around for the nine months it would take for *The Naked and the Dead* to be published. In September of 1947 he and Bea left for Paris to study at the Sorbonne on the GI Bill of Rights. As he later said, it was "a way of getting two hundred dollars a month to live on." Between them Mailer and Bea actually received $150 a month, $75 each, from the GI Bill, but they had money left over from their combined $3000 savings from the service. Bea remembers feeling comparatively rich.

Government money was not the only reason for Mailer's odyssey to the City of Light, even though living there was undeniably cheaper than living in New York in 1947. For a young novelist Paris was the inevitable center of postwar literary activity. Just as his World War I predecessors, Hemingway, Fitzgerald, and Dos Passos, had come to the French city after their war to live in self-imposed exile from the anti-intellectualism of America in the 1920s, so Mailer went to partake of what Paris had to offer.

The era of Gertrude Stein, the Dadaists, Sylvia Beach, and James Joyce had by now given way to that of Sartre and the Existentialists. But this did not stop a throng of young American writers from coming to Paris in search of the intellectual ghosts of the Lost Generation. Although Mailer was one of the first of his literary peers to make the pilgrimage to Paris, by the early 1950s a colony of young American writers would descend on the city to write their novels and start small literary magazines.

The Paris Review, founded in 1953, attracted the more glamorous expatriates: George Plimpton, Peter Matthiessen, Thomas Guinzberg, John Marquand, Jr., William Styron, and Terry Southern. Richard Seaver, who had published Mailer's Harvard novella, *A Calculus at Heaven*, edited a small Parisian literary magazine called

Merlin. James Baldwin arrived in Paris in the early 1950s, and by the end of the decade James Jones would make the city his home. Some of Mailer's generation would remain in Paris, but he had no desire to play the longtime expatriate. He was far less nostalgic than many of his peers about following in the footsteps of the preceding literary generation. It was America he wanted to write about, not France. Paris was just a brief cultural detour.

Stanley Geist, a fellow Harvard man who was a few years older than Mailer, had also arrived in Paris in 1947. He saw Mailer frequently and remembers his attitude toward the Paris experience. "There were a number of young Americans around who were trying to relive the 1920s, but Norman had his own ideas, and he was a little less stuck on literary mythology than the other people," Geist says.

French novelist Jean Malaquais, whom Mailer would meet that year at Geist's home, described Norman's attitude in much the same way. "Paris has been a beacon for painters and writers for decades. It is in some sense a must for young artists. But Norman is very much an American writer. I don't think he ever wanted to be an expatriate; there is no vagabond streak in him." Bea recalls no discussion about being a part of a lost generation. "We were just a bunch of kids enjoying ourselves being young. The war was over, and we were in another country," she says.

The Mailers stayed briefly at a cheap hotel in Paris, then found a furnished apartment on the Left Bank for twenty-four dollars a month. Although it was dusty and had mice, it was furnished with a piano, which appealed to Bea, who as a Boston University music major had become an accomplished pianist. The Paris apartment, which had a living room, a den, and a bedroom, was larger than the one on Remsen Street. The bathroom only had a toilet and a sink; the bathtub was in the kitchen. Bea remembers that the first time she and Norman tried to take a bath together they almost suffocated. French water heaters were then operated by gas, which had a tendency to rob the air of oxygen. Bathing in Paris was so precarious then that people either did not bathe at all or they went to the public baths once a week, as did Mailer and Bea.

The Mailers became friendly with Mark Lindenthal, a fellow Harvard man, who, like Geist and Mailer, had come to Paris on the GI Bill. Lindenthal had been a navigator on a bomber and had been shot down and sent to a Nazi prison camp. His European perspective on the war was intensely interesting to Mailer. The three Harvardians came to know each other when they enrolled at the Sorbonne with two hundred other American GI's that September. The popular course that Mailer and Bea signed up for was Cours de la Civilisation Française, a yearlong survey covering French language, literature, history, and philosophy. Out of the two hundred American students only eight, including Bea, finished. "They decided no one in the States would know what they were doing, so they didn't do much work, and the attrition rate was tremendous," she recalls.

Mailer dropped out after only a few sessions, and in the tradition of American expatriates, including Hemingway and Fitzgerald, he began frequenting the Café des Deux Magots with the other American students. Everyone's primary interest, Bea recalls, was to see whether Jean-Paul Sartre or Simone de Beauvoir would show up. Catty-cornered across the Boulevard St. Germain was the Café de Flore, which the existential couple frequented. It became a ritual for one of the Americans to spot someone in the café who looked like Sartre or De Beauvoir. Everyone would then rush across the street to see if it were actually they. Neither author was ever spotted in the flesh, but the anticipation made it worth the game.

Sartre's fame as the father of modern existentialism was just beginning to spread in those early postwar years. *No Exit* had just been translated into English in 1946. *Nausea* would not be translated until 1949, and the classic *Being and Nothingness* would not be read by an American audience until 1953. But the significance of Sartre's existential philosophy was already making a clear impact on these young Americans abroad, including Mailer.

As Stanley Geist recalls, "Everyone who was young in Paris at that time, whether French or American, had a certain fascination with Sartre. It didn't have to do with existentialism but with the picturesque personages of 1947 in Paris. Everybody was infected by existentialism, but no American, including Norman, had read a page of Sartre's philosophical work."

Despite his early ignorance about the existential movement, Mailer would develop his own homegrown brand of that philosophy. In fact he would refer to his second book, *Barbary Shore*, published in 1951, as the "first of the existentialist novels in America." The intuitive basis for that claim was clearly formed during his year in Paris, when existentialism, as an idea, was absorbed by many Americans through a strange but apparently effective process of osmosis.

Although most of Mailer's Paris friends were fellow Americans, he formed some close friendships with Frenchmen. One French couple, Paul and Odette, got both Mailers interested in painting. Paul was an artist from a middle-class family who, like Mailer, was determined to live in a garret. An accomplished moocher of meals, Paul operated in a sublime manner. When he invited Mailer and Bea to dinner, he asked them to bring the wine, bread, and cheese. He would do the rest. The "rest" involved taking a ham bone, some split peas, an onion, and salt and, when combined with the Mailers' contribution, creating a feast for almost no money. Bea remembers these Paris experiences fondly: "I spent one of the happiest years of my life there. I was young; I was enthusiastic. We had so many friends."

One of these friends, Jean Malaquais, was making a profound and enduring impression on young Norman Mailer. Malaquais, an immigrant to France from Warsaw, was a brilliant anti-Stalinist Marxist philosopher, a novelist, and the former secretary to André Gide. He had received the Prix Renaudot for his second novel, *The Man From Nowhere*. His impressive third novel about France during the war, *World Without Visa*, had been published shortly before Mailer arrived in Paris. Fifteen years older than Mailer, he was a classic French intellectual whose political sophistication was far greater than that of the twenty-four-year-old American. Mailer had never met anyone like Malaquais, but to the cultured Frenchman Mailer seemed "a boy scout, both intellectually and mentally; like somebody from a kibbutz."

Malaquais had been a tourist in America a couple of months before he and Mailer met. The two inevitably began talking about American politics, specifically the Henry Wallace movement, which Mailer vehemently supported. As Malaquais remembers: "Norman was young; he was throwing himself headfirst into a political turmoil about which he didn't have the slightest understanding. He thought in terms of the Cold War, the danger with Russia. There was another war looming on the horizon, and his reaction was visceral. There are people called pacifists, but he wasn't a pacifist. He didn't think in personal terms either, but in terms of God, Liberty, and the Constitution.

"Norman had a classical petit-bourgeois, middle-class concept of elections," Malaquais adds. "You elect a representative, a civil servant as President, and if you don't like them, you vote them out of office. I told him this was nonsense, that crooks get reelected. On that score we had differences, because for him an election meant democracy. But he didn't even know the difference between direct democracy and elective democracy."

Malaquais became Mailer's political mentor, and slowly he laid the groundwork for Mailer's broader perception of political reality. But Malaquais steered clear of Marxist theory because he felt that Mailer was such a *naïf*. His horizons would have to be expanded bit by bit. "When I met Norman in Paris," recalls Malaquais, "he knew nothing about the history of the Russian Revolution, of the Russian movement going back to the 1880s. In Western Europe all students are political animals, but in America a writer is a writer is a writer. Mailer grew up without a political orientation and didn't have the curiosity. But that curiosity began in Paris, and he became very interested. Being young and perturbed on an intellectual level by the Cold War, he was open-minded to a degree. He was willing at least to confront and combat."

Mailer was in fact becoming so engrossed in his political discussions with Malaquais that when the two of them and their wives went to an American Ringling Brothers circus which was visiting Paris, no one could focus on the three rings. All of them, including Bea, spent the entire time discussing politics.

Malaquais introduced young Mailer to Boris Souvarine, one of the founders of the Communist Party Central Committee in Paris. As early as 1935 Souvarine had written a seminal biography of Joseph Stalin, *Stalin: A Historical Perception of Bolshevism*, casting the Russian premier as the devil incarnate. Although by the late 1940s many American intellectuals had rallied around this anti-Stalinist view, Mailer was simply baffled by Souvarine and never argued with him.

Mailer did, however, argue with Malaquais. As the sessions with Malaquais continued, the teacher tried to convey his idea that the further to the left a government in the Western world was, the greater the chance for embezzlement and swindling, and the greater the hold of the government on men of goodwill. If the left-of-center Democrats came to power in the United States in the guise of Henry Wallace, he told Mailer, the danger of armed conflict would be greater than if the Republicans won. Republicans, he explained, historically acted on a simple concept of greed and would keep trade avenues open. Liberals had a more complex perspective and would try to blackmail the Russians, causing a more dangerous interplay. "I tried to convey to Mailer," Malaquais says, "that the Wallace movement was exactly the opposite of what he thought it would be. He reacted strongly. Norman was semi-intellectual. Being an American youth and given his middle-class Brooklyn background, he was inclined toward a pseudohumanism or liberalism."

Mailer would continue to react strongly against much of Malaquais's teaching, but the disciplines of radical thought were firmly introduced to Mailer in Paris. By the time he returned home, he had a new belief in collective political action, as well as a more sophisticated sense of politics. Mailer had also adopted the European idea that a writer does not exist in a vacuum and must be politically engaged.

While Mailer was shedding layers of his bourgeois background in the City of Light, he was totally isolated from the excitement that was building around his book in America. "He was very timid at that time," Stanley Geist recalls. "He showed me the proofs of *The Naked and the Dead* like an insecure young man who wanted some reassurance. He was, after all, a newcomer, and he wasn't at all sure of his ground."

❦

In New York, Rinehart was convinced it had a potential success on its hands and was preparing an unusual publishing campaign for *The Naked and the Dead.* Stanley Rinehart was determined to see the book triumph, and Mailer's novel was a perfect vehicle for a creative new marketing strategy.

Three months before the novel's publication on May 8, 1948, reproductions of the line drawing on the book's jacket were strategically placed in bookstores and in advertisements with no mention of the book's title or the author's name and with no advertising copy whatsoever. The pen-and-ink drawing was of a soldier's face shot through with bullet holes, and as the publication date neared, the picture increased in size in successive stages. This kind of marketing hype is now more commonplace in publishing, but in 1948 it was a daring move on the part of Stanley Rinehart and his advertising director, Helen Murphy. As Adeline Lubell recalls, "Everyone was both startled and shocked. But it worked because by the time the book was published, the jacket had become famous." It also won an advertising award for Helen Murphy.

In addition to the advertising campaign five hundred advance paperback editions of the novel were sent out to key people. In the late 1940s it was rare for large numbers of advance galleys to be sent out, because of the expense, and a lavishly printed paperback edition was unheard of. Norman A. Hall, then a sales representative for Rinehart, remembers that he even sent advance paperback editions to salesmen in other publishing companies so that they would talk about the book to bookstore buyers.

Hall, now retired, says *The Naked and the Dead* was one of the two or three books he could really pitch with conviction in all his years of selling. Despite the fact that it was a first novel, had an unusually high cover price of four dollars, and was about the war, Hall was not surprised when Rinehart advanced some ten thousand copies to bookstores before publication. "When I was given the manuscript to read, I stayed up until three in the morning finishing it. I knew it would be a best seller," he says.

As publication date approached, the publishing world was alerted that Stanley Rinehart was personally behind this book and had written an unprecedented piece of flap copy. It consisted of a personal "word to the reader" from Rinehart: "Twenty-seven years ago I was fortunate enough to be associated with the publication of John Dos Passos's *Three Soldiers*. In no year since have I felt the same surge of excitement for a war novel—not until the manuscript of Norman Mailer's *The Naked and the Dead* was readied for publication. . . ." Rinehart went on to compare the book to Thomas Boyd's *Through the Wheat*, Remarque's *All Quiet on the Western Front*, and Hemingway's *A Farewell to Arms*. The keynote was set for many of the reviewers.

The day *The Naked and the Dead* was published, Mailer was still in Paris, missing the excitement being generated by his novel in New York. The reviews immediately announced an important new American writer. In the May 7 edition of the daily *New York Times* Orville Prescott called *The Naked and the Dead* "the most impressive novel about the second World War that I have ever read. . . . Mr. Mailer is as certain to become famous as any fledgling novelist can be." Prescott, who was considered a conservative critic, complained about Mailer's "unnecessarily offensive" language but went on to call him a "conscientious student of John Dos Passos" and praised his "brilliant self-assurance."

On May 8 Maxwell Geismar in the *Saturday Review* prefaced his comments by saying, "Just when we have stopped talking about the new literary voices of the 1940s, they seem to be appearing." Although Geismar decried the "final lack of emotional impact" in the novel, he concluded by saying, "Mr. Mailer is a new novelist of consequence."

A day later, on May 9, *The New York Times Book Review* ran a piece by David Dempsey, who called the book "undoubtedly the most ambitious novel to be written about the recent conflict . . . It bears witness to a new significant talent among American novelists." *Time*, on May 10, compared the book to Tolstoy's *War and Peace*, while *Newsweek*, on the same day, called Mailer "a writer of unmistakable importance."

Rinehart duly dispatched all the reviews to Mailer in Paris as they appeared, and it became clear to the young author that he had been accepted as a major voice in the literary world. Adeline Lubell, who received a number of letters from Mailer during this period, recalls his attitude. "Norman both expected it and feared it wouldn't happen," she says. "I think he was redeemed. He was not part of the literary set, and he yearned to be."

That spring Mailer could have had no way of knowing just how large a part he would come to play in that literary set, or indeed in modern American letters. More than a decade later Diana Trilling would look back on *The Naked and the Dead* as having represented "the hot breath of the future." She hailed the author as having perceived the changes taking place in history—the "loss of faith" in the orderly process of social development, the "increasing social fragmentation," and the "diminishing trust in individual possibility."

On the eve of Mailer's literary debut Fanny, never one to be excluded from her son's life, arrived in Paris with Norman's father, Barney. Barney was on his way to Poland on behalf of an American Jewish group that was helping Polish Jews immigrate to America. Fanny, of course, had come to see her boy wonder. The senior Mailers found a nice apartment on the Right Bank with a view of the Eiffel Tower, and when Mailer's sister, Barbara, arrived in Paris that spring, the whole family was reunited in the glow of Norman's success.

With the prospect of royalties coming in Fanny, Barbara, Bea, and Mailer decided to take a trip to Switzerland and Italy after Bea had finished her exams at the Sorbonne. Mailer's rich uncle, David Kessler, wired them enough money to buy a Renault for the tour. In the early summer of 1948 the foursome set off through the south of France, over the Alps, to Como, Italy. As they were crossing a particularly precarious mountain pass, Bea remembers Fanny exclaiming, "If anyone ever told me I'd be crazy enough to come on this trip, I would have told them it was impossible."

By the summer's end the four were on their way back to Paris when Mailer decided to stop off at an American Express office in Nice to see if he had received any more news about his book from the States. He emerged from the office loaded with letters and a cable. The wire informed him that *The Naked and the Dead* was number one on *The New York Times* Best Seller List, where it would remain for eleven consecutive weeks. Another letter informed him that Lillian Hellman wanted to adapt the novel for a Broadway play.

"We got more and more hysterical reading the mail inside that car," Barbara recalled. "Norman opened a cable and giggled, 'Gee, I'm first on the Best Seller List.' " She adds, "That was the last time Norman could feel he was himself and not Norman Mailer."

He was twenty-five years old, and he was famous.

• IV •

FROM SUCCESS TO THE SHORES OF FAILURE

Three months after the publication of *The Naked and the Dead*, in mid-August of 1948, Norman and Beatrice Mailer flew from Paris back to the United States. By the end of their first week in New York it was clear that their lives had been irrevocably altered. The book had been at the top of *The New York Times* Best Seller List for two months, and the literary establishment and the press were impatiently curious about the precocious twenty-five-year-old who had leapt from obscurity into such an exalted position.

Everything Mailer now did, said, even wore, was scrutinized as literary fame closed in on him. Mailer had hungered for this moment, but nothing he had learned at Harvard or in the war had prepared him for the emotional reality of international success. At first he reacted to it with an excessive humility born out of old middle-class habits. Novelist Calder Willingham, who met Mailer that fall, remembers him as a generous, ingenuous young man, the well-mannered person Fanny and Harvard had taught him to be. "He was new and fresh," Willingham says. "He had come out of Harvard and the army and had written this book, but he wasn't hip. Of course, later on he became very sophisticated and knowing, but at that time he was still very naïve."

One of the first adjustments Mailer had to make to his new success was getting used to having money. *The Naked and the Dead* had earned substantial royalties since its publication in early May. It would sell 197,185 copies in hard cover by the following May with gross royalties of almost $100,000, a substantial amount in 1949 for a twenty-five-year-old. Mailer liked the feel of wealth but defiantly refused to change his bohemian life-style.

Rinehart staffers delight in telling the story of Mailer's first royalty check; it was a sure sign of Mailer's image of himself at the time. With a large check from Stanley Rinehart in hand, Mailer immediately walked into a bank across the street from the publisher's offices and asked for an officer. He wanted to open an account. The banker took a disdainful look at Mailer's youthful face and disheveled garb—an old T-shirt and sneakers—and suspiciously asked him how much he planned to deposit. Mailer casually handed him the check and watched as the banker's jaw dropped in disbelief.

The press was just as fascinated with Mailer's sudden wealth as he was. In August he commented on the money to writer Horace Sutton. "It gives you a fantastic security," Mailer said. "If I keep on living in the manner to which I've been accustomed, the money would probably last for fifteen or twenty years. If I live according to my present scale, it would last a day and a half."

Mailer may have boasted about his new wealth, but Bea remembers ruefully that their physical surroundings did not improve. On their return from Paris they moved into a thirty-dollar-a-month furnished attic room in the same Brooklyn boardinghouse where Mailer had written most of *The Naked and the Dead.* Considering her husband's new fame, Bea's tolerance was remarkable. The attic room had no kitchen, and the couple usually ate at Fanny's apartment or with Mailer's Uncle Dave. They had given up the Remsen Street apartment before they moved to Europe, so the boardinghouse may simply have been an expedient choice. But Bea thinks otherwise: that there were more romantic motives for a best-selling author to live in an attic. "Norman was always living out his bohemian fantasies," she says. "But I knew we wouldn't be there long." In October Mailer was already justifying his bohemian life-style to the press. He was suspect of possessions and found apartments depressing, he told *New Yorker* writer Lillian Ross.

Mailer had no sooner returned from Paris when he discovered that fame attracted the famous. Not only the public but literary celebrities as well were suddenly courting him. Playwright Lillian

Hellman, the distinguished author of *The Children's Hour*, *The Little Foxes*, and *Watch on the Rhine*, had been sent galleys of *The Naked and the Dead* by Rinehart the previous spring. "I sent an immediate blurb to Rinehart," she remembers. "The publishers didn't ask for a blurb, but I sent one anyway because I thought the book was so wonderful." Miss Hellman wanted to convert the novel into a play and had taken an option on the theatrical rights while Mailer was still in Europe. It was Lillian Hellman's interest in *The Naked and the Dead* that had brought Mailer home from France. During his first week back he had a series of conferences with her, and Hellman found him totally cooperative.

Hellman's adaptation of *The Naked and the Dead* was slated to open the following February with Kermit Bloomgarden as the producer. But after writing the first act in the fall of 1948 Miss Hellman discovered she couldn't finish it. "I decided I didn't know where I was going or how to do it, and I stopped," she recalls. "But Norman and I became very close friends. He came up to Pleasantville with Beatrice to see us. My chief memory of Beatrice is that her petticoat was pinned up with a large safety pin which showed at the bottom."

Mailer's own clothes had already become a subject of intense interest to the New York literary press. At a cocktail party Rinehart threw that summer to show off their new prodigy, Mailer arrived without a jacket or tie, wearing a faded tan sports shirt, baggy pants, and scuffed shoes. "He looked," said Horace Sutton, who attended the party, "as if he had just run over from a stickball game on Avenue A." Today Sutton adds: "It was as if he was thumbing his nose at the prestigious group of critics who had gathered to meet him."

The way Mailer dressed at his literary debut soon took on the proportions of myth. By October Lillian Ross had written in *The New Yorker*, "We'd heard rumors that Mailer was a rough-and-ready young man with a strong antipathy to literary gatherings and neckties." She reported that at the August cocktail party Mailer was actually wearing sneakers and an old T-shirt. When she finally met Mailer that fall and saw that he was neatly turned out in gray tweed, shined shoes, and a red-and-white striped tie, Ross couldn't help asking him if he had any deep-seated prejudices about dress. "Actually," Mailer responded, "I've got all the average middle-class fears." He pointed out to her that before the notorious cocktail party he had actually been playing in a ball game and it was hot. "I figured anybody with brains would be trying to keep cool."

Mailer had tried to explain away his casual dress, but by February the myth of Mailer's stickball-player look was becoming literary history. In a *Saturday Review* profile Rochelle Girson added to the legend. "Norman Mailer, Harvard degree or no," she wrote, "is not prone to primp in speech or dress. He made his bow to a cortege of silk-tied critics in a rumpled T-shirt." Mailer was now learning about the intense, often trivial scrutiny awarded a new literary celebrity. Stanley Rinehart's personal secretary, William Sladen, remembers that Mailer complained about it to Rinehart. He was worried that all the New York papers were presenting him as a truck driver. "Well, Norman," Rinehart couldn't help replying, "You *look* like a truck driver."

Mailer's appearance at *The New Yorker* offices dressed in gray tweed shows that the Brooklyn enfant terrible was capable of playing the Harvard gentleman. But he was also holding tenaciously to an anti-celebrity stance, claiming that his success was making him feel uncomfortably like a movie idol. "Whenever I make an appearance," he told Lillian Ross, "I have thirty little girls crowding around me asking for my autograph. I think it's much better when people who read your book don't know anything about you, even what you look like. I have refused to let *Life* photograph me. Everyone keeps asking me if I've ever been psychoanalyzed. The answer is no, but maybe I'll have to be by the end of another five years. These are rough times for little Normie."

It seems out of character for the man who would become such a notorious self-promoter to resist media hoopla in 1948. But only months after his return to the States Mailer had already sensed the unreality of his situation. "Early success changed my life for a long time after *The Naked and the Dead*," Mailer told the author. "I kept walking around saying, 'Nobody treats me as if I'm real.' I believe I could write about an heiress because I felt something that was equivalent to that. That is, no one wanted me for my beauty, only my money. In my case it was that no one wanted me for myself and my five foot eight inches. Everyone wanted me for my celebrity and therefore my experience was not real.

"And so all the habits I had formed up to that point of being an observer on the sideline were shattered and suddenly if I went into a room, I was the center of the room," Mailer adds. "In those days — I was only twenty-six or twenty-seven — I was the only one among my peers who had succeeded. Regardless of how I carried myself, everything I did was taken seriously, and critically. I complained bitterly to myself about the unfairness, until I realized it was fair: that it was my experience. It is the simplest remark in the world to make to yourself but to get to that point can take ten years."

The young author also had to cope with book reviews. They were generally profuse with praise, but often, he was convinced, for the wrong reasons. Having been unable to respond to his critics while in Paris, Mailer was now determined to let some reviewers know that their interpretations of *The Naked and the Dead* were misguided. At the literary cocktail party in August he complained to Lewis Gannett, a distinguished critic for the *Herald Tribune*, that a piece written by Robert Ruark in the New York *World-Telegram* was all wrong. Ruark had written that after reading *The Naked and the Dead* young men of draft age could happily enter the war. Ruark had interpreted *The Naked and the Dead* as a prowar book, but Mailer felt that his strong antiwar message was obvious to any intelligent reader. "My first reaction was that I never wanted to write again, it seemed so futile, so silly. I might as well spend my time doodling."

Two weeks later, while Mailer and Bea were visiting Bea's mother, Mrs. H. I. Silverman, at her Boston home, the author was interviewed by *The New York Star* and complained about reviewers who called his book a documentary. "I don't think," he said, "the book is at all a documentary—a piece of realism. For one thing, the number of events that happen to this one platoon couldn't possibly have happened to any one Army platoon in the war." Mailer called the book "highly symbolic." It represented many concepts to him: "things like death and man's creative urge and man's desire to conquer the elements, fate."

Mailer was learning how strongly reviews affected him, whether they were complimentary or not. His retorts to reviewers were sincere, but they also masked an insecurity about *The Naked and the Dead*. "I was painfully aware of its flaws from the day I wrote it," he later said. "I felt like an imposter. And when these profuse reviews came in, I walked around haunted by a sense of 'Look, I know I don't belong. I don't deserve to be there.' " This was gentlemanly and humble, but it was also one of the last times in his life when Mailer was to feel that humility was a profitable emotion.

❦

On his return from Paris, the Norman Mailer who had been politicized by Jean Malaquais suddenly became vocal about the international situation. He was troubled by the Cold War, and his fear of a real conflict between the United States and Russia had sharpened.

In Europe he had seen what he believed were the disastrous results of the anti-Communist Truman Doctrine and its offshoot, the Marshall Plan.

In Italy, Mailer observed the postwar reconstruction through his newly radicalized eyes. "Italy is pretty bad right now, a pretty ugly country," he said on his return. "The Marshall Plan definitely is keeping in power the smartest, dirtiest, old-time politicians, the broken-down aristocracy that would normally have been kicked out. Italy would be better off under communism than under the kind of very bad capitalism they have there. You don't have to be a Communist to see that."

Although Mailer had joined the Progressive Citizens of America before leaving for Europe, he had been suspicious of collective political action, naïvely thinking of himself as an anarchist. But with his Paris teachings in mind he now decided to become an activist-writer and devote his new celebrity to the 1948 presidential campaign of former Vice President Henry Wallace. Wallace was running on the Progressive Party ticket, a revival of the Teddy Roosevelt party name, in a three-way race with President Truman and the Republican candidate, New York governor, Thomas E. Dewey. Wallace's anti-Cold War stance dovetailed with Mailer's own hope for a postwar rapprochement with the Communists.

The young author-turned-activist announced his conversion in a Rinehart press release: "At this particular period I don't think a writer can avoid being political to a great degree," Mailer said. "There's been a regrettable tendency in the last decade in America to be unpolitical as writers, and I think it's partially accountable for the poverty of American letters in this period."

The 1948 presidential election was only two months away, and Mailer threw himself into the Wallace for President campaign. Bea, who was equally enthusiastic about Wallace, began working in the New York headquarters on Fifth Avenue, where she canvassed by telephone. She clearly remembers their political attitude at the time. "Norman and I wanted better relations with Russia, and we wanted to stop the Cold War," she says. "Truman wasn't about to do it, and Dewey would have been worse than Reagan. So Henry Wallace seemed like a viable alternative. Polls showed Wallace had a big following. We had hopes he would be elected. We thought all the Democrats were going to vote for Wallace, including my parents and Norman's parents."

Commentary editor Norman Podhoretz, then a nineteen-year-old undergraduate at Columbia University studying with Lionel Trilling, recalled seeing Mailer for the first time when the author was campaigning for Wallace at a college rally. "He on the platform," Podhoretz said, "a slight, thin, nervous figure speaking bumblingly for Wallace, I in the audience listening, appalled." Podhoretz was dismayed because he felt that Wallace's campaign had largely been taken over by "Communists" and "fellow travelers," while most intellectuals of the time, including Lionel Trilling, were staunchly anti-Communist. At the time Podhoretz and Mailer were at opposite ends of the political spectrum, although by the late 1950s their views would begin to come closer together.

Two weeks before the election Mailer had made eighteen speeches for Wallace, and a dozen more were scheduled. He even took a brief two-week campaign trip to Hollywood to enlist the support of the movie community. Dancer Gene Kelly remembers meeting him there for the first time. "My wife Betsy was working for Wallace," Kelly recalls, "but I was a strong Truman man. We saw Mailer several times while he was campaigning here, since my home was always the center for New York expatriates. I remember that Hollywood received Norman very well because he'd just published a striking novel." Kelly and his wife made a return visit to Norman and Beatrice in their small boarding-house apartment in Brooklyn Heights shortly afterward. "We liked him, and we liked Beatrice," Kelly recalls. "They were very kind and courteous to us."

If Kelly thought of Mailer fondly, some others did not during this heated political era. On the Hollywood campaign trip Mailer ran into Irwin Shaw, whose book *The Young Lions* had rivaled *The Naked and the Dead* as a best-selling war novel that year. Despite their simultaneous successes, there was little feeling of fraternity between them, politically or otherwise.

"We got into a dispute," Shaw recalls, "because I was against the Wallace campaign. I was afraid Dewey would be elected as a result of splitting the Democratic vote between Truman and Wallace. Since then Norman has said some nasty things about me, but he says nasty things about everybody. Mailer always tries to push himself up by denigrating others." Shaw is referring to a comment Mailer made about *The Young Lions* a decade later. The "considerable merits" of Shaw's novel, Mailer claimed, were tainted by "overambition, opportunism, and a lack of understanding about Europe's past."

There was resistance to Henry Wallace in Hollywood in 1948, but his supporters included a large leftist faction, and Mailer's campaign trip was considered a success. Back in New York Mailer joined the writers' chapter of the Independent Citizens' Committee of the Arts, Sciences and Professions. It had been founded in 1944 by Hannah Weinstein to help Roosevelt's wartime reelection campaign and was now promoting the Wallace candidacy with the help of such celebrities as Lillian Hellman, Howard Fast, Dore Schary, Leonard Bernstein, and Frederic March, all noted for their left-liberal viewpoint.

Mailer, too, was involved. "As a writer Norman was interested in freedom of expression," Weinstein recalls. "He used to sit in my office at the Hotel Iroquois, where he wrote things for the campaign, and we'd talk. He was darling and anxious to get involved. He was very interested in what was going on and in the world—how he saw it and how it affected him. He had great drive and energy."

On October 8, Mailer used that energy to involve himself in a political controversy. He wrote a story for the *New York Post* about George Parker, a teacher at Evansville College in Indiana, who had been asked to resign two days after he had presided at a rally sponsored by the Vanderburgh County Citizens for Wallace Committee. Mailer spoke to the president of Evansville College, Lincoln B. Hale, and did some research on the town while he was there. As he wrote in the *Post*, "Nearly all the townspeople I talked to thought that Wallace was a Communist. . . . The storm which was to swirl around Parker had its origins, I believe, in the anti-Wallace hysteria which was developed calculatedly in the city."

The issue of Communist control of the Wallace candidacy was becoming pivotal in the election. Mailer denied he had met any Communists in the Progressive Party campaign, but a number of leftist intellectuals felt that Wallace had been duped by the Communists and they refused to vote for the candidate. Mailer's continuing belief in Wallace might seem like the naïve idealism of a twenty-five-year-old, but it also showed his early disposition to avoid intellectual fashion and follow his own convictions, even if sometimes wrong-headed. Norman Podhoretz later made an astute observation about Mailer's politics: "He must always work everything out for himself and by himself, as though it were up to him to create the world anew over and over again in his own experience."

Calder Willingham, who had published his well-received novel

End As a Man the year before, was shocked by what he felt was Mailer's political naïveté. Willingham had written to Mailer after *The Naked and the Dead* was published, but the two writers met for the first time during the Wallace campaign when Mailer and Bea visited Willingham's apartment in Flatbush, Brooklyn. After dinner they talked about Wallace, and Willingham predicted that both Mailer and the voters would become disillusioned with the "popular front" which supported the candidate.

"I had been around a little bit more in the New York literary radical circles, and I knew Dwight Macdonald and many of the others," Willingham remembers. "The fashion for the literary intellectuals in those days was anti-Stalinist. But Norman didn't know that—not yet. I told him, 'Look, what about the Moscow trials?' He had hardly heard of them. He looked at me—he was always a very quick, alert person—with an inquisitive expression on his face seemingly asking, 'Can this fool know something I don't?' "

Willingham's dire forecast for the Wallace candidacy was accurate. On November 4 he won only 2.37 percent of the total ballots, an ignominious 1,157,140 votes. Beatrice Mailer speculated that people were so afraid of Dewey's winning that they refused to come out for Wallace, voting instead for Truman. "Even people working for Wallace voted for Truman," she now recalls. Despite the disastrous defeat, Bea and Mailer, along with a handful of other Wallacites, couldn't resist going to the Republican election headquarters at the Roosevelt Hotel on election night. "We watched all the Republicans in their sables and tuxedos crying because Dewey hadn't been elected," Bea says.

❦

Wallace's defeat ended Mailer's brief affair with collective political action. "The Progressive Party, as an organization, was almost as stupid as the army," he later said. But his political interests were far from dead. Over the next two years Mailer's sympathies would grow increasingly radical, but less conformist, largely because of the influence of his French Marxist mentor, Jean Malaquais.

Malaquais had arrived in New York a month before the presidential election. The two had not corresponded since Paris, but Mailer quickly went to see him to resume their discussions. There was still a severe housing shortage in New York, so Bertram Wolfe, a founder of the American Communist Party, helped Malaquais find an apartment in his own building on Montgomery Street in Brooklyn. The Frenchman became part of Wolfe's circle of friends, which at the time included Dwight Macdonald, the editor of *Politics* magazine. Malaquais found that he was considerably more purist about his Marx than this group. As he now recalls, "They were all left liberals by that time, already on the other side. But at one point they were the Marxist light in this country."

Mailer and Malaquais would meet in each other's Brooklyn apartments, and occasionally the two would get together in Jamaica, Vermont, where Norman and Bea had rented a house so they could ski. Mailer wanted to know what he should read to further his political education, and Malaquais suggested such works as *The History of the Russian Revolution*, *The History of the French Revolution*, and *The History of the Working Class in America*. But he never asked Mailer to read any Marx. He viewed Mailer as an influential and enthusiastic new leftist but a lightweight in political theory. He still felt Marx was too "hard" for the young novelist.

Their conversations no longer dealt with the American electoral system but with the concept of state capitalism. Malaquais was a fervent anti-Stalinist who believed the current Communists were counterrevolutionaries, the distorters of Marx's socialist vision. "Norman couldn't understand the proposition that Russia practiced state capitalism and that this had nothing to do with socialism," Malaquais says. "I told him that the basic test is to ask oneself, 'If labor is bought and sold on the market like any commodity, is there or isn't there socialism?' The answer is obviously no."

Although Mailer was slowly succumbing to the Frenchman's view, he continued to test Malaquais. One day he brought Charles Devlin, who had helped him with *The Naked and the Dead*, to Malaquais's apartment. He told Malaquais that Devlin was extremely knowledgeable about Russian production and distribution. After talking to him for a while Malaquais decided that Devlin's views were "laughable." "He was a didactic and simplistic kind of man who went by the book," Malaquais recalls. "If the Central Committee told him tomorrow that Stalin had always been Hitler's spy, he would believe it. It was child's play to destroy him; Mailer shouldn't have brought him."

Malaquais's influence on the impressionable young Mailer was not fully known until March 1949, when some members of the New York intellectual community were startled to learn that his politics had undergone a radical change. On the weekend of March 25 to 27 the National Council of the Arts, Sciences and Professions sponsored a cultural and scientific conference for world peace at the Waldorf Hotel. The U.S. State Department branded the conference a Communist sounding board and permitted only twenty five foreign delegates to attend, most of them from Russia and satellite countries.

The conference began Friday night with a banquet at the Waldorf for two thousand guests. While a thousand anti-Communist pickets paraded outside, celebrities such as Lillian Hellman, Russian composer Dmitri Shostakovich, and Dr. Harlow Shapley of Harvard spoke at the dinner. The following day Mailer was one of the main speakers at a panel session on writing and publishing. Other panelists included F. O. Matthiessen of Harvard, Howard Fast, and Russian writer A. A. Fadayev. Poet Louis Untermeyer was the chairman. In the audience were several leaders of the New York literary establishment, including poet Robert Lowell, Mary McCarthy, Dwight Macdonald, and Edmund Wilson. Seated together in the same audience were Beatrice Mailer and Jean Malaquais.

An international peace conference seemed the perfect vehicle for Mailer's antiwar sentiments. The audience was confident that the young author of *The Naked and the Dead* would make an impassioned plea for the Soviet position, attack the Marshall Plan, and brand President Truman as a villain. On several occasions when Untermeyer turned to introduce a new speaker, voices were heard shouting, "Mailer!"

When the author finally stood up to speak, he was white-faced. When he began, everyone, including Bea and Malaquais, was astounded by his remarks. "I have come here as a Trojan horse," Mailer said. "I had deliberated about coming here and speaking. I don't believe in peace conferences. They don't do any good. So long as there is capitalism, there is going to be war. Until you have a decent, equitable socialism, you can't have peace.

"I am going to make myself more unpopular. I am afraid both the United States and the Soviet Union are moving toward state capitalism. There is no future in that. The two systems approach each other more clearly. All a writer can do is tell the truth as he sees it, and to keep on writing. It is bad, perhaps, to inject this pessimism here, but it is the only way I can talk honestly." Mailer had been a folk hero when he stood up to speak. When he sat down, he was loudly booed.

"That's when Norman broke away from being a fellow traveler,"

Bea Silverman recalls. "At the time it happened, I felt Norman was selling out, because I was more radical than he was. I was still a fellow traveler. We didn't know much about the Stalinist regime at that point. We knew about the purges, but you could rationalize. I told Norman afterward that now that he had money and was on his way up the ladder of success, it had changed him. Jean had influenced him."

Malaquais, however, was equally surprised by his protégé's turnaround to his own way of thinking. He had no idea that his influence had penetrated so deeply. As he now says, "Norman was no longer the small boy who believed in the Constitution." Mailer had intellectually committed himself to the concept of revolutionary socialism, and he had finally staked out what he believed to be the consummate answer to the perils of the postwar world. For the next year and a half he would work feverishly at translating that political vision into a new novel.

Norman Podhoretz would later point out that Mailer was undoubtedly the sole American liberal who responded to the Cold War by rushing to embrace revolutionary socialism. The hostile reaction at the Waldorf conference showed that this position was unpopular among many leftist intellectuals, but there were some, like Irving Howe, who were in favor of Mailer's new anti-Stalinist view. Howe, a socialist intellectual who later founded *Dissent* magazine, remembers being "delighted" by Mailer's comments.

"I had been aware of Norman before that," Howe now recalls, "as more or less a young fellow traveler politically, a supporter of the Wallace movement and so on. His speech at the Waldorf distressed the people who were running the conference but delighted me because it was pretty close to my anti-Stalinist point of view. And I was immediately able to recognize the intellectual fingerprint of who was behind that speech—Jean Malaquais. As soon as Norman started spouting about state capitalism, I knew Malaquais was responsible. But I didn't know until then that Malaquais had been pumping him, working on him." Howe now views Malaquais as "on old-fashioned Marxist sectarian" but admits he served an important purpose by breaking Mailer away from Stalinism.

Howe was so pleased with Mailer's remarks at the conference that he went up to him afterward and complimented him on the honesty of his speech. Mailer's response was surprising. "Norman said the kind of thing I've never totally appreciated," recalls Howe.

"He said, 'Oh, nobody's really honest.' I thought that was a bit of fake humility." Howe decided to say nothing, and the two agreed to get together at some point. But it wouldn't happen for another four years, when Howe approached Mailer about starting *Dissent*.

❦

Mailer later complained that after his return from Paris he felt "prominent and empty." He had written of his one big experience—the war—but what was he to write of now? He was also undergoing the disorienting experience of fame. As Mailer was thrust onto the literary stage, all the careful novelistic habits of being an anonymous observer that he had learned at Harvard and in the war were suddenly shattered. When he walked into a room, Mailer himself was now the focus of attention. People were no longer reacting to him but to his new fame, and he began to feel that his experiences, no matter how exhilarating, were not real. Mailer's abrupt success had so altered his personal reality that to write of his past at that point in his life would have been impossible.

It would take Mailer years to come to grips with his new view of himself and gain the experience he needed to write. "My celebrity made it impossible to get that experience," Mailer now explains. "But then I realized that there was something else that might be equally valuable. I was having a form of twentieth-century experience that was going to become more and more prevalent: I was separated from my roots. I was successful and alienated and that was a twentieth-century condition. This got into all my work after that, in one way or another, and will go on forever at this point. That alienated personality interests me more than someone who is rooted.

"I realized that the kind of writing I was going to do from then on was going to be altogether different from the writing I thought I would do," Mailer adds. "You see, after *The Naked and the Dead*, I thought I would ideally write huge collective novels about American life. One about a labor union, one about a small or medium midwestern town. But I discovered that I knew nothing about labor unions and nothing about midwestern towns and I had no characters left. I had used them all up in *The Naked and the Dead*."

Mailer realized that if his past was useless as a theme and he was unable to be an anonymous social observer, he would have to forge an imaginary future for himself. It was to be one formed largely by Jean Malaquais's revolutionary socialist teachings and by Mailer's own fear of another world war. That, he decided, would be the basis of his new novel.

The book would be called *Barbary Shore*. The protagonist, Michael Lovett, is a young unpublished writer suffering from amnesia after World War II. He has no future unless he chooses one for himself, and he chooses politics, specifically the politics of revolutionary socialism.

Mailer began writing *Barbary Shore* in earnest after the Wallace defeat. Although he had told a number of journalists that he had been working on the novel in Paris, Bea doesn't remember him doing much writing there. Mailer himself admitted that Paris wasn't conducive to work. "It was like a Chekhov comedy," he told Horace Sutton. "Everyone stood around doing nothing and saying 'Gee! I have to do some work this afternoon.' "

Mailer, in fact, could not have begun serious work on *Barbary Shore* in Paris, because he wasn't emotionally or intellectually ready to write the book that later emerged. He had yet to absorb Malaquais's lessons fully, had yet to go through the Wallace campaign, and had still to experience the shock of celebrity that awaited him in America with the publication of *The Naked and the Dead.*

Barbary Shore is set in the Brooklyn Heights boardinghouse where Mailer wrote *The Naked and the Dead.* The novel describes young Michael Lovett's unfolding involvement with another boarder, an ex-member of the Central Committee of the American Communist Party named McLeod. McLeod fears his former comrades as well as another boarder in the house, an FBI agent named Hollingsworth. McLeod's fear is due to something he stole, an unidentified "little object" which remains a mystery throughout the novel but which is clearly a symbol of hope. Another boarder in the house is a strange, incoherent girl named Lannie Madison. Lannie is an informer and a fervent Trotskyite who has become insane due to the death of her political hero. Through Lannie, Hollingsworth and McLeod, Mailer attempts to dramatize the bitter, failed dream of the Trotskyites, what he considered the inherent fascism of the American government, and the future hope of revolutionary socialism.

Lovett's growing involvement with these characters leads him to rediscover his own history and to come to some understanding of the contradictions in the modern world. McLeod, like Malaquais to Mailer, becomes Lovett's spiritual father, and Lovett grows to believe McLeod when he says, "With the integration of the worker into the state economy of the two opposed colossi, the perspective of Barbarism draws ever closer." The only alternative to "mankind in barbary" is "revolutionary socialism." Thus the title *Barbary Shore.*

❦

In the summer of 1949, while he was writing *Barbary Shore,* Mailer and Bea went to Hollywood. Mailer had decided to become a screenwriter and hoped that Hollywood might also provide background for future novels. If Mailer's odyssey to Paris after the war was the inevitable journey of a young novelist following nostalgically in the footsteps of the Lost Generation of World War I, Hollywood was the traditional lure for the young best-selling author of sudden fame. The silver screen had seduced some of the best of the literary generation before Mailer, but the lesson of Fitzgerald's despairing descent into alcoholism was not lost on him. Mailer indulged his ambition and went to Hollywood, but from the moment he got there he steeled himself so completely against its temptations that he was able to accomplish nothing.

Ever since his return from Europe Mailer had told the press that he would like to write for the movies or make his own film. To emphasize that it was not a sudden interest born of fame, he told a reporter that he had made a fifty-dollar surrealist movie at his home in Brooklyn before the war. Bea also remembers his early interest in films. "At Harvard," she recalls, "we all thought movies were a great art form. Now Norman had written the great novel, and he wanted to write the great movie." Mailer wanted to sell *The Naked and the Dead* to the movies, but only if he wrote the screenplay, Bea says. No one was willing to buy the film rights under those circumstances, so when Samuel Goldwyn offered him a contract to write an original screenplay, he readily accepted.

In June 1949 Mailer and Bea, who by this time was seven months pregnant, moved into a modest two-bedroom wood-paneled house on Marley Drive in the hills above Laurel Canyon. The hills were rustic, wooded, and secluded, although they were almost directly above Hollywood's center of gravity, Schwab's drugstore. A number of writers and directors lived in the vicinity, forming an artists' colony which still exists today. The homes were without swimming pools or other trappings of celebrity, but the Mailers' house had a small yard in front, and it was more spacious than their furnished room in Brooklyn.

Mailer immediately wrote Jean Malaquais, who was then teaching at New York University and the New School for Social Research, and asked him and his wife to join them in Hollywood. Malaquais had been an assistant film director in France, and Mailer wanted his help on the script he was writing for Goldwyn. Malaquais and his wife bought a car and spent the next three months driving across country before they arrived in Hollywood in September and installed themselves in the Mailers' home. Mailer's first child, Susan, had been born just a few weeks before, and Bea was remarkably gracious under the circumstances. Initially she had not liked Malaquais, finding him "self-centered, arrogant, and pompous." But in Hollywood she was eventually seduced by his "brilliance and precision of thought." "I even fell a little bit in love with him," she now recalls. Not surprisingly he was named Susan Mailer's godfather.

Soon after the Malaquaises arrived, both couples moved into a much larger house a few streets above Sunset Boulevard. Although this house had servants' quarters and a large garden, there was still no requisite Hollywood swimming pool. As Malaquais points out, "It was not a typical Hollywood house. It was a pleasant place, but nothing special." Neither Malaquais nor Mailer was ready to fall into the Hollywood cliché.

Mailer and Malaquais soon met with Samuel Goldwyn and gave him a verbal synopsis of an original story they had created. The story was loosely based on Nathanael West's novel *Miss Lonelyhearts*. West's novel concerns a Christlike advice-to-the-lovelorn newspaper columnist who can do nothing to help the suffering souls he sees around him and is emotionally buffeted by his cynical world-weary editor. Mailer's story was about a television advice-to-the-lovelorn columnist whose program is sponsored by an enterprise which sells plastics for burials. As Malaquais says, "It seemed an extraordinary proposition: People write letters to seek out help, and the sponsor buries people. It created a kind of dichotomy between people who were drowning and somebody waiting for their corpses."

After listening to their story Goldwyn wrote up a contract for fifty thousand dollars for the finished version and gave them three offices on the studio lot in which to write. Two offices were for Mailer and Malaquais, and one was for secretaries. Both men were amused by the unstated implication that they could have whatever kind of secretaries they wanted, including girls to sleep with.

After a month Mailer and Malaquais had ninety pages of script finished and once again met with Goldwyn. According to Malaquais, Goldwyn was willing to buy the script and produce it, but he wanted to bring in "hack writers" to rearrange it so that American virtues were extolled and the ending was happy. "He wanted it changed," says Malaquais, "so that good sentiments would be rewarded and bad sentiments would be punished." As Goldwyn was talking to the two writers, he grabbed a button on Malaquais's jacket and kept pulling it as he explained that when Americans do things, it comes from the heart, but when Frenchmen do things, it comes from the head. By the end of the conversation Goldwyn had pulled the button off the jacket.

Mailer and Malaquais considered Goldwyn's proposal unacceptable. "We sold him an idea," says Malaquais. "We wrote it down, and that was that. We were not going to let ourselves be bought out or outmaneuvered. So we said no and broke a fantastic contract on principle."

Bea remembers the Hollywood scenario somewhat differently. She says Goldwyn didn't want the script at all but offered Mailer five thousand dollars to shelve the project. "Norman refused," recalls Bea, "and walked off with the screenplay. He felt if it wasn't good enough, why was Goldwyn going to give him five thousand dollars to keep it? I agreed with him."

Two decades later Mailer looked back on that time with some bitterness. "Out there in Hollywood," he wrote, "I learned what pigs do when they want to appropriate a mystery. They approach in great fear and try to exercise great control. Fear + Control = Corporate Power."

Mailer's breaking of the Goldwyn contract became the stuff of legend in Hollywood, where it was assumed that no one would throw away money on principle. Mailer and Malaquais confounded everyone even further by insisting that they would produce the film themselves. Goldwyn had already lined up Charles Boyer and Montgomery Clift to act in the project, so the two writers approached the actors about starring in their production. Boyer and Clift were willing, but neither Mailer nor Malaquais knew how to raise the money to produce the film, and the project was finally dropped. Clift, however, became a good friend of Mailer's. Ironically, years later he starred in another adaptation of *Miss Lonelyhearts*.

The studio now sensed that Mailer would not play their way. But he was still the first important novelist of World War II, and Hollywood ached for a great war picture. Malaquais had also published war diaries, so the twosome were considered literary specialists on the war. Despite the Goldwyn contretemps, Malaquais remembers that they must have had at least fifty meetings with various producers. Every one of them wanted a war picture that was "happy," but the two writers would not compromise.

One Hollywood director, Robert Rossen, asked Mailer to write a screenplay for Humphrey Bogart, but Mailer refused. "He was always turning down things," Bea recalls. "He always felt he would compromise himself. He was so puritanical that he wouldn't even do a radio talk show with some actress because he would have to say 'Drink Pepsi Cola.' His integrity was almost pathological."

Mailer was so anxious to protect himself against the lure of Hollywood ambition that he wore integrity as a kind of chastity belt. "I think," Bea says, "that he was so afraid of instincts in himself that would make him into what he actually later became that he checked them abnormally." Malaquais, however, had nothing but respect for Mailer's integrity. "Faulkner and Fitzgerald crumbled in that town, but Norman did not. He's a fighting rooster, and he just hits back."

Despite his reputation as a "difficult" writer, Mailer was constantly being invited to the homes of such Hollywood celebrities as Charlie Chaplin. In addition to being a famous war novelist Mailer was one of the few literary celebrities in Hollywood who had no compunction about being identified with the left. At the time Senator Joseph McCarthy was beginning his anti-Communist campaign, and the specter of the Hollywood Ten had caused the left to lose support in the motion-picture community. "Norman was an important acquisition for them, and they courted him strongly," Malaquais reflects. "Before that they had whoever they wanted, Dos Passos, Steinbeck. But in that atmosphere Mailer was one of the very last."

Actor-dancer Gene Kelly and composer Saul Chaplin remember socializing with Mailer in those days. Chaplin recalls that they were all part of a group whose focus was the Actor's Lab, a left-wing acting and teaching organization similar to the WPA Theater in New York. About ten of the group's members would often get together at Mailer's house for dinner. "That meant somebody put sliced ham on the table and some cheese, and you had a buffet," Chaplin says. "There was no sitting down, but that's the way all of us entertained." In retrospect Saul Chaplin is struck by the fact that Mailer left no indelible impression on him. "It wasn't like he was the life of the party or always on or had strong opinions, nothing like that," he says. "He was reserved, spoke quietly, and was pleasant to be around. He seemed nothing like the Norman Mailer who has since emerged."

Mailer also met Dorothy Parker during his stay in Hollywood, although the young novelist and the notorious wit of the Algonquin Round Table never became close friends. They were first introduced in Parker's room at the Chateau Marmont. During the visit the naïve Mailer was startled when Parker praised an agent to his face, then tore him apart as soon as he left the room. "After that meeting," Mailer later said of himself, "Mailer always did his best to be the last to leave Dottie Parker's sitting room at the Chateau Marmont."

A more sophisticated Lillian Hellman laughed at Mailer's concern over how he might be treated once Parker's door had closed. "Norman," she told him, "everyone knows that Dottie will talk about you after you leave the room. It will amount to no more than the compliments she's just given you. Everybody who cares about Dottie knows that's the price to pay."

That year in Hollywood, Mailer met one person, a young actor, who was to become a close ally and a lifelong friend. Mickey Knox was from Brooklyn, and when a mutual acquaintance brought Mailer to Knox's house, the two immediately took to each other. "Norman then was not the kind of fellow he is now," Knox recalls. "He was shy and much quieter. He was very young and suddenly found himself in a world that if not overwhelming was certainly much different from anything he had ever known. He was very timid."

But despite Norman's shyness, Knox remembers huge parties at Mailer's house, where the cream of the Hollywood acting community—Charlie Chaplin, Marlon Brando, Gene Kelly and his wife Betsy, and Montgomery Clift—gathered. "Norman had an enormous reputation in that town," says Knox, "as the first young writer to come out of the war."

Knox introduced Mailer to Harold Hecht, who wanted to produce *The Naked and the Dead* as a movie. Hecht, a former agent, had joined Burt Lancaster as a partner in Lancaster's new movie company, and when he met Mailer at Knox's house, he immediately took an option on the novel. Knox recalls that John Garfield was eager to play the role of Sergeant Croft.

Hecht began preproduction work on the film but immediately ran into problems. "Harold had a lot of trouble with the government," recalls Knox, "because you couldn't make a war picture without getting tanks and uniforms and guns. They refused to give all this to him unless he changed the title and made various changes in the story." As the problems mounted, Hecht was forced to call Mailer and tell him he didn't know what to do. Mailer made an unprecedented offer. He would buy back the book. "Harold almost kissed his feet, because it was a lot of money," Knox recalls. Years later Knox asked Norman why he had done it. "Well, if Hecht had kept it, the movie never would have been anywhere near the book," Mailer replied. *The Naked and the Dead* was not produced as a movie until 1958, when Mailer sold it to Charles Laughton and Hollywood producer Paul Gregory, who in turn sold it to Warner Brothers. The film, which starred Cliff Robertson and Raymond Massey, was a disaster.

While Mailer was making his unsuccessful forays into the world of cinema, he was also working hard on *Barbary Shore*. Bea remembers that he would take his typewriter into the tiny, empty maid's room and close himself off for hours. Malaquais confirms that Mailer usually worked on the novel in the morning and would then surface about 1:30 or 2:00 P.M. for lunch.

Mailer never showed Malaquais the manuscript of *Barbary Shore* while they were in Hollywood because he was wary of the Frenchman's criticism. Malaquais had stayed on in Hollywood several months after the Goldwyn debacle in order to work on the French translation of *The Naked and the Dead*, and he had made copious notes criticizing the manuscript because he felt there were serious problems with both the structure and the prose. "Norman has a baroque twist to his writing," Malaquais now says. "He can't say a nose is a nose is a nose. He always uses flashy images." Mailer would not let Malaquais read *Barbary Shore* until after it was published, but even so, the book is dedicated to him.

While Mailer was busy writing and trying to make an impact on the Hollywood community, Bea was becoming increasingly despondent about her own situation. She had enjoyed motherhood for the first few months after Susan was born, but she soon became bored with that role. Being married to a famous man, she was discovering, made everything even worse. One became a nonentity, an appendage, and without a separate and sustaining career self-respect was easily lost. As the Hollywood celebrities courted her husband and politely ignored her, Bea became increasingly disoriented and depressed. The problem had grown serious by June 1950, when Norman and Bea decided to leave Hollywood.

The town had clearly cast its pall over the young couple. Those first shining moments of true celebrity, of mingling with famous movie actors and directors had eroded into a far less glamorous reality. Mailer had failed to make a movie or even write a screenplay. His second novel, after two long years, was not going smoothly, and Bea was very unhappy. Fame could offer them no refuge from their problems, for it was fame that had helped to create them. Hollywood had lived up to its notorious reputation for wooing the young and the hopeful, then discarding them.

❦

In June 1950 the Mailers left Hollywood and retreated to the beaches of Provincetown, Massachusetts, where Mailer rented a big house on a hill, one of a series of homes he would enjoy there over the next three decades. Mailer had begun his first novel in Provincetown, and like a homing pigeon, he would return to the town again and again throughout the years to work or just relax. That summer, as the Korean War broke out and anti-Communist feeling in the United States grew, Mailer continued to work every day on his novel about revolutionary socialism. His old Harvard mentor Robert Gorham Davis and his wife, Hope Hale, who lived in nearby Wellfleet, visited the Mailers briefly. Despite Bea's growing depression, they remember a happy domestic scene, with little Susan crawling between them on the floor.

In the fall the Mailers bought a large white one-hundred-and-fifty-year-old farmhouse in Putney, Vermont, where Mailer intended to settle down to the life of a gentlemen writer and put the finishing touches on *Barbary Shore*. Almost immediately, however, there were complications with Bea, who was by now seriously depressed. She made futile efforts to engage herself, first by practicing the piano again and then by painting. "I started to paint, like all unhappy women when they don't know what to do with themselves," Bea recalls. "But I wasn't interested in it; I'm not a painter." Since creativity was integral to the value system she shared with her husband, it never occurred to her to take up a nonartistic pursuit.

"I was miserable in Vermont," Bea says, "absolutely miserable. Here I was with this darling little girl, the house was gorgeous, and we had very interesting friends—writers and artists. Putney was a New York away from New York. But I was a very depressed woman. It just wasn't my bag to be the wife of a famous man without a life of my own."

Mailer was aware of how unhappy his wife was, but there was little he could do. He did try to help her with career decisions and Bea fondly remembers one particular effort. One day Mailer brought her a little pocket book on careers. He had gone through it himself, looking for a solution, and he seemed to have come up with a prophetic one. "You know, Bea," he said, "you should become a doctor. You have all the characteristics of a doctor."

Bea now admits that if she had become a doctor right then, instead of waiting until after the divorce, the marriage might have been saved. But even then she must have sensed that the dominance of her husband's personality and the intrusion of fame would make it difficult for her to hold her own in his world. Mailer understood this as well. Years later, when he was asked why he and Beatrice had broken up, he could only reply, "Success."

Mailer was later able to see that he had been living with what he called a "premature Women's Liberationist." "She was a very strong woman," he recalled. "She profoundly resented the female role into which my success had thrust her. You see, when we married, she was, if anything, stronger than me. She was perfectly prepared to go out and work for years in order to make enough money for me to stay at home and write a good many books. And if that happened, we probably would have been a happy couple of that sort, she the strong one, I the gentle one. Then what happened? I became successful so suddenly I got much more macho. . . . I suddenly felt like a strong man. That altered everything between us."

Bea at first refused to recognize the inevitability of their separation. "I was so traditional in some ways that the idea of divorce never entered my mind, the idea that I could get out of it," she says. But it was clear that fall in Vermont that the marriage was disintegrating rapidly.

Mailer not only was anticipating failure at home, but was beginning to realize that his writing career was imperiled. Calder Willingham remembers receiving a poignant letter about *Barbary Shore* from Mailer in Vermont. Willingham had written Mailer asking for a loan: He was in the Virgin Islands getting a divorce and was destitute. Mailer, with a generosity so typical of him in those days, wired him $200, which , as Willingham points out, "was quite a hunk of money then." In the letter Mailer revealed his feelings about the novel he was working on. "He said," recalls Willingham, " 'I'm going to stay here in Vermont building stands for power tools for the rest of my life.' He was having awful problems with *Barbary Shore*. The second novel is always a hurdle when you've had a lot of attention with the first one."

Mailer's fears about his new book soon proved justified. When he delivered the manuscript of *Barbary Shore* to Rinehart that fall, nobody in the publishing company really liked it. Everyone who read the manuscript sensed that it was a poor follow-up to *The Naked and the Dead*. The first printing and the advertising budget were scaled down, and there would be no promotional hoopla as there had been for *The Naked and the Dead*.

"We were all aware that *Barbary Shore* wouldn't be successful," recalls Norman Hall, the Rinehart sales representative who had stayed up all night reading *The Naked and the Dead* three years earlier. "The house was not one bit enthusiastic. It was a very obscure and difficult book, and to me it was hardly to be understood. It was very hard for a salesman to go out after a big success like *The Naked and the Dead* and say to clients, 'This guy has gone one better or even as good.' Any salesman who does that kind of thing pretty soon loses his reputation. We had to play it down; there's no question about that."

Mailer was by now fully aware of the problems *Barbary Shore* posed. He had taken a conscious gamble in this second novel by creating a style which was radically different from that of his much-praised *The Naked and the Dead*. The Kafkaesque allegory which emerged in *Barbary Shore* was alien to the literary traditions Mailer had absorbed at Harvard and had drawn on so successfully in his first novel. Furthermore the books' semisurreal style was so tied to Mailer's revolutionary socialist view that the critics were unable to separate the two. When *Barbary* was published in the spring of 1951, China had just entered the Korean War, and nobody wanted to hear about socialist virtues. That the novel collapsed at the end into a tedious and dogmatic political tract did not help its reception either.

The reviews of Norman Mailer's second book were in stark contrast to the praise given *The Naked and the Dead*. They were almost universally bad. "It is likely to be said," wrote Anthony West in *The New Yorker* in June 1951, "that a bad press is the price Mr. Mailer has had to pay for making the courageous gesture of writing and publishing an overtly socialist book. The truth is that it has a monolithic, flawless badness, like Mussolini's play about Napoleon, that lifts it clear out of the political arena."

Time magazine, in its May 28 issue, was no kinder. "Using the stereotypes of the tortured confessional, the state spy, the bureaucratic machine, universal fear and insecurity, he achieves at best a small-beer *Nineteen Eighty-Four.* At worst, he talks like a highbrow caught with his IQ down. . . . Mailer nails his flag to the mast as a sort of last-of-the-intellectual-leftists. But his novel, paceless, tasteless and graceless, is beached on a point of no fictional, or intellectual, return."

A slightly more positive view was offered by Harry Sylvester in the May 27 *New York Times Book Review*, but the end effect was almost the same. "At best, the result is not unlike a good modern painting, a yellow mist through which the reader sees only the essential shape and line, and in which a guilt, similar to that informing 'The Trial,' is felt. At worst, Mailer can be very dull and, in his insistence on the lost purity and nobility of the communist left, sentimental and untrue."

Although Mailer would later try to dismiss these reviewers, the fact that Jean Malaquais, the ideological mentor of *Barbary Shore*, did not like the book either was a stunning blow to his ego. "It's a political tract, not a novel," Malaquais says. "You don't make a novel with political themes or you have to be a genius. I didn't like the book, and I told Norman so."

For years Mailer would continue to defend *Barbary Shore* as the "richest" of his first three novels. But Mailer later conceded that he had tried for something beyond his reach. "I was two personalities: one the successful writer, the other this guy of twenty-six, twenty-seven, still trying to work things out for myself," he confessed. At the age of twenty-seven, after having been suddenly hurtled to the summit of literary success, Mailer was tasting the first bitterness of failure. Despite his worldwide fame, he could do nothing to alter his wife's deepening depression or his publisher's growing coolness. To rebuild, he would have to look for other avenues of experience.

• V •

BREAKING OUT

The devastating critical reception of *Barbary Shore* sent Mailer into a deep depression for a year. During this time he managed to write only short stories, in all of which he reverted to the style of *The Naked and the Dead*.

Even before *Barbary Shore* was published in the spring of 1951, Mailer sensed that a pastoral life in Vermont with a depressed wife was not the ultimate existence. He was stifling in rural domesticity, and as Calder Willingham speculates, he became bored with Bea because she wouldn't indulge his yearning for a new adventure. "Bea had her own idea of things, and she wasn't going to follow along in Norman's wake," Willingham says. "Norman suddenly thought of running around with other women, and there was just no way he was going to stay married." That winter Mailer left Bea and headed for Greenwich Village, the heart of American bohemia in the early 1950s. By April Bea and their infant daughter, Susan, had also departed Vermont, headed for Mexico and a new life.

Daniel Wolf, a close friend of Mailer's who would found *The Village Voice* with him four years later, recalled the author's arrival in the Village. "Here he had this nice, big, white house in Vermont," Wolf stated. "He'd picked out his surroundings. He was going to live the life of a normal, young American writer who had succeeded." But unexpectedly Mailer showed up at Wolf'sVillage apartment one night and told him he needed a place to stay because he was breaking up with Bea. Wolf knew this was no idle threat: "Norman was making one of his big moves."

Mailer had originally met Wolf through Jean Malaquais in 1948, when the Frenchman was teaching at the New School and Wolf enrolled in one of his classes. Eight years older than Mailer, Wolf was known around the Village as a brilliant conversationalist. He dropped out of the New School in 1950 and spent a number of years working at odd jobs. By 1954 he would have written sections of *The Columbia Encyclopedia* on Greek, Roman, and Arabic philosophy, composed press releases for the Turkish Information Service in New York, and been a freelance writer and editor. It was through Mailer that Wolf would meet his future wife, Rhoda Lazare, who had been a close friend of Barbara Mailer's since their youth in Crown Heights. And it was through Wolf that Mailer would meet *his* second wife, Adele.

The night Mailer showed up at Wolf's apartment, the two of them proceeded to down most of a bottle of whiskey together. At 11:30 Wolf decided to phone a girl he knew for Mailer. The girl Wolf had in mind was Adele Morales, a Spanish-Peruvian painter who lived in a cold-water flat on East Sixteenth Street and who supported herself by making store-window dummies.

Adele had been the girl friend of Edwin Fancher, another New School student who would later join Wolf and Mailer in starting *The Village Voice*. Fancher had received a master's degree in psychology from the New School and had set up a therapy practice in the Village. After Adele broke off her relationship with Fancher, she had an affair with beat writer Jack Kerouac, but this was winding down by the time Wolf called her on behalf of Mailer. Wolf sensed correctly that Adele would be the radical change Mailer was looking for.

When Wolf called Adele, she said it was too late in the evening but added that she would like to meet Norman Mailer some other time. She had read *The Naked and the Dead* and admired it. Mailer, however, was adamant about meeting Adele that night. "Tell her I'll pay for the cab," he insisted to Wolf. Finally she relented. Ten minutes after she arrived at the apartment, Wolf passed out in the next room. When he woke the next morning, he found Norman and Adele still up and in the middle of a deep conversation. In time, Adele Morales would become Norman Mailer's second wife, and for the next tempestuous decade the couple would be inseparable.

Beatrice had in many ways been like Mailer's mother—strong, bright, Jewish, and intolerant of Norman's macho antics. But Adele was quite different: a dark, sensuous Latin, who, at least initially, was a strong woman without a sense of her own strength. She had gone only to Washington Irving High School, and her limited education gave her a certain insecurity which permitted her to passively follow Mailer's intellectual lead. Yet as an artist Adele had her own unconventional imagination and she would learn to play Mailer's psychic games with innovation. Although these games would eventually get out of hand as Mailer's vision of the "orgiastic and violent" intensified, in the beginning Adele offered Mailer an exciting and mysterious departure from the dominant women he had known. "Adele's an Indian," Mailer has said, "primitive and elemental."

Adele's responsive sensuality stimulated Mailer's evolving sense of freedom and his growing desire for the forbidden. "That early period with Adele was probably his happiest time," Wolf later said. "She opened him up. He saw in her a direct involvement with life." In courting Adele, Mailer was clearly charting a course away from his bourgeois Brooklyn background and his mother's apron strings, but it is ironic that Mailer's need for a strong woman would not diminish. In Adele he would eventually create a woman so strong and competitive that his masculinity once again became threatened.

Soon after Mailer met Adele, Wolf found him an apartment in a building that adjoined his own, at 41 First Avenue, near Second Street on the Lower East Side. Wolf was then living at 39 First Avenue in a railroad flat five flights up. Wolf's and Mailer's apartments were connected on the outside of the building by a fire escape which was in constant use. Wolf's apartment, which was in the front of the building, shared a toilet with the back apartment. When Mailer first moved in, there was a dancer living next to Wolf, but she soon turned her apartment over to Adele. The connecting fire escape was now used more than ever, and until Adele moved in with Mailer, the two would visit each other in this unusual way.

Mailer had actually taken two apartments on the top floor of 41. He broke through the wall between them to make one long if narrow loft. He installed a bathtub himself, did all the plumbing, and fixed the place up. His friend Mickey Knox, who was then back in New York for a time, was amazed that Mailer did the work himself even though he could afford help. "Well," Norman told him, "it's my house, I'm living here, and I want to do everything myself." But despite Mailer's improvements, Tobias Schneebaum, who moved into

Adele's apartment at 39 First Avenue after Adele moved in with Mailer, insists that it was still ghetto living. "Norman's apartment was really a dump. It was a filthy old tenement building," he says.

The setting didn't stop Mailer's literary and movie friends from climbing five dingy flights to engage in riotous drinking parties and conversations that would make Mailer's tenement apartment a vital postwar salon. Some were new friends, such as Vance Bourjaily, whose first novel, *The End of My Life*, published four years earlier, had established him as a major young luminary. When *Barbary Shore* was published, Bourjaily had written Mailer, telling him that it was a fine novel despite what the critics said. Bourjaily was conscious of how difficult it was to follow a first novel. He had written and thrown away his own second book, and it would take him seven years to publish another. Mailer replied to Bourjaily's letter by postcard, inviting him to come to a party.

"Probably the reason I decided to write Norman at all," Bourjaily says, "is because we were both in John Aldridge's book *After the Lost Generation*. It began to look as if something might be happening on the critical front that would draw us postwar writers together into a kind of group. I wanted to get to know some of the other people."

John Aldridge's influence as a literary critic was considerable. He was only a year older than Mailer, but with the publication of *After the Lost Generation* in the spring of 1951, his reputation soared. As Bourjaily noted, he was the first to group the post-World War II writers together in a recognizable literary generation. Aldridge looked at the most significant World War I writers—Hemingway, Fitzgerald, and Dos Passos—and compared them to the new writers who had emerged since World War II: Bourjaily, Mailer, John Horne Burns, Irwin Shaw, Merle Miller, Gore Vidal, Paul Bowles, Truman Capote, and Frederick Buechner. In Aldridge's view none of these younger writers could match the standards of the Lost Generation. This new generation had arrived at the end of a transition in society, he felt, and did not have the fresh perspective of protest which favored the writers of the 1920s.

While Hemingway, Fitzgerald, and Dos Passos confronted the sense of loss and the meaninglessness of the First World War, the younger writers were already well-schooled in futility. Aldridge also pointed out that the language of the novel had already been transformed by the Lost Generation. Once again the younger writers were stymied. All they could do was repeat now-outmoded stylistic formulas. What the new generation could do, Aldridge said, was enlarge the narrow perspective of the World War I novelists into a more comprehensive social view.

Aldridge felt that Mailer was the first of the World War II novelists to examine the moral and philosophical premises of war. Or at least Aldridge believed Mailer had made a brave attempt at it in *The Naked and the Dead*, although he had ultimately failed: "The good are humiliated or suffer fatal deception; the evil are made ridiculous; and the mediocre ride to victory on an accident. Instead of rising through successive stages to a supreme indignity, the novel descends through a series of reductions to an absolute zero." Aldridge thought Mailer had failed in "the abstract truth of the master design," but he did not deny the emotional power of *The Naked and the Dead*. "No novel since *The Red Badge of Courage* and *War and Peace*," he wrote, "has contained a more vivid or terrifyingly accurate picture of the conditions of actual warfare, and certainly no novel of our time since *U.S.A.* had projected its theme on a more variegated background of human experience."

Aldridge's *After the Lost Generation* was published the same week as *Barbary Shore*, and the two authors were curious to meet each other. It was Bourjaily who arranged the get-together, and the three young men spent a long evening together at Bourjaily's apartment on Grove Street in the West Village in the summer of 1951, only a few months after their books were published. Aldridge remembers that Mailer was saddened by the reception of *Barbary Shore*, especially since his review in *The New York Times Book Review* was on page five and Aldridge had been given the cover. But the critic and the author became friends, and Mailer later called on Aldridge when problems arose with his third novel.

Bourjaily was instrumental in introducing Mailer to a number of other people, many of whom would become his longtime friends. A young theater producer named Lewis Allen, who then worked for producer Robert Whitehead and who later became one of the producers of the Broadway hit *Annie*, met Mailer through Bourjaily. The three frequently saw each other in the early fifties, and all later spent time together in Mexico in 1954. Allen and his future wife, screenwriter Jay Presson Allen, also lived near Mailer in Connecticut in the late fifties, as did Aldridge.

Through Bourjaily, Mailer met another great war novelist, James Jones. Both Jones and Bourjaily had been edited by Max Perkins at

Scribner's, and when the famous editor died in 1947, the two writers were taken over by another Scribner's editor, Burroughs Mitchell. Jones first came to New York several months after *From Here to Eternity* was published in February 1951, but he knew no one in the city. Mitchell brought him and Bourjaily together. When Jones told Bourjaily that he wanted to meet Norman Mailer, Bourjaily immediately took him to Mailer's East Village loft.

Mailer had read the galleys of *From Here to Eternity* the previous fall in Vermont. Larry Alson recalls that when he and Barbara were visiting, Mailer was sick in bed with a cold and feeling awful, but he was avidly reading the end of Jones's book. "I've just come across the most tremendous guy," he told Alson. "He knows more about the army than I will ever know. This is a big, big book." When Jones and Mailer finally met, the two war novelists instantly took to each other. As Bourjaily says, "Jim was nice and unpretentious with a James Cagney type charm, and he and Norman liked each other. There was no cock fight or anything like that between them."

A few weeks later Mailer brought along his Hollywood friend, actor Montgomery Clift, to a party at Bourjaily's Grove Street apartment. Jones was introduced to the actor, who would later star as the protagonist, Prewitt, in the film version of *From Here to Eternity.* "For years afterward," recalls Bourjaily's wife, Tina, "Clift kept saying in movie magazines that it was at that party that he and Jones decided to do the movie of *From Here to Eternity* together."

Another of Mailer's Hollywood friends was Marlon Brando, whom he brought along to a number of the Bourjailys' parties. Clift and Brando also became fixtures at Mailer's own parties, and Tobias Schneebaum remembers Clift sitting by himself in a corner of Mailer's loft appearing very withdrawn. Larry Alson's impression of Brando was that of a self-satisfied star standing in the middle of one of Norman's parties looking at the guests with bemusement and saying, "Just who *are* these people?"

The cast of characters in the Mailer salon was an eclectic one. Lillian Hellman would frequently climb the five flights to his parties with her fur coat dragging over the filthy stairs. Louis Auchincloss made his way down from the Upper East Side. Hortense Calisher, Alberto Moravia, Susan Sontag, William Styron, and Calder Willingham also joined their celebrated peers at Mailer's soirees. Jones was a frequent guest at the parties before he went back home to Marshall, Illinois; he and Mailer could sometimes be seen hand wrestling. "They were heavy drinking parties," recalls Bourjaily, "noisy and good-natured. Pot was not part of the scene yet. We were all young, and there was lots of flirtation, lots of drinking and yelling and laughing and good-time party behavior."

Louis Auchincloss noted that the parties were dominated by Mailer's personality. "Norman developed a little court around him," he recalls. "I was reminded of the man who went to an evening at Victor Hugo's. The great author sat on a kind of dais in silent thought. At last he was heard to murmur: *'Quant à moi, je crois en Dieu.'* In the background someone else murmured, *'Quelle merveille! Un Dieu qui croit en Dieu!'* "

Mailer's court was undoubtedly reassuring to him after the failure of *Barbary Shore*. The parties were a salve to his ego, and they were also a way of observing, even experimenting in social interaction. Unlike some of his literary friends who stuck mainly to their own kind, Mailer invited all types of people to his gatherings. Judy Feiffer, the former wife of cartoonist Jules Feiffer, remembers that by the mid 1950s Mailer was throwing provocative parties by bringing together unlikely people. The evenings either produced superb conversational riffs, or else they fell flat, but she sensed that there was artistry in his choice of guests.

One incident at a Mailer party gave everyone pause. About forty people had gathered in Mailer's loft when, during the course of the evening, five hoods from the neighborhood banged on the door demanding to be let in. The guests all crowded around the door and backed them out. A half hour later the door was kicked open, and the hoods burst into the room with bottles and clubs. Mailer dashed bravely up to them.

Calder Willingham vividly recalls what happened next. "One of them knocked Norman down with his fist, like in a John Wayne movie. Norman was stunned on the floor. Then another one, a nut, grabbed a hammer. There was a little dreamy-eyed poet standing there watching this, and the nut—who had glasses that magnified his eyes like the bottom of a Coca-Cola bottle—knocked the poet down to the floor like a steer. Then Norman started getting to his hands and knees, with blood coming out of his nose. This guy whammed Norman on the head with his hammer, and we thought he had killed him. Meanwhile everyone was standing there stunned and watching when Adele suddenly screamed bloody murder. She was the first one who took action. She ran at the guy, and they withdrew. Norman was knocked cold. He didn't know where he was." The next day Mailer's window was riddled with bullets from a shotgun.

Eight years later, when Mailer was attempting to explain in *Advertisements for Myself* why the protagonist of his third novel, *The Deer Park*, seemed overly delicate when he, Mailer, was not, he used the party scenario as an illustration of his own physical prowess. Mailer's version of the evening is slightly different from Willingham's. He insists that he had taken two cracks on the head with a hammer but had still been able to fight back.

❦

In addition to bringing together eclectic groups at parties Mailer and Bourjaily thought it might be interesting to create a more formal salon, to have a group of writers meet each Sunday afternoon at the White Horse Tavern on the corner of Hudson and West Eleventh streets in the West Village. Bourjaily believes the original idea was Mailer's and that Norman definitely chose the place. In the late forties the favorite Village literary hangout had been the San Remo bar on the corner of Bleeker and MacDougal streets, catering to such clientele as beat writers William Burroughs, Allen Ginsberg, Gregory Corso, and Jack Kerouac. The scene then moved to the Minetta Tavern and a bar called Louis near Sheridan Square, which William Styron frequented. As soon as Mailer started his White Horse group, however, that tavern succeeded the others as *the* Village hangout.

Daniel Wolf believes that it was he who originally suggested that Norman make it a Sunday-afternoon tradition to go to the White Horse. "Norman found that if you invited people to your house, it was not that easy to get rid of them," he said. The White Horse "had a pleasant atmosphere; it was the right setting—the 'real' Village; it was an old bar and had a quiet neighborhood quality."

Soon after Mailer began his Sunday-afternoon salon, poet Dylan Thomas began drinking at the White Horse, but at night. He had heard it was a place where writers went. For some reason the tavern eventually became better known as Dylan Thomas's hangout than as Mailer's, and English majors from northeastern colleges took treks to the White Horse in search of the Welsh poet rather than the World War II novelist.

The whole enterprise seems out of character for the Harvard undergraduate who thought literary salons were pretentious. But after the failure of *Barbary Shore* Mailer felt he had to be at the literary center. The idea of a writer's group was also a romantic one, harking back to Hemingway in Paris and to Sartre at the Deux Magots and the Café de Flore. "It was a yearning we all had," says Vance Bourjaily, "a kind of common yearning at the time. Paris of the twenties was what we had in mind, and various people made attempts at it, including us."

Hortense Calisher remembered the very first White Horse meeting in 1952. "Word had been passed around to writers who often met at Vance and Tina Bourjaily's that 'Norman' wanted us to meet of a Sunday and get some needed café discussion started, the bar chosen being The White Horse on Hudson Street. . . ." she wrote in her book, *Herself*. "The day we first go, in a group of about ten, of which I recall for sure only Mailer, the Bourjailys and Frederic Morton, the bar and its usual patrons, mostly the remainders of indigenous Greenwich Village Irish, are no more unhandy with us—don't we *know* whether we want a glass or a stein?—than we are with ourselves. The White Horse doesn't yet know it is going to be a literary pub. And we have the sad sense, or I do, that stuff like this is hard going in America.

"At one point Mailer takes out a dollar bill, and pleads for somebody to start an argument going with him, 'on anything.' Nobody much takes him up on it (I couldn't, though I sympathized with what he was after in getting us together. He knew only one way to advance or conclude an argument with any woman—and a dollar was a small price for it). Nothing memorable having been said by anybody, we leave, unsure that we have consecrated the place."

Even though Calisher attended only one White Horse meeting, it was rare for a woman novelist to be a part of the group at all. As author Frederic Morton now says, "They were mainly stag affairs." But at the original meeting Morton also remembers that Cyrilly Abels, then editor of *Mademoiselle*, came along with Louis Auchincloss. Morton, who had already published two novels, *The Hound* (1947) and *The Darkness Below* (1949), and who had come out with *Asphalt and Desire* that year, had met Mailer before *Barbary Shore* was published. The introduction was through Morton's editor, Hiram Haydn, who was then at Crown and who would go on to Bobbs-Merrill and Random House.

While the White Horse idea was still germinating, Mailer had called Morton and said, "Look, I'm going to start a sort of literary club down at the White Horse Tavern. Come on down." It sounded interesting to Morton, but he was somewhat embarrassed at the first meeting when the other writers jeered at him for ordering ginger ale instead of liquor. Everyone drank at those sessions, although Morton remembers that it wasn't really a hard-drinking crowd. "We sometimes got pretty raucous, but the afternoon setting moderated the tone."

Morton attended about ten of the conclaves. "They were very self-conscious because they were supposed to be literary. Bitching about publishers is what I mostly remember, but I suppose that's most natural to writers." In addition to Morton, the mainstays of the White Horse group were Mailer—who always came without Adele—Bourjaily and sometimes his wife Tina, and Calder Willingham. Lewis Allen came a few times, as did William Styron and Louis Auchincloss. Daniel Wolf came only once. "I hope we were just hanging out," says Bourjaily. "I wouldn't like to think we were talking about literature."

The subtle machinations of literary politicking could hardly be avoided at the White Horse, and Mailer was already intent on testing other writers' loyalties to him. One Sunday as Bourjaily and Mailer were on their way to meet Calder Willingham at the White Horse, Mailer said, "Watch what I'm going to do to Calder." When they arrived Mailer's manner turned stern. He looked at Willingham and said, "Calder, I've heard what you've been saying about me." Willingham, who had a reputation for being a gossip, became anxious, even defensive as he tried to remember what he had said about Mailer. For ten minutes Mailer put on an act of being hostile over a supposed rumor. Then he smiled and told Willingham he had heard nothing.

Mailer's relationship with Willingham was a special one. Calder was the first real southern writer Mailer had ever met. He had an ineffable style of talking, a soft, elongated drawl which fascinated the boy from Brooklyn. Just as Mailer had first adopted the more cultured intonations of the Harvard Brahmins, then the drawl of the Texas rednecks in the army, he would use Willingham's southern inflections now and then.

The White Horse group was small but did not long remain insular. Bourjaily and John Aldridge were putting together an annual collection of original writing by the best young authors of the day. The series was called *Discovery.* The first issue, which contained a war story of Mailer's, was published by Pocket Books in 1952. Bourjaily's work on the collection brought him into contact with many young writers, and as Tina Bourjaily points out, "Every new writer gravitated toward *Discovery* and toward the White Horse group. It was a time in New York when all the young writers knew everybody, and it was very exciting."

Bourjaily was also on the executive committee of the Authors Guild, whose president at the time was Merle Miller. Miller presided over his own literary circle, composed mostly of Guild members, but occasionally his group would merge with Mailer's. Miller introduced Bourjaily to Herman Wouk, who told Bourjaily he wanted very much to meet Mailer. Bourjaily brought Wouk down to the White Horse one Sunday, and the two famous Jewish authors shook hands. "Wouk was very courtly, and Norman was friendly," recalls Bourjaily, "but I don't think they ever saw one another again."

Merle Miller's group, which also included John Hersey, was active in conventional politics, and all its members were strongly behind the 1952 Adlai Stevenson presidential campaign. By this time Mailer's infatuation with collective political action was over, and most of his circle had the same political orientation as he. "Norman was not in conventional politics at all," says Bourjaily. "Our group was more leftist and independent and unregistered. There were those who were pretty political, but by and large we weren't affiliated with any party."

In addition to Merle Miller's circle, there was a *New Yorker* crowd which centered mainly around A. J. Liebling, Jean Stafford, and Louis Auchincloss. Auchincloss felt a little self-conscious on the occasions when he made his way down below Fourteenth Street to attend the White Horse gatherings, but he still retains a special fondness for Mailer because of a comment Mailer once made. "The fact that I was a Wall Street lawyer, a registered Republican, and a social registrite was quite enough for half the people at any one party to cross me off as a kind of duck-billed platypus not to be taken seriously," Auchincloss stated. "I did not realize how much I wanted to be included until Norman Mailer congratulated me on a short story entitled 'The Gem-like Flame,' which had appeared in a periodical called *New World Writing*. He gave me the only true compliment that one writer can give to another. He said that he would not have minded having written it himself. I was so pleased that I went right home. I wanted to leave one such assembly with a happy impression."

William Styron also gravitated into Mailer's new circle. Mailer had met Styron in late 1951 at a small luncheon given by producer Robert Whitehead, Lewis Allen's boss. Styron had published his highly acclaimed first novel, *Lie Down in Darkness*, only months before *Barbary Shore*, and he had been catapulted into the major literary leagues as swiftly as Mailer had been three years before.

Although Styron was part of no formal group, he and a number of his friends frequented the Mailer salon at the White Horse around the time when James Jones arrived on the scene. John Marquand, Jr., who originally introduced Styron to Jones, remembers a few afternoons at the West Village pub. Two others in Styron's group, John Maloney and Sigrid de Lima, also became part of the literary coterie. Both Maloney, a young editor at Bobbs-Merrill, and De Lima, a Scribner's novelist, had taken Hiram Haydn's creative-writing class at the New School with Styron in the late forties. Not surprisingly Vance Bourjaily remembers referring to Styron's group as "the New School crowd."

Before James Jones returned to his home in Marshall, Illinois, Mickey Knox remembers that he, Jones, Styron, and Mailer were becoming close friends, not only meeting on Sundays at the White Horse but night after night touring Village bars together. After one such night, Knox remembers, Styron suddenly stopped on a street corner and put his arms around Jones and Mailer, saying, "Hey, fellas, isn't it wonderful? The three greatest young American writers, and here we are together."

❦

Mailer was now in the protective environment of an expansive and important literary set. But if his social life was growing, his work was not. After the failure of *Barbary Shore* he sensed a difference in his writing, a deadness of style he could do nothing to remedy. He started on a new novel, a "mechanical" novel about Hollywood, but after a month of work he realized that it was the worst writing he had ever done and gave up the project.

The winter of 1951–52 was a low point in Mailer's career. He dispiritedly took up writing short stories about the war in the style of *The Naked and the Dead*. It was the only time Mailer ever regressed in his work, retreating to the safety of an earlier success. He took little pride in these stories, but they offered him quick bursts of concentration and a freedom from the torturous responsibilities of a novel. He would start one in the morning and if he didn't finish it the same day, he would turn to another. In a few weeks he was able to write ten stories, but his output was of little consolation. He was beginning to feel he had nothing left to write about. At one point during that depressing winter Mailer thought of becoming a psychoanalyst or even going into business to garner new experience for a novel.

Mailer was having serious doubts about whether he was a writer at all, but he did not display his anxiety. In fact Vance Bourjaily remembers being extremely impressed by his discipline in turning out the short stories. "Norman and I were talking, and Norman said, 'Well, I think I'll do some short stories,' " Bourjaily recalls. "I was surprised, for it was the move of a man with a program for himself, and I had never thought of writers as being like that. My feeling was that in spite of the defeat of *Barbary Shore* he was still riding pretty high and thought it was time for a guy of his stature to make a contribution to the American short story. It's probable that Norman's literary position seemed so much stronger and better than my own that I just assumed he was riding high."

In his two previous novels Mailer had the war and the Cold War to react against. Now his alienation found no focus, and he was floundering. Indeed the general intellectual temperament of the early 1950s was one of complacency and nonalienation. Jobs had become plentiful, and most intellectuals, perhaps for the first time in Modern American history, were being happily assimilated into the bosom of the establishment.

At the time Mailer possessed one significant asset. He had begun a new kind of life with Adele, one of freer sensuality and of emotional, not political, complexity. It was slowly sharpening his understanding of new sociological forces at work in American society. As early as 1952 Mailer was beginning to zero in on the heart of what was to become the prim Eisenhower fifties: conformity and sexual repression. He was on the threshold of an intuitive, perhaps prophetic, intellectual transition, although even he did not fully realize it at the time.

What Mailer did sense was the extent to which he was courting society, even "crawfishing" before it. He saw that he was increasingly ingratiating himself with the literary set and with magazine editors and agents who might buy or sell his short stories, his only literary production at the time. It was a small incident with one magazine editor which alerted Mailer to the dangers of compromise. In early 1952 Vance Bourjaily told Mailer an anecdote which Mailer subsequently transformed into a short story. Called "The Paper House," it was about a Japanese geisha girl who threatens to commit hara-kiri after her GI lover ridicules and dishonors her. The story ends with the wise geisha ridiculing the GI. Mailer submitted the work to a women's fashion magazine, and during the week it was being considered, Mailer and some of his friends invited the editor of the magazine to a party the writer was giving in his new apartment.

Mailer and Adele had moved into a place at 14 Pitt Street which they painted battleship gray. Pitt Street was in a Lower East Side slum area down by the Williamsburgh Bridge and was as unlikely a setting for a renowned author as Mailer's previous apartment. As Larry Alson's mother would say to Fanny, "I can't believe that Norman is going back to the place we tried so hard to get out of!"

The meeting with the magazine editor took place as scheduled in the new apartment. The idea was that once she and Mailer were introduced, the story would be accepted. Unfortunately the meeting was less than harmonious, and by the time the editor left it was clear that the magazine would not take the piece. Mailer was angry: at her, at the literary establishment, and at himself, fed up with trying to insinuate himself diplomatically into a short-story market which thrived on established decencies. He knew that despite the humiliation of *Barbary Shore* he had to return to the novel, the form that had once placed him at the center of the world literary stage.

• VI •

THE DEER PARK: A NEW PERCEPTION

Mailer's next work, his third and most controversial novel, *The Deer Park*, would be three years in the creation, the most trying and frustrated period of his life. It was to be his spiritual trial: years dominated by sensuality, drugs, confusion, disturbing insights into his own violence, and a recurring, morbid depression that had settled on him with the abject failure of his last book.

Barbary Shore had been a personal political examination, an attempt to take his unformed socialist ideas and affix them to a plot. Mailer had hoped to use fiction to illuminate his strange, individualistic perception that the Western world had a totalitarian core not very different from that of the tyrannical East. Even though the book was to fail as fiction, Mailer's polemic theory of repression in America was to be embraced by radical youth almost twenty years later, during the American cultural revolution of the late 1960s and early 1970s.

After *Barbary Shore* Mailer needed new insights to fuel his next novel. If *Barbary Shore* was basically political, *The Deer Park* was to be basically sensual. The move from stable Vermont to the bohemian Village, from intellectual Bea to elemental Adele, from middle-class values to underground leanings was the beginning of that new experience. It was one that would lead Mailer to hot sex and hot jazz and to marijuana for inspiration, drinking for release, and Seconal for sleep. The Harvard-trained writer of formal prose was now attempting "an entrance into the mysteries of murder, suicide, incest, orgy, orgasm and Time."

It would be a wrenching rite of passage, one which began when Mailer devised a plan for what was to become *The Deer Park*. The morning after his embarrassing meeting with the magazine editor, Mailer woke with an ambitious concept. He decided to write eight related novels beginning with a common prologue. Still depressed but encouraged by Adele, his sister Barbara, and friends Lillian Ross of *The New Yorker* and Dan Wolf, Mailer worked feverishly on the prologue for a month, finally producing "The Man Who Studied Yoga." Set in a Queens housing development, the prologue recounts a day in the life of a forty-year-old frustrated minor artist and old leftist named Sam Slavoda. Sam writes comic strips while indulging an ambition to create a great novel. Versed in Freudian psychoanalytic jargon, Sam admits to having fantasies of murdering his wife, Eleanor, but never accepts the fact that she is just a nag.

One Sunday a group of Slavoda's friends—all old leftists with no new dream—descend on the apartment to use Sam's movie projector. One of them has obtained a pornographic film, and they are all embarrassingly anxious to watch it. At the end of the second viewing Sam wonders whether they will have the orgy "which tickles at the heart of their desire." He knows they won't, since they are all too reasonable and responsible, and he thinks of the Deer Park of Louis XV, where the most beautiful maidens of France were brought as "ladies of pleasure awaiting the pleasure of the king."

After the others have left, Sam and Eleanor play the movie again while they make love, but Sam's mind is too divided by anxieties to enjoy it; he falls asleep thinking about his novel. As the narrator says, he is "a man who seeks to live in such a way as to avoid pain, and succeeds merely in avoiding pleasure."

Mailer's sad, poignant depiction of the Slavodas and their civic-minded friends, locked in conformity and resorting to Freudian psychology for their answers when they truly ache for sexual satisfaction, marked the beginnings of a pivotal transition for the writer. The eight novels Mailer originally had in mind were to represent the eight stages of Sam Slavoda's dream that night, centering around an

Irishman named Sergius O'Shaugnessy. Mailer intended O'Shaugnessy to be a mythical hero who would travel through the worlds of pleasure, business, communism, church, the working class, crime, homosexuality, and mysticism, all subjects which Sam had touched upon that one Sunday. Mailer also intended to arrange the time scheme so that various characters would reappear in different novels at different ages.

The Deer Park was to be the first of these novels. Mailer began writing it in the spring of 1952 in a rented studio room in an old high-ceilinged building, Ovington Studios, on Fulton Street in Brooklyn, about a half mile from the rooming house where he wrote *The Naked and the Dead*. Drawn from his Hollywood experience two years earlier when McCarthyism was strong and Mailer's political radicalism was acute, the novel has a political framework. Specifically, it is the story of a liberal movie director, Charles Francis Eitel, who is blacklisted by the studios for refusing to name his Communist friends at a Congressional hearing but who then relents and talks in order to work again. As Mailer delves further into his story, the sexuality of his characters begins to play the more significant role, replacing politics as the touchstone of personal destiny. It was an evolution closely paralleling Mailer's own life.

Antitotalitarianism would play a key role in *The Deer Park* as it would in all his books. But here the concept of totalitarianism was expanded to sex itself. Sex in the modern world, as Sam Slavoda had observed, was no longer a source of pleasure but a source of power. And nowhere was the sex-power game more prevalent in America in the early 1950s than in Hollywood.

The Deer Park is set in Desert D'Or, a fictitious resort town, similar to Palm Springs, a few hundred miles from the "Capital," Hollywood. When Mailer was just beginning the novel, Mickey Knox recalls that he and Norman drove across country because Mailer wanted to pick up some "atmosphere." Once they reached the West, Mailer asked Knox if it would be too much out of the way to stop off at Palm Springs. They went, and as Knox says, "We weren't even there a day, and it was amazing to me when I read the book how he had gotten the damn place down: all the trees and architecture."

The hero-narrator of the novel, Sergius O'Shaugnessy, is a young would-be writer with no roots, not unlike Michael Lovett in *Barbary Shore*. While Lovett had suffered from amnesia after the war, Sergius is an orphan. Mailer's new hero, however, is much more physically defined than Lovett. Sergius is a six-foot Irishman with blond hair and blue eyes who has the build of a light heavyweight and the looks of a movie star. Sergius had been a decorated first lieutenant in the air force, but he suffered a nervous breakdown when he realized he had been killing hundreds of people with his bombs. Images of the burned flesh of his victims has left him sexually impotent—a classic Hemingway device—although his prowess is duly restored with the help of a blond movie star, Lulu.

Sergius, ironically, is not a real Irishman. O'Shaugnessy is just an assumed name. And as he says, "There is nothing in the world like being a fake Irishman." But after enough fights with the boys at the orphan home he knew he had a right to call himself Sergius O'Shaugnessy.

Sergius's tale is linked with Mailer's own sense of himself as somehow being Irish, even to the point of affecting a brogue on occasion. Mailer is proud of this Irish alter ego—a tough, barroom image that hides the nice Jewish boy from Brooklyn. The heroism, masculinity, and proletarianism Mailer sensed in the protagonist of James T. Farrell's *Studs Lonigan* is part of this Irish perception of himself. Sergius O'Shaugnessy becomes something of a hard-drinking stud in the novel after regaining his potency, paralleling Mailer's own emergence as a drinker and a lover. The boy from Brooklyn was creating a new persona not only for his book but for himself, another dimension of his increasingly complicated personality.

Although Sergius is clearly intended to speak with Mailer's voice in the novel, the dramatic focus quickly shifts to Charles Eitel, the once-successful movie director who has been blacklisted. In a deep depression over his lack of work, Eitel begins an affair with an unlikely woman: an uneducated sensuous Latin named Elena Esposito who has recently been rejected by producer Collie Munshin. Collie is the son-in-law of the head of Supreme Pictures, Herman Teppis.

Eitel's affair with Elena increasingly occupies center stage in the novel. Although Elena is unschooled and somewhat coarse, she wants to learn from Eitel. She will change herself for him and do what she thinks pleases him, including experimenting sexually with other couples. Eitel knows that Elena is intellectually his inferior, but her potent sexuality and primitive understanding as well as her essential human dignity supports his ego at a time when he is creatively frustrated. He is at work on a movie script which is similar to Nathanael West's *Miss Lonelyhearts*, just as Mailer had once been.

In Mailer's exploration of the sexual relationships between Sergius and Lulu and Eitel and Elena, he took pains to avoid the sensational and tried to make the reader focus on the moral implications of the actions of his characters. But in the early 1950s no description of sexuality, however skillfully evasive, was readily accepted. One particular description of fellatio in a scene between Herman Teppis and a call girl named Bobby was to cause a furor:

> Tentatively, she reached out a hand to caress his hair, and at the moment Herman Teppis opened his legs and let Bobby slip to the floor. At the expression of surprise on her face, he began to laugh. "Just like this, sweetie," he said, and down he looked at that frightened female mouth, facsimile of all those smiling lips he had seen so ready to be nourished at the fount of power and with a shudder he started to talk. "That's a good girlie, that's a good girlie, that's a good girlie," he said in a mild lost little voice, "you're just an angel darling, and I like you, and you understand, you're my darling darling, oh that's the ticket," said Teppis.

In December 1952 Mailer handed in *The Deer Park* to Rinehart with a subtitle he had crossed out: "A Search for the Obscene." Most of the editors who read it were not pleased. At this point the book was still part of Mailer's gargantuan eight-novel scheme, and *The Man Who Studied Yoga* was attached as a prologue. Almost everyone felt the manuscript was unwieldy and obscure and did not work as a novel.

But Mailer disagreed. He felt that this was his most important work to date and refused to accept Rinehart's negative judgment. When Mailer demanded an outside opinion, the house agreed and told him he could pick a critic of his choice. Mailer chose his friend John Aldridge. The critic was contacted by John Selby, editor-in-chief of Rinehart, who wrote: "At the suggestion of Norman Mailer we would like to send you his new novel, *The Deer Park*, for an outside reading. . . . It should be considered an entity in itself although it is the first in a series of eight. We hope you will be able to read this for us and give us your opinion on matters of taste, construction and similar considerations."

"I was terribly high-minded in those days," recalls Aldridge, "and I wrote back and said very sternly that I would be willing to give my frank opinion, but they must take into account the fact that I'd met Mailer and liked him. I told them I would make every effort to obliterate that fact and write about the book with complete objectivity. I also said that I was writing this report for them, the publisher, and not for the writer, that I would give them a reader's report rather than a report a critic might give to help a writer with his problems. They said fine. So I wrote the report in that way, and then with great glee they went waving it in Mailer's face."

In his four-page report, which was sent to Rinehart on January 6, 1953, Aldridge began by saying that if the editors were worried about obscenity, they needn't be, since the novel wouldn't disturb "anyone above the level of 16-year-old daughters and 70-year-old grandmothers."

"I think the trouble with *The Deer Park*," Aldridge continued, "is that it has no morality at all, neither as great fiction nor pornography. . . . it presents a series of situations in which the obscene literally cannot be found no matter how strenuously the characters court it. This is the real theme of the book, and Mailer is careful never to deviate from it. But the result of his singlemindedness is that the experience he presents is precisely as dull, mechanical, monotonous, passionless and unobscene to the reader as it is to the characters."

Aldridge went on to point out that nobody has ever believed the obscene is worth looking for anyway, adding that Mailer's viewpoint was unfortunately indistinguishable from his characters'. But it was Aldridge's closing point which would anger Mailer the most. The critic felt that it was "a very bad show" for Mailer to let anyone see the manuscript in its present condition. A writer shouldn't show anyone his work, Aldridge believed, until it is as close to perfection as he can bring it. "Since this manuscript did leave Mailer's hands," Aldridge wrote, "and since critical and editorial advice was requested, I'm forced to conclude that Mailer felt an uncertainty and insecurity about the work which ought to have told him that there was something badly wrong. But it should have sent him back to the workshop, not to you or to me."

After Aldridge's negative report to Rinehart, Mailer had no choice but to agree to rewrite the book. He decided to abandon the eight-novel scheme, simplify the novel he had, and turn the prologue into a separate novella. Mailer's ambition to do a long epic novel, however, would never fade. By 1959 he was once again promising a big book. The public's anticipation of a major work would be kept alive by Mailer throughout his career. It also sustained the notion, in himself and others, that he *could* do it.

Mailer was angry at Aldridge for his report, and on January 12, 1953, he wrote the critic a two-page single-spaced letter castigating him for writing something which was in no way helpful. Aldridge, he said, could at least have tried to show him how the book might have been improved. "You really and truly act like an idiot," he wrote, "or worse, like a sort of General MacArthur delivering harsh pronunciamentos from your high and lonely peak, deriving your pleasure, I suspect, from the bitter notion that you've been true to yourself and hang the consequences." Mailer went on to scold Aldridge for his final point, saying that there are certain writers who try out their stuff on friends and other writers who don't. "You seemed to treat the manuscript as a *fait accompli*," he wrote, "as if it were already published and how shameful to release a work in that condition. When the fact of the matter—as you know damn well—is that *The Deer Park* is very much a first draft and what I'm interested in is exactly how to improve it."

"I had to write back an equally long, stern, eloquent letter," recalls Aldridge, "saying I didn't write the report with that in mind but for an entirely different purpose. We had a rather brisk exchange of letters between us during January and February. My problem with him from that point on has been that he felt—maybe because he put so much of himself into the book, and he had such trouble with it—that this was really his best novel. But I think both Mailer and I were ill-used by the publisher in this instance. They were obviously wanting very much to have ammunition for what they were going to do anyway."

Shortly after his first letter to Aldridge, Mailer went on a skiing trip to Canada with Adele and Vance Bourjaily. Adele was just learning to ski, while Mailer was already quite good. "He has a characteristic of getting into things like that with a great deal of intensity and becoming quite proficient quite quickly," notes Bourjaily. "He's a pretty good man physically, and he brings the same kind of concentration to learning something athletically that he brings to writing."

On the trip Bourjaily remembers that he and Mailer had a talk about the use of obscene language in literature. Surprised that Mailer seemed to be retreating from his defense of the obscene words in *The Naked and the Dead*, Bourjaily argued that dialogue must be realistic, that characters shouldn't have to talk in Victorian circumlocutions. For instance, Bourjaily said, if two young men meet each other the night after a date, he would have one of them say, "Did you get laid last night?"

"I wouldn't," Mailer replied. "I'd have them say, 'Did you make love last night?' "

"It was so strange that I remember it vividly," recalls Bourjaily. "What Norman seemed to be churning over in his mind at that time was a more severe and classical approach to language."

Mailer never mentioned his problems with Aldridge or Rinehart to Bourjaily, but he was obviously thinking through his new challenge. He was aware that the frank sexuality he was beginning to explore in *The Deer Park* would pose enough problems without the added onus of explicit language. If he had broken through the taboos of four-letter words in the late 1940s, it was something else again to challenge, head-on, the sexual restrictions of the early 1950s.

On February 6, 1953, a week after Mailer returned from Canada, he wrote Aldridge again. This time his tone was considerably softer, saying that they simply had failed to have a meeting of minds. "Norman is marvelous in that way," says Aldridge. "He doesn't hold grudges for that long. He sort of wrote the whole thing off by saying what I wrote wasn't helpful to him, and he didn't agree with any of it anyway, and that's that." Mailer also told Aldridge that he had never discussed their disagreement with Vance Bourjaily; at the time both Bourjaily and Aldridge were coediting *Discovery* and were not only friends but working associates. As Mailer put it, "Any intrusions of my problems upon both of you would be messy."

At the end of Mailer's letter to Aldridge he spoke of trying to get into the Mickey Jelke trial which was then going on. Jelke, the rich son of a prominent meat-packing family, had been accused of being a pimp for a number of call girls. Mailer's sudden interest in the Jelke trial is significant, for during the next year, as he began revamping *The Deer Park* in New York and Provincetown, he added an important new character: Marion Faye.

Faye is a brilliant, depraved, pot-smoking pimp, the son of an illicit union between his lower-class mother, Dorothea, and a European prince. Faye's hedonism is based on a strange code of moral ethics. It is Faye, for instance, who convinces Eitel not to name names in the Hollywood Communist investigation. When asked a decade later by a *Paris Review* writer how Faye emerged, Mailer would say, "The book needed something which wasn't in the first draft, some sort of evil genius."

The character of Faye represented an important step in Mailer's developing social philosophy. Faye is seen by Mailer as a satanic saint and represents the first sketchy prototype of Mailer's hipster, the man who in the face of collective death relentlessly pursues the immediate gratification of his desires by any means possible. In Faye, Mailer also introduces a new mystical element, the obsession with good and evil, or God and the devil. It is Mailer's first involvement in religious themes and an expression of his evolving concept of God as an existential being. At this point Mailer was coming to believe that God is not all-powerful but is an embattled being at war with his antagonist, the devil. It is therefore only through man's heroic actions that good can prevail over evil.

In May 1954, after a year of strenuous work on the second draft of *The Deer Park*, Mailer again showed it to his publisher. Rinehart's reception was almost as chilly this time as it had been earlier. The editors agreed that the novel was tighter, more self-contained, and that there could be no question of rejecting the book for its stylistic or structural flaws. But there was still the question of the book's sexual frankness, which they all knew was extremely radical for 1954. Stanley Rinehart, however, really had no choice. He had locked himself into a contract according to which Rinehart & Company, Inc. had to pay Mailer his ten-thousand-dollar advance whether they published the book or not.

Without enthusiasm Rinehart agreed to bring the book out the following February. But they asked Mailer if they could delay paying him the first half of the advance, due upon delivery of the manuscript, until the book's publication. It was a suspicious move, but Mailer, thinking it would improve relations, agreed. He and Adele left for a six-month vacation in Mexico, believing the book would be published in February. An acute sense of anxiety would nag Mailer during all those months.

The stress of writing *The Deer Park* was beginning to take its toll. Mailer's liver, which had gone sour in the Philippines, was in bad condition, aggravated by drinking and by the strenuous work on *The Deer Park* after a year of debilitating depression. Mailer and Adele had finally married that spring, and whatever the emotional highs, there was the added stress and responsibility of that new union. An extended trip to Mexico would give Mailer a chance to relax, to recoup his health and energy.

❦

In Mexico, Mailer and Adele moved into a beautiful three-hundred-year-old restored house in San Angel, an old village west of Mexico City. Vance and Tina Bourjaily lived nearby in Mexico City's

Passeo de la Reforma, and Lewis Allen had come down to Mexico with a stunning model, Bette Ford, who was also an avid bullfighter. Mailer's first wife, Bea, now remarried, had been living in Mexico for three years with Mailer's only child, Susan.

Mexico was a welcome respite, but it was to become more than that—a catalyst that would accelerate changes in Mailer's personality that were already taking place. Depressed by Rinehart's dismal reception of his novel, Mailer began to smoke pot in earnest. He had first started smoking marijuana in the Village and had used it occasionally in Provincetown to relieve the pain of rewriting *The Deer Park*.

A nineteen-year-old aspiring writer, Anthony Tuttle, who was part of a literary circle in nearby Wellfleet composed of Dwight Macdonald, Mary McCarthy, Edmund Wilson, and Robert Gorham Davis, remembered Mailer's use of marijuana in Provincetown the previous summer, 1953. Tuttle was then playing drums in a jazz quartet at a bar called Louis' in North Truro. One night Mailer came over and said to Tuttle, "Have you ever heard of reefer?" Tuttle said that he had heard of it but had never tried it. Mailer then took out a cigarette, tore it in half, emptied the tobacco, and poured some grass into the paper. He gave it to Tuttle. "It was the most spectacularly exciting thing that ever happened to me," recalls Tuttle. "When I went home that night, I put that half-joint carefully in a drawer, as if I had most of the cocaine in Peru. But it turned out to be bad dope; I didn't get stoned."

Marijuana became Mailer's spiritual refuge in Mexico. "Down in my deep depression with a bad liver, pot gave me a sense of something new about the time I was convinced I had seen it all," Mailer later said about the days in Mexico. When Jean Malaquais later asked Mailer where he had found God, he answered: "On marijuana."

Henrique (Hank) Lopez, then a young attorney who has since become a successful writer, was friendly with the Mailers in Mexico. He recalls an evening when Mailer and Adele were stoned on marijuana and tried to get him to use it. The threesome were in a car headed toward a burlesque house in one of Mexico City's seedier districts. When they got there, Mailer drove into a dead-end alley and told Adele to pull out three joints. Lopez confessed he didn't know how to inhale and that the whole thing would be lost on him. Mailer laughed. "You're a fucking fake Mexican. I've never heard of a Mexican who doesn't smoke pot. Give me back the roach, I'm not going to waste it on you." He then told Lopez that maybe they could get him high by osmosis. He and Adele proceeded to blow marijuana smoke in his face. "They were being so kind," says Lopez, "that I faked a high."

Pot was opening Mailer's senses, but, as with drinking, it did not always produce a felicitous state. "Norman was very destructive in those days," a friend recalls. "When they went down to Mexico, all kinds of sexual adventures went on that I think finally destroyed the relationship between Norman and Adele."

It was in Mexico that Mailer's personality began to develop its potential for violence. Adele warned Lopez of Mailer's violence that evening when the threesome were headed for the burlesque house. "Watch out, he'll pick a fight. He always picks a fight when he's high on pot," she told Lopez. Actually Mailer was benign that night, and as he watched the sexual undulations of the dancers, he joked with Lopez: "I hope you're not a tit man like Vance [Bourjaily]. I'll tell you the most important place. It's the navel."

Mailer had displayed his animal spirits at Harvard in tearing down the goalposts after a game. But in Mexico a fascination with more serious forms of violence was beginning to emerge. Lopez gave a party at his apartment on the Rio Hudson for the members of the Center for Mexican and North American Writers to which the Mailers and the Bourjailys were invited. Author Warren Eyster, who later won the National Book Award for *No Country for an Old Man*, brought along an ex-prisoner who had just gotten out of jail for killing his wife. "Norman became terribly fascinated with this guy," recalls Lopez, "and spent a good deal of the evening asking him, 'How did it feel? What was the exact reaction you had just before you pulled the trigger?' Norman had this incredible desire to know what everyone else felt, wanting to viscerally live the situation."

One evening at a party at the Mailers, there was a sense of impending violence, Lopez recalls. During the evening Adele and Tina Bourjaily went into the kitchen to prepare food. As Adele was slicing salami with a large knife, she began talking to Tina and gesticulating with her hands. Mailer suddenly came into the kitchen through a swinging door, and by sheer accident Adele's knife was pointing directly at his stomach. Mailer looked at his wife and said, "You don't dare, baby."

"Norman was playing, but they were always playing their little games," Lopez comments. "When Norman subsequently stabbed

Adele in 1960, Vance and I were together the next day. Vance said to me, 'I guess you're the most unsurprised guy in the world.' 'Yeah,' I answered, 'their little game just slipped.' "

The Mexican environment was also conducive to Mailer's growing sense of the importance of physical prowess. It was in Mexico that summer that Mailer developed his idiosyncratic way of walking, like a sailor who has just come off a ship. Lopez remembers that at parties he would stand in a corner and periodically brace himself much like a boxer against the ropes. This physicality found a perfect outlet in bullfighting, which for Mailer was a Hemingwayesque ritual. Virtually every Sunday, Mailer, Adele, Bette Ford, and Lewis Allen went to the bullfights together, and Mailer became fascinated by the sport. Lew Allen had to return to New York, but Bette Ford stayed on to continue her bullfight training.

Lopez, Mailer, and Bourjaily would frequently play fronton tennis with Bette, a game much like jai alai, to help keep her in shape. Afterward she would give them instructions in bullfighting. Mailer admired the female bullfighter, and decided that he, too, should fight a bull. One day Bourjaily, Lopez, and Mailer all agreed that they would rent a small bullring and hold their own fight. They talked about it for many weeks, and Mailer was clearly excited by the idea. Unfortunately nothing came of it before Mailer had to return to New York to follow up on *The Deer Park*. After he left, Bourjaily and Lopez were each invited to different bullfighting ranches to attend a *tienta*, a testing of cows to see if they are good enough to breed with the bulls. As it turned out, each of them got a chance to fight a cow, and they couldn't resist calling Mailer in New York to tell him about it.

As Lopez recounted his session on the phone Mailer was deadly silent, offering only a few monosyllabic grunts. By the time Bourjaily began his account, Mailer had had enough. He hung up the phone. Bourjaily immediately called him back only to find that Mailer was furious. "You sons of bitches, you dirty double-crossers," he yelled at them. "We were supposed to do this together." Years later, at a party at George Plimpton's, Mailer would put on a farcical demonstration of Bourjaily fighting the bulls. When Bourjaily heard about it, he told Lopez, "You know, I don't think Norman's ever forgiven us for the bullfight."

Mailer's love of the physical has since become one of his trademarks. Yet as war buddy Francis Gwaltney observed, Mailer has to work hard to be aggressive. His early life in Brooklyn did not prepare him for the macho image he was intent on developing. Lopez noticed this in Mexico. After a game of fronton tennis Mailer, Bourjaily, and Lopez began to swap stories about their youth. Lopez told of witnessing a gang bang in Denver, where he had grown up. He also told Mailer and Bourjaily the story of a penis-measuring contest in which the winner was given a broom to mount. Mailer was flabbergasted by these childhood stories, and when Lopez and Bourjaily asked what he had done as a boy he hesitated. "Christ," he finally said, "I was going to Hebrew school every afternoon."

❦

When Mailer and Adele returned to New York City, they moved into a beautiful duplex at 320 East Fifty-fifth Street. He seemed to be setting the stage for the enthusiastic reception of a renowned writer's third novel. Everything was preceeding on schedule. By November the first advertisement for *The Deer Park* was given to *Publisher's Weekly*. Then, with less than three months to publication, Stanley Rinehart told Mailer he would have to delete six lines of the vague description of fellatio between Herman Teppis and the call girl.

Although Mailer was convinced that Stanley Rinehart had read the book the previous spring, Ted Amussen, who had returned to Rinehart from Holt as editor-in-chief after the book was in galleys, believes differently: "I don't think until I arrived there that either of the Rineharts—Stanley or his brother, John—had bothered to read it. Then finally Stan did read it while it was in galleys and came across that scene of fellatio, which apparently shook him. He wanted the whole thing out. He said he was concerned about what his mother would think, since she was on the board of directors. It was a point well taken, because Mary Roberts Rinehart would have had hysterics about that scene, although actually it was so written that I didn't even know what was going on."

Mailer initially gave in to Rinehart's demands. He agreed to change a couple of words and rewrite a line. Then, feeling he was a moral coward, he changed his mind. He called Ted Amussen the next day to say he wanted the original words put back in. A day later Stanley Rinehart stopped publication of the book and broke Mailer's contract.

Amussen was given the chore of telling the news to Mailer. He remembers the meeting vividly. "I got in touch with Norman, and we went somewhere and had drinks. I told him what had happened, and

I told him why. He tried to persuade me out of it, but I said I had no choice, that was what Stanley wanted. Then Norman stood up, reached in his pocket and found a handful of change, and threw it on the table. He said, 'Okay, you son of a bitch, that's the end of that,' and walked out."

That same night Mailer called William Styron, who had recently returned from Europe with his new wife, Rose. Mailer had shown him *The Deer Park* in manuscript, and Styron had written a long letter back saying, "I don't like *The Deer Park*, but I admire sheer hell out of it." On the basis of this Mailer asked Styron if he would call his own editor, Hiram Haydn, on his behalf. Haydn by this time had moved from Bobbs-Merrill to Random House.

Mailer submitted the book to Haydn at Random House, but it was turned down. Haydn subsequently had lunch with Mailer and told him that it had been his decision not to do the book. What he did not mention was that it was Bennett Cerf, the president of Random House, who had had the most intensely negative reaction to it. In fact when the book was finally placed at G. P. Putnam's Sons, Cerf called Walter Minton, the son of the company's president, and urged him not to publish it. "Cerf said that once again we would draw down the shade of censorship upon the book industry," Minton recalls. "I asked him if he had heard from Mr. Joyce's shade recently." Cerf, of course, was famous for having published James Joyce's *Ulysses* in America and winning a federal court decision on December 6, 1933 that the book was not obscene.

Cerf had also had a hand in Alfred A. Knopf's rejection of the book. After Random House had turned down *The Deer Park*, Mailer had gone to see Blanche Knopf, Alfred's wife. William Koshland, who was then corporate secretary of Knopf and a member of the board of directors, was in that original meeting. He remembers Mailer telling Blanche Knopf, "Well, you've always said you wanted to publish me, and now you've got a chance."

Blanche Knopf subsequently read the book, along with Koshland, senior editor Phil Vaudrin, and another editor, Harold Straus. All were enthusiastic and wanted to publish it, although there was some debate about what should, or should not, be deleted. It was sent to Knopf's attorneys, the firm of Stern and Reuben, and a meeting was called to discuss the fine points. Mailer, his lawyer-agent Charles Rembar, two attorneys from Stern and Reuben, and William Koshland and Harold Straus attended. Rembar, who was Mailer's cousin and a close friend, had acted exclusively as Mailer's lawyer before problems with *The Deer Park* arose. But he now moved in to negotiate all Mailer's literary dealings.

At the Knopf conference, Mailer was willing to make small concessions but would agree to no major changes. They were almost at the point of a final agreement when trouble arose. Cerf called Alfred Knopf to ask him if he knew what was going on at his own company. Knopf had heard nothing about the Mailer book, but over the following weekend he made it clear to Blanche that the book would not be published by Knopf. He then called in Koshland, Straus, and Vaudrin and asked them what they were trying to do to Knopf's reputation. As he told Koshland, he could understand his aiding Blanche, but what made him think anyone would want to read a novel about Hollywood? According to Koshland, Knopf never read *The Deer Park* manuscript himself.

While Mailer was making these difficult forays into the publishing world, Ted Amussen at Rinehart was trying his best to place the novel. In addition to talking to Bennett Cerf and Blanche Knopf, Amussen spoke to John Farrar and Robert Giroux. But he failed to arouse interest. As he now points out, "It was a time when publishers just wouldn't consider that kind of book. It was another world."

Charles Scribner, Jr., who also turned down *The Deer Park*, remembers when the novel came to his company through Burroughs Mitchell, James Jones's editor. He and Mitchell discussed the book superficially, although Scribner never read it himself. "Burroughs was not a person to be squeamish about content," Scribner now reflects. "After all, we had published Jones and a lot of other people who were ahead of their time in that area. We probably turned it down for a combination of reasons: not thinking it was anywhere close to *The Naked and the Dead*, a feeling that it was too expensive, and perhaps a feeling that it might create some censorship problems. If we had thought it was a tremendous book, we wouldn't have been worried about the price or the censorship. Those difficulties could be thrashed out. It was that we weren't that deeply impressed by the book as a book."

Later, in March 1956, James Jones and Mailer would argue about the Scribner's rejection in a brief correspondence. Jones wrote, "I think your book was turned down [by Scribner's] because it was a pretty bad book, and though I've read both the galleys and the finished version, I don't see how you helped it very much. Now it's very possible I'm wrong about *The Deer Park* and I'm willing to admit I may be. But as far as I'm concerned it's not a good book, and in fact isn't as good by far as *Barbary*, which I liked very much—when read as an allegory, and not as a novel which of course it is not. . . ."

As the celebrated author of *The Naked and the Dead* was undergoing this humiliating odyssey through a total of seven publishing houses—including Harper & Row, Simon & Schuster, and Harcourt Brace—G. P. Putnam's Sons suddenly voiced interest in the novel. A young assistant editor, Peter Israel, who was later to become Putnam's president, heard the manuscript was available and told the advertising manager about it. It was a smart move, for the advertising manager was then Walter Minton, the son of the ailing president, who would be running the company himself by the following year.

Walter Minton had been an avid fan of Mailer's ever since he had read *The Naked and the Dead* in a special advance edition six years earlier. Exactly the same age as Mailer, Minton was also a veteran of both Harvard and the army and felt a strong affinity for the author. "After I read *The Naked and the Dead*," Minton recalls, "I told my father that it was one of the best books I ever read. After that my father ran into Stanley Rinehart at the Publisher's Lunch Club and told him, 'My son thinks that you're publishing one of the great works of American fiction.' Rinehart said, 'Oh, yes, *The Naked and the Dead* by this fellow Mailer. How old is your son?' My father told him twenty-four. 'That's nice,' said Rinehart, 'but I hope some of his older compatriots who have the money to buy the book agree with him.' "

When Minton heard from Peter Israel that Mailer had a new novel that was making the rounds, he immediately called Charles Rembar, who told him that Mailer had promised to show the novel to another house. Mailer was indeed planning to next offer *The Deer Park* to Viking. Minton wouldn't be dissuaded. "But you don't understand, I'll publish it," he told Rembar. "I not only said this without having seen it," Minton now says, "but I said it without having the authority, because I wasn't then running Putnam."

Minton's commitment to buy the book sight unseen is not as strange as it seems. He was convinced that any novel by Mailer which had been turned down by so many publishers would sell just because of the controversy. He also knew that Putnam's desperately needed some good books. Although the *Atlantic Monthly* later pointed out that Putnam's paid Mailer the largest advance for a novel in their one-hundred-eighteen-year history, Minton didn't feel that ten thousand dollars was too much for Norman Mailer.

When the book finally came in, everyone at the house was enthusiastic, a welcome reception for Mailer, who had been buffeted from house to house. Ted Purdy, the editor-in-chief who would work with Mailer, liked it. Minton put on added pressure to get it through. "We knew about the problems," says Minton, "but after reading it I was convinced it was the best novel that's ever been written about Hollywood. I was absolutely astounded not that Stanley Rinehart found it objectionable but that Random House and Simon & Schuster turned it down. It never occurred to me for an instant that there would be any censorship activity."

Before Mailer arrived at Putnam's doorstep, Stanley Rinehart did something that permanently altered Mailer's view of the publishing world. He refused to pay the ten-thousand-dollar advance he contractually owed to Mailer. Mailer had grudgingly given Rinehart credit for taking such an expensive moral stand when he halted publication of *The Deer Park*, but he now felt that Rinehart was trying to cheat him. It sickened him that his romantic fantasy of the publishing world of Max Perkins and Scott Fitzgerald, when houses and editors held on to major authors no matter what they wrote, was now just that, a fantasy. Even by 1954 publishing had begun to undergo its postwar change from a gentleman's occupation to a profit-oriented corporate industry.

❦

The personal transformation that had begun in the Village and had accelerated in Mexico now became intensified as Mailer seemed to turn against a society that had rejected him, even toyed with him. "I was out of fashion and that was the score," he later wrote. "I was finally open to my anger. I turned within my psyche I can almost believe, for I felt something shift to murder in me. . . . All I felt then was that I was an outlaw, a psychic outlaw, and I liked it."

Mailer became involved in heavy pot smoking and took in Harlem jazz almost every night, making friends with black musicians and feeling the impact of jazz on the subculture, a phenomenon he was later to address in his essay "The White Negro." If Mailer had been foolishly locked into dead romantic literary images, he was now becoming ultra-hip.

Marijuana became his "secret weapon." The drug boosted his confidence and his ego at a time when his reserves were low. As he later said, "Mary Jane . . . was the back door to sex, which had become again all I had and all I wanted. . . . Sex was the sword of history to this uncommissioned General, for only when sex triumphed could the mind seize the hip of new experience." By the late 1960s marijuana would become the secret weapon of an entire counterculture, but Mailer had discovered its reputed visionary and sexual powers before many others, and his writings about it contributed to the drug's vast dissemination a decade later.

During this fevered winter of 1954–55 his fascination with violence became even more pronounced, and old friends saw a new side of Mailer emerge. One night not long after *The Deer Park* had been placed with Putnam's, William Styron got a call saying that his friend John Maloney was in jail for stabbing his girl friend during a quarrel. Maloney wanted Styron and Mailer to come and get him. They did, and in the cab with Styron and his wife Mailer kept talking about the incident, obviously intrigued by Maloney's irrational act.

Mailer was changing so fast and so many mental connections were being made by him on the high tides of pot that he began to write a journal of ideas, a wild log of fanciful projects. He wrote a hundred thousand words of this journal in only eight weeks and compared his prolific output to that Sigmund Freud had achieved with the help of cocaine. By February the journal had begun to taper off, but his mind was clearly restive.

Putnam's was anxious to bring *The Deer Park* out in June, but in his new mood Mailer suddenly decided to make a few changes in the page proofs. Nobody at Putnam's liked the idea, especially Walter Minton, who thought the book would attract more interest if it was exactly the same as the supposedly notorious Rinehart version. But Mailer insisted, and once he began to make his minor changes, he came to see—from his new perspective—that the book's style was wrong. The first-person narrative was too formal for a protagonist who had been an orphan and an Air Force pilot. It was, Mailer decided, "a timid inhibited" book.

With his new outlaw perceptions he was suddenly annoyed at the literary restrictions that had previously harnessed him. As Mailer began to tear into Sergius O'Shaugnessy's voice to create a prose that was rougher, he felt that he was learning about language for the first time. "Usually it takes you twenty years to learn that much about editing," Mailer explains. "I began to see how much the very sound of a word alters just about everything in a sentence. I was coming in touch with the sort of literary experience that Flaubert and Henry James had when they were older and much more developed and better able to take advantage of that sort of knowledge."

High on pot, Mailer felt that the changes he was making in the manuscript were momentous, but it wasn't long before he realized he was tiring. More pot, Seconal, Miltown, Benzedrine, liquor, and two packs of cigarettes a day kept him going, though the punishment of the drugs left him even more exhausted than he had been in combat. The insights kept flowing, but Mailer was paying the price. "I consumed vast tracts of my brain," Mailer recalls about this period of heavy drug usage. "I was doing to my brain what Barry Goldwater was recommending we do to the foliage in Vietnam. I think parts of my head have been sluggish ever since. I learned a tremendous amount about writing but I paid a prodigious price."

Now the reviewers crept into his mind, and his anxiety over their reaction made him tone down provocative sexual language and leave out sentences that were legally precarious. A few words were even changed in the six lines that had originally caused his rupture with Rinehart: "Fount of power" in the fellatio scene was changed to "thumb of power." Mailer knew that he needed a success badly, since all his habits, even his rebellion, depended on success. But he knew that by making these concessions he was risking, for the first time in his life, the loss of what he called "the incorruptible center" of his strength.

As the weeks wore on, Mailer's energy waned. Publication was delayed from June to August and finally to October, yet he couldn't stop his relentless work on the novel. August 1 was the final deadline, but by July, with five times the usual dose of Seconal in his body, Mailer's dulled mind could only work an hour a day before giving out completely. He managed to make the August deadline, feeling that the book was close enough to the way he wanted it.

After he finished the rewrite, Mailer and Adele immediately left for a few weeks of recuperation in Provincetown, where he was able to wean himself from pot and Seconal. But as soon as he arrived back in the city, Mailer took some mescaline. In the "pleasure garden" of that trip he wrote the last lines of *The Deer Park*.

Six weeks afterward the book was published. The reviews were mixed, although the bad ones outweighed the good. Orville Prescott in the daily *New York Times* was hostile: "*The Deer Park* in the last analysis is only a dreary story about the noisome affairs of a group of degenerate characters. . . . Rarely have I been so glad to finish a book as I was when I finally reached the last page. . . ." But John Brooks, writing for the *Times Book Review*, generally liked the work: "Though it is not a wholly successful novel, it is studded with brilliant and illuminating passages and, by and large, it is good reading. . . . Mailer would seem to have the instincts of the artist, which is to say, among other things, that his approach to his material is at bottom moral."

Time attacked Mailer's "subpoena envy," while *Newsweek's* review was favorable. Brendan Gill in *The New Yorker* noted, "Only a writer of the greatest and most reckless talent could have flung it between covers." Malcolm Cowley agreed that it was both "serious and reckless."

A number of reviewers, such as John Hutchens of the New York *Herald Tribune*, intimated that Mailer had eliminated all the truly erotic parts of the first draft in the Putnam edition. This irritated Walter Minton as much as it did Mailer. Minton eventually came to feel that the book's notoriety before publication actually hampered its sales.

"The notoriety attracted a lot of attention," Minton reflects, "but at the same time it cast the novel as a dirty book by an author who didn't have the reputation to carry it. And anybody who went into it expecting a dirty book was liable to be disappointed. The reception *The Deer Park* got had a lot to do with what happened to the book before, and to a certain degree they were reviewing that rather than the book itself. I've always felt that had Rinehart gone ahead and published it, they might have had even more success than we did."

As it turned out, *The Deer Park* did relatively well. It sold over fifty thousand copies and rose to number six on the *Times* Best Seller List before dropping off at Christmastime. The fact that the book was neither a raging success nor an abject failure depressed Mailer, for he had shed psychic blood over this third novel, and no one was responding in kind. He had achieved a "draw," an insulting reception to his third try at greatness.

Six weeks before *The Deer Park* was published, Mailer sent an inscribed copy of it to Ernest Hemingway in Havana, hoping that his endorsement would boost the book's reception. During the excruciating rewriting of his novel Mailer had begun to agree even more strongly with Hemingway's notion that it was more important to be a man than to be a great writer. After the tiring moral stands he had taken throughout the ordeal, he had also begun to sense that he was one of the few writers of his time who was truly emulating Hemingway's discipline. But by asking Hemingway for a blurb Mailer was undermining that discipline, and he knew it. As a result his inscription to Hemingway was belligerent, challenging, even hostile. He said that if Hemingway answered with "crap," well, then, "fuck you." Papa Hemingway never even saw the note. Weeks later the book came back in the mail unopened with *Address Unknown* stamped all over it in Spanish. Hemingway must have bought a copy himself in the next couple of months, though, for in December 1955 he wrote to his friend Wallace Meyer from Cuba: "In *The Deer Park*, Mailer really blows the whistle on himself."

A few days after Mailer had sent the book off to Hemingway, he sent copies to more than a dozen other writers for comments, including Graham Greene, Cyril Connolly, Philip Rahv, and Alberto Moravia. Moravia was the only one who responded. It was the ultimate confirmation of Mailer's sense of uncertainty and failure, one that had been building for several years.

Walter Minton now reflects that if Rinehart had gone ahead with the book and if it had been a greater success, it might have changed Mailer's subsequent approach to writing fiction. He believes that as a result of *The Deer Park* Mailer has been tentative about writing novels ever since. Mailer himself says: "If anything, I probably regret the way I edited *The Deer Park*."

Indeed, Norman Mailer would not write another novel for ten years. But during that time he would create a public persona so vivid and outrageous, so seething with frustration at what he viewed as establishment repression, that not only would he remain visible in the literary world but he would help to lay the psychic groundwork for a new generation of alienated youth.

• VII •

THE VOICE

By the fall of 1955, at the age of thirty-two, Mailer was physically and emotionally exhausted. His odyssey of the past seven years, from the summit of worldwide acclaim in 1948 to the stultifying failure of *Barbary Shore* in 1951 to the bloodletting draw of *The Deer Park*, would have made a man of lesser ambition retreat. Mailer had moved perilously close to nervous collapse as he made his third frenzied bid for greatness. But rather than admit defeat and seek a time for healing, Mailer quickly moved back onto the stage in a startling new incarnation.

Mailer had just fought what he believed to be a brave if nightmarish battle with the literary Goliaths over the importance of *The Deer Park*. He was angry, convinced there was something wrong with an American establishment that so mercilessly oppressed creative souls such as himself. In a brilliant tactical stroke Mailer fused his own bitterness with a collective condition of modern times that he felt affected everyone and was propelled to action again. There were undoubtedly phalanxes of similarly oppressed souls out there who needed a leader.

As he put it, "I said, 'My God, we are not inferior. And they are killing us . . . because they don't know what they're doing. They're running the machine, and they don't know how to run it. I seemed to feel we could run it better. . . . Once you've decided nobody knows how to run the machine, you suddenly see yourself running it. And then you become very curious about yourself. You start making all sorts of experiments. I put myself in a laboratory."

His experiments with expanding his self now had a concrete focus. If his novels couldn't change society, he would—through the sheer force of his will and creative alchemy. He would devise a public personality so provocative that it would demand attention for his ideas. If Mailer the failed novelist could not move the culture with his fictional imagination, he would make his own life a story that others would have to follow. It would inspire the underground army of similar souls which Mailer suddenly envisioned around him to nothing less than revolution against the oppressors. Far from retreating, Mailer was now ready to offer himself as the leader of an all-out war against sexual and moral repression.

Mailer, as a self-proclaimed oracle, needed a public platform, and his old friend Dan Wolf accommodated him. While Mailer had been revising *The Deer Park* the previous year, Wolf and Ed Fancher had been talking about starting a newspaper in Greenwich Village. They wanted to publish an avant-garde, bohemian weekly which would be essentially a writer's paper and would fill the cultural gap left by *The Villager*, a weekly which was basically an attractive showcase for local ads. "In the fall of 1954 there was a lot of talk about a new paper, and we started discussing it seriously at the beginning of 1955," Fancher recalls. "At one point Dan said, 'We have very little money, but I think Norman has some. Should I ask him?' I said sure."

Wolf approached Mailer in the spring of 1955, and the author was immediately intrigued by the idea. He agreed to match Fancher's original investment of five thousand dollars. For that he became a 30 percent founding stockholder, sharing equally with Wolf, who was to be the editor of the paper, and Fancher, who would be the publisher. Charles Rembar, who drew up the corporate papers in the spring of 1955, took the remaining 10 percent in lieu of a fee. There was still the question of what the paper would be called; even today there is disagreement about who came up with the name.

"Norman thinks he suggested the name" says Fancher, "but I remember there was a schoolteacher I knew who mentioned the name *Village Voice* to me. We had a list of about twenty possible names, and that was added on to it. But Norman may have been the one who said, 'I like that best, let's go with it.' " Mailer's version, however, is that while he was revising *The Deer Park* in order to find Sergius's voice, he suddenly thought the Village needed a "voice" as well. Thus the name *The Village Voice*.

Immediately after, Mailer returned to his struggles with *The Deer Park*. Neither Wolf nor Fancher heard from him again during those hellish summer months when Mailer was strung out on drugs finishing the book. On their own the editor and the publisher started the paper and hired their first staff. John Wilcock was hired as news editor, and Jerry Tallmer became the first associate editor and film critic. By October 26, just as *The Deer Park* was appearing in bookstores, the first issue of *The Village Voice* hit the newsstands.

The publication date of the *Voice* coincided so closely with the publication of Mailer's novel that it was not until a month later, when most of the reviews of *The Deer Park* were in and Mailer's mood was dark, that he approached the *Voice* and made an auspicious debut in its pages. Mailer bought space in the paper for a half-page advertisement for *The Deer Park* which he had composed himself. It was an unusual ad, made up entirely of the worst pans he had received to date. "All over America," the ad opened, "*The Deer Park* is getting nothing but RAVES." It then went on to chronicle the debacle: "The year's worst snake pit in fiction"—Frank O'Neill, *Cleveland News;* "Sordid and crummy"—Herman Kogan, *Chicago Sun Times;* "Moronic Mindlessness"—John Hutchens, New York *Herald Tribune*." And so on.

The ad marked the beginning of the outrageous and outraged gambits Mailer would defiantly make use of over the next two decades. He was quickly shedding the modest personal habits that had carried him through Harvard, the war, and initial fame. He was sharpening the double-edged psychic razor of the absurd. "Up until that point, I'd been a nice young literary man," he later recalled. "My manners were the equal of anyone's, I had worked hard at them. I was like any other reasonably intelligent young writer who came from Brooklyn, and was Jewish, and had gone to Harvard." But now the tide had turned against him, and he was fighting back as the self-styled "psychic outlaw." By provoking reactions to his own behavior, he hoped to draw attention and instigate a revolution of cultural sensibilities. It was risky, but it was a more promising approach than writing another failed novel.

Mailer's *Deer Park* advertisement should have told Wolf and Fancher that their friend's scarred psyche was moving in dangerously provocative directions. By the late fall of 1955 Mailer began showing up at the *Voice* on a regular basis, playing at various jobs while making bold resolutions about what should be done with the paper. Mailer even offered his services as the circulation manager. "He could see that Dan and I were out of our minds just keeping things going," says Fancher. "We didn't know what we were doing, and we were overwhelmed by it since neither of us had any background or knowledge in newspapers. So Norman volunteered to take over the circulation."

The paper was then being distributed by a commercial company, but everyone was unhappy with them. When a *Voice* employee, Fred Fleck, suggested an investigation of their circulation problems, he and Mailer went out for two weeks to check newsstands. They came back feeling that something had to be done. Fleck convinced Mailer that they should fire the distributor and do it all themsevles. Mailer agreed, but on their first night out Fleck and Mailer got into an argument, and Fleck quit. "Norman continued to do it all by himself for three or four weeks," recalls Fancher. "He was very diligent and covered all the major newsstands as far as I could see. But it was ridiculous for Mailer to be wasting his time driving all over the Village distributing papers."

Mailer rose before the sun every Wednesday morning and drove in Jerry Tallmer's old car to various drop-off points throughout lower Manhattan. Not only did he deliver the paper, but he cajoled the owners of the stands, mostly old Jewish ladies, to take a few more copies than usual. *Village Voice* historian Kevin McAuliffe recounts a telling story about Mailer's circulation days. Editorial assistant Florence Ettenberg remembers delivering several bundles of back issues with Mailer during his tenure as distributor. The *Voice* had taken a stand at an international show in the old Wanamaker building, and Mailer was responsible for stocking the stand with free back issues. As Ettenberg and Mailer lugged bundles of the papers across town to the show, Ettenberg suddenly broke out laughing in the middle of the street. Mailer asked her what was so funny, and she replied, "Someday I'm going to tell my grandchildren that I delivered papers with Norman Mailer." He laughed right along with her. "That's right," he said. "And they're going to ask you, 'Was that before or after *The Naked and the Dead?*' And you're going to say—AFTER!"

Mailer was circulation manager of the *Voice* for a month before another distributor was found and he was relieved of his chores. This left him free to comment on and complain about the paper's editorial policy, which annoyed Dan Wolf, who did not share Mailer's view of their mission. Mailer wanted the *Voice* to be outrageous. He felt it would never grow unless it adopted a revolutionary stance that would reach an audience commanded by no other paper. If the *Voice* failed, it failed; but the gamble should be taken. Wolf and Fancher, however, were convinced that to make the *Voice* successful, they first had to get ads.

"Our ideological differences weren't a big issue at the beginning, but they developed over a period of time," says Fancher. "Norman, as time went on, said that the *Voice* should be very radical, full of sex and drugs. Dan and I pointed out that we were working seven days a week, twelve hours a day, trying to put this paper out. We had no money, we were losing a thousand dollars a week, and it had to be commercially viable, or it was going to go down. We had a big investment in seeing it survive, but we felt that Norman's attitude was that it wouldn't survive and so it should go out in a blaze of glory like a big firecracker." The argument would grow more heated over the next six months.

By the beginning of 1956 not only Mailer's restiveness but the paper's financial problems had to be dealt with. The money problem was resolved by bringing in a fourth partner, Howard Bennett, whom Fancher had known at the New School. In return for fifteen thousand dollars Bennett received Charles Rembar's 10 percent interest in the paper and an additional 5 percent from each of the other three partners—so that all four had a 25 percent share in the stock. Fancher and Mailer also contributed another ten thousand each.

With the money question settled, everyone turned to the Mailer problem. What does one do with an internationally renowned author who owns part of a newspaper? Mailer himself suggested that it might be a good idea for him to write a weekly column. Wolf and Fancher liked the idea, sensing that it would allow Mailer to release his frustration and help them to contain his radical ideas without altering the entire *Voice*. His name would also be an important draw.

But Mailer had more serious plans for his journalistic debut. High on pot and desperate to regain his place as a hero of his time, Mailer saw the *Voice* column as nothing less than "the declaration of my private war on American journalism, mass communications, and the totalitarianism of the totally pleasant personality."

"What he wanted at the time was a big explosion that would make the scene," Wolf later recalled. "He felt that if you just pressed the right button, all these people would come up from the underground." Not only was finding the right stylistic button to prove difficult, but Mailer's initial approaches alienated his readers.

Mailer's first column for the *Voice* was published in mid-January 1956. It was twice as long as it was supposed to be, and he handed it in after the deadline. It was called "QUICKLY: A Column For Slow Readers." The war was on. Insulting Villagers as "venomous" and "frustrated," Mailer told them "the only way I see myself becoming one of the cherished traditions of the Village is to be actively disliked each week."

Despite Mailer's assault, some of his readers, including Mailer's old friend Norman Rosten, voiced a certain admiration for the column. "Read 'Quickly' slowly—and to my astonishment it had some very good things," Rosten wrote the paper. "Even some logic. What have you done to Mailer?" Then, alluding to the picture that ran with the column showing Mailer in a plaid lumber shirt with masses of black curls, Rosten added, "But for Chrissakes get him a haircut."

In the first column Mailer also publicly aired his ideological differences with the paper's policy, calling it "remarkably conservative." Although Dan Wolf was not pleased, Ed Fancher realized Mailer's provocative stance was actually good for the paper. "We needed to get attention, so we thought the fact that the column was radical and abrasive was a good thing," Fancher says. "It generated a lot of talk, and we favored that. We didn't want the whole paper to do the same thing, but it was a good column for that purpose."

Mailer's next column was a long serious essay on communication. It dealt with the falsities of gossip columnists, the lack of true communication by the mass media, and the question of obscenity, or the lack of it, in newspapers. Ed Fancher read it just before it went to the printer and suggested to Mailer that it might be difficult going for readers. Mailer didn't change the column, but he added a caveat to his readers. "The column this week is difficult. . . ." he cautioned. "If you are not in a mood to think, or if you have no interest in thinking, then let us ignore each other until the next column."

Mailer's little warning brought in a barrage of angry letters from readers, including an especially irate one from a reader.

> Outside of getting yourself a 'reputation' by gutlessly imitating (prim term for thievery) Dos Passos in your ONE & ONLY book, and now *again* imitating by stencilling yourself upon the very overworked, tired, boring, creaky, mimeographed Henry Miller in your column, well, why you consider yourself anything but an adequate journeyman writer is a

> serious inner disturbance you ought to take up with an analyst. The very obvious trouble with you is that you really suffer from illusions of grandeur: sometimes you must think you're the indisputably great Norman Mailer. It's a cinch your romance with yourself will be recorded as one of the most magnificent love stories in history. . . ."

Other letters were no more laudatory. "This guy Mailer," wrote another reader, "he's a hostile, narcissistic pest. Lose him."

On the basis of a few positive letters Mailer somehow convinced himself the tide had turned in his favor. The following week he decided to coax his audience with a little humor aimed at American columnists. Entitled "COMMUNIQUES FROM THE MARSH MEDIA," the piece parodied such figures as Hedda Hopper of the *Daily News*, who became "Cheddar Chopper of the N.Y. Daily Nose"; Dorothy Kilgallen of the *New York Journal-American* was reduced to "Dorothy Kill-Talent of the N.Y. Churlish-American"; Max Lerner became "Wax Burner," and so on.

Mailer's readers were hardly ready to be seduced by his wit. Indeed, most of them, in the subsequent issue of the *Voice*, responded to the warning in his second column. "Burp: A Column for People Who Can Read by Normal Failure," wrote a reader. It was finally becoming clear to Mailer that his readers might be more hostile than he anticipated. In the next four columns he tried to cajole them again with humor.

By column eight, in the February 29, 1956 issue, he was back to serious observations, on psychoanalysts versus novelists. For the past year he had been analyzing himself, he admitted. "If I were ever to look for an analyst I would be inclined to get me to a Reichian." This was Mailer's first mention of his fascination with Wilhelm Reich, the Freudian dissident who believed in the therapeutic value of the orgasm.

Although Wolf had hoped the column would keep Mailer distracted from meddling in the running of the paper, the author continued to protest, demanding that the *Voice* engage in more radical coverage. As Kevin McAuliffe noted, "As his moods got blacker, he became more and more impossible. Cover this. Cover that. Cover Sex. Murder. Dope. Revolution." John Wilcock remembers that as he was laying out the dummy of the front page one week, Mailer arrived to oversee the operation. Wilcock was furious. "You can fire me," he yelled at Mailer, "but if you have the front page, you do it. I quit." The ploy worked and Mailer backed down.

Ironically Wilcock was perhaps the one staffer who might have sided with Mailer, had his support been enlisted. He believed in taking gambles with the paper and actually liked Norman's columns. But Mailer regarded Wilcock as irrelevant. "My impression is that I was an insignificant jerk to Norman," says Wilcock, "some little employee hanging around. Norman was a very egotistical, big-headed, self-important writer at that time—with a lot of justification, because he was a big star, and he owned part of the paper. But he wanted autonomy to do things he wanted to do without even understanding everyone's role in relation to the paper. He wanted to be involved, but his ego made him overplay it and bludgeon his way through.

"I had a certain respect for his talent, but that was muted by his lack of professionalism. I was a newspaperman and had worked on tabloids since I was sixteen, so when I came to the *Voice*, I was already experienced. My feeling about people writing for newspapers was that they would follow the norms of newspaper conduct—that they would be edited and turn their stuff in on time and wouldn't cause extra work for others. My earliest impression of Mailer was that he did not have his column ready on time. He would literally drive out to the printer in New Jersey while we were having the paper printed. Not only did we have to typeset the column, but we couldn't cut a word of it, not a comma. That anyone could be so unprofessional was too much. Maybe because he was successful so early he tended to believe that everything he wrote was holy."

Ed Fancher believes it was these procedural problems that caused the staff's most serious altercations with Mailer. "Norman would bring in his copy at the absolute last possible moment, and this drove Jerry Tallmer wild," Fancher says. "Tallmer was responsible for processing the copy and really bore the brunt of the paper. He was very resentful that Norman brought his copy in so late and that Norman acted like a prima donna. Not a line could be cut. We had a small paper, only twelve pages, and if Norman's copy ran long, it meant Jerry would have to cut an ad or somebody else's copy. Norman seemed to be very insensitive to the problems of putting together a whole paper."

It was the typographical errors in Mailer's printed column that finally exacerbated everyone's temper. "Four of us," recalls Fancher, "had to drive out to the printing plant in Elizabeth, New Jersey, at two in the morning Monday night, and none of us had slept for forty-eight hours. After the copy went into the machines, it had to be proofread while the printers were screaming around us. There was tremendous pressure on Jerry, and it was inevitable that he had typos. But when the typos began to appear, Norman got very paranoid and thought that Jerry was doing it or the printers were doing it or somebody was doing it to destroy him."

Jerry Tallmer, now a critic on the *New York Post*, was irritated by the pressures Mailer created at the *Voice*. "He wanted the paper to be more hip, covering drugs and aspects of the Village which were far out, outré, and leaning toward the lower depths," recalls Tallmer.

Since everyone on the paper had a different view of what it should be, tempers naturally flared. Mailer's insistence on doing it his way once caused Dan Wolf to snap at him, "Norman, for a socialist you're acting like the worst capitalist in the world." Jerry Tallmer concurs, adding: "He was like a cartoon boss, beating the slaves."

The hostility between Tallmer and Mailer was intensified by the author's obvious dislike of Tallmer's long theater reviews. "I think," Tallmer says, "that Norman thought of me as a perpetual college boy, although he himself is a perpetual college boy of a different kind. Norman was writing all this stuff about hip and cool and acting very hot. I tried to outcool him whenever I could."

One incident caused Mailer to dislike him even more intensely, Tallmer now believes. At the time the *Voice* had a very chaste format with typography done by the artist Nell Blaine. Mailer felt the look of the paper was part of its problem. "He prided himself on knowing something about art," Tallmer recounts. "In fact, he once told me he knew about art because he was married to a painter." On this occasion Mailer wrapped himself in a black cloud and disappeared into the back room for two days, hard at work on some secret mission. When he finally emerged, he had restyled the logo of the paper by hand. He had created a new typeface, and wandering in and out among the letters of the logo were tiny sketches of what Mailer believed were true Village types: junkies and Bowery bums.

"He was quietly bursting with pride," recalls Tallmer. "He called Dan and me up to to the front office at 22 Greenwich Avenue. 'What do you think of it?' he said. We all looked at it, and there was a long, profound silence. Finally I said, 'Well, it's okay, Norman, but I think it's a little high school.' That tore it. From that moment on he never trusted me again."

By column eleven Mailer had had another spat with Wilcock over a ploy the author had devised in connection with his choice for President in the November 1956 election between Adlai Stevenson and Dwight Eisenhower. The previous issue had featured an announcement, by Wilcock, that ten dollars would be paid to whoever could guess Mailer's choice for President—not necessarily one of the major party candidates—and that a clue would be printed in Norman's column that week. The announcement also mentioned that Mailer's choice was in a sealed envelope pasted on the *Voice* window on the second floor of 22 Greenwich Avenue, where anyone could see it from the street.

Mailer's preference had indeed been sealed in an envelope and placed in the window, but it was directly above Wilcock's desk, which annoyed Wilcock. In addition Mailer had put no specific clue about the candidate in the previous week's column. He had indicated to Wilcock that there were hints in all of his columns taken together, and Wilcock had misconstrued what he meant. In column eleven Mailer made amends and dropped a few elusive clues: "Candidate X must of course be Hip, and yet not display himself unduly as a hipster. Perhaps we can assume that he was one of the germinal influences in the birth of the hipster."

In column twelve he announced that his choice for the Democratic presidential candidate was Ernest Hemingway, chosen for his "charm," his "war record," his ability to "speak simply," and particularly for his lack of experience. Mailer then used the space to talk about Hemingway's macho image, an obsession that had helped shape his personality as a sixteen-year-old freshman at Harvard. "This country could stand a man for President, since for all too many years our lives have been guided by men who were essentially women," Mailer wrote.

A year later Mike Wallace would challenge Mailer on this subject of "womanly men" on his television show, *Night Beat*. It was Mailer's first television appearance, and under Wallace's questioning he charged that President Eisenhower was "a bit of a woman." After the show Adele said, "Well, we may be dead tomorrow, but it was worth it."

In this prefeminist era Mailer's hero worship of Hemingway did not bring protest from female readers, but it raised the ire of James Jones. "If you have ever made a really close study of Hemingway through his work as I have," Jones wrote him, "you will know what I mean by immature. The consensus of his philosophical outlook might be worded thusly: Say and do everything you can that will make Hemingway look good, even if it does make a lot of other people look bad."

Jones was concerned about Mailer's new role as a columnist and how it was affecting both his work and his ego. "I still believe there are great books in you, *great* books," he said in the same letter, "if you can ever get them out. But I certainly doubt very much if you'll ever do it while writing a fucking column for *The Village Voice*. That's another serious mistake in judgment you've made, I feel. Certainly, I know that my own ego-vanity could never survive such an operation, and in spite of what you say I'm positive yours is at present ballooning—both for the admiration you get and for the dislike you get, just as my ego would."

Other friends, such as publisher Lyle Stuart, were equally concerned that Mailer was squandering his talent by writing the *Voice* columns. Stuart had met Mailer a few years earlier at the home of Mailer's brother-in-law, Larry Alson. Mailer wanted to meet Stuart because he had been reading his iconoclastic newspaper, *Exposé*, which had subsequently been renamed *The Independent*. Stuart was notorious at the time for attacking such sacred cows as the Catholic Church, Walter Winchell, and Senator Joseph McCarthy. "Norman fancied himself as a heroic character, and here I was actually doing these things," Stuart says.

In 1956, when Mailer's columns were appearing in the *Voice*, Stuart had lunch with Mailer's lawyer, Charles Rembar. He pleaded with Rembar to get Norman to stop what he was doing. "He was playing to the Village audience to show how bright and brilliant he was," says Stuart, "and I wanted him to be a narrative fiction writer. I felt if he continued to do books like *The Naked and the Dead*, he would become a latter-day Charles Dickens, a very readable writer who had something to say and could say it. I was concerned because I thought he was throwing away a certain talent. Rembar commiserated with me but said he couldn't do anything with him."

If other friends were worried about the route Mailer's stubborn ego had launched him on, so were Wolf and Fancher, and their relationship with him was deteriorating rapidly. Mailer had begun to ally himself with Howard Bennett, who was as critical as he of the paper, which added to the in-house tension.

❦

By late April Mailer's relationship with his old friends was close to enmity. But he was beginning to find a true voice in his columns. On April 25 he wrote a column on the hipster. It was in response to a letter from a reader who had written him, "Tell me, what is your definition of a Hip person? A third rate rape artist or a boy who digs Shakespeare, Milton and Freud?" "Could be either," Mailer wrote in his sixteenth column for the *Voice* and then went on to develop a thesis that would eventually win him intellectual accolades.

"Hip is an American existentialism," wrote Mailer, "profoundly different from French existentialism because Hip is based on a mysticism of the flesh, and its origins can be traced back into all the undercurrents and underworlds of American life, back into the instinctive apprehension and appreciation of existence which one finds in the Negro and the soldier, in the criminal psychopath and the dope addict and jazz musician, in the prostitute, in the actor, in the—if one can visualize such a possibility—in the marriage of the call-girl and the psychoanalyst."

In this column Mailer had drafted the first sketchy blueprint of what would become, one year later, his seminal essay on hipsterism, "The White Negro." Although Mailer admitted that by April 1956 the concept of hip had already infiltrated American consciousness, he would be the first to synthesize the various strands of the thesis and become its chief intellectual exponent.

Mailer may have intuitively gauged the importance of this column, but the raging battle that erupted over it between himself, Wolf, and Tallmer had to do not with any ideas in the piece but, once again, with a typographical error. When the paper ran the column, the final sentence read as follows: ". . . Because Hip is not totally negative, and has a view of life which is predicated on growth and the nuisances of growth, I intend to continue writing about it for at least the next few weeks." The problem was the word *nuisances*. Mailer had originally written it as "nuances of growth," and when he saw the typo, he was outraged, convinced, as usual, that someone had deliberately sabotaged what was clearly his most important column to date.

Jerry Tallmer had proofread that sentence after a typically grueling 4:00 A.M. trip to the printer and a ninety-hour work week. He noticed nothing wrong with the word. It was not misspelled, it made sense of a kind, and he decided to let it run. When he arrived at the office the following day after only a few hours of sleep, the phone rang. It was Mailer. He screamed at Tallmer for the typo, and Tallmer screamed back. The editor then sat down and wrote Mailer a stiff note, saying, in effect, he had better not do that anymore. Mailer wrote back an equally abrasive note saying, "Ok, Jerry, but next time take your finger out of your ass."

It was the final blow after months of friction between Mailer and everyone at the *Voice*. "It was a combination of Norman being in a very bad state, very frustrated, very angry about *The Deer Park*, and just blowing up over the typos," recalls Fancher. "I think at a certain point Dan felt he'd had enough. After the last typo incident Norman called up Dan in an absolute rage, and Dan told him he'd taken enough of that kind of abuse. That was the break. I thought it was a crazy thing. If Norman had been in a different psychological state, it wouldn't have happened."

The result was a decision that the next column would be Mailer's last. Mailer, however, would not bow out gracefully. His final column, which ran on May 2, began with a discussion of Samuel Beckett's play *Waiting for Godot*, which was then running on Broadway and causing some controversy. As theater critic for the *Voice*, Tallmer had already reviewed the play and praised it as "the most serious piece of writing to come our way since the death of Joyce."

Mailer opened his column with the admission, "I have not seen *Waiting for Godot* nor read the text, but of course I have come across a good many reviews of it. . . . What amuses me is the deference with which everyone is approaching Beckett. . . . I . . . suspect that the complex structures of the play and its view of life are most attractive to those who are most impotent. . . ." By writing this directly after his argument with Tallmer, Mailer seemed to be accusing the reviewer of impotence. "I thought that was directed at me, and I still do," Tallmer says. "It seemed glaringly obvious, especially since I had been the guy who promoted this play."

Mailer's column didn't end there. In his farewell he described the typo incident that had caused the final rupture with the *Voice*, claiming that the incident was obviously used to divert attention from a more serious difference of opinion about where the paper should be heading: "They wish the newspaper to be more conservative, more square—I wish it to be more Hip. . ." Mailer wrote. "Since I am a minority stockholder and have no real voice in the control of anything except my column, I have decided that this contradictory association can go on no longer. . . . I regret only that it became impossible to go on writing about the nature of the Hip and the Square, for that was fascinating to me, and I had finally found the subject (yes, after all these columns) which I wished to explore. . . ."

Mailer could not end without adding an encore. In this case it was a poem that had appeared in *The Deer Park* called "The Drunk's

Bebop and Chowder." Inspired by Joyce, the poem followed its own linguistic rules. "Let us see how many typos there are in this," Mailer taunted Tallmer.

In the issue in which Mailer's last column appeared, Dan Wolf printed an editorial commenting on Mailer's resignation, stating that they had always given Mailer "complete editorial freedom" and that they would not censor his final column.

On this same day, May 2, 1956, a new agreement was drawn up among the four stockholders. Until then, Bennett and Mailer had owned 50 percent of the stock, and Fancher and Wolf had owned an equal amount. For a long time the paper had been close to bankruptcy, and the financial records were in a state of chaos. Mailer had brought in his father, Barney, to act as accountant, but this clearly was not working out. "Norman didn't appreciate the fact that we were close to bankruptcy," says Fancher, "and he was the only one of us who was financially well off. When we asked him for more money, both he and Bennett took the position that they didn't want to put in more money because they didn't have confidence in our leadership. So I said, 'Okay, you don't want to accept our leadership, I'll put in more money, and we'll have the majority.' "

Fancher did invest additional money, for which he received another 10 percent of the company. This gave Wolf and Fancher a controlling 60 percent as opposed to Mailer and Bennett's 40 percent. An agreement was reached whereby a minimum of four thousand dollars in liquid assets had to be maintained by Wolf and Fancher or control of the *Voice* and 20 percent of their stock would revert to Mailer and Bennett. Until that happened, Mailer and Bennett agreed to stay away from the office and not to try to influence editorial policy.

Mailer's brief tenure as a newspaper columnist was over. So, for a time, was his friendship with Wolf and Fancher. It would take years for the wounds to heal, but by then the world was catching up to Mailer's vision, and the *Voice* was becoming a leading proponent of that changing view. Mailer would write again for the paper from time to time, and the paper would often write about its irascible founding father.

Two days after Mailer left the paper, he finally read *Waiting for Godot*. Unnerved that it was better than he had thought, he went to see the play. The play depressed him even more deeply, for he could see Beckett's artistry emerging even in the Broadway production. He knew he had been wrong in his last column. His depression was not alleviated by Adele, who taunted him on the way home from the play, saying, "Baby, you fucked up." Ashamed of himself for the views he had proffered in his final column, Mailer decided to make amends.

In the next day and a half he wrote a three-thousand-word piece on *Godot* in which he humbly apologized for his column attacking the play. Mailer then paid to have it published in the *Voice*.

❦

The *Voice* fiasco left Mailer further depleted of creative energy, and by the summer of 1956 he was in another of his deep depressions. Fearful that his talents as a novelist had totally withered, and worried that his first attempt at becoming a public personality had been a failure, he left for Paris with Adele. He knew he would have to rid himself of a few self-destructive habits if he was to learn to work all over again. That summer while he and Adele were living at the Hotel Palais Royale he kicked both Seconal and Benzedrine. But his despair was such that even signing the hotel guest book was an emotional whiplash. As he stared at Truman Capote's signature, Mailer ruefully realized that his own signature was "so dim in its fashion that year."

His longtime political mentor, Jean Malaquais, had been back in Paris for some time. He had written Mailer a long letter about *The Deer Park*, admitting that he did not like it but stressing that writers shouldn't always have to produce an outstanding work. The two got together in Paris to thrash this out, but no one in Paris that summer, including Malaquais, correctly gauged the depth of Mailer's depression. Just as Vance Bourjaily had misread Mailer's previous depression in 1951, so James Baldwin, who was in Paris that summer, would now fail to understand Mailer's true mood.

Baldwin met Mailer for the first time that June at Malaquais's home in Paris. Although Baldwin's *Notes of a Native Son* had come out the previous year to a stunning reception, he was now facing his own abyss of despair: a broken love affair and the torture of returning again to the typewriter. From the depths of his own personal hell he misperceived Mailer as "confident, boastful, exuberant, and loving—striding through the soft Paris nights like a gladiator."

In Paris, Mailer and Baldwin argued about the myth of Negro sexuality. Mailer was developing his concept of "hip" and by the following summer would publish "The White Negro." This encounter with one of America's best black authors should have been an important testing ground. But at the time Baldwin was becoming tired of both white America's romance with the Negro and the pretensions of white men like Mailer, who somehow felt psychically black and hip.

"So," Baldwin recalled in his 1961 *Esquire* piece, "The Black Boy Looks at the White Boy," "it did not seem worthwhile to challenge, in any real way, Norman's views of life on the periphery, or to put him down for them. . . . He [the white man] will face in your life only what he is willing to face in his. . . . And matters were not helped at all by the fact that the Negro jazz musicians, among whom we sometimes found ourselves, who really liked Norman, did not for an instant consider him as being even remotely 'hip' and Norman did not know this and I could not tell him. . . . They thought he was a real sweet ofay cat, but a little frantic."

Baldwin did not change Mailer's conviction that sensuality was more heightened in blacks than in whites. As Mailer told Paul Krassner, editor of *The Realist*, in October 1962, "I'm willing to bet that if you pushed Jimmy hard enough, he'd finally admit that he thought that the Negroes had more to do with sexuality than the white—but whether he really believes that or not, Baldwin's buried point is that I shouldn't talk this way because it's bad for the Negro people."

Neither Mailer nor Baldwin knew that the other was facing a personal crisis in Paris that summer of 1956. After Baldwin dropped Norman and Adele off at their hotel he would wander through the underside of Paris, "drinking, screwing, fighting" until morning. And Mailer, withdrawing from Seconal, would get up at four in the morning and wander around the streets until dawn, often arriving at an Algerian bar at five, where he would watch the workers drink wine for breakfast.

If Baldwin envied Mailer his love that summer, as he said he did, he shouldn't have. Mailer's relationship with Adele had begun to sour and would grow progressively more violent over the next four years. A subtle shift of balance had taken place in their union. While Baldwin saw Mailer as the confident young gladiator, Adele recognized the deep depression her husband was in. In March 1961, a week before his marriage to Adele ended for good, Mailer wrote a prose poem about their Paris sojourn entitled "Summer 1956," which he dedicated to Hemingway. It chronicled the evolving brutality of their marriage and spoke of Adele as a "Spanish lady" with "murderous Indian blood."

As he mined deeper into his obsessions with sex and violence, Mailer had pushed Adele to be as brave and sexually inventive as he. Adele had grown tough under his tutelage, and she came from fighting stock: Her father was a professional boxer, and she knew the lexicon of the ring. If Mailer wanted a courageous competitor, he now had it. But that also meant that he had to stay in shape, and that summer, in Paris, Adele very clearly had the edge. And she was pregnant.

When they arrived back in New York later that summer, Mailer was still having acute symptoms of Seconal withdrawal. The pace of the city seemed too brutal for them and their coming child. The couple decided to move to the country, to find an environment in which Mailer's overwrought, overdrugged brain could be refueled, a place where the enervating battles of the difficult 1950s might be left behind.

• VIII •

A WHITE NEGRO IN CONNECTICUT

In the fall of 1956 the Mailers visited Lewis Allen, who was then living in Washington, Connecticut, and who had just married writer Jay Presson. Mailer and Adele liked the area and decided to buy a rambling farmhouse nearby. It was to be the beginning of a new social and intellectual scene for Mailer, but not the end of his fear that his career had been severely damaged, perhaps even destroyed.

In addition to the Allens, the Mailers' new circle of Connecticut friends included John Aldridge and his wife, Leslie, who had recently divorced Clay Felker. The Aldridges lived on the back road from Washington to Roxbury in Arthur Miller's former house, one which he had shared with his wife, Marilyn Monroe. The Millers had gone to England to shoot the film *The Prince and the Showgirl*, so Mailer was not to meet the woman with whom he would become obsessed and about whom he would write two books. William and Rose Styron, who also lived in Roxbury, were an added incentive for Mailer's move to the countryside.

As soon as he arrived in Connecticut, Mailer concentrated on getting into shape. For the next four months he gave up his traditional two packs of cigarettes a day, and although he blew up to a hundred and seventy-five pounds, he began to box in earnest. In the barn studio behind the house he set up two punching bags, one heavy and one light, right next to his desk. Mailer had frequently boxed with his father-in-law, but this was the first time he seriously conditioned himself for the sport. It was the beginning of an abiding interest in boxers and boxing, one which had its origins in his early fantasy of becoming the contemporary Hemingway.

Novelist Chandler Brossard remembers that when he came to Connecticut for a long weekend visit, Mailer asked him to put on the gloves and fight. Mailer had met Brossard recently, when the latter had interviewed him for a magazine called *Gentry*, and the two had gotten along. The morning before the interview Mailer had told Brossard that he had never read his work, but afterward he admitted that he had in fact read it and had liked it. Mailer's evasiveness annoyed Brossard, but it is not insignificant that Brossard was the author of *Who Walks in Darkness*, a novel published in 1952 which melded the concepts of existentialism and hip. One of the early usages of the word *hipster*, in fact, was in a blurb on Brossard's book jacket cover. Moreover, Brossard's book was about a Negro who passes for white.

Since Mailer was now formulating his own piece on hip, "The White Negro," there was a natural affinity between him and Brossard. Mailer also had heard that Brossard used to box and had been trained by the same man who taught Hemingway. He was clearly excited by this and wanted to test their respective physical skills. Brossard, as a semiprofessional, rarely fought with amateurs, and he tried to convince Mailer that if they boxed, one of them might get hurt. Mailer repeatedly denied that he could get hurt, but he let the matter drop. "Violence and pain are a form of engagement to Norman, of reality," says Brossard. "Really smart, tough people don't do that, but Norman wanted bloody emotions, and I sensed that he liked 'rough trade.' "

Lewis Allen also remembers that Mailer tried to box with him, but he refused as well. One night at a party the Mailers gave, Norman took Allen out to the barn to show him a new exercising gadget. "It was one of those rollers with a board across it," recalls Allen. "We all had one of those things at the time, but Norman, not being content with mastering that, put movable footboards on it so he could also turn right and left. Then he made it so the whole board revolved. It was very tricky, and he wanted to show me how he could do it. Of course he spun around and flew up in the air and landed on his nose and almost knocked himself out.

"He was bleeding from the nose and really groggy, so I said, 'We better go back to the house, Norman, and wash up.' As we were walking back, he said, 'I'll tell you what. When we get back to the house, let's tell everybody we had a fight out there, and you knocked me out.' When we got back, Adele asked what happened, and Norman replied, 'We had a fight, and Lew knocked me down.' For the rest of the evening Adele kept staring at me and saying, 'Lew, Lew.' "

Mailer's Connecticut friends remember that period as one of the most difficult in his life. "Norman was ready to take offense at anything," recalls Jay Allen. "His whole nervous system was exposed, and his nerve ends were out on stalks. He was on pot all the time and primed."

Leslie Aldridge concurs. "When I think of that period, I think of it as a time when Norman was mainly interested in physical combat, proving he was strong. He seemed to pick a fight with everybody." She remembers one evening at the Mailers' house when Norman tried to get her and her husband stoned. The Aldridges went upstairs and smoked marijuana furiously, but it had little effect on them. Later that evening in the living room Leslie Aldridge was talking to Adele when she happened to look at her own watch. Adele got very incensed and said, "Don't look at your watch when you are talking to me." "Norman's ears pricked up," recalls Leslie, "because at that point he loved fights. He said, 'All right, let's have a real fight.' He tried to get Adele and me to have a physical fight. I don't know whether he would have gotten a sexual or an ego kick out of it, but he was clearly disappointed when we decided not to fight."

Another evening, this time at the Styrons', Mailer walked up to Bennett Cerf, Styron's publisher. "You're not a publisher, you're a dentist," he told him. The confrontation ended with Mailer and Cerf slugging it out in the flower beds outside the house. Still other Connecticut friends recall Mailer shadowboxing in the aisles on the train from New Milford to New York, obviously high on some drug.

Frederick Christian, a writer who lived near Mailer, later realized that Mailer was making a connection in his mind between violence and creativity. As Mailer himself later told Mike Wallace, "I've noticed . . . that violence and creativity do seem to have some sort of twinlike relation." The first night that Christian and his wife were invited to Mailer's house for dinner, the author's behavior seemed to bear this out. "When our conversation turned to another writer," Christian recalled, "he asked, 'Do you think you could take him?' He meant, 'Could you lick him?' . . . During the nights I saw him in New Milford, he seldom discussed writing. He seemed to live principally for pleasures of the moment—rather dubious ones at that."

Although Mailer's behavior disturbed a number of his friends, Chandler Brossard was sympathetic, realizing that he was at a very low point. "He was drinking a lot and taking a lot of drugs," Brossard recalls. "He had no money, and he was discovering he didn't write fiction very well anymore, and that's a bad place to be. It's the worst place. That's when you think of killing yourself. There's an analogy to boxers: They reach a certain point where training is agony for them, and if that gets out, that person is marked. You've lost it, you can't handle it anymore." Mailer would later admit that during this period "I began to live with the conviction that I had burned out my talent."

To compensate for the dread of losing his talent, Mailer started to direct his creative energies toward real people rather than fictional characters, manipulating them into his own imaginative situations. "Norman invented you and then addressed his invention," recalls Jay Presson Allen. "If you weren't deadly sure who he had invented, you didn't have the right dialogue, and then he was provoked by the fact that you didn't know the lines. His riffs were always unnerving because I never knew what I was supposed to be talking about. I finally had to say to him at one point, 'Norman, if you don't stop acting up, I'm going to tell everyone what a nice person you are.' "

Chandler Brossard felt equally uneasy about the mythology Mailer had constructed around him. But because Brossard was an early incarnation of hip, the two conspired more closely. "Norman was unique in the sense that if he liked you, he was totally there for you, totally game," Brossard says. "He'd say, 'You name it, and I'll play it.' That's very rare in the literary world. I always thought of Norman as an unemployed and unemployable Hamlet. He was like a hermit crab looking for the shell of another to get into, not only in an interpersonal way, but as a click on. Norman is not self-sustaining." Mailer and Brossard played a cool game together. One New York editor remembers that at a party at Mailer's home the two of them came up to him with a hipper-than-thou attitude and rudely asked him if he was "plugged in."

Brossard drew close to Mailer, but his relations with Adele were strained. "She and Norman had a very deep-seated violent relationship, very deep, and Norman was very explicit about it," says Brossard, "When she kept baiting me, I finally told Norman, 'You're going to have to get Adele off my back because she's really annoying me.' Norman was amused by it and said, 'Yeah, she can get like that, but I'll take her outside and knock her down a few times.' What he actually did, in an angrily playful way, was drag her off to the side and instruct her to stay away from me."

Several of Mailer's other friends felt that Adele was acting provocatively only in order to please Norman and seem more exotic. At the same time she was alienating a number of people. As Lew Allen explains, "I think there was an intellectual pressure on her from Norman and his friends which wasn't her bag. She was a painter. She reacted to that pressure by pushing." Frederick Christian recounted: "There always seemed to be tension between Mailer and his wife. I cannot recall a time when I ever saw one address the other directly. Or, for that matter, *look* at each other. I was not really surprised when I heard of the stabbing."

Even Mailer's old war buddy, Francis Irby Gwaltney, was aware that something serious was happening to his friend, and he wondered if Adele was partially the cause. As he wrote to his editor at Random House in the fall of 1956, "Norman and I have been drifting further and further apart. I called him some time ago and talked with him, but he seemed strangely interested in besting me in a 'You're short on intellect' conversation. There was also a lot to indicate that I might be short on talent. I will agree that I'm pretty damned short on both of those items, but it cuts hell out of me to have somebody close to me tell me so. . . . I'd like to know what the hell is happening to Norman that makes him act like he has. He's making a fetish out of being rude." Gwaltney then speculated that Mailer's marriage was contributing to his unease. Gwaltney's insight was undoubtedly close to the mark. Mailer's relationship with Adele had clearly reached a destructive stage.

It was in the midst of this scene that publisher Lyle Stuart arrived for a weekend visit in the late winter of 1956–57. To Stuart, however, all outward signs seemed peaceful enough. Adele was pregnant and on March 16 would give birth to Norman's second daughter, Danielle. Little Susan was visiting Mailer and romped in the New England snow with her father's large standard poodle, Tibo. Mailer, if slightly pudgy, seemed in good spirits as both he and Stuart took home movies of the setting. Knowing that the author was increasingly absorbed with the physical, Stuart even persuaded him to take jujitsu classes in New York, which Mailer diligently did. In fact when Mailer later heard that his jujitsu professor had a book which Stuart wanted to publish, he agreed to match Stuart's fifteen-hundred-dollar advance and be a partner. The book proceeded to do so well that, as Stuart now says, "I lost track after I paid Norman twenty-two thousand dollars."

One night during that weekend Stuart and Mailer stayed up to talk after everyone else had gone to bed. Their conversation turned toward freedom in the mass media. Stuart told Mailer there was no idea he wouldn't print in *The Independent*. Mailer agreed that Stuart might print anything, but if he were to write, say, a piece on integration in the schools, he doubted whether the largest newspapers would print it. Stuart challenged him to write it in order to find out.

That night before he went to bed, Mailer, sluggish from not having written for months and determined to be provocative enough not to be ignored, wrote four paragraphs implying that the reason the white man hates the idea of Negroes gaining equality in the classroom is that the white man knows the Negro has sexual superiority.

Lyle Stuart liked the piece but realized that in order to get other papers to run it, he would have to drum up some controversy. He sent the essay to William Faulkner, one of Mailer's lifelong literary heroes. Faulkner's answer was brief but devastating: "I have heard this idea expressed several times during the last twenty years, though not before by a man. The others were ladies, northern or middle western ladies, usually around 40 or 45 years of age. I don't know what a psychiatrist would find in this."

Since Faulkner had challenged not only his intellect but his manhood, Mailer was propelled to write an overly defensive reply to the great author. He called Faulkner "timid" and said that his, Mailer's, own ideas had been confirmed by a mulatto pimp and a whorehouse madam in South Carolina. He concluded, "I'm a bit surprised that William Faulkner should think a psychiatrist could ever understand a writer." Stuart sent the Faulkner-Mailer exchange to a number of people, including Eleanor Roosevelt, who replied, "I think Mr. Mailer's statement is horrible and unnecessary." Other responses were no more favorable, and when Stuart sent the entire exchange to six southern newspapers, not one picked up the story.

But it was Faulkner's rejection that gnawed away at Mailer. The young Harvard undergraduate who had read *The Sound and the Fury* late into the night with awe couldn't help but recognize the bold presumption of his stance. Mailer would have to articulate his ideas a lot better if a writer of Faulkner's stature were to take serious note of him.

❦

For the next month, sick with the fear that he had lost his talent, Mailer wrote his now celebrated essay "The White Negro." It was a brilliant analysis of the inchoate hip consciousness Mailer was perceiving around him, even actively forging in his own life. Written in 1957, it was also stunningly prophetic. The strands of theory and experience that Mailer strung together in the essay would help form the basis of the new counterculture which emerged in the late 1960s. Fighting his own lonely battle against the establishment, Mailer had presaged the mass adoption of marijuana, youth rebellion, mysticism, the black revolution, violent confrontation, existentialism, antitotalitarianism, antimilitarism, all of it enveloped in a pastiche of Freud and Marx, a mix that was to become the new religion of the upcoming generation.

Mailer argued that with the specter of the atom bomb and collective death a new kind of American existentialist had come into being, the hipster. He lived with the terms of death by seeking out the rebellious imperatives of the self, what Mailer called "the psychopath in oneself." The Negro, with his sensuality and his jazz, he claimed, is the source of this outlaw mentality. Centuries of discrimination had led him to develop primitive, uninhibited sexuality, and for Mailer the sexual act was the primal existential one. When the Negro joined with the other postwar disenfranchised, the bohemian and the juvenile delinquent, the hipster was born.

Unlike the rational French existentialists, the hipster is essentially religious or mystical. His God, says Mailer, is "energy, life, sex, force, the Yoga's *prana*, the Reichian's orgone, Lawrence's blood, Hemingway's 'good,' the Shavian life-force; 'It'; God; not the God of the churches but the unachievable whisper of the mystery within the sex."

Even though Mailer drew heavily on psychoanalytic thought in shaping his idea, he characterizes the hipster as anti-Freudian. The hipster, Mailer says, is a "philosophical psychopath" whose nature is to live "the infantile fantasy" in order to diminish the tensions of those infantile desires and so be free to remake himself. And, as Mailer points out, the language of the hipster is "a language most adolescents can understand instinctively, for the hipster's intense view of existence matches their experience and their desire to rebel."

The one part of Mailer's ideology that would cause him both immediate and long-range problems was his defense of personal violence. Theorizing that rage can be dangerous to creativity when it is turned inward against the self, Mailer claimed that externalizing that violence is both therapeutic and cathartic. If one cannot purge one's violence, one cannot love, Mailer theorized. He would also maintain that individual acts of violence are better than the collective violence of the state. This premise would be attacked by critics throughout his life, especially after he stabbed his wife in 1960 and after his protégé, convict Jack Abbott, stabbed and killed a waiter in 1981 after Mailer helped effect his release from prison.

"The White Negro" would become a major cause célèbre when Irving Howe published it with great fanfare in the summer of 1957 in *Dissent*. But to a few who saw the seventeen-page piece before it came out, the terrain Mailer was covering was totally new, even alien. John Aldridge remembers that Mailer showed him the rough draft of the essay in Connecticut before it went to *Dissent*. "I was totally uncomprehending of what he was trying to do," Aldridge recalls. "I told him he should do something about the style because it seemed to me overblown. He needed to edit it carefully. Now when I read it over, I realize there was a lot there that I simply didn't have enough perspective then to see. It's a very prophetic piece."

Lew Allen received one of the few privately bound editions of "The White Negro" which Mailer printed and gave to friends. As Allen recalls, "He talked about it a lot. I thought it was interesting and possibly farfetched. But Norman was obsessed with it over quite a period."

Irving Howe was excited by the essay when he received it, but he had some serious reservations about Mailer's defense of violence. He particularly objected to a passage in which Mailer speaks about two hoodlums beating in the brains of a candy-store keeper. As Mailer wrote, "One murders not only a weak fifty-year-old man but an institution as well, one violates private property, one enters into a new relation with the police and introduces a dangerous element into one's life."

"I still feel," says Howe, "that I should have sent it back to

Norman objecting to that passage and saying, 'For Christ's sake, what are you saying here? At least reconsider it.' But I didn't. When you put out a little magazine like *Dissent* with a small circulation and you get something which can pass for a scoop—and 'The White Negro' was by our lights a scoop—it's hard to be sufficiently intransigent or principled to send it back. And of course the piece attracted an enormous amount of attention, mostly positive. I think people were excited and impressed by the pyrotechnics of it, by the brilliance of the analytical segments, and didn't ask themselves what the significance of some of this was. Most of the people who read it were deeply impressed with his knowledge of social types and social phenomena which we ourselves knew very little about, for Norman is very gifted in analyzing what is going on among segments of the population we don't know."

Most intellectuals praised the social insight Mailer had brought to the definition of hipsterism, but they did object to the same passage that disturbed Howe. The following year, in a piece he wrote for the *Partisan Review*, "The Know Nothing Bohemians," Norman Podhoretz, soon to be the editor of *Commentary*, called it "one of the most morally gruesome ideas I have ever come across, and [one] which indicates where the ideology of hipsterism can lead." But by 1959, after meeting Mailer, Podhoretz had become one of his most ardent backers among the intellectual set, even if still critical of Mailer's interest in violence.

"Bored with my own sensibly moderate liberal ideas," Podhoretz recalled, "but with Marxism and all its variants closed off as an alternative, I saw in Mailer the possibility of a new kind of radicalism—a radicalism that did not depend on Marx and that had no illusions about the Soviet Union. Soon there would be others, but at that moment there was no one else in sight who held out the same tantalizing possibility.

"It was not the particular doctrines he preached that attracted me; on the contrary, I thought he was being simply foolish in constructing a theory of revolution with the psychopath playing the role Marx had assigned to the proletariat. But this very willingness to risk looking foolish in the pursuit of something very large and ambitious was exactly what I admired about Mailer."

Podhoretz was not alone among intellectuals in recognizing the revolutionary political role that Mailer had given to the hipster. Alfred Kazin and Diana Trilling would also make note of it. As

Trilling wrote in 1963 about "The White Negro": "It is the doctrine which, enshrined in the place that Marxism once had in his system of thought, allows Mailer to probe modern society on a level deeper than that of political and economic determinism."

"The White Negro" stirred up a torrent of intellectual debate and even changed the perceptions of some powerful establishment critics. It was natural that Mailer was obsessed by the essay for some time. In essence it was the definitive articulation of all he had been groping for in *The Deer Park* and had failed to communicate. "The whole theory of hip," says Norman Podhoretz, "was a way of inflating the significance of *The Deer Park*. It was a way of claiming virtues and meanings for that novel that it didn't really possess on its own, much like Capote's use of the idea of the nonfiction novel."

Mailer's obsession with the ideas in *The Deer Park* was far from over. The following year he would write a play based on the novel as well as two sections of a long epic novel, which itself was never finished or published, in which Marion Faye and Sergius O'Shaugnessy reemerge as characters.

In the play *The Deer Park*, Marion Faye has been inevitably given a more pivotal role. The setting has changed from Hollywood to Hell, and both Faye and Charles Eitel had been prison inmates. Lewis Allen, who was then working for theater producer Robert Whitehead, remembers hearing the first drafts of the play in Connecticut. "Norman would come over and read it out loud," he recalls. "I remember three or four versions of it. I thought it was quite brilliant, but not yet shaped dramatically or professionally. I've always thought that what Norman wrote the easiest was the best, and what he slaved over was reaching for something he maybe necessarily didn't get. But some of it was brilliant." Mailer would eventually stage three productions of *The Deer Park*, one of the Actors Studio in 1960, one in Provincetown in the summer of 1966, and one in New York at the Theater de Lys in 1967, none of which received real critical acclaim.

Of the long epic novel only two sections were ever published. The prologue, entitled "Advertisements for Myself on the Way Out," was printed in the *Partisan Review* in the fall of 1958 and again in Mailer's semiautobiographical compendium, *Advertisements for Myself*, in 1959. A dark, Faustian drama of murder and suicide with Marion Faye as the protagonist, it fictionalized some of the tenets of the "The White Negro." The other segment of the novel, an erotic piece called *The Time of Her Time*, was printed as a novella in *Advertisements*. The novella represented Mailer's most vitriolic and humorous attack on Freudianism, although by the early 1970s certain feminists were claiming that it was Mailer's bitterest assault on women.

In *The Time of Her Time* Sergius O'Shaugnessy has returned to New York from Hollywood via Mexico. This tall, blond swaggering Irish alter ego of Mailer's now teaches bullfighting by day and sexually entertains Greenwich Village girls by night. One of the girls he meets is a frigid Jewish college student who spouts Freudian jargon and who challenges Sergius to give her the sexual satisfaction she has never had. Using his "avenger" in a grim, all-out effort to overcome her "civilized" resistance to the primitive in herself, Sergius finally succeeds in bringing her to orgasm. But rather than being grateful, her ego flares and she leaves him, saying: "Your whole life is a lie, and you do nothing but run away from the homosexual that is you." The vanquished Freudian has struck back.

The Time of Her Time contained some of the most graphic sexual descriptions Mailer had yet written, and when he tried to include the story in *Advertisements for Myself* Putnam's voiced some objection. Mailer subsequently wrote to a number of critics, including his former Harvard professor Robert Gorham Davis, asking their opinions of the story. Davis took the occasion to send Mailer a sermon on his attitudes toward women. "He seemed to have to turn his relations with women into a battle," Davis says, "and was sometimes very cruel. But I don't think I influenced him. He responded but didn't agree with what I wrote." Putnam's finally decided to print *The Time of Her Time*.

Mailer's belief in the orgasm as the ultimate act of self-realization was now fully evolved. It sprang in part from his growing fascination with the work of Wilhelm Reich. In *The Time of Her Time* Reich and Freud battle it out in the bedroom, with Freud the neurotic loser. Although Mailer had been influenced by Freudian technique, as evidenced by his many years of "self-analysis," his hip philosophy could no longer accommodate Freud's civilizing restraints. But Wilhelm Reich, with his belief in sexual energy and the primacy of the orgasm, was a perfect substitute for Freud.

Not surprisingly Mailer was one of the first writers to construct his own Reichian orgone box, a device in which one sat in order to absorb the unseen psychic energy. In his barn studio in Connecticut, Mailer devised an interesting variation of the box, one which Lew Allen remembers. "One day Norman asked me to go out to the studio with him and see what he had been building," says Allen. "In the studio there were dozens of these big wooden eggs which Norman had built himself. They were beautifully finished, and there was a big one that opened like an Easter egg. He climbed inside and closed the top of the egg."

Vance Bourjaily also saw the eggs when he came up with his wife for weekend visits. He realized they were a variation of the Reichian orgone box, but it was the quality of the workmanship that impressed Bourjaily. "Norman had this well-equipped machine shop with electric hacksaws, and he could weld anything," he says.

Bourjaily also remembers that on one weekend visit he brought along his jazz trumpet, which he had been learning to play. Mailer had rented a tenor saxophone. The two of them put on a record of Thelonious Monk, and while Bourjaily performed free form, Mailer would "honk." "He didn't think of himself as being able to play," says Bourjaily. "He just rented this saxophone as a tribute to hip music."

Bourjaily was aware that Mailer's work was moving in a radically different direction from that of most of the post-World War II writers who, with himself, had been grouped together in John Aldridge's book *After the Lost Generation*. But as part of that generation, Bourjaily understood the pressures to change to meet new literary challenges, particularly from the younger writers. "I think what happened to Norman happened to all of us, but he made much more of an effort to accommodate himself to it," he says. "What happened was that in the late 1950s, instead of the postwar group being what fascinated the critics and journalists, it was suddenly the beat generation. We all felt we were being left behind before we really had our innings. The implication was that we were all done, and here were the new guys who really had something to say. Norman's impulse was very much 'If I can't beat them, I'm going to join them,' and he did accommodate himself to it, and successfully."

By the summer of 1958 hipsters and beatniks were being lumped together under the label the Beat Generation, but Mailer took pains to explain the differences between them. The beatniks dressed in a "slovenly" manner, whereas the hipsters had a certain "chic." Beatniks were more of the mind than the body and were "sentimental," whereas hipsters were more "Faustian." But he would also add, "If there are hipsters and beatniks, there are also hipniks and beatsters like Ginsberg and Kerouac."

The lines of demarcation were confusing, but Seymour Krim, a

Village Voice writer and later the author of the influential collection of essays *Views of A Near-Sighted Cannoneer*, met Mailer in the summer of 1958 and saw him as distinctly different from such beat writers as Ginsberg and Kerouac. "Norman had been through the army, Harvard, and had very strong middle-class roots," Krim says. "He wasn't a pushover when it came to money or success, and I remember he once said to me about publishers, 'You know, all I have is my name,' and he meant to milk that for as much as he could get out of it. In that sense he was very different from the beats. My hunch is that if he hadn't had *The Deer Park* bounced around and felt a loss of faith, things would have been different. I think Norman has an opportunistic streak in him as a part of a very complex personality, but he was also flexible enough and curious enough to reach out into new areas, while other postwar writers were much more fixed in their attitudes and themes. Styron and Jones, for instance, would never permit themselves to absorb the beat phenomenon except critically, whereas Mailer did."

❦

The tension between Mailer and other postwar writers, specifically William Styron and James Jones, was in fact coming to a head. Mailer had been seeing a lot of both authors during his Connecticut stay, and at the same time that he was moving away from them intellectually, and from fiction in general, he wanted very much to be included in their social scene. This was especially true of Jones, for whom Mailer had affection because of his personal simplicity and his great war novel, *From Here to Eternity*.

Styron and Jones, however, had drawn very close to each other by 1958, and Mailer was entering the triangle as the odd man out. This stimulated Mailer's jealousy and exacerbated his fear that he was a failed novelist. It also caused him to play one of them against the other. According to Mailer there were nights at Styron's house in Connecticut when Styron would read aloud the worst passages of Jones's new book, *Some Came Running*, and Mailer would join in the laughter, feeling, as he said, "a touch sick with myself." Other times Mailer would tell friends, including Chandler Brossard, that he couldn't stand Styron.

Jones, too, would engage in this ego sparring. Larry Alson was present at Mailer's house in Connecticut when Jones asked Mailer, "Do you think Styron is in the same league as us? Is he as big as we are?" According to Alson, Mailer replied, "Of course he is; what are you talking about, Jim?" And Jones answered, "Well, I read his stuff, and I'm not too sure."

The jealousies among these three literary egoists led to the events which began March 13, 1958, the day Mailer sent Styron a scathing letter accusing him of having made a derogatory remark about Adele. Styron had made what he thought was an innocuous remark about Mailer's wife, and Mailer's letter seemed to him to be out of proportion to the actual comment. Mailer wrote the equivalent of: "Listen Billy Boy or Bully Boy, sources closer to you than you know told me what you said about Adele, and I want you to know that none of this is true, and it's despicable." The letter continued in a vitriolic tone.

Lew Allen, who eventually read Mailer's letter, recalls: "It was really threatening, and Bill was scared, really scared. But the irony is that just before that Norman had read Styron's novel *The Long March*. I heard him say several times that Bill was *the* writer of that generation, and it was the best thing he had written."

The day after Styron received Mailer's letter, Styron went to see his wife, who was in the hospital having her second child. Jones and his wife Gloria had also come to the hospital to visit, and all four talked about Mailer's letter at length. Jones and Styron concluded that whatever had triggered it probably had something to do with their three-way friendship. Gloria and Jim Jones left for Paris four days later, but in a subsequent letter to Styron, Jones indicated that his feeling for Mailer had changed. Jones even implied that he didn't want to see Mailer again. Styron's immediate decision was to stay completely away from Mailer. As Jay Allen now says, "It was a really serious, ugly break." And it was the beginning of a feud with Styron and Jones that would intensify by 1959, when Mailer published *Advertisements for Myself*, in which neither writer was treated kindly.

Mailer had lost one friend and alienated another but he had written "The White Negro," one of his great works to date, and he seemed to be thrashing his way out of failure. His turbulent but strangely productive Connecticut days had come to a climactic close.

• IX •

THE MESSIAH AND THE NEW JOURNALIST

In the fall of 1958 the Mailers left their pastoral Connecticut environs and returned to New York City, where they rented an apartment at 73 Perry Street in the West Village, near the White Horse Tavern.

"The White Negro" had not done for Mailer what *The Naked and the Dead* had accomplished, but in the nine years since the novel's publication it was the first of Mailer's works to be acclaimed. It was to be the beginning of a new career, a second chance for Norman Mailer, who would now emerge as perhaps the best subjective journalist of his time.

Until the spring of 1959 Mailer devoted himself to a series of short pieces, covering everything from Picasso to the mass media. He began collecting these new essays, along with previously written pieces, for his compendium, *Advertisements for Myself*, which would be published the following fall. Walter Minton, now president of G. P. Putnam's, had agreed to publish this miscellany, although to him it wasn't as serious an endeavor as a new novel by Mailer. "*Advertisements* was a book that had validity and that Norman wanted to do," Minton says, "but it wasn't what I liked to see him doing. I don't think it was presented as a major work. To me, it was just a collection."

A number of critics would share Minton's view, but the project's seeming lack of ambition was deceptive. Although outwardly the book was just an eclectic assemblage of Mailer's past work—including pieces from Harvard, his war stories, bits of his novels, the *Voice* columns, "The White Negro," the play *The Deer Park*, and the prologue to his new novel—the autobiographical narrative which linked these pieces was the first real evidence that Mailer had found a new voice, perhaps the first that was truly his own.

By 1958 Mailer was aware that the style of *The Naked and the Dead* was borrowed from Dos Passos and Farrell, and the other writers he had read at Harvard. The success of that novel had only served to hamper him in his search for a central voice that was uniquely his. Rather than mass-producing similar best-selling prose, he had been groping for a personal style, a journey that initially took him through the critical debacle of *Barbary Shore*, then through *The Deer Park*, where the first signs of the future Mailer were seen.

"The White Negro" had been a liberating influence, and at the age of thirty-five Mailer was finally able to create an authentic style. He knew he had achieved success without truly mastering his métier. He had experienced the frustrations and bitterness of learning how to write while enduring the harsh glare of the literary spotlight.

The first-person narrative style that emerged in *Advertisements* was intimate, egotistical, psychological, macho, and angry but it strove for honesty. As in his life, Mailer himself was the central character. This discovery of a personalized narrative opened Mailer to new possibilities, and for the next decade almost all his work would be nonfiction, with Mailer first as the subjective observer, then as the central protagonist. "I think really the watershed book was *Advertisements for Myself*," Mailer says today. "I thought that was, oddly enough, the first book written in what became my style. I never felt as if I had a style until that book. When I developed that style, for better or for worse, a lot of other forms opened to it."

Mailer's finding of his own voice was probably closely related to the advent of the New Journalism. "These days everyone is laying claim to having started the New Journalism," Mailer now says. "Truman Capote is screaming. Tom Wolfe has been writing manifestos about it for the last ten years. And Lillian Ross, who actually started it, has been silent. But I think that if I started any aspect of that New Journalism—and I did—it was that of an enormously personalized journalism in which the character of the narrator was one of the elements in the way the reader would finally assess the experience. I had felt that I had some dim intuitive feeling that what was wrong with all journalism is that the reporter tended to be objective and that that was one of the great lies of all time. Now it is more comfortable to write that way. You can't go through *The Village Voice* and not find a story that isn't written that way."

It is typical of Mailer that even though he was making a major transition in his work, he was only dimly aware of it at the time. Mailer would insist throughout *Advertisements* that he was at work on a major epic novel, and he would flash his ego around outrageously to back up the gambit: "I have been running for President these last ten years in the privacy of my mind . . . ," he wrote. "The sour truth is that I am imprisoned with a perception which will settle for nothing less than making a revolution in the consciousness of our time."

Mailer was taking a huge risk in displaying his ego so blatantly; his personality was now inviting attack. No longer was he a private writer protected by literary decorum. Mailer knew his public persona would now have to be equal to his projected literary one if the myth he was creating was to be sustained. The challenge was to make him more macho, more vulnerable, even more aggressive in his private life.

❦

During the summer of 1959 in Provincetown, Mailer attracted an entourage of flattering male followers who posed no threat to his ego and who acted as loyal buffers between him and the outside world. The Provincetown entourage was only the first in a series of Mailer royal courts, often made up of boxers. By the following fall an ex-middleweight fighter named Roger Donoghue would be a close Mailer follower, and by the early sixties ex-Golden Gloves boxer and editor Buzz Farbar would be added to the group, as would the prominent fighter José Torres. Mailer's longtime friend from Brooklyn, actor Mickey Knox, was also part of this evolving circle.

The Provincetown entourage included diverse types. One member of the group was Bill Walker, who ran a famous coffeehouse in Washington, D.C., called Coffee and Confusion and who later became Mailer's self-proclaimed bodyguard during his New York mayoral campaign of 1969. Another was Dick Dabney, who wrote for *The Washington Post Weekly*. A young poet, Lester Blackiston, was also part of the group. Bill Ward, who that summer started a literary magazine called *The Provincetown Annual*, met Mailer when he solicited a piece from him. Mailer gave him an essay from *Advertisements* entitled "Eye on Picasso," which was published in the annual's first edition, in August 1959.

Another member of this entourage was Village writer Seymour Krim, who had met Mailer the previous summer through Dwight Macdonald's ex-wife, Nancy. Krim had been invited for a weekend in Provincetown by Mrs. Macdonald, and he remembers he had stopped at a gas station near North Truro when Mailer roared up in his Thunderbird. Nancy Macdonald introduced them. Mailer balled up his fists, and as Krim now recalls, Mailer looked him "right in the eye with a crazy twinkle," and told him he couldn't get started on a new book unless he had a fight.

This macho pose didn't alienate Krim. As another New York writer who was into hip, he had vast respect for Mailer's essay "The White Negro." By the summer of 1959 Krim was an avid participant in Mailer's Provincetown group, which he characterizes as "a gang of post-Beat kicks-oriented writer-fighters and wild-assed gallants from Washington, D.C., P-town and the East Village." Most of them—not Krim—were younger than Mailer, and they all looked up to him as the hero of their hip cause.

During the summer of 1959 Mailer's "crew" would get together for endless drinking parties at the rented house on Commercial Street, where Mailer was frequently seen drinking directly from his bourbon bottle, or at a local bar called the Old Colony, which was also on Commercial Street. Krim remembered well Mailer's activities that summer: "Mailer arm-wrestled, shadow-boxed, sucked on pot, downed his Bellows, exploded energetically (I've seen him lift a woman and windmill her around his head without sweat to either party) and generally had a ball in the shoulder-punching warmth of this barracksroom camaraderie."

To Mailer, Provincetown was then, and is still, what Key West and Cuba were to Hemingway, part of his immutable legend and the stage where Mailer indulges his obsession with physicality as he seeks to surpass the macho Hemingway legend. If Hemingway had his bullfights, his game hunting, and his fishing, Mailer had fast cars, fast boats, arm and thumb wrestling, hang gliding, endless boxing, rope walking, and softball and jogging.

Although most of the Provincetown gatherings in 1959 were essentially all-male affairs, Adele was occasionally included in the festivities. Krim remembers one evening when Mailer invited him and a few other people over to watch a pornographic movie, and Adele was there. At one point during the evening—for no apparent reason—Adele approached Krim and threatened to snip off his tie. "She was capable of doing it," Krim says, "but Mailer stopped her. I think she just wanted to get a rise out of me. It was provocative. I found Adele attractive, mercurial, unpredictable, perverse, a flirt, and wanting recognition. Because Norman had such an ego, it wasn't easy for any of Mailer's wives not to be dominated by his personality, and I think Adele had a tremendous need for approval and status of some kind."

Adele did gain a certain kind of recognition one night that August. It was apparently at the instigation of her husband, and the attention she received was of dubious value. The Mailers were attending a Provincetown party given by a man named Bobby Olaffson. Everyone was quite drunk, and in the middle of the evening Adele walked over to a tall, blond woman named Harriet Sohmers, who was Bill Ward's girl friend and an editor at *The Provincetown Annual*.

Out of the blue, according to Sohmers, Adele said, "If you're not chicken, come outside." Sohmers was startled, but she followed Adele outside, whereupon Adele slapped her in the face. Sohmers was drunk enough to hit her back rather than retreat. As she now recalls, "We ended up rolling around punching each other out with Norman and all the other guys at the party watching us and cheering us on. It was dreadful, and as I was led limping away by Bill Ward, Norman screamed insults at me, one of which was 'cancer hole.'

"It had always been common knowledge that Mailer liked to watch women fighting or wrestling," Sohmers says. "I always felt he resented me because of my size, and he was always challenging me to arm-wrestle with him, which I never did." But Sohmers also admits that she may have provoked Mailer's wrath a month before the fight. She had just begun to live with Bill Ward that summer, and she was resentful of the endless male meetings Mailer held: "This whole macho thing that was going on," as she puts it.

At one point in July she walked into one of these sessions at the Old Colony and, to be provocative, intimated to Mailer that he was really a homosexual. "It was definitely a nasty crack," Sohmers says, "and he was furious at me, and Bill was furious at me. But a few days after that I ran into Norman at the Old Colony again, and he said, 'Look, Harriet, I know we don't like each other too much, but when the great struggle comes, you and I will be on the same side of the barricades.' "

❦

Mailer's concern about who would man his side of the barricades was growing. As he made his new bid for public recognition with *Advertisements*, his anxiety about who was for or against him began to take on an aggressive edge. And it would sharpen after the publication of *Advertisements*, for new enemies would be made with that book.

When *Advertisements* was published in the fall of 1959, the reviews did little to lessen Mailer's insecurity. Few critics commented on the development of his style, or if they did, it was to object to Mailer's egotism. Some of the more favorable reviews compared the book to Fitzgerald's "The Crack-up" and recognized the erratic brilliance of the autobiographical narrative. But almost all the critics admonished Mailer for wasting his novelistic talents on such a minor effort.

"The maddening thing about all this obsessive bilge," wrote *Newsweek*'s critic on November 9, "is that it is mixed with so many evidences of a vigorous and sophisticated mind that the book as a whole is a fascinating performance." *Newsweek*'s summing up was more direct: "A great gift squandered." Harry T. Moore in *The New York Times Book Review* made much the same point on November 1: "In this volume Mr. Mailer, at 36, shows once again that he is the most versatile if not the most significant talent of his generation . . . perhaps one day he will be able to concentrate his various talents to produce the big important novel he still seems capable of writing."

Time was almost totally negative. On November 2 its critic said: "His book gives no sure sign that the wreck is under effective repair." Granville Hicks added to the criticism in the November 7 *Saturday Review*, "I'm not at all sure he can do what he wants to do, but perhaps he can, and in any case I wish he would get about it instead of frittering away his time."

Mailer had set himself up for attack by egotistically boasting in *Advertisements* that he was in the process of writing a fictional masterpiece. The critics were saying, as was his publisher, Walter Minton: "Well, get to it." The result was that *Advertisements* was not taken as seriously as it should have been. It was a devastatingly honest portrayal of the cult of American success and its deleterious effects on the writer. One such effect was evident in Mailer himself: the development of an overly large ego in order to survive celebrity.

Critics such as Alfred Kazin, who did note the book's power in this regard, objected precisely to that ego. In the November 26 *Reporter* Kazin stated that not only was Mailer "hungry to make his mark again in one big smashing outrageous way," but he was measuring himself against his competitors instead of "the moral abstractions of courage, duty, grace, etc." Kazin concluded: "What will become of him God only knows, for no one can calculate what so overintense a need to dominate, to succeed, to grasp, to win, may do to that side of talent which has its own rule of being and can never be forced."

Gore Vidal was also disturbed by the giant Mailer ego. In a review for *The Nation* on January 2, 1960, he wrote: "If there is anything in Mailer's new book which alarms me, it is his obsession with public success. I suspect Mailer may create more interest in himself by having made this 'clean breast of it' than he would have got by publishing a really distinguished novel. The audience no longer consumes novels, but it does devour personalities." But unlike Kazin, who thought that Mailer was openly fighting his competitors in *Advertisements*, Vidal saw Mailer as being diplomatic: "I noted with some amusement that despite the air of candor, he makes no new enemies in this book. He scores off those who are lost to him anyway, thus proving that essentially the work is politic."

Vidal was obviously getting back at Mailer for a piece in *Advertisements* entitled "Evaluations: Some Quick and Expensive Comments on the Talent in the Room." In that essay Mailer attacked Vidal for being a "narcissistic" writer who had difficulty creating real characters. Vidal wasn't the only victim of Mailer's scorn: James Jones, William Styron, Truman Capote, Jack Kerouac, Saul Bellow, Nelson Algren, J. D. Salinger, Paul Bowles, Vance Bourjaily, Chandler Brossard, Anatole Broyard, Myron Kaufmann, Calder Willingham, Ralph Ellison, James Baldwin, and Herbert Gold were all grazed by Mailer's analytical lance. Many of these writers were, of course, friends. Mailer was hardly scoring off those who were lost to him anyway. And of these writers only five came off relatively well: Capote, Broyard, Kaufmann, Ellison, and Brossard.

In the January 30 issue of *The Nation* Mailer responded to Vidal's allegation that *Advertisements* was "politic." "Only a fool brags of making new enemies," Mailer wrote, "but I was bruised to the bone by this quick assertion, and when Vidal called a few days later to discover my reaction to his piece I gave documents to the man, page and paragraph about the new enemies I had made, and by God yes I think even Gore V. would admit this day he was hasty."

Mailer's essay had indeed aroused animosity, and literary feuds began to fester. Calder Willingham was one of the first to see the piece while it was still in galleys. In fact it was Norman who showed it to him at a party at Mailer's West Village apartment. Sidling up to Willingham, he asked him if he would like to read something from his forthcoming book. Innocently Willingham began to read: "Calder Willingham is a clown with the bite of a ferret, and he suffers from the misapprehension that he is a master mind. . . . He lacks ideas, and is as indulgent to his shortcomings as a fat old lady to her Pekinese."

After reading the passage Willingham looked at Mailer and said, "Norman, that's not complimentary to me. You're being competitive and hanging other writers in this goddamn piece." Perhaps to justify the evaluation to himself, Mailer had another confrontation with Willingham that evening. In front of several people Mailer accused him of never paying back the two hundred dollars he had borrowed in 1950 when he was in the Virgin Islands getting a divorce. When Willingham protested that he had paid it back, Mailer said to him, "You know, Calder, you're an immoral who-cares kind of character. It's not in style to protest that you paid me back." Willingham was so angry and embarrassed that he made a bet with Mailer: If he couldn't find the cleared check endorsed by Mailer, he would pay him double. If he did find it, Mailer owed him another two hundred dollars.

When Willingham got home, he found the check, which had been endorsed over to Mailer's mother, Fanny. He put the check in the mail to Mailer with a note saying, "Norman, you accused me in front of a whole lot of people of being a deadbeat, and it's not true. This is a myth in your own mind. You send me $200." Mailer sent the check, which Willingham then tore up, but their friendship was no longer the same.

"He had changed by then from the boy I had seen in 1948," Willingham now recalls. "He had become aggressive, although not quite as belligerent and pugnacious as he became later. His career was going nowhere. Here was a guy who had written three novels, the first a brilliant success, and the next two which hadn't done anything. Then he starts writing the *Voice* column and for *Dissent* and then he made a character, a persona, out of himself. If he couldn't make it by writing fiction, he would just storm the walls and tear the whole thing down. He would raise so much hell that you'd have to notice him. That's what he did, and it's one way to do it."

Willingham would continue a friendly if strained relationship with Mailer until 1963, when he wrote a biting account of Mailer in *Esquire*. Mailer never forgave Willingham. "I think he has an attitude," says Willingham, "and he learned this from Adele, that either you're with me or you're against me, and if you're against me, then you're the enemy, and there is no qualification about it. You're in with Norman or you're out."

❦

James Jones, William Styron, and James Baldwin were all in Paris when *Advertisements* came out. When a copy of the book reached Jones, he invited Styron and Baldwin to his apartment to read Mailer's evaluations of them out loud. They were all stunned by the comments. Mickey Knox, who happened to be in Paris and on hand that evening, found himself the butt of their wrath. "They really bloodied me," he recalls, "because I was always a surrogate for Norman. I was under attack all night. At one point Jim got the book and said, 'You see what he wrote about my friend Bill? I'll show you what he wrote.' I replied that I had already seen it, but he opened the book and got behind his bar, which was an actual church altar, and began reading. Bill started twitching and said, 'Okay, Jim, that's enough, Jim!' "

Although in his critique Mailer spoke warmly of Jones at first, calling *From Here to Eternity* "the best American novel since the war," he went on to say that Jones "has sold out badly over the years" and added that Jones should stop "trying to be the first novelist to end as a multi-millionaire." Mailer had not forgiven Jones for siding with Styron during the Connecticut contretemps.

The piece affected Jones profoundly. His wife Gloria recalls that Jones kept a copy of *Advertisements* on a sideboard in the dining room of the Paris apartment. Whenever any of the authors Mailer had attacked came through Paris for a visit, Jones would have them write their comments in the margin of the book near Mailer's evaluation of them. The copy was subsequently lost, but in yet another copy of *Advertisements* Jones clipped out reports of Mailer's stabbing of Adele from *The Paris Herald Tribune* and pasted them on the inside cover. It provided a constant reminder for Jones of the difficulties Mailer was having.

Despite the feud, a certain love existed between Mailer and Jones. In 1965 a rapprochement of sorts was attempted at a party at John Marquand's New York apartment on East Fifty-seventh Street.

As Marquand recalls, "A lot of people came, and Jones and Mailer showed up. This was when Mailer was having his fight with Styron, and nobody was speaking to each other, and they were all going to kill each other. Mailer and Jones went off into a separate room, and they were out for a conspicuous amount of time. I was concerned that the furniture was going to be attacked. First Mailer came out by himself, and he was obviously quite moved. He didn't seem angry; he seemed purged, almost as if there were tears in his eyes. Five minutes later Jones came out, and they didn't speak to each other again. They went to separate corners of the party. Jones later said to me, "It was something we had to get straight.' Even later he said, 'I love him, but I don't like him.' "

When William Styron read Mailer's evaluation of him in Jones's Paris living room in the fall of 1959, he was clearly prepared for the worst. He was, in Vidal's words, "already lost" to Mailer. But still, the intensity of Mailer's attack was unexpected. "I wonder," wrote Mailer, "if anyone who gets to know him [Styron] well could wish him on his way? . . . I must speak against the bias of finding him not nearly as big as he ought to be." Mailer went on to compliment Styron on his first two books but of the third, *Set This House On Fire*, which Styron was then writing, he said: "The reception will be a study in the art of literary advancement. For Styron has spent years oiling every literary lever and power which could help him on his way, and there are medals waiting for him in the mass media."

In 1962 Styron replied to Mailer in Myrick Land's book *The Fine Art of Literary Mayhem*. "Any 'feud' which exists has always, for some queer reason, seemed far more important to Mailer than it has to me," Styron said. The enmity between Styron and Mailer, although lessened, still exists and has become the stuff of literary legend, as Mailer might have guessed it would when he first began their quarrel.

Of the Paris trio Baldwin was the first to confront Mailer. His evaluation of Baldwin had been briefer and less damaging than the others, although Mailer did write that, "Baldwin is too charming a writer to be major." The black author was tempted to send him a telegram from Paris, but then he realized Mailer probably expected him to act that way. He decided to play it cool. As Baldwin said in *Esquire* in 1961, "His judgment of myself seemed so wide of the mark and so childish that it was hard to stay angry. I wondered what in the world was going on in his mind. Did he really suppose that he had become the builder and destroyer of reputations . . . ?"

A few months later, as Baldwin recalled it, he was back in New York, and he confronted Mailer at the Actors Studio, where a reading of the play *The Deer Park* was being staged. They went to a bar, where Baldwin asked him why he had written those things about him. Mailer at first answered that he thought there was some truth to his comments, but then added with a grin, "You're the only one I kind of regret hitting so hard. I think I—probably—wouldn't say it quite that way now."

Mailer and Baldwin remained friends, although in his 1961 *Esquire* piece, "The Black Boy Looks at the White Boy," Baldwin speculates that Mailer's political ambitions had driven the writer into a state of moral confusion which resulted in the stabbing of his wife.

❦

With *Advertisements* Mailer was receiving the attention that he had hoped for, but he was also getting critical heat. His blatant public ambition rankled the literary establishment, where power is supposed to be gained through one's art, not through the cult of personality. Gore Vidal's review of *Advertisements* in the January 1960 *Nation* attacked Mailer on this point, introducing the idea of Mailer as a messiah. "His drive," wrote Vidal, "seems to be toward power of a religio-political kind. He is a messiah without real hope of paradise on earth or in heaven and with no precise mission except that dictated by his ever-changing temperament.

"I am not sure finally that he should be a novelist at all, or even a writer, despite formidable gifts. . . . One of the few sad results of the collapse of the Judeo-Christian ethical and religious systems has been the displacement of those who are absolutist by temperament and would in earlier times have been rabbis, priests, systematic philosophers. . . . Those who once would have been fulfilled in Talmudic debates . . . have turned to writing novels, and worse, to the criticism of novels."

Vidal's characterization of Mailer as a messiah had touched a critical nerve. In 1962 Diana Trilling elaborated on this provocative idea. "His moral imagination," she wrote in *Encounter*," is the imagination not of art but of theology, theology in action. . . . Mailer is an anti-artist, deeply distrustful of art if only because it puts a shield between the perception and the act. His writer's role, as he conceives it, is much more messianic than creative." And she concludes: "If we listen closely, we perhaps hear his insistence as less the expression of personal authority than a call to a time when religion was still a masculine discipline—a call, that is, to a Hebraic world, still molded in the image of the stern father, Moses. From Moses to Marion Faye, with a stop-over at Marx."

Mailer's Marxist mentor, Jean Malaquais, today calls Mailer one of the least Jewish-conscious writers in America. In a literal sense this is true, but Malaquais fails to see Mailer's Old Testament underpinnings, which by 1959 were coming into sharper view. Living in the secure Jewish environment of Crown Heights and attending Hebrew school as a boy, he had been indelibly impressed by the rich symbolism and moral authority of the Old Testament. He had repressed these influences at Harvard, but now, as he learned more about the amoral mutations of modern society, he was partially reverting to his ancestral values.

As Mailer retreated to a kind of moral primitivism, he came to scorn anything that infringed on man's capacity for individual heroism, even godliness: technology, modern architecture, and contraceptives. Since his moral scheme was based on the stern patriarchal image of Moses, or even Jehovah, women were necessarily seen as mysteries. They were to be revered, as he revered his mother, Fanny, but they were subsidiary to the mythic work at hand. It is not very surprising that Mailer should have six wives and eight children, emerging as a supreme patriarchal figure. It was also inevitable that by the early 1970s he would have a confrontation with the feminists, who presented as much a threat to his sense of primitive masculine moral order as he to their political advancement.

Mailer faced an inherent problem in his messianic call: He was trying to use traditional moral values to shape a modern revolution. H. L. "Doc" Humes, a novelist and cofounder of *The Paris Review* who became friendly with Mailer in the late 1950s, saw this dichotomy in Mailer, but he believes it is one reason why he has become such an important "bridge figure" to the postwar generation. "Norman," he says, "has himself said that he would probably be happiest teaching at a yeshiva. He has that Talmudic approach to life and reality which is part of the social conditioning of the thirties and forties. He can remember the Depression and the war with great clarity, whereas many of us postwar writers who were a few years younger cannot. His main contribution to literature is that he's a bridge figure for many of us. Dreiser through Hemingway through Mailer—all bridged the period between the neo-Victorian and the modern age."

As a stern patriarchal figure who fought his way to the literary mountaintop, "Papa" Hemingway was clearly a man of heroic proportions to Mailer. In the introduction to *Advertisements* he wrote of his admiration for the master: "Every American writer who takes himself to be both major and macho must sooner or later give a faena which borrows from the self-love of a Hemingway style." But Mailer intended to better Hemingway. Mailer the Messiah would try to outdo Hemingway the Hero.

Mailer and Hemingway almost met shortly before *Advertisements* was published. But what could have been a celebrated fabled encounter between two champions, one the embodiment of upper-middle-class Anglo tradition, the other a feisty Talmudic challenger, never came to pass. Mailer by this time had become friends with George Plimpton, one of the founding editors of *The Paris Review*. Plimpton, who had returned to New York, was noted for throwing large, eclectic literary parties at his town house on Seventy-second Street near the East River. It was at one of his own parties that he met Mailer.

"Norman came here to a party, and we all went out afterward," Plimpton now recalls. "He was at that stage—not that it ever left him—where he admired people who do something skillfully, and it didn't matter what it was. After this party he saw me backing my Mercedes sports car down Seventy-second Street at a terrific clip. I was told he was tremendously taken with this for some reason. Of course, he was also interested in boxing and some of the other things I'd done, such as *The Paris Review*, so there was a sort of kinship. I've always admired him enormously, although sometimes he made me quite nervous because he was at that stage where you weren't certain what was going to happen, what was going to set him off or what the various keys were to his stability."

This volatility interfered with Mailer's meeting Hemingway. Hemingway was in town visiting Plimpton, and the two of them, along with A. E. Hotchner, Hemingway's biographer, were having dinner when Plimpton tried to demonstrate to Hemingway what Mailer liked to do at the time, which was thumb wrestle.

"Hemingway was very bad at it and didn't like the game particularly," recalls Plimpton, "so he just began applying pressure with his grip. I remember being lifted right out of my seat by the force. It was that day that I had asked Hemingway if he would like to meet Norman, and he said, 'Yes, that would be interesting.' But Hotchner, who was with us, said, 'No, don't.' I think he thought it was either going to be uncomfortable or that they wouldn't get along. So I couldn't continue with this invitation. I think Norman was very upset because I had told him what I was going to do, and he wanted very much to meet Hemingway. He stayed by the phone, waiting. They probably would have had a lot of fun, although this was a time in Norman's life when he was hugely competitive, so it might not have worked out at all."

When *Advertisements* was actually published, Hemingway and Plimpton bought the book together. Hemingway would later characterize it in a letter to *The Paris Review* editor as a "ragtag assembly of [Mailer's] rewrites, second thoughts and ramblings, shot through with occasional brilliance." Papa was hardly ready to relinquish his crown to the boy from Brooklyn.

❦

Although responses such as Hemingway's were clearly not what Mailer had hoped for, the publication of *Advertisements* was gaining him greater recognition, even notoriety. An excerpt in *Esquire* increased this new visibility. The piece exposed the psychic mauling Mailer felt he had undergone at the hands of the literary establishment with *The Deer Park*. Entitled "The Mind of an Outlaw," it set Mailer up as an antiestablishment figure who was bravely battling the callous giants of publishing, all of whom were running scared from the threats of censorship. Since Mailer revealed his heavy usage of pot, Seconal, Benzedrine, and finally mescaline, he was also seen by some as a new literary cult hero.

A young editor at *Esquire*, Harold Hayes, had bought the first-serial excerpt because he had read "The White Negro" in *Dissent* and was interested in *Advertisements*. In addition Mailer's new work seemed tailored to the editorial profile the magazine was trying to develop. As Hayes says, "This happened to intersect with the desire of the young editors of that day to try to make the magazine a bit more vigorous and more literary, particularly more literary in terms of our generation rather than the generation that dominated the magazine from the earliest years through the fifties. Mailer was one of a number of writers we were looking to. Baldwin was another, and Styron, and Vidal a little later. They were a group that represented a very significant advancement in their literary attitudes toward this country and toward things that were going on."

The Mailer excerpt, published in November 1959, was one of the pieces that set the future tone for the magazine, although in retrospect Hayes is amazed at the number of demands Mailer made during the negotiations. Through Mailer's lawyer, Charles Rembar, Hayes had to agree to mention the piece on the cover, above any other announcements. In addition Mailer himself would choose what was to be used from *Advertisements*, and he would title the piece. As Hayes recalls, "I had long conversations with Rembar about his terms. The thing that was unprecedented was that anybody would tell us what to do with our cover. Also, in those days we insisted on our right to title and subtitle our own pieces. Mailer's were very rough terms.

"But," Hayes adds, "Mailer was very astute. He pulled out the one piece—which he titled "The Mind of an Outlaw"—that if we had been sharp and aware, we would have chosen. It was the one he thought worked for *Esquire* at the time, and he was dead right. Moreover, I think he gained immensely by that intersection at that moment—that is, his arrival in our magazine when it was trying to become what it later became. It propelled him into a different dimension in his career."

The arrival of Mailer at *Esquire* was indeed a turning point for the writer. The following spring Clay Felker, another young editor at *Esquire* who later went on to found *New York* magazine, asked Mailer to write about the Democratic National Convention, launching Mailer on a career of political journalism that would eventually win him a Pulitzer Prize and a National Book Award.

The circumstances under which Felker proposed the political piece to Mailer were quite casual, even accidental. Felker had gone to a jazz nightclub called the Five Spot, which he used to frequent. He had written an article for *Esquire* entitled "Upper and Lower Bohemia" and as a result had come to know the owner of the club, Joe Termini, quite well. The Five Spot was jammed that night, but Termini always saw to it that Felker got a table. Termini also assumed that Felker knew Norman Mailer, who was there that night with Adele, Mickey Knox, and Adele's sister, whom Knox later married. Termini decided to seat Felker at Mailer's table.

"I was very uneasy," Felker recalls. "I had never met Mailer before, and he and Adele proceeded to get into a terrific fight. Norman wasn't saying anything, but Adele was exploding all over the place, saying things like, 'We're all shit; we don't add up to anything. You guys think you're significant, but it's all shit.' I'd never seen a fight like that before—the bitterness on her part and her language stunned me. Norman was smiling and almost totally silent. He seemed to be kind of amused by it, and this drove her into greater furies, because he wasn't fighting back. She was really goading him, saying that all their lives were worthless.

"At one point she said, 'I want to get out of here,' so Norman threw the car keys onto the table, and she took them and left. The others stayed. So there I was left alone with Norman and the others, and we started to talk. I talked about the one possible common denominator I could have with him, which was his doing something for *Esquire*. I asked him if he had ever thought about journalism, and he said he had."

"Have you ever covered politics?" Felker asked Mailer.

"No," Mailer replied, "but I'd like to think about it."

"What about covering the upcoming Democratic National Convention?"

"That was the origin of the thing," says Felker. "It stemmed from sheer embarrassment on my part. Part of it, too, of course, was that I had read his pronouncement in *Advertisements* that he had been running for President in his mind and wanted to create a revolution in the consciousness of our times. Pundits were going around saying the upcoming election would mark a turning point in American history and usher in a revolutionary age, so I thought, 'What is more natural than turning loose the revolutionary mind on a revolutionary event?' "

As a result of this impromptu exchange between Felker and Mailer, in mid-July 1960 the author went to Los Angeles to cover his first political convention. It would be, as Felker had anticipated, an historic moment in American politics. John F. Kennedy would be nominated over Adlai Stevenson, heralding in a new political era. Felker agreed to go to Los Angeles with Mailer because the writer felt he needed someone to introduce him to politicians. "A lot of people who are doing journalism for the first time," Felker says, "feel they need entry and accreditation to a publication or somebody to set things up. They don't realize how easy it is, but Norman obviously caught on immediately."

As it turned out, Mailer knew a number of people at the convention on his own. Everyone, of course, recognized his name and was flattered by his presence. "The Democrats fascinated him," Felker recalls, "and they in turn were fascinated by him." Not only were Arthur Schlesinger, Jr., and Max Lerner willing to interpret the machinations of the politics for the novice journalist, but politicos themselves traded information and ideas with him. Back-room operations not normally accessible to reporters were opened up long enough for Mailer to see what was going on.

When Mailer first arrived in Los Angeles, he had no idea of how he was going to write about the convention. Felker remembers that Mailer picked him up at the airport, and as they drove to their respective hotels, the author said, "The only political writing I know anything about is Marx. I'm not exactly sure how to go about it." But during the convention itself Mailer went up to Felker and told him, "I know how to do this now."

After Kennedy's nomination Mailer flew to Provincetown and began to write his article. In early August he called Felker and asked him to come up and take a look at the first part to see if it was all right. Felker flew to the Cape, and after reading Mailer's first efforts he knew he had an important piece. "I said to him, 'This is terrific; this is great,' and in fact it was much better than I expected."

Mailer had done far more than simply cover the convention. He had essentially grafted the ethos of "The White Negro" on to John F. Kennedy, sculpting Kennedy as the hero, the prince of the "unstated aristocracy of the American Dream." To Mailer, Kennedy had come to represent a romantic liberation from the sterile dullness of the 1950s. The writer sought to portray the politician as a modified archetype of his own hipster hero.

The choice between Kennedy and the Republican nominee, Richard M. Nixon, was a clear one in Mailer's mind. "So, finally, would come a choice," Mailer wrote, "which history had never presented to a nation before—one could vote for glamour or for ugliness, a staggering and most stunning choice—would the nation be brave enough to enlist the romantic dream of itself . . .?"

Mailer had discovered his new existential hero in life rather than in fiction. But the dynamic myth he was so brilliantly weaving around Kennedy gave him momentary pause: Did the reality of the man measure up to the heroic image Mailer was constructing? Perhaps to verify his own perceptions, Mailer went to Hyannis Port that August to interview the candidate.

As Mailer waited in the compound living room before his first interview with Kennedy, he talked briefly with Jackie Kennedy and the surrounding entourage, which included Arthur Schlesinger, Jr., and his wife Marian, Jackie's brother-in-law, Prince Radziwill, writer Peter Maas, photographer Jacques Lowe, and press secretary Pierre Salinger. Mailer was feeling unnerved that day, for it was hot and he was wearing a black suit, the only unwrinkled one he had found in his closet. He had also had a raging fight with Adele at breakfast because all his summer shirts were in the laundry and he was forced to wear a heavier button-down. Chatting with the elite Kennedy group under the circumstances was disconcerting, and Mailer felt "like a drunk marine who knows in all clarity that if he doesn't have a fight soon it'll be good for his character but terrible for his constitution." Jackie, however, was charming to him. Mailer liked her that day, finding, prophetically, that she had "perhaps a touch of that artful madness which suggests future drama."

The initial interview with Kennedy was short but relevant to the subjective scheme Mailer was developing in his piece. The first thing the future President said was that he had read Mailer's books. "Yes," he said, "I've read . . ." There was an uncomfortable pause during which Mailer realized no title had come immediately to his mind. But then Kennedy said, "I've read *The Deer Park* and . . . the others." As Mailer would point out in his *Esquire* piece, this "startled me, for it was the first time in a hundred similar situations, talking to someone whose knowledge of my work was casual, that the sentence did not come out, 'I've read *The Naked and the Dead* and . . . the others.' If one is to take the worst and assume that Kennedy was briefed for this interview . . . it still speaks well for the striking instincts of his advisors."

Kennedy's remark about *The Deer Park* was indeed well-rehearsed. As author Peter Maas who was there, recalls, there was even a problem in getting Kennedy to talk to Mailer at all. "Pierre Salinger had gone along with letting this interview happen," says Maas, "but he was getting a lot of heat from Kennedy about it. Kennedy was suddenly saying, 'Why do I need an interview with Norman Mailer?' Other Kennedy advisers were very concerned about it. They saw Norman as an unguided missile and weren't sure when the piece was going to come out. From their point of view it was full of land mines. At that time in his life Norman was not viewed as Mr. Stability.

"I said to Pierre, 'Look, I know a perfect way to handle Norman. The one thing he cannot stand is somebody coming up to him and saying, Mr. Mailer, I loved your novel *The Naked and the Dead.* He just goes up the wall. The book he likes best is *The Deer Park*, and if you really want him eating out of your hand, have Kennedy say this. But string it out a little. The timing has to be just right.'

"Pierre told me afterward that Kennedy got up and walked toward Mailer with his hand extended and said, 'Mr. Mailer, I really loved your book—' and then he paused. Pierre said you could almost see Norman getting uptight. Suddenly Kennedy said, '*The Deer Park*,' and, according to Pierre, Norman just melted."

Mailer's dress for the occasion stood out. "Everybody was running around in cutoffs and sandals," says Maas. "One of the things I had always noticed about Norman is that he wants to be different. This time he apparently decided not to be different, and he was different in spades. He had on a three-piece suit, and it was a hot day, and everyone was dressed in beach garb except Norman. He was sweating, but he never took off his jacket."

Since Kennedy didn't have much time, a longer interview was scheduled for the following day. The candidate told Mailer to bring along whomever he liked. Norman deliberated and brought Adele, whose enthusiasm for Jackie Kennedy further cemented Mailer's psychic links to the future first couple. He went back to Provincetown and added a few paragraphs to his piece, "secretly relieved to have liked them, for . . . how would I have rewritten it if I had not liked him?"

❦

In early September Mailer handed the article in to *Esquire* with the title "Superman Comes to the Supermarket." As he gave it to Felker, he told him it was the most important thing he had done since "The White Negro." The *Esquire* staff was equally excited. With only forty-five days until publication they cleared away nine pages for it to run in. *Esquire* usually required a three-month lead time, but Mailer's piece, they knew, had to run in the November issue to reach the newsstands by October 15, three weeks before the presidential election. There was clearly no time to develop any graphics, so Harold Hayes suggested to Felker that he write interstitial summary headlines—in the mode of nineteenth-century chapter headings—to break the piece up visually. The very same day Mailer handed in the article, Felker wrote the headlines and the story went into production.

A problem immediatley arose with Arnold Gingrich, the publisher an editor-in-chief of the magazine. Gingrich decided he didn't like the title; he wanted to change the word *Supermarket* to *Supermart*, believing "Superman Comes to the Supermart" was more alliterative and had the right rhythm. There were several other underlying reasons for the change. As Felker recalls, "Gingrich would sometimes rebel against our running the magazine, because we were changing it quite rapidly. He didn't like that, so occasionally he would come in and make some little change to show he still had authority. But he also didn't like Mailer, and he thought the piece was junk. He kept putting it down and saying, 'This isn't writing; it's just smearing anything on the page that comes into his head.'"

Harold Hayes also remembers Gingrich's feelings about Mailer but points to another cause for the disagreement. "Mailer's posturing seemed ludicrous inside the magazine, ludicrous," Hayes recalls. "The blustering and the Hemingway machismo. *Esquire* had published Hemingway, and Gingrich had edited his copy, so he wasn't about to be intimidated by some self-proclaimed literary giant who was really on his way up and hadn't yet achieved that stature. Gingrich just decided no, he was going to call the piece 'Superman Comes to the Supermart,' and he did."

The younger staff members were upset, feeling that Mailer's title was fine. But Felker knew it was more improtant to let the piece run than to quibble with Gingrich, especially since the editor was now threatening not to publish it at all. Mailer had no idea of the real trouble his article was in, and when he received his check with an invoice that read "Superman Comes to the Supermart," he immediately called Felker to complain. To appease him, Felker assured Mailer the word *Supermarket* would be put back in.

Three days before the issue came out, however, Mailer ran into Felker at a party, and the editor told him the change had not been made. "You can't tell a writer," Felker says, "that the editor of a publication doesn't like his piece. So I was in the middle of an uncomfortable situation because I couldn't explain to Mailer why this minor change took place in the title. I remember feeling very unhappy about it, but I was also very surprised that he was so upset by a title."

When Mailer finally saw the published article in mid-October, he wrote a biting letter to *Esquire*, which was printed in the January 1961 issue. In the letter he objected to the title change, the "intercalated small headlines," and a ten-year-old photograph of him which ran in Felker's "Backstage at Esquire" column. "You gotta treat the hot writer right or you lose him like you just lost me," Mailer wrote. This was the beginning of several disagreements with the magazine, and although his relations with Felker were more or less severed, he would start writing for *Esquire* again two years later.

When "Superman Comes to the Supermart" was published, it had not been mentioned on the cover because of Gingrich's opposition. It caused a stir nontheless. "Everybody talked about it," Felker recalls. "It made an enormous impact and caused a lot of young writers to begin to think about politics." Harold Hayes adds, "That really set the tone for many, many things to come for him and for us."

Pete Hamill, then a young journalist working at the *New York Post* who would become Mailer's friend by the following year, recalls the impact of Mailer's "Superman" article. "When it came out, it went through journalism like a wave," Hamill says. "Something changed. Everybody said, 'Uh, oh. Here's another way to do it.' Mailer had altered the form, and you said, 'Okay. It's not the same, and you've got to deal with that.' Everybody in the business, guys my age, were talking about it. Norman took political journalism beyond what the best guys—Mencken, Teddy White, Richard Rovere—had done. Rather than just a political sense there was a moral sense that came out of the piece."

Mailer himself understood the importance of the article. As he said in *The Presidential Papers* in 1963, "This piece had more effect than any other single work of mine, and I think this is due as much to its meretriciousness as to its merits. I was forcing reality, I was bending reality like a field of space to curve the time I wished to create. . . . Around New York there was a turn in sentiment; one could feel it; Kennedy now had glamour."

Mailer's work strengthened the Democratic candidate's image, but with his grandiose ego Mailer went so far as to believe that he had actually won the election for Kennedy. This conviction propelled Mailer into a "Napoleonic mood," in which, he later admitted, his sense of reality was "extravagant." The piece on Kennedy and the convention had given Mailer his first heady sense that he might have the power to directly affect political reality through his work. But Mailer knew that the real power to effect change in society lay with Kennedy, not with Mailer, and in politics, not in writing about politics. Mailer had set Kennedy up as the existential hero who mirrored his *own* ambitions. The writer now wanted to claim some of that heroism for himself.

The Kennedy article had intensified Mailer's messianic nature. The man who had said he had been running for President for years in the privacy of his mind and who had just transmuted a handsome young politician into a hipster hero saw the possiblity of turning writing into action. Just as he had imitated Hemingway and become an internationally acclaimed novelist, now Mailer was being seduced by the aura of John F. Kennedy and dreamed of political power.

After the *Esquire* piece was published, Mailer decided to run for mayor of New York City.

• X •

THE STABBING

Mailer had found a new, truer style and had developed more confidence in his work. But the timing of his mayoral bid, on the Existential Party ticket, still was not propitious. If politicians are judged on their charisma and their ideas, they are also measured by the nature of their personal lives. During the past six months Mailer's life had been publicly marred by several incidents which raised doubts about his emotional stability.

The previous May, Mailer had helped lead a group of people who went to City Hall Park in the midst of an air-raid drill and refused to take shelter. Then, only one week after Mailer had returned from the Democratic Convention in July 1960, he was in a Provincetown courtroom defending himself against a drunk-and-disorderly charge. The incident had taken place on the evening of June 9 at about 1:10 A.M. After pub crawling Mailer and Adele were walking to their summer rental, the Hawthorne House, a beautiful large Provincetown landmark set on a hill. As they made their way through the deserted streets, a police car was making its silent rounds.

Like many summer resorts, Provincetown has two conflicting cultures: the natives, in this case either Protestant New Englanders or Catholic Portuguese fishermen, and the summer people, a group of writers, artists, homosexuals, and beats, many from New York. The difference between the two cultures created certain tensions, and the summer people believed that the Provincetown police sided with the natives and came down hard on them.

When Mailer saw the police car gliding up the street, he became defiant. He mockingly yelled out, "Taxi! Taxi!" Adele, aware of the possible consequences, wisely said, "Be quiet, you damned fool!" But once again Mailer yelled, "Taxi!" The police car went slowly around the corner and then circled back, pulling in front of the Mailers as they were about to cross the street.

Two policemen got out, and one of them asked if Mailer had yelled "Taxi." Mailer said he had. "Does this car look to you like a taxi?" one of them asked. Mailer exacerbated the situation even further by replying, "Well, you know—that thing on the top." The policeman told Mailer to move on, but by now the author's ego was challenged, and he brazenly answered, "I'll move on when you get out of my way."

This did it. The two cops grabbed Mailer and shoved him into the car while he yelled at Adele, "You're my witness, I'm not resisting arrest!" When they got to the police station, however, Mailer's passive resistance turned slightly more active. The two policemen attempted to "assist" Mailer into the station house, but Mailer tried to duck away from and sidestep their firm grasps. In the process one of the cops fell, and then a billy club came down on Mailer's head from the rear. As Mailer told the *New York Post* several weeks later, "I kept standing but I think it took a bit away from my pride to resist because the form my thoughts next took were liberal rather than radical: Give up a little or they'll beat your head in."

Mailer had to have thirteen stitches as a result of the clubbing, and he was put in a cell without a bed or toilet. When one of the two policemen came to tell Mailer that he had actually cut his head on a car bumper, Mailer asked him if he was Catholic. He said he was. "You'll go to hell for lying!" Mailer yelled at him.

At 3:30 A.M. Adele arrived with the fifty-dollar bail, but when she saw her husband's bandaged head, she was incensed. "Look what you've done to my husband. You'll wish you'd never begun this." She was right, for the policemen had not realized that Mailer was a prominent writer, nor could they have known that he would eventually defend his own case. Mailer's rationale for conducting his own defense was that an out-of-town lawyer would be resented whereas a local lawyer would not attack the police. Mailer wanted the Provincetown police to get what he believed was coming to them.

On the morning of the trial, July 23, 1960, Mailer and Adele, who was dressed in somber black, decided to use the old family sedan, rather than the new Triumph TR-3 Mailer had recently bought, to drive to the courthouse. Adele was even sent back inside to put on stockings when Mailer discovered she wasn't wearing any. Mailer's old friend Dwight Macdonald, who lived nearby, was with them. He was covering the trial for *The New Yorker;* a host of other writers were there from various publications.

"Adele was terribly nervous about testifying," Macdonald recalls. "But Norman told her he would only ask her simple questions, like 'Did I have steak for dinner?' She eventually came through it okay. Norman also invited all of his hippie friends to come to the trial and there was a terrible moment when the judge discovered one of them smoking pot in the rear and had him put out.

"But the judge was absolutely marvelous. He kept saying, 'You don't know the rules, so we'll give you plenty of leeway, Mr. Mailer.' Norman himself alternated between his Harvard accent and his southern drawl, depending on the voltage he required."

Mailer had written certain questions on cards in advance of the trial and had hoped to use them when questioning the officers. Two such questions were: "Are you aware that people in the town believe they have a bullying and brutal police force?" and "Do you know that the nickname for the police here is the Gestapo?" But Judge Gershom Hall, a circuit-court judge from nearby Harwichport, pointedly told Mailer that these questions were not pertinent. Mailer found it difficult to refrain from interpretation and kept drawing conclusions as he posed his questions.

"The judge," Macdonald remembers, "kept telling Norman that he mustn't call the police chief a "cobra." Norman said, 'Well, I'll try not to, but if I do, it's complete absence of mind on my part and I beg pardon in advance." As Macdonald noted in *The New Yorker*, "It was the legal vs. the novelistic mind."

Mailer could not resist asking one of the officers: "Do you ever have bad dreams about violence?" before the judge stopped him. Mailer eventually took the stand himself and described his "rumble" with the police, admitting he may have acted "a little coy" with them. "I was a little high," he went on, "but I don't get drunk on four drinks. That night, I was irritable because I had stopped smoking two days earlier. I was worried about myself when they began hitting me. I have a bad temper. They may have thought I was a dangerous beatnik; maybe they look at television too much."

In his summing up Mailer was surprisingly moderate, a sign of what some consider his essentially bourgeois nature, one which eventually seeks compromise, even reveals a kind of hidden modesty. "A middle ground may apply here. A man has had a few drinks and is sassy, but I question whether this is a cause for arrest. . . . I don't want to be flowery. I've been coming here ten times in the last fifteen years. I like Provincetown, and there's no reason it can't have a police force that is as good as the rest of the town."

After a brief recess Judge Hall found Mailer guilty of drunkenness but innocent of disorderly conduct. After admitting that the police had been a little too thin-skinned, the judge turned to Mailer and added, "I advise you in the future to show more respect to the police." The case was dismissed from court but not from the public's mind. It became the stuff of notorious legend. This was fine for Mailer's growing reputation as the Peck's Bad Boy of literature but awkward for a prospective mayoral candidate, no matter how unseriously his candidacy was viewed.

❦

The air-raid and taxi incidents took place some months before Mailer's decision to run for mayor, so one might argue that he had yet to prepare himself for the larger responsibilities he was so anxious to assume. But in the following months Mailer's belligerence did not seem to wane. By the fourteenth of November, five days before he intended to announce that he was running for Mayor, Mailer was again arrested on a disorderly conduct charge, this time in New York City, the town he hoped to run.

The incident took place sometime after midnight at Birdland, a club at 1678 Broadway, at Fifty-Second Street. Mailer, who had come to the club with a girl, was presented with a bill for $7.60, and when he tried to pay by credit card, the manager, Oscar Goodstein, explained that the law forbade liquor purchases on credit. According to Goodstein, Mailer then hurled profane language at him. Goodstein called the police, and Mailer was soon arrested. The next day in the Magistrates Court he pleaded not guilty, and a hearing was scheduled for November 22. As he left court, Mailer told reporters, "The guy thought I was rude, but of course I was not." This was two days after

Mailer, with other writers, had drafted a petition to Governor Rockefeller asking for an inquiry into New York police operations.

Mailer was intent on pursuing his mayoral bid despite his notoriety, but only a few sporadic attempts at shaping either a platform or a constituency had been made. George Plimpton recalls that Mailer, accompanied by his large poodle, had occasionally turned up at his door at one in the morning to get him to go campaigning, but it was always too late. Writer Noel Parmentel, Jr., remembers that he, Seymour Krim, and poet Allen Ginsberg were informally designated press secretaries, although the only position paper ever drawn up was one which called for Police Athletic League jousting tournaments to curb juvenile delinquency.

Novelist Doc Humes had become a close acquaintance of Mailer's by this time and was actively involved in the mayoral campaign. The two men were neighbors: The new apartment at 250 West 94th Street that Norman and Adele were living in was a sublet Humes had gotten for them in his building. Humes remembers Mailer's state of mind at the time. "It was a period when he was grim-faced every day. He wasn't sleeping well, he was using a lot of Demerol and alcohol, and he had collateral worries about his work."

Humes points out that despite Mailer's desire to win the election, he refused to pay attention to the mechanics of the campaign. "Norman was taking the race very seriously," Humes reflects. "He wanted to win. I was trying to get him to run on a conceptual platform with the intention of losing, but the idea of doing anything to lose is very difficult for Norman to accept. It was difficult to get him to even focus on the mechanics. He was very romantic in his approach to the campaign."

Mailer had written one position paper of sorts and intended to read it at the official announcement of his campaign scheduled for Tuesday, November 22, 1960. It was an open letter to Fidel Castro, calling him "worthy of Cortes" for "sending the wind of new rebellion to our lungs." Mailer went on to describe America's own tyranny, indicating that the American reaction against Castro, which by then had grown acute, was due to the fear that he would incite a rebellious spirit here. Mailer also contended that the Communists were using Cuba as a foil, hoping America would attack the island so that the rest of Latin America would be alienated. This kick-off speech to Mailer's campaign was an oddly prophetic statement which foreshadowed the Bay of Pigs, but it had little to do with running the City of New York.

If Mailer's political platform was dubious, his constituency was even more so. Mailer wanted to meld the dispossessed of the city—junkies, prostitutes, victims of police brutality, the whole "Third World" of New York—with the social, political, and artistic elite in whose circles he traveled. Only Mailer's visionary mind could have hoped to synthesize these disparate elements under his aegis without any kind of political base.

❦

On the evening of November 19, 1960, Mailer hosted a large party in his apartment to informally announce his candidacy for Mayor. That night he realized his dream of political power might not be fulfilled. George Plimpton remembers that on that afternoon, while he was watching the Yale-Harvard football game on television, Mailer kept calling him. He wanted Plimpton to bring several people to the party that night. "He wanted people in power," recalls Plimpton. "He wanted to impress his constituency. The fire commissioner. The police commissioner. Then he wanted me to get Saduradin Aga Kahn, who had an important position at the United Nations, Tammy Grimes, who was to represent Broadway, and, for some odd reason, Brendan Behan. God knows what he was supposed to represent. There were about seven of them in all, and they all had positions which Norman felt would enhance him in the eyes of this vast other group he had invited to the party, a sort of Third World that he wanted to represent in his mayoralty campaign.

"He felt that if he could only get the prostitutes and the junkies and all these people who usually don't vote, he'd really have a constituency. The people I was supposed to bring—and maybe others were assigned to bring other people as well—were meant to be impressed by Norman's constituency, and the constituency was likewise supposed to be impressed by the important people Norman knew."

Plimpton obligingly interrupted his football game to make the phone calls, but of the people Mailer wanted, the only one who agreed to come was musician Peter Duchin. When Plimpton and Duchin arrived at Mailer's sprawling upper West Side apartment later that evening, *New York Post* columnist Leonard Lyons was already on his way out. Anywhere from a hundred to three hundred people were milling through the rooms at various times, and among the literary people, boxers, minor politicians, and fringe figures only a few recognizable celebrities such as actor Anthony Franciosa could be spotted. There were also several notable literary guests, including Allen Ginsberg, Norman Podhoretz, Delmore Schwartz, critic Richard Gilman, Lewis and Jay Presson Allen, and Seymour Krim, but the power elite of New York was conspicuously absent. The Third World figures, many of whom Mailer didn't know personally, dominated the scene. As George Plimpton recalls, "None of the powerful people came, and Norman's constituency, who probably wouldn't have cared anyway, got drunk. The party was an utter disaster; the thought must have been running through Norman's head at the time."

As the party wore on and the drinking got heavier, an undercurrent of violence began to develop. Richard Gilman remembered the scene: ". . . fights quickly broken up in corners, sexual stalkings and contretemps, envies and jealousies staging themselves as group therapy." By midnight Mailer, sensing his lack of control, became increasingly belligerent. In his column the next week Lyons would write that Mailer had been in the living room clutching a photograph of himself taken at Birdland the night he was arrested. "If you want to see it," Mailer challenged a guest at the party, "try to take it from me." Lyons added, "It's been quite apparent, for more than a year, that the gifted writer needed psychiatric help. He seemed to be ever wanting to fight everybody—including City Hall."

"There was a strong element of pathology, not only on the part of Norman but in other people who were around," recalls Doc Humes. "It was a spooky evening. You could cut the tension with a knife. It was exactly the kind of atmosphere that Norman in his state should have avoided."

Larry Alson remembers a strange incident at the party. Someone offered Mailer a job as a "color" commentator for the New York Yankees, which was the last thing a seriously depressed writer with mayoral ambitions needed to hear. Alson also recalls that people at the party kept coming up to Mailer and challenging him to fight. He responded, and the threat of violence was soon beginning to emanate from Mailer himself. He went down to the street and tried to provoke his ex-boxer friend Roger Donoghue into a fight even though the party had been held partly in honor of Donoghue's birthday.

Other friends were also challenged to fight. As Random House editorial director Jason Epstein recalls, "I got to the party, and Norman tried to box with me. I don't know anything about boxing, so I just held my hand out as if to make him go away. I didn't touch him, and he fell over. Later he had gone downstairs and was chasing George Plimpton up the street, kicking George in the leg like a little dog chasing a pony."

Plimpton describes a scene of mayhem on the street below. "When one left the party, there was Mailer down on the street fighting people as they came out of the apartment house," he remembers. "He was in pretty bad shape. He wanted to fight with everybody; he was sick of them, and of course they had had a rotten time. Donoghue had popped him, and he wanted to fight me. There were a couple of policemen across the street who should have locked him, or all of us, up, which would have been a break because then Norman wouldn't have gone through what he did."

Lewis and Jay Allen, sensing the violence, also decided to leave. "The party was getting very rough," says Lew Allen, "and Norman was being very belligerent. When Jay and I left the party, he rode down in the elevator with us to get us a cab. He was very high-strung and got in a fight with somebody in the elevator who wasn't even from the party. He had a bloody nose by this point." Norman Podhoretz concurs that the atmosphere had turned sour. "It was a very ugly night. There was a lot of bad feelings in the air, most of it emanating from Mailer."

In the midst of this debacle Adele approached Harriet Sohmers, the woman she had fought with the previous summer in Provincetown, and said she wanted to talk. Sohmers was instinctively alarmed, but Adele allayed her fears. She took Sohmers into their large, old-fashioned white-tile bathroom and locked the door. "I want to tell you that Norman made me do that in Provincetown," Sohmers recalls Adele saying. "It was all his idea, and I felt terrible about it." Sohmers said she forgave her, and they both embraced, but Sohmer's main recollection is that Adele seemed frightened that Mailer would discover them together.

At about three in the morning, with only twenty guests remaining, Mailer acted out a little drama which parodied his own lack of a political power base. He commanded his guests to divide into two lines, one for those who were for him and one for those who were against him. When no one moved, he pushed almost everyone, including Adele, into the line of nonsupporters. Then he ordered the remaining few, including the family maid, Nettie Marie Biddle, into the supporting line. He kept insisting under his breath that the maid was the only one who had never betrayed him. Slowly the guests were able to separate themselves from this embarrassing spectacle and started to go home.

Only a handful of people were left by about 4:30 A.M., when a very drunk Mailer walked in from the street with a black eye, a torn lip, and blood all over his fancy bullfighter's shirt. Adele took one look at him and spoke sharply. The accounts of her comment vary. George Plimpton was told that she said the equivalent of "You look like you've been rolled by a couple of sailors in the back streets." Others remember it as "You look like a woman with lipstick on your mouth." As Plimpton now says, "The whole evening was predicated on this sociopolitical thing that failed, and the last thing to be disappointed about is the one person who should stand by you."

This was the culmination of a disastrous drunken evening in which Mailer's ego had been severely battered. He took out a two-and-a-half-inch-long penknife and went at his wife, stabbing her in the upper abdomen and back. One stab wound was later described as three inches deep and three quarters of an inch wide, a "thrust near the heart."

Doc and Anna Lou Humes, who lived in an apartment downstairs, were asleep when a bleeding Adele was brought down to them on a mattress. Nobody wanted Mailer near her. She was put on a couch in their dining room and covered with blankets while Anna Lou Humes held her hand. "We didn't move her," recalls Doc Humes. "That was probably the thing that saved her life. We held her so she couldn't move." While Mrs. Humes consoled her, Adele moaned repeatedly and said, "Things like this don't happen to people like us. They happen to black people in Harlem and Puerto Ricans but not us." Over and over Adele said, "I can't believe this."

Humes instantly got on the phone and contacted a physician, Dr. Conrad Rosenburg. "The position of everybody," Humes now says, "was that we weren't going to volunteer anything unless asked. The effect on the Mailer child, the family, the psychological damage that might ensue, the publicity, all these factors were taken into consideration."

Dr. Rosenburg arrived and immediately took Adele to the University Hospital at Second Avenue and Twentieth Street by ambulance. She was admitted at 8:00 A.M. Sunday, about three and a half hours after being wounded. After arriving at the hospital Adele, to protect Mailer, told the attending physicians, including Rosenburg, that she had fallen on glass in their apartment, but the physicians were suspicious when they saw the severity of the wounds.

They notified the police, who were unable to talk to Adele that Sunday because she was undergoing an emergency operation. But by Monday afternoon, when her condition had stabilized, she reluctantly admitted to Detective Francis Burns that her husband had stabbed her. She told the detective she could give no reason why. "He was depressed. He just came at me with a funny look in his eyes. He didn't say a word. There was no reason. He just looked at me. Then he stabbed me."

❦

After Adele was taken to the hospital early that Sunday morning, Doc Humes went back up to Mailer's apartment to see if he could help him. "He was in a semisomnolent state," recalls Humes. "He wasn't just drunk; he was out of it totally. I don't think he really knew where he was." The Mailers' youngest daughter, Elizabeth Anne, who was then only a year and two months old, was in the apartment, and she was quickly brought down to the Humes place. Humes called Mailer's sister, Barbara, and her husband, Larry Alson, and told them to come and get the child. "Everyone was very concerned," says Alson, "because the baby was in the apartment with Norman, and they wanted us to get her out."

Later on that Sunday, before Adele was operated on, Mailer showed up at the hospital and had a lengthy discussion with the surgeon, Alson recalls. According to Adele's subsequent account in *The New York Mirror*, she told Detective Burns that Mailer had sneaked into her hospital room at 3:30 A.M. Monday morning and cautioned her not to talk to the police. She also told Burns that Mailer planned to visit her that Monday night, but she pleaded with him not to. "I don't want to see him; don't let him in," she told the detective.

While Adele was relating this to Burns on Monday, Mailer was taping a bizarre television interview with Mike Wallace in which he described the knife as an instrument of manhood. Mailer reiterated his intention to run for mayor of New York City and talked about the problem of juvenile delinquency, saying it would not be resolved by disarming the young hoods. "The knife to a juvenile delinquent is very meaningful," he told Wallace. "You see, it's his sword—his manhood." He suggested a better solution would be to hold annual gangland jousting tournaments in Central Park, "which would bring back the Middle Ages." When Wallace innocently asked about his black eye, Mailer grinned. "Yes," he said, laughing, "I got into quite a scrape Saturday night." Mailer's sense of reality had become more than "extravagant." He seemed to have lost all bearing.

Mailer visited his sister and brother-in-law shortly after the Wallace taping, and they pleaded with him to see a psychiatrist. Mailer actually met with an analyst that afternoon, but according to Larry Alson, "he gave a diagnosis of the situation which was far from the truth." The diagnosis never went on the record. As Mailer later told writer Brock Brower, "Let me say that what I did was by any measure awful. It still wasn't insane. My whole feeling was that prison was far better than the mental hospital. I felt, just generally, that any man who was at all sensitive, who spent a year in an asylum, would come out insane."

Mailer decided to deliberately seek arrest. That Monday night at 10:30 he was found sitting quietly on a bench outside Adele's hospital room. Detective Burns, who had been waiting for Mailer, told him that he had spoken to his wife and was placing him under arrest. When he searched Mailer and found the penknife, Mailer told him he "always carried a knife." Burns later testified that Mailer denied stabbing his wife and said he wouldn't make any comments without a lawyer.

Mailer was taken to the West 100th Street police station and held overnight pending his appearance in Felony Court the following day. During this time Dr. Conrad Rosenburg, who had treated Adele, briefly interviewed Mailer to determine his mental condition. Rosenburg's report was read to the court on Tuesday: "In my opinion, Norman Mailer is having an acute paranoid breakdown with delusional thinking and is both homicidal and suicidal. His admission to a hospital is urgently advised."

Magistrate Reuben Levy of the Felony Court read Rosenburg's report into the record as Mailer, wearing a storm coat, stood silently beside his lawyer, Irving Mendelson. After the report was read, Mailer told the court he wished to speak. "Naturally," he said, "I have been a little upset, but I have never been out of my mental faculties. I only saw Dr. Rosenburg for thirty seconds or a minute. It's important for me not to be sent to a mental hospital, because my work in the future will be considered that of a disordered mind. My pride is that I can explore areas of experience that other men are afraid of. I insist that I am sane."

Magistrate Levy was not swayed by Mailer's testimony. "Your recent history," he said, "indicates that you cannot distinguish fiction from reality. In your interest and the public interest I have to commit you." That day Norman Mailer was admitted to Bellevue for psychiatric observation. Seymour Krim, who was in the courtroom, remembers Fanny Mailer's response when the reporters crowded around her. "My boy's a genius," she told them. "It was almost," says Krim, "as if she believed he was above the law. She was equally proud, defiant, and not ashamed in the least about expressing herself."

As soon as it was learned that Mailer had been committed to Bellevue Hospital, Channel 13, the local public television station, rushed the taped interview of Mailer and Mike Wallace onto the air that Tuesday night. The following day *New York Times* television critic Jack Gould angrily wrote: "It is hard to see the purpose of the showing beyond catering to morbid curiosity. Surely when a court rules that there may be uncertainty over an individual's ability, TV can wait until his case is clarified." But the *Times* itself was chronicling this case every step of the way, as were a number of other papers. Mailer had in some way been victorious. He had thrust himself into public consciousness more swiftly and completely with this one nightmarish act than he could have done with perhaps a decade of serious, sustained work.

Despite Fanny Mailer's defiant attitude in support of her son, Mailer himself was worried about having to go to Bellevue. As a college undergraduate he had run away from a job in a mental institution after one week. Moreover, Mailer's own psychological circuits were finely tuned to perceiving, even heightening, psychopathy in himself and others, and the task of proving himself sane when others were looking for insanity was especially unnerving. But after only two weeks in Bellevue a doctor named Jordan Lachman had, as Mailer put it, "the guts to let me out." In early December, Mailer was released on twenty-five hundred dollars bail after having been pronounced legally sane.

❦

On December 20 Mailer appeared in a Manhattan court to answer the earlier charges of disorderly conduct which had been leveled against him by the manager of Birdland. The original court hearing had been scheduled for the day that Mailer was sent to Bellevue, then postponed. At the new hearing the restaurateur, no doubt sensitive to Mailer's larger legal problems, withdrew his charges, and Mailer promised to pay the bill. Outside the courtroom he told reporters that Adele was "feeling fine" and that she would be in court the following day.

On December 21 Norman and Adele appeared together at Felony Court on Centre Street, where Adele refused to sign a complaint against her husband. Speaking through her lawyer, Sol Gelb, she said, "I have no complaint to make against anyone." Mailer's new lawyer on the case, Joseph Brill, asked that the case be adjourned until December 29, saying that there were certain points of law he was "researching" and that Mailer had only recently been granted bail. Magistrate Walter H. Gladwin agreed to Mr. Brill's request.

On December 29, amidst cries of "Cheek to cheek, Norman," Mailer and Adele were photographed smiling together in the press-room of the Centre Street courthouse, where two decades later Mailer would defend convict Jack Henry Abbott to a hostile press. Shortly afterward Mailer's lawyer moved for dismissal on the grounds that there was no complaint. It was denied, but the press had picked up a new drift to the case. Picture captions in the New York dailies read: "Adele and Norman Mailer Sit Arm in Arm" and "A Picture of Togetherness at Court Today."

The actual hearing did not take place until January 12, 1961, when Mailer and Adele again appeared at the Felony Court. The first witness called was Adele Mailer, who wore a soft-green velveteen dress and a simple necklace. She was asked by Assistant District Attorney William F. Reilly if she wished to sign a complaint against her husband. "My husband and I are perfectly happy together," she replied, "and I don't wish to make any." The prosecutor then handed her a police affidavit and asked her whether the allegations against her husband were true. Adele read it and returned it to Reilly, saying, "I just can't answer that. . . . I don't know."

When Magistrate Gladwin asked her to explain what had happened, Adele began, "There was a party and some people and I really don't remember . . ." The prosecutor then began to shoot questions at her: "Do you remember being cut?" "Do you recall being taken downstairs?" "Was your husband drinking?" Each time Adele replied that she didn't know or couldn't remember. When the penknife was shown to her and she was asked if she had seen it before, she replied,

"No." At the prosecutor's request Magistrate Gladwin declared her a hostile witness.

Mailer's lawyer, Joseph Brill, had no questions for Mrs. Mailer. The prosecution then called Dr. William Mackler, the physician who had treated Adele in the hospital. He described the wound and was excused with, again, no questions from Brill. Then the Mailers' housemaid and Detective Burns were called. At the end of the testimony defense lawyer Brill called for dismissal of the charge of felonious assault on two grounds: that no proper complaint had been made and that a prima facie case had not been presented. Magistrate Gladwin denied both motions and declared that the case be forwarded to the grand jury since, in his opinion, "a probable crime" had been committed.

On January 30, 1961, Mailer was indicted by the New York County Grand Jury on two counts of felonious assault and one of possession of a dangerous weapon. The bill was handed up to General Sessions judge Joseph A. Sarafite, and the arraignment was scheduled for February 2. On that day Mailer pleaded not guilty to both counts, and his lawyer was given two weeks to file motions attacking the validity of the indictment.

❦

Only four days after this, on the evening of Monday, February 6, Mailer returned to public life, giving a reading at the Young Men's Hebrew Association Poetry Center on Ninety-second Street and Lexington Avenue. The YMHA, which had also featured T. S. Eliot, W. H. Auden, and Marianne Moore that season, had invited Mailer to appear on its stage before what his friends would come to call "the Trouble." He had signed a contract with the Y shortly after returning from the Los Angeles convention in July, and it stipulated that he would read on February 6.

It was a welcome opportunity for Mailer, who felt the need to refocus public attention on his work rather than on his legal difficulties. He knew that the New York literary vultures would be out, circling his fragile psyche, ready to swoop down at the first signs of timidity. But Norman Mailer was not about to bow, troubles or no. Facing the prospect of a jail term for stabbing his wife, almost any other public figure would have conducted himself with decorum, but Mailer adopted a stance of bravado. Years later he would say that it was "better to expire as a devil in the fire than an angel in the wings." That night he played devil to the audience.

The auditorium of the Y was filled with seven hundred people curious to see how Mailer would deport himself. In a show of unity, Adele Mailer was also present. Mailer began by reading an assortment of nonfiction prose and bits of his play and then turned to some poems that he had begun after the stabbing.

Most of these poems were composed while Mailer was soaked in drink. Written in indecipherable longhand on little scraps of paper, they were then reworked the following morning. He would continue to write poems throughout that year, and as he mended, they gave a certain cohesion to his life. A collection of the fragments would be published the following March 1962 by Putnam's under the title *Deaths for the Ladies and Other Disasters*. The themes ranged from women to politics, but the emotional power behind them was clearly the stabbing. The most famous of these poems is called "Rainy Afternoon with the Wife":

So long
as
you
use
a knife,
there's
some
love
left.

The poems Mailer read that night were explicitly sexual, and he warned the YMHA audience in advance that they contained obscenity. Mailer also admitted that they were very bad poems but pointed out that the reading of bad poetry heightens an audience's appreciation of good poetry. After reading the first of these poems, he asked for a show of hands by those who found it offensive. A few hands were raised, but no one left the auditorium. As he continued reading, more hands were raised, but in general the audience encouraged him by laughing, occasionally even cheering. Then suddenly, while he was in the middle of reading a poem, the curtain came down in front of him.

The last two lines of the offending poem read as follows:

Dear Kike
I wish you were a dyke.

A few minutes later Mailer returned to the stage and informed the audience that the management had objected to his poems. While he didn't like the situation, he felt it would be best if everyone left quietly. As he disappeared behind the curtain, the crowd started cheering for Mailer, demanding that the management come out. When Mailer finally reappeared, beat poet Allen Ginsberg joined him on stage. Both asked that the audience leave, under protest, which they could demonstrate by a raising of hands. When the audience continued to cheer, Mailer asked for quiet, pointing out that any trouble might make it worse for him in his trial with its threat of eleven years in prison.

The following day *The New York Times* quoted Dr. William Kolodney, the educational director of the YMHA, who had ordered the curtain rung down, as saying he had taken action to end "a recital of wrong, obscene images and vocabulary which broke the limits of good taste from any point of view." He added, "People were laughing the way they do at dirty jokes in smoking cars."

Poet Allen Ginsbergwas angered by Kolodney's statements and wrote him saying it was "evil" to blame Mailer when the audience clearly was sympathetic with what he was doing. "I am not an intimate of Mailer nor, actually, a literary ally, since I wish he would turn his attention away from paranoiac sociology toward pure apocalyptic prophesy," Ginsberg asserted. But, he added, Mailer's consciousness that night was moving in the right direction. For that reason, Ginsberg felt, Kolodney's censorship was deplorable.

Mailer's reading was undoubtedly part bravado, but it was also an honest reflection of his own disordered state at the time. Although Dr. Kolodney had told the press it was the poems he objected to, he later amended this, saying he primarily objected "to the climate of Mr. Mailer's program as produced by commentary." But the newspaper accounts were already out, and Mailer's friends were afraid that they would influence the court and that he would be sent to jail.

It is not surprising that on March 9, in a sudden about-face, Mailer pleaded guilty to third-degree assault. Mailer told the press that he had decided to make this plea because he feared a trial would bring harmful publicity to his wife and children. Judge Mitchell D. Schweitzer set the sentencing date for April 28. Mailer could be sent to jail for a year and fined five hundred dollars, but finally on May 10 Judge Schweitzer postponed the sentencing until November 13 and put Mailer on probation. As the judge explained, Mailer had an "explosive temper," particularly after drinking, and the court wanted to see "whether a person like him will comply with a degree of supervision." Mailer's lawyer assured Judge Schweitzer that his client "has been and will be productive at the genius level."

Mailer and Adele had retained the public semblance of togetherness in order to help Mailer's legal situation, but once the crisis was over there was no longer anything to hold them together. They separated that March. As Mailer later said about their marriage, "The man wasn't good enough. The woman wasn't good enough. A series of psychic stabbings took place." The ten-year union was over.

In court on November 13, 1961, almost one year after the stabbing took place, Mailer received a suspended sentence with a probation period not to exceed three years. Mailer's lawyer told the court that during his supervision Mailer had behaved well, was working on a new book, and could make a contribution to society. Judge Schweitzer confirmed the probation report and noted that Mrs. Mailer had requested that the court be lenient with her husband. The headlines now read: "Norman Mailer Goes Free in Knifing Case."

❦

Eighteen years later Mailer would say of the incident: "A decade's anger made me do it. After that, I felt better." The stabbing had been, in its own horrific way, a catharsis; Mailer had been increasingly fascinated with his own hostility throughout the fifties. It had been a grueling decade for Mailer, one in which his anger had grown in direct proportion to the failure of his own best hopes.

If the forties had buoyed his talent and his dreams of heroism, the fifties had systematically crushed them. Mailer had fought back by instinctively mirroring the violence he felt was being done to him and by audaciously seeking out the most revolutionary antidotes to establishment strictures. In waging this personal battle against looming failure, Mailer had helped to shape the rebellious ideology of a new postwar radicalism, which would surface around the country in the sixties. With Kennedy's election, a new decade and a new era had dawned, one which Mailer had helped usher in with his *Esquire* piece. That November he voted in a presidential election for the first time since 1948. Mailer, of course, had dropped his idea of running for mayor of New York that year, but by the end of the decade he would renew his bid.

In stabbing Adele he had acted out the ultimate psychopathy he had expressed in "The White Negro." After the stabbing Mailer was no less provocative, but his rage was muted, and he had become aware of the depth of his own dark impulses. The Faustian advocate of psychopathy in the fifties would now evolve into an apocalyptic pundit in the sixties, a decade that would embrace rather than reject him.

• XI •

ENTERING THE SIXTIES

> At periodic moments in our history, our country has paused on the threshold of a new epoch in our national life, unable for a moment to open the door, but aware that it must advance if it is to preserve its national vitality and identity. One feels that we are approaching such a moment now. . . .
>
> The beginning of a new political epoch is like the breaking of a dam. Problems which have collected in the years of indifference, values which have suffered neglect, energies which have been denied employment—all suddenly tumble as in a hopeless, swirling flood onto an arid plain. . . .

These prophetic words, written by Arthur Schlesinger, Jr., in 1959 in an essay entitled "The New Mood in Politics," heralded a new decade, the sixties, which was to radically transform the direction of the political left and have a profound impact on the sensibility and career of Norman Mailer. Although the seeds of Schlesinger's "new political epoch" had been planted in the 1950s, when the older ideological left—the Socialists and the Communists of the 1930s—all but disappeared during the Eisenhower years, it was not until the sixties that the new movement emerged. Known as the New Left, it had its roots in the beats' drug and antiestablishment culture, in the Cuban revolution, in the evolving civil rights movement, and in such cultural prophets as C. Wright Mills, Paul Goodman—and Norman Mailer.

Like Mailer, the New Left was to be an ecumenical political and ethical mixture, avoiding narrow ideological labels. As Jack Newfield pointed out about the New Left in *A Prophetic Minority*, there is "an indifference to ideology, discipline, economics and conventional political forms. . . . It contains within it, and often within individuals, elements of anarchism, socialism, pacifism, existentialism, humanism, transcendentalism, bohemianism, Populism, mysticism and black nationalism."

Mailer, in "The White Negro," had been one of the first to synthesize these elements, but some New Leftists refused to see him as a comrade-in-arms. He was, they felt, not an activist but a writer observing from the sidelines. But years later such youthful activists as Jerry Rubin, Abbie Hoffman, and Jack Newfield recognized their debt to Mailer as a prophetic father of their movement. "How could they not dig Mailer?" Newfield asked in *The Village Voice*. "Mailer, who preached revolution before there was a movement. Mailer, who was calling LBJ a monster while slide rule liberals were still writing speeches for him. Mailer, who was into Negroes, pot, Cuba, violence, existentialism . . . and hipsters while the New Left was still a twinkle in C. Wright Mills' eye."

If the New Left had its origin in the 1950s, its first manifestations appeared in the spring of 1960 with lunch counter sit-ins, peace marches, a riot against the House Committee on Un-American Activities, and a "Fair Play for Cuba" advertisement in *The New York Times* protesting America's attitude toward Fidel Castro's alliance with the Communists. The ad was signed by a number of writers, including James Baldwin, Truman Capote, and Norman Mailer.

Lyle Stuart, who had been writing sympathetic pieces on Castro for his iconoclastic newspaper, *The Independent*, recalls that the *Times* ad marked the beginning of his own interest in the Fair Play committee. "Castro was a hero to everyone at that point, and he was still a hero to 95 percent of the Cuban people," Stuart says. "I guess Norman saw him as very admirable, courageous, and colorful. Castro was also perfectly suited to Norman's own romanticism."

Kennedy's election in November 1960 indicated a further shift in the political arena, which Mailer was one of the first to note in his "Superman" piece for *Esquire*. Jack Newfield believes Kennedy's defeat of Nixon was essential to the birth of the New Left. "If Nixon had won in 1960, I think the earliest protests would have been crushed in a McCarthyite paroxysm and the New Left aborted," he wrote. "Kennedy provided a friendly umbrella for the New Left to grow under and held up a vision of social idealism, represented by the Peace Corps, which led students to take the logical next step—into SNCC and the SDS."

But in April 1961, only five months after Kennedy was elected, the United States made an inept attempt to help anti-Castro rebels invade Cuba, precipitating the Bay of Pigs debacle. "Fair Play for Cuba" demonstrations sprang up, and Mailer joined one massive rally at Manhattan's Union Square. Some historians believe that this opposition to Kennedy's Cuban invasion marked the real beginnings of the New Left. It also gave Mailer a chance to align himself with the movement before it was intellectually fashionable, when no one could have predicted how widespread the New Left would become by the late sixties.

On April 27, 1961, only ten days after the Bay of Pigs invasion, Mailer published an open letter to Kennedy in *The Village Voice*. It was his first *Voice* contribution since he had left the paper in 1956, but the *Voice* had since moved further to the left and now shared Mailer's own political radicalism. Addressing the President as "Dear Jack," Mailer chastised JFK for listening to his CIA advisers on Cuba, implying that the chief executive would have been better served had he sought the counsel of Norman Mailer. It is America's artists, not the CIA, who preserve freedom, he told the young President. To substantiate his point, he enclosed the open letter he had written to Fidel Castro in November 1960, in which he had voiced the hope that Castro and Kennedy might meet to iron out their differences.

Shortly after the Bay of Pigs, Mailer even briefly thought of more direct action: going to Cuba himself to talk to Castro. The idea arose during a lunch with Lyle Stuart. The publisher had visited Cuba several times and knew Castro quite well. When Mailer implored Stuart to take his open letter directly to the Cuban premier, Stuart suggested that Mailer come to Cuba with him and give the letter to Castro himself. "Norman was very excited by the idea," Stuart recalls. "He asked me a lot of questions about Fidel, wanting to know what kind of fellow he was personally and how I felt about him."

Mailer agreed that he would go to Cuba with Stuart on his next trip. After Stuart arranged for a visa, which took a few months, he called Norman to say he was going down to Cuba in two weeks. Did Mailer still want to go? "Norman came up with something that was so transparent an excuse about not going that I did something dreadful: I laughed," Stuart says. "He was obviously frightened. It seemed funny to me, but things were never the same between us after that."

❦

If Mailer the writer was entertaining political ideas that would develop into revolutionary themes for the 1960s, Mailer the man was seeking to protectively align himself with the establishment. In early 1962, a little more than a year after he stabbed Adele and only a few months after he was put on probation after stretching society's tolerance to the breaking point, Mailer made a surprising match with Lady Jeanne Campbell, daughter of the Duke of Argyll and the granddaughter of the powerful British press magnate Lord Beaverbrook.

Many saw his marriage to Lady Jeanne Campbell as a search for respectability after his notoriety with Adele, but in some ways Lady Jeanne was the perfect complement to Mailer at the time. While Adele mirrored Mailer's emerging sexuality and rebellion in the early fifties, Lady Jeanne confirmed his sense of stature in the new liberal atmosphere. She also guaranteed the writer increased visibility in the media. It was not insignificant that Mailer was said to have stolen Lady Jeanne away from the media giant Henry Luce.

"Lady Jeanne," says Midge Decter, "had the blood of the Argylls in her, and she had also been Henry Luce's lady. That was irresistible to Norman. London society fascinated him, and she did as well. But she was a fairly simple, limited girl who had this role thrust upon her. His novelist's interest was piqued by mastering Lady Jeanne and her world."

Lady Jeanne Campbell and Adele Morales were essentially as different as two women could be. A large-boned English aristocrat, Lady Jeanne had none of Adele's Latin sensuality. Well-schooled, Lady Jeanne was a columnist on her father's paper, *The Evening Standard*, and was socially prominent in media circles and the better New York and European drawing rooms. If Adele had evolved into a strong woman under Mailer's tutelage, Lady Jeanne came equipped with a fierce independence. She was not inclined to follow Mailer's more imaginative lead, and it would be a stormy marriage from the start. As Mailer would later comment: "At least I can say I went two rounds with the best light heavyweight the British ever sent over." Lady Jeanne would echo that sentiment: "We managed to empty a room quicker than any couple in New York."

They were introduced by Marion Javits, the wife of New York's former senior U.S. senator, at a large Christmas party at Gore Vidal's, where Mailer managed to gaze Lady Jeanne down after a twenty-minute staring match. "The night I met him," she recalled, "I knew I was going to marry him and have his child." George Plimpton later commented that these staring matches with women were not uncommon for Mailer at the time. "There was hardly a social occasion at which he did not challenge someone to a confrontation of some sort," he wrote. "With females, he involved them in a staring contest—in which he and the person opposite stared into each other's eyes until one or the other gave way. Mailer always seemed to win, the girls never knowing quite how to react, usually glancing away out of embarrassment. . . . As for Norman, I supposed he did it to establish his dominance, like Mowgli staring down Shere Khan, and he apparently got a lot of satisfaction out of it."

Mailer and Lady Jeanne had one daughter, Kate, Mailer's fourth child, who was born on August 21, 1962, only three months after it was confirmed that the two had wed. The marriage had taken place secretly several months earlier, after Mailer's Mexican divorce from Adele. Lord Beaverbrook had disapproved of the match, and as a result of her decision to marry Mailer, Lady Jeanne reportedly forfeited a sizable sum of money. Some put the loss at close to ten million dollars.

In the late spring of 1962, after a European honeymoon jaunt, Mailer and a pregnant Lady Jeanne moved into 142 Columbia Heights, a brownstone building in Brooklyn. Mailer had decided to buy the house while he was still with Adele, but "the Trouble" intervened. This would be Mailer's New York residence for the next two decades. The Brooklyn boy had come home.

The Columbia Heights house was a four-story brownstone. Mailer took over the top floor, with its two bedrooms and large living and dining area overlooking the East River and the New York Harbor, as living quarters. He intermittently wrote in a small studio on the third floor of the building, which over the years would also serve as an office for his secretary, a guest room, and a storage closet. After Kate Mailer was born in August, Lady Jeanne and the baby moved into the ground-floor garden apartment. She upholstered the entire area, including the walls, in a flowered fabric which Mailer later derisively referred to in his fourth novel, *An American Dream*. "It had the specific density," he wrote, "of a jungle conceived by Rousseau."

Writer Seymour Krim had lunch with Mailer and Lady Jeanne shortly after they were married. "She was not physically quite as sparkling as Adele," he recalls, "but as far as poise, presence, and general amiability go, I think I liked her. Mailer seemed relaxed with her, and she was somewhat under wraps. She let Norman take center stage. The marriage seemed odd to me, but at the same time I was impressed by it because how many of us knew Jewish-American novelists who were married to British nobility? It struck me as quite a feat. But I think Norman has always been intrigued—due to the associations of his Harvard days—with upper-crust things. He always reserved the right to be the earthy Jew in relation to it, to have it both ways: admiration and disapprobation. I think they're both parts of his experience."

Mailer's brother-in-law, Larry Alson, saw the marriage as the only truly impulsive match Norman ever made. "He lived with all his other wives for a time before marriage. After he found that it was working, he thought it was right to dignify the arrangement. But this was different. If you look at his work, one of his fantasies is nobility." Bea Silverman now views Mailer's marriage to Lady Jeanne as the next step up the gentile social ladder which he had been ascending since Harvard. "She was the ultimate *shiksa*," Bea says.

The match clearly confounded the New York literary crowd, who, after the stabbing of Adele, were intrigued by the union of Mailer and Lady Jeanne. "Their courtship, their marriage, their breakup, their divorce in 1963, the old Juarez routine—people were fascinated by all this and talked about it all the time," Tom Wolfe later recalled.

❦

Mailer's new alliance with the establishment was gaining him the visibility he sought. It also enhanced his masculine myth: The world now saw him not only as a man who had stabbed his wife but as one who had subsequently married a favored member of the English aristocracy. Some editors had begun to think of Mailer as a reigning expert on women, and *Playboy* invited him to partake in a discussion of the "womanization" of America for their June 1962 issue. For the first time Mailer voiced his concern about contraception, suggesting that women might have a biological aversion to it. This was one of several provocative ideas which would later bring Mailer into conflict with a new enemy, the feminists. "There's been a change in the minds of most men about the function of marriage," he said in the *Playboy* discussion. "It isn't that they're necessarily becoming weaker vis-à-vis their wives, it's that they've married women who will be less good for them in the home and more good for them in the world. . . . What [a man] wants is a marvelous courtesan with social arts."

Clay Felker at *Esquire*, who had worked with Mailer on the JFK piece, now saw him as the perfect writer to interpret the elusive first lady, Jacqueline Kennedy. Despite Mailer's argument with *Esquire* in 1960 over the "Superman" article, Felker couldn't resist approaching him. "You've got to remember," says Felker, "that it was not long after Norman had stabbed Adele. That was the reason he received the Jackie assignment. The United States and the world were in a tizzy about Jackie. They had discovered this glamorous first lady. It was natural to put Mailer up against her." Because of the author's tense relationship with Felker, it was Harold Hayes who actually worked with Mailer on the piece. Mailer started writing in March 1962, while he and Lady Jeanne were honeymooning in Villefranche, France, and continued the work in Paris. The article was completed in New York in May.

Mailer had one problem with the piece: The first lady refused to be interviewed. He had sent her a strange letter in the fall of 1960 after she had complimented him in a handwritten note on his "Superman" piece about her husband. In the note, she wondered if Mailer's "impressionistic" treatment of the present could be applied to the past. Mailer wrote Mrs. Kennedy back saying he thought it was possible. He was thinking of doing a biography of the Marquis de Sade and the "strange honor of the man." As he later admitted: "I suppose this is as close to the edge as I have ever come."

Despite his flippancy, Mailer was surprised that the first lady had turned him down for an interview. "The vanity was no doubt outsize, but one thought of oneself as one of the few writers in the country," Mailer said. "There was a right to interview Mrs. Kennedy."

Mailer was feeling defensive, a stance which *Ragtime* author E. L. Doctorow, who would become his editor at Dial three years later, believes is the best stimulus for Mailer's work. "There is a pattern in his stuff where very often a really good piece will begin as he attempts to extricate himself from a jam," Doctorow says. "There's some mechanism there whereby his best forces can be elicited by his getting into situations that he has to write his way out of."

The Jackie piece for *Esquire*, entitled "An Evening with Jackie Kennedy," was provoked by only a mild rebuff, but this was enough.

He felt that the charming young woman he had met in Hyannis Port two years before had now become a poseur. Her voice, Mailer wrote, was "a quiet parody of the sort of voice one hears on the radio late at night, dropped softly into the ear by girls who sell soft mattresses, depilatories, or creams to brighten the skin." She was a phony, Mailer concluded, and it was a sad image for America.

Hayes remembers that the Jackie Kennedy piece raised a storm when it was published in July 1962. Kennedy's press secretary, Pierre Salinger, immediately called the magazine to object. "Salinger," says Hayes, "felt the piece was unfair and untoward and improper for the magazine to do. But he did nothing more than state his dismay over it. Then we got a fascinating parody of the piece that was sent in anonymously from the White House. We didn't run it, and we should have, but we found out subsequently that it was done by Kennedy's speech writer, Richard Goodwin, acting as the self-appointed defender of the honor of Mistress Kennedy."

Far from disturbing the *Esquire* editors, the reaction from the White House was received with elation. "We were astonished and pleased," says Hayes, "that we would be taken so seriously—that we'd get a call from the White House protesting anything. It was a great boost for us." Although the editors might have appreciated Mailer's appraisal of Mrs. Kennedy, many readers did not. The magazine received an onslaught of letters objecting to Mailer's portrayal of their sanctified institution, the First Lady.

If Mailer was heightening *Esquire*'s visibility that summer, the reverse was also true. Mailer decided that the magazine might become a forum for writing regularly on a variety of subjects, and he approached the editors about starting a monthly column to be called "The Big Bite." "I got the feeling," recalls Harold Hayes, "that the columns were to be a big bite out of life. He had an omnivorous appetite, and it was exciting for us not to know what was going to happen in the next one."

Mailer had written frenzied attacks on the mass media in *The Village Voice* five years earlier, but he was now learning how to manipulate the press in more subtle and effective ways. There would still be assaults on newspapers and television, but they would be handled with moderation, and his audience was becoming more inclined to listen. He would try not to alienate his readers with self-destructive anger.

Mailer was learning something about survival as the nation

At the piano in the office of *The Harvard Advocate*, President Bruce Barton, Jr., entertains fellow staffers, including a young Norman Mailer, shown standing second from right.

Dust jacket of *The Naked and the Dead*.

Portrait of the author of *The Naked and the Dead*. The book was published in 1948 and became an instant best seller.

Mailer with his first wife, Beatrice Silverman. The couple met while they were both undergraduates in Boston. "Bea" is now a psychiatrist in Florida.

Assembled for a "world peace" conference in New York on March 25, 1949 were, from left to right: A. A. Fadayev, secretary-general of the Union of Soviet Writers; Norman Mailer; Russian composer Dmitri Shostakovich; playwright Arthur Miller; and British delegate Dr. Olaf Stapledon. Mailer surprised the group with his strong anti-Stalinist viewpoint.

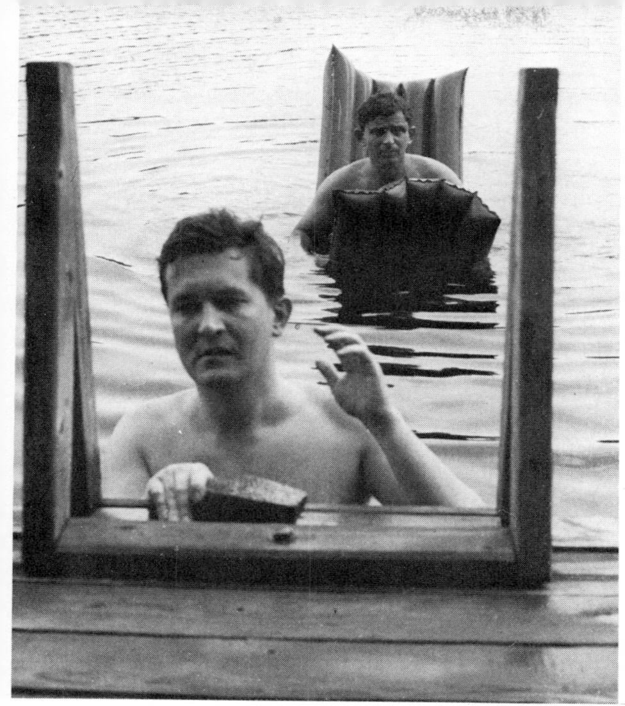

Mailer (on raft) and author William Styron in Connecticut, circa 1958. Mailer and Styron have since been engaged in an intense, bitter feud.

Sporting a beard, Mailer is shown seated alongside his second wife, Adele, Gloria Jones, and fellow World War II novelist James Jones, author of *From Here to Eternity*, in 1958.

Jailed on a charge of stabbing his wife Adele, Mailer is escorted from his cell at New York's West 100th Street police station on November 22, 1960. Mailer received a psychiatric examination at Bellevue Hospital and was later released on probation.

Mailer poses with Adele following his hearing on felonious assault charges on December 21, 1960. At the court hearing, Adele refused to sign a complaint against her husband.

Mailer and Dan Wolf, two of the three cofounders of *The Village Voice*, are shown in the *Voice* offices. Mailer fought his colleagues for a more radical policy for *The Voice*.

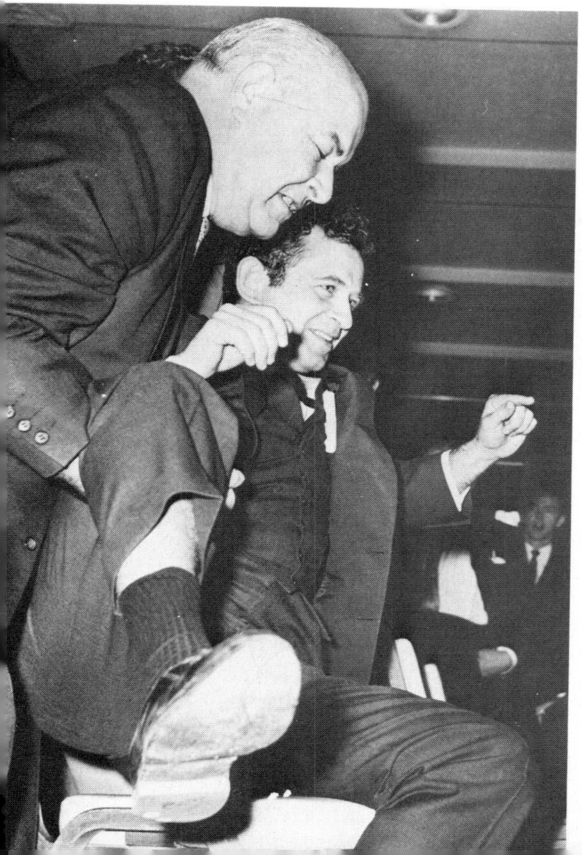

A security guard ejects Mailer from Sonny Liston's press conference in Chicago, September 26, 1962, after Mailer invited himself to the dais to support the cause of Liston's opponent, Floyd Patterson.

Mailer, who considers himself a writing "champ," tests his physical strength against former world heavyweight champion Muhammad Ali.

Mailer shown at the Republican National Convention in 1968, which he covered for *Harper's* magazine.

Mailer at the march on the Pentagon in October of 1967. Mailer's report on the event, *Armies of the Night*, won the Pulitzer Prize for non-fiction.

Mailer, his fourth wife, Beverly, and his sons Michael Burks and Stephen McLeod on the balcony of their Brooklyn Heights home in 1969.

The futuristic city built out of Lego blocks by engineer Mailer is displayed in his Brooklyn Heights home. The model was featured on the cover of Mailer's *Cannibals and Christians*.

mmy Breslin and Mailer concede defeat in New York City's primary ections on June 18, 1969. Mailer sought the Democratic nomination for ayor while Breslin ran for city council president. Unlike his staff and nning mate, Mailer believed that he would win the race.

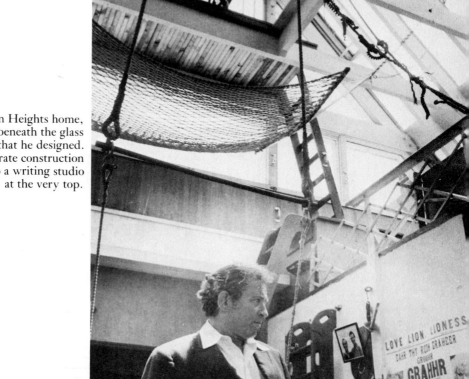

his Brooklyn Heights home, ailer stands beneath the glass wood gable that he designed. The elaborate construction leads to a writing studio at the very top.

Mailer shares the dais with feminist author Germaine Greer during the March, 1971 Town Hall debate. Mailer faced four advocates of Women's Liberation.

Fanny Mailer with her son at his gala fiftieth birthday party at the Four Seasons restaurant in New York in February, 1973. Fanny is the only one to whom Mailer readily defers. Mailer's fourth wife, Beverly, has said that Fanny "is the *only* Mrs. Norman Mailer."

At a press conference at the Algonquin Hotel in July, 1973, Mailer discusses his controversial book on Marilyn Monroe, *Marilyn*. In it, Mailer offered a conspiracy theory of her death.

posite) Boxer Mailer demonstrates his ls in the ring against his friend and ner light heavyweight champion José res. Mailer studied boxing under res, who considers him the equivalent Golden Gloves contender.

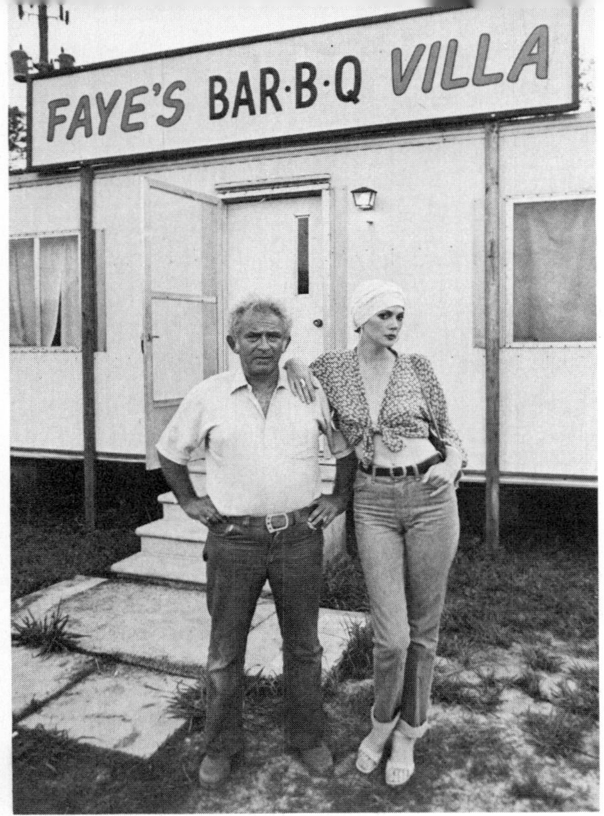

Norris Church, who became Mailer's sixth wife, poses with him in Americus, Georgia, near Jimmy Carter's home in Plains, in 1976. The former Arkansas schoolteacher came to New York with Mailer only weeks after they met.

Jacqueline Kennedy Onassis chats with Mailer at a cocktail party in October, 1978. Mailer interviewed J.F.K. for *Esquire* during the 1960 presidential race, but was later refused an interview by the First Lady.

Mailer, Truman Capote, and Dotson Rader clown at a Random House party.

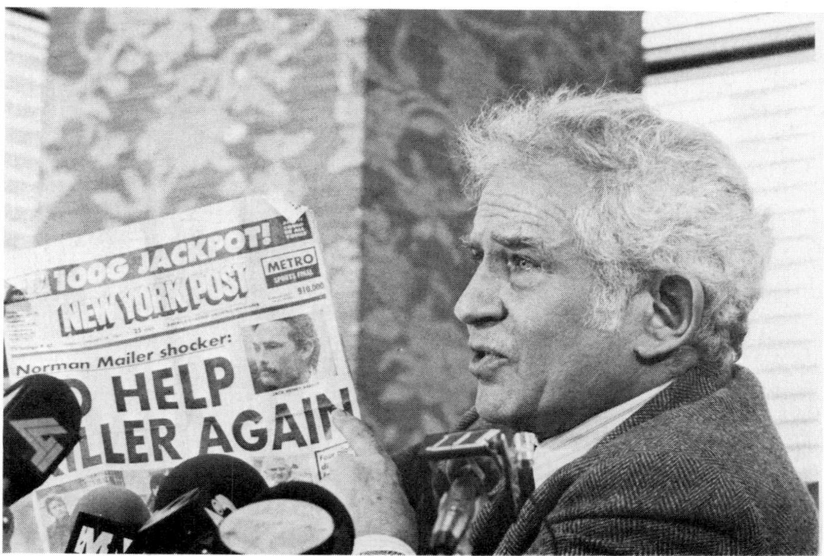

Mailer displays a headline in the *New York Post* at a press conference in January, 1982, where he announced his plans to sue the *Post* for its coverage of his role in the trial of convict-author Jack Henry Abbott.

At their rented home on Maine's Mount Desert Island, Mailer and Norris Church are shown with their son, John Buffalo, Mailer's eighth child.

In the summer of 1979, Mailer poses with Norris Church, left. At the right is his third wife, Lady Jeanne Campbell, daughter of the Duke of Argyll.

Mailer is shown with all his children, except for Susan Mailer, his eldest child. From left to right: Michael, Danielle, Betsy, Kate, Stephen, Matthew Norris, Maggie, and John Buffalo.

In 1982, Mailer and Norris Church watch a show of Valentino's fashions at the Metropolitan Museum in New York. Mailer was so taken by Norris's beauty when they first met, that he turned his back and walked out of the room without a word.

turned the corner into the 1960s. As he started his *Esquire* columns, he confided to Paul Krassner of the *The Realist* that he intended to join the enemy, or at least appear to. "If anyone is a leftist, or a radical . . . the thing to do . . . is to devote his life to working subtly, silently, steelfully against the state. And there's one best way he can do that. He can *join* the mass media. He can bore from within. . . . Few of us are strong enough to live alone in enemy territory. But it's work which must be done." For the next decade Mailer would effectively do just that.

Mailer's first column for *Esquire*, which was published in the November 1962 issue, opened with a caveat to his readers. "Your columnist would warn you," Mailer wrote, "these pieces will be written two months before publication. The art is to anticipate what might be interesting in sixty days. I was talking about this with a columnist. 'Write your column so that it can still be read with pleasure ten years from now,' he said. Good advice. I will try to entertain some of you. I will try to drive others a little closer to their deaths."

The column actually dealt with death, specifically the suicides of two of Mailer's prime fantasy figures, Ernest Hemingway and Marilyn Monroe. It also covered concerns that would occupy Mailer in the coming decade. They were to become his metaphors for collective ills: sewage, plague, cancer, housing projects, fallout, mass media, and science.

Some of these ideas were articulated after this column was written, when, in September 1962, Mailer debated William F. Buckley, Jr., the editor of the conservative *National Review*, on the role of the right wing in American life. A Chicago theater producer, John Goldin, promoted the evening, billed as a political debate between a conservative and a hipster. But Mailer's views had evolved considerably since his "White Negro" days. He had moved beyond hipsterism and was now concerned with some of the broader issues of the New Left.

Almost four thousand people assembled in the Medinah Temple in Chicago to hear Buckley and Mailer on the evening of Saturday, September 22. Mailer's opening speech was a sweeping summary of future concerns of the left. Distinctions, he said, were beginning to disappear; authenticity was diminishing. As a result, the country was beginning to suffer from "a plague." The insidious effects of this plague were to be found everywhere: Modern architecture was becoming homogeneous; mysterious new diseases were surfacing; nature was being polluted with artificial chemicals; emotions were being distorted by motivational research; educational systems were not teaching students how to think; faith was bankrupt; and the language was being sullied.

The right wing, Mailer argued, was sensitive to this plague, but they tended to blame it on collectivism. In this Mailer was not sure that they were totally wrong. But here he made a decisive tactical maneuver. He pointed out that the right wing's—and specifically Barry Goldwater's—insistence on military superiority over the Russians caused such a domestic economic drain, with two thirds of every federal dollar going into the defense budget, that there was "no alternative to an ever-increasing welfare state."

Mailer's answer was to end the Cold War. Vietnam had yet to take hold of the country's imagination, but Mailer would make a point that the left would repeat in the years to come: "Let communism come to those countries it will come to. Let us not use up our substance trying to hold onto nations which are poor, underdeveloped, and bound to us only by the depths of their hatred for us."

Mailer concluded by saying the real war was not between West and East but between the conservative and the rebel, "authority and instinct," between two views of God. The conservative's view is that the rich and the poor are born in their place. The rebel's view—Mailer's view—is that society is caught up in a war between God and the devil and that "man must serve as God's agent, seeking to shift the wealth of our universe in such a way that the talent, creativity, and strength of the future . . . will show us what a mighty renaissance is locked in the unconscious of the dumb."

In the ensuing debate with Buckley, Mailer, his fists clenched in a fighter's stance, fielded the conservative's verbal jabs with characteristic vigor. When Buckley asked, "Are you prepared to say that it is distinctly the right wing that wants to win the Cold War?" Mailer shouted back, "No, it is the right wing that wishes to blow up the earth." When Buckley asked why, Mailer responded, "You think it is better to be dead than Red." Buckley retorted: "Is it not better to be alive and free?" "Yes," Mailer agreed, "but the way to be alive and free is to end the Cold War." Discussing Mailer's view of God, Buckley asked, "Why is the right wing not concerned with God's displeasure?" Mailer answered that the right wing was not religious. Buckley then inquired who, besides Nehru, was religious. Mailer replied that he was.

On the following Monday *The New York Times* excerpted parts of this debate on the front page of its second section, concluding that it had been a draw. Mailer was not pleased. He was convinced that he had won; people had even told him so afterward. When he read the *Times* piece, Mailer later recalled, "Something pent up for years, dictatorial and harsh, began to slip through my good humor."

The timing of the news article was significant, for the day after it appeared, Mailer was to cover the Floyd Patterson–Sonny Liston heavyweight championship fight in Chicago for *Esquire* in lieu of writing a February column. It would be a disastrous fight. Patterson, the favored establishment black, was knocked down by Liston, the rebel black, in the first round.

In the *Times*'s coverage of the Buckley debate, Mailer believed he had found his enemy. Not only would Mailer open his piece about the fight, entitled "Ten Thousand Words a Minute," with a searing indictment of newspaper journalists, all of whom worked for "the Goat," Mailer's term for the American newspaper, but he also would equate *The New York Times* with the liberal establishment, which, in the end, he thought, it had defeated its own hero, Floyd Patterson.

Having located the enemy, Mailer could turn to the two fighters. Although he secretly admired Sonny Liston as the hip, Faustian black, the psychic outlaw who had once gone to jail for breaking a cop's leg, Mailer finally sided with Patterson, the establishment hero. Mailer had cast Liston as representing evil and Patterson, the heroic defeated black, as representing good. Patterson and Liston had emerged as symbols of the struggle that was taking place in Mailer himself.

Mailer decided that he could not stay on the sidelines of such an important conflict. Instead he would step in and become the protagonist of his own story. He arranged a press conference for the day after the fight, stating that he would do publicity for a second Patterson-Liston fight since he was the only man in America who believed Patterson could win. Unfortunately, Mailer's own press conference conflicted with one Liston was holding that day. He decided to walk up to Liston's pressroom, where he sat himself on the dais before the fighter arrived. According to Mailer, two house detectives told him to leave, and when he refused they lifted the chair he was sitting on off the dais. When Liston arrived at the conference, Mailer badgered him about Patterson while the press shouted, "Shut the bum up."

Liston tried to quiet them. "No, let the bum speak," he said. Mailer went to the dais and confronted Liston.

"You called me a bum," Mailer declared.

"Well, you are a bum," Liston replied. "Everybody is a bum. I'm a bum, too. It's just that I'm a bigger bum than you are. Shake, bum."

"Once more I had tried to become a hero, and had ended as an eccentric," Mailer wrote about the encounter. "There would be an argument later whether I was a monster or a clown. Could it be I was indeed a bum? I shook his hand."

Pete Hamill, who was then writing for the *New York Post*, and who had met Mailer just before the historic Patterson fight, attended the legendary conference. "The poor writing slobs were arguing with the TV people, as usual, when suddenly there was a big storm going on with Norman up there on the stand and others pulling him off," Hamill recalls. "I remember him being pulled, not carried, off the stand. I was sort of appalled by it. At first I thought the cops would hurt him for no good reason when they pulled him down. His brain is too valuable. I wasn't prepared for that kind of show."

Mailer would spend seven weeks writing the piece on the Liston-Patterson fight, four of them lost on a false start. He finished in time for publication in the February 1963 issue of *Esquire*. The editors were again delighted.

Hayes remembers that he wanted to run a wire-service picture of Mailer being ejected from the Liston press conference, but when he wrote Mailer for permission the author answered, "Certainly not." "It was interesting," reflects Hayes, "the way Mailer viewed himself as a serious person with respect to a piece as against his personage as an antagonist when he became an actor."

Pete Hamill also admired Mailer's article on the fight. "Mailer's piece showed how the novelist's gift is important to journalism," he says. "Mailer did it in a particularly modern way by putting himself at the center of the action. The modern sensibility is really about the artist rather than his characters, and that's what Norman showed. I think Norman intuitively understood that neither Patterson nor Liston appreciated the drama of the fight, so he thrust himself into it. He had to have a piece of that drama, and for a moment he became a protagonist."

This role of Mailer as a protagonist was to become a familiar one in the 1960s. In "Superman" he had created a poetic image of JFK that went beyond the news. But he had remained an observer. In his fight piece, Mailer was to extend the New Journalism by making himself an active participant in the story, a technique that would shape his style and eventually earn him a Pulitzer Prize for *Armies of the Night*.

❦

"Who knew any longer where Right was Left or who was Good and how Evil had hid?" Mailer wrote in his fight article. In December of 1962 Mailer again took up the questions of good and evil, God and the devil, as he began a column for *Commentary*, the prestigious journal of the American Jewish Committee.

For the first time Mailer was publicly dealing with the question of his own Judaism. His column was to be an existential exploration of Martin Buber's *Tales of the Hassidim*. Norman Podhoretz, editor of *Commentary*, recalls that this was Mailer's idea. "I don't remember what impelled him to do the column," Podhoretz says, "but my influence may have had something to do with it. I actually took him to a Hassidic synagogue on the eve of Yom Kippur at his request. He wanted to see what it was like, and he was fascinated." Mailer originally wanted to write a monthly column, but Podhoretz was "a bit uncertain about the idea" and prevailed upon him to accept a bimonthly arrangement.

To apply his radical existential-religious attitude to a prominent Jewish theologian like Buber and in a magazine like *Commentary* was obviously risky. At the same time, it assured Mailer new visibility among the powerful New York Jewish intellectual community, and perhaps would even gain him their respect.

Midge Decter, who is married to Norman Podhoretz and was then working on her husband's magazine, notes that by this time intellectuals were changing their minds about Mailer. "Mailer's relation with the serious intellectual community and the community of successful pop writing was always ambiguous and ambivalent—until the literary intellectual community changed course and followed him. By 1963 people were beginning to say, 'Hey, wait a minute; this guy really means it.'

"I think he got interested in Hassidim naturally. There is a mystical tradition in Judaism, and Norman thought he might find something in Judaism which would conform with his general theory. I think in the end he discovered that Judaism was not what he hoped he could make it be."

Although Mailer had successfully grafted the hip ethos of the

White Negro onto John F. Kennedy, it was a trickier proposition to impose his existential view of God and the devil on Judaism. In his *Commentary* columns Mailer contended that for centuries Jews have been obsessed with the question of whether they belong to "a God of righteousness or a Devil of treachery." Their flight from this confrontation has led them out of religion and into philosophy, psychoanalysis, social action, and the arts. Mailer, however, did not sanction such a flight. He felt it merely diluted the paradox of the Jews. Rather he proposed absorbing these traditionally Jewish concerns into new existential guidelines.

Both God and the devil exist, Mailer stated. The Nazi concentration camps have proven that God is not all-powerful but is actually an existential being who can only discover his powers through the history of man. Therefore it is only through the moral heroism of man that God can defeat the devil. Throughout the next decades, acting as a prophet, Mailer would contest this devil, who, he said, is a "monumental bureaucrat of repetition" whose purpose is to "waste substance." The devil's aesthetics are evident, he suggested, in the plastic materials of "a new airline terminal, a luxury hotel, a housing project, or a civic center."

As Mailer gained popularity in the 1960s, his admirers as well as his critics tended to dismiss his evolving ideas, whether about God and the devil, cancer, excrement, or plastic, as eccentric excesses. Midge Decter, however, thinks they were all conceived in earnestness. "Mailer was serious about this stuff—about God and the devil and existentialism and shit—he was dead serious," she says. "But in a way, accepting him and making him a kind of guru figure—because the collection of groupies started very quickly—was a way of not taking it seriously. People were constantly trying to turn his ideas into metaphors, and that drove him crazy. A lot of people who professed to be his greatest admirers in those years didn't take his ideas seriously. You'd say, 'What about the devil?' and they'd say, 'Oh, well, you know . . .' "

Norman Podhoretz remembers that the response to the *Commentary* pieces was mixed. "Some people thought he was overreaching in the sense that he was talking about things he knew nothing about. But a lot of people were pleasantly surprised. On the whole it was a successful venture."

Although Mailer has always seen himself as somehow quintessentially American, his secretary, Anne Barry, a gentile from New England who began working for him at the time of the *Commentary* columns, sees him as ultimately Jewish. "I was just a little green kid from New Hampshire, but he was certainly Jewish to me," she says. "Anyone who would write about Martin Buber and *Tales of the Hassidim* had to be Jewish. It was also his freedom, his humor, the willingness to look things that are unpleasant in the eye, a reluctance to make things look nice—these are Jewish qualities, and they come through in his work as well as in the man."

Barry had met Mailer in the spring of 1962, after she wrote the author from Radcliffe to inform him that she was doing her senior paper on him for Erik Erikson's course on life stages. Her thesis was that Mailer, at the age of 39, was having an identity crisis. "I came to New York with the paper written but discovered it was all wrong. He was not having an identity crisis. After a while I realized he had a sense of humor. I had managed to read all his works without realizing that." Barry received an A on the paper, nevertheless. "In later years, whenever Norman gave me trouble, I threatened to publish it," she says.

During the fall and winter of 1962-63, Mailer worked hard on his columns for *Commentary* and *Esquire*. He had by now switched to writing in longhand. "He thought it helped his style of writing," Barry says. She would take his longhand manuscripts, type them triple-spaced, give them back to Mailer for editing, and then type them again double-spaced. At this point Mailer was working in the third-floor studio or at a large blue table in the living room on the fourth floor at 142 Columbia Heights. Barry used one of the two bedrooms on the fourth floor as an office. "He was a very hard worker," she recalls. "He'd start working between nine and ten in the morning and continue until lunch. Then he might go back to work or take time off and do letters."

Roger Donoghue also remembers the author's extraordinary discipline. "He always worked no matter what. He could be out all night, and I'd call at noontime and talk to his secretary, and he'd be working. I'd say, 'Oh, come on, he's just sleeping.' She would say, 'Well, if he is, who is giving me these papers to type?' It was like clockwork. I've been pals with Budd Schulberg and Nelson Algren, and they would work like hell night and day for a month, and then things would go. But Norman put those four or five hours in no matter what."

By May 1963 Mailer had written seven columns for *Esquire* and three for *Commentary*. Not only was the critical establishment beginning to take serious note of Mailer, but a new generation was responding to his work. Director James Toback, then a student at Harvard, later recalled: "Everyone I knew at Harvard read *Esquire*, one reason being a monthly column of Norman Mailer's, 'The Big Bite.' For years Mailer had been promising that 'something large' would come of him, and all of us had hoped so, for he seemed, alone among living American writers, potentially Gargantuan. He could fight, speak, act and marry with a kind of overwhelming dexterity that sent waves of excitement into our imagination. That he had stabbed his wife (and got away with it) and been observed at Bellevue actually enhanced the image. . . . We looked for an intellectual hero who transcended, even flouted the respectability of intellectualism. . . . We suspected Mailer could become the hero of our generation. And yet the promise had not yet been realized."

❦

Norman Mailer had not written a novel for eight years, and it was fifteen years since his masterpiece, *The Naked and the Dead*, had been published. Even as he refined his journalism into formidable social commentary, he was aware how keenly his public anticipated another work of fiction. In April 1963 Mailer recounted in his "Big Bite" column a discussion he had had the previous summer with Gore Vidal about the decline of the novel and the petty backbiting that went on among novelists.

"Gore," Mailer said laughingly, "admit it. The novel is like the Great Bitch of one's life. We think we're rid of her, we go on to other women, we take our pulse and decide that finally we're enjoying ourselves, we're free of her power, we'll never suffer her depredations again, and then we turn a corner on a street, and there's the Bitch smiling at us, and we're trapped." Mailer then went on to announce that in the next issue of *Esquire* he would discuss ten novels: *The Thin Red Line* by James Jones; *Set This House on Fire* by William Styron; *Naked Lunch* by William Burroughs; *Catch-22* by Joseph Heller; *Rabbit Run* by John Updike; *Letting Go* by Philip Roth; *Another Country* by James Baldwin; *Henderson the Rain King* by Saul Bellow; *Franny and Zooey* and *Raise High the Roof Beam* by J. D. Salinger.

The July 1963 issue of *Esquire* was devoted entirely to literature. Mailer's article, which featured a picture of him, taken by Diane Arbus, in a boxing ring, was called "Some Children of the Goddess" and resembled his "Evaluations" piece in *Advertisements*, though it was perhaps more reflective. In this essay Burroughs, Heller, and Bellow all came in in first place, Updike and Roth were awarded a middling second, and J. D. Salinger was a poor last.

Styron was the object of Mailer's most antagonistic personal attack. He called Styron's new novel, *Set This House on Fire*, "the book of a man whose soul has gotten fat." The two had been feuding ever since their Connecticut days, and by now Mailer's intense dislike of Styron had become something of an obsession. It was in the "Goddess" piece that Mailer made public Styron's disloyalty to Jones, the time in Connecticut when Styron recited the worst passages of *Some Came Running*. This was Mailer's way of trying to weaken the Styron-Jones relationship and reclaim Jones for himself. His treatment of Jones in "Goddess" was gentle compared to his comments on Styron. He called *The Thin Red Line* merely "a holding action, a long-distance call to the Goddess."

Even though Mailer was jealous of Styron's friendship with Jones and angry at Styron's remark about Adele, these feelings could not fully account for his assault on the southern novelist. More likely Mailer's hostility was provoked by his belief that Styron represented the true traditional novelist—what Mailer ached to be and now sensed he might never be. Styron's entire life-style also reflected the success of his literary labors. Styron was accepted by the literary establishment and had even been invited to the White House.

Calder Willingham remembers that Mailer even tried to provoke Styron into a fistfight after the "Goddess" column was published. The incident took place in 1963 at an *Esquire*-sponsored writers' conference in Princeton, New Jersey, in which Styron, John Cheever, Ralph Ellison, Philip Roth, Willingham, and a number of other writers participated. Mailer also showed up.

"Norman came in the door," recalls Willingham, "and as he walked by Styron, Bill said, 'Hi.' Norman leaned toward him and deliberately bumped him hard with his shoulder as if to say, 'Let's have a fight.' " By this time Styron had come to see that this feud was far more important to Mailer than to him, and he did not respond. Although Mailer's provocation aroused Styron's anger, years later he would call Mailer a figure of "pathos."

The Styron-Mailer quarrel is still intense. Mailer sometimes speaks as if he covets Styron's more traditional literary accomplishments. "If I had no economic necessity, I would have written about maybe one and a half times as many pages as Bill Styron," Mailer now says. "That's because I'm one and a half times more energetic than old Bill. I would have written books that were more like Styron's, too, in the sense that they would be more literary and more well-rubbed. And I would have spent more time on them. I would have polished them. I would have lived with them. I would have sighed over them and I probably would have taken them more seriously than I did take them, although I have taken them seriously."

Mailer's critique of James Baldwin's *Another Country* was almost as brutal as his assessment of Styron's novel. He called Baldwin's new book "abominably written." Mailer had seen Baldwin the previous fall at the Liston-Patterson fight in Chicago and had noted that a "bad feeling" seemed to surround their relationship, perhaps as a result of Mailer's comments about him in *Advertisements* and Baldwin's retort in *Esquire*. But Baldwin does not now agree that there was any chill between him and Mailer at the heavyweight fight. As for Norman's attack on his novel in "Goddess," Baldwin dismisses it. "I don't want to get involved in all that nonsense," he says. "It's Norman's problem, not mine. I have other things to do. I have nothing against Norman. He was and is my friend."

Mailer had diplomatically left Gore Vidal out of "Goddess." Unlike some of the other writers who had been mauled in Mailer's critique in *Advertisements*, Vidal had remained friends with Mailer. When Mailer was released from Bellevue Hospital after the stabbing, he had visited Vidal at his country home and asked help in reestablishing his reputation with such literary men as Saul Bellow and critic F. W. Dupee. Vidal and Mailer had also made a professional pact not to speak ill of each other.

By 1970, however, the relationship would deteriorate. Vidal was then quoted in *Women's Wear Daily* as having made a disparaging remark about Mailer's hatred for women. Mailer responded by telling the paper that while he had been married five times and had seven children, including five daughters, Vidal had never married and had no children. "These statistics of course prove nothing unless it is to suggest that the reason Vidal may have married no lady and fathered no child is due perhaps to his love of women and his reluctance therefore to injure their tender flesh with his sharp tongue," Mailer said. Their mutual sniping had escalated into open warfare by the summer of 1971, but in 1963 they still nourished their friendship, or perhaps their nonaggression pact. Their caustic jibes were aimed at others.

Calder Willingham was less willing than some of the other

writers to turn the other cheek to Mailer. At the *Esquire* conference, Mailer told Willingham that he hadn't liked his new book, *Eternal Fire*. "He was quite nasty to me," Willingham recalls. "I casually called him a jerk. I meant nothing by it, but Norman suddenly bridled and turned to me and narrowed his eyes and said, 'That's the second time you've called me a jerk. Don't push your luck!' It was clear he was ready to have a fistfight. I said to him, 'Gee, Norman, I thought I knew you well enough to speak informally; I didn't intend any insult.' He then became kind of surly and left."

Willingham was not one of those insulted in the "Goddess" article, but he had been attacked in *Advertisements* and now he sought to return Mailer's fire. In the December 1963 issue of *Esquire* he answered Mailer's "Goddess" with a piece entitled "The Way It Isn't Done: Notes on the Distress of Norman Mailer." Willingham accused Mailer of being obsessed with notoriety, a charge that was to be repeated by others over the years. "I cannot imagine a more truly splendid example of how not to be a writer than that provided by Mailer in this murky, disorganized, and downright incoherent essay; even the relatively comprehensible parts of it reek with the odor of an acute literary illness," wrote Willingham. "The real victim of Mailer's attempted assassination of his fellow writers is Mailer himself. A compulsion to win glory and fame is a dreadful curse."

Harold Hayes now says that the editorial decision to run Willingham's rebuttal was a natural one. "Mailer went around with a chip on his shoulder asking anyone to knock it off," Hayes states. "He was fair game. And therefore the magazine happily participated. One might argue that he even invited it."

Willingham later realized that criticizing Mailer for not behaving as a novelist was a waste. It was becoming highly apparent that Mailer was developing a new type of literary role. "The route he's followed," Willingham says, "is not necessarily that of a novelist but of a literary figure, a commentator. He's fulfilled a role in which his verbal pyrotechnics, his dexterity, his inventiveness, and daring have endeared him to many. I didn't take that into account when I did that piece for *Esquire*. I later wrote Mailer in Provincetown to tell him this, but he claims he never got the letter."

❦

During the same month that Mailer wrote his "Goddess" article, May 1963, he once more invited notoriety by staging a public reading, his first since the unfortunate YMHA presentation two years before.

His choice of auditorium was Carnegie Hall, the ultimate symbol of accomplishment. As Mailer told Millicent Brower of *The Village Voice* the day before the reading, which was to take place on Friday, May 31, "Carnegie Hall has a grand tradition. It's the home of virtuoso performers. Of course, I could've gone to Lincoln Center, but that's a nexus for cancer pushers."

Mailer divulged that the real reason for the performance, which was being staged by Richard Fulton, was economic. "It's a benefit," he told the *Voice* writer. "It's a benefit for Norman Mailer and his new novel. To raise enough money to give him a little time to work on the book." When Brower interjected that some people believed he was an "exhibitionist nut," Mailer, who had been pacing, abruptly sat down.

"My name arouses too many different kinds of reactions in too many different kinds of people," Mailer countered. "Besides, this evening is taking place on one of the worst dates of the year, May 31. It's the day after Memorial Day. Half of the people I want to be there are going to be out of town, and half of the out-of-towners who think I look like a circus geek will be paying their hard money to glower at Dad."

Mailer's premonition about the audience was not far off. After he emerged on the huge, bare stage dressed in a dark-blue suit, he perched himself on a solitary stool and looked out dismally at the small group. "Now I know," he quipped in his machine-gun diction, "what Robert Frost meant when he said, 'Hell must be a half-empty auditorium.' " The hall was in fact less than half full, but more people came in as the evening wore on. As Richard Kluger facetiously pointed out in *The Washington Post Book Week*, "One had the feeling vans were prowling the Village and areas beyond rounding up stray hipsters and rushing them uptown to make the house respectable."

"The reading was supposed to make him money, but I'm sure it didn't," Midge Decter says. "It was like all of Mailer's foolish—and by that I mean extraliterary—activities. Somebody had talked him into it." Decter recalls that the audience was surprised when Mailer appeared in his dark-blue suit. "They were prepared for this enfant terrible, radical and bohemian, which was stupid. Of course he would be there as a serious person in his blue suit."

Mailer began by reading from some of his most recent political nonfiction. His former Harvard professor Robert Gorham Davis, who was among the crowd, recollects that he was not taken with Norman's performance. "He wanted to present himself existentially to the audience. It was rather painful, as I remember. He didn't quite know what he was doing then, and he talked a lot about cancer." Norman Podhoretz, who was also there, concurs: "I seem to recall that the evening was not particularly successful, even slightly embarrassing."

Part of the embarrassment stemmed from questions posed by the audience. One young man stood up and asked, "Have you given up creative writing to become a political essayist?" In a provocative twist of logic, Mailer replied, "Would I be up here now talking about politics if I'd given up on my creative writing?" Mailer rushed to point out that he was working on a novel and assured the audience that what he wanted most was "to become a great novelist, believe it or not." Most in the audience, and elsewhere, believed it.

Midge Decter relates that another person at the reading asked Mailer what he thought of homosexuality. "I think it is a vice," Mailer responded. "There was this gasp and a moment of silence and bewilderment," Decter states. "The questioner asked him to repeat what he had said, and Mailer said louder, 'I think homosexuality is a vice.' Then he made a little speech about how people are free, and people who are homosexuals opt for it. It was not some disease they suffer from. This was so unheard-of and outrageous an idea, especially coming from him. People thought he was a bohemian wild man and would say, 'Anything goes, man.' Of course that's not Mailer's view of life at all. It was one of those perfect moments of incomprehension between Mailer and his audience."

Although the Carnegie Hall reading was a bid for recognition, Mailer would reconfirm his image as a rebel by the evening's end. It was part of his balancing act, one in which he simultaneously supported the establishment and rebelled against it, a technique he would cleverly use throughout the decade. At the beginning of the recital Mailer had promised his audience an "existential caper" at its close. The "caper" consisted of Mailer reading a paragraph from his contract with the hall that stipulated that no obscene language was to be used. In fact the management had hired a special security guard to take Mailer off the stage if he violated the agreement. Tucking the contract in his breast pocket, Mailer proceeded to read one of his poems containing several four-letter words. With that he left the stage, this time before the curtain could be brought down.

"The Carnegie Hall Caper added to the legend taking shape about him," wrote Richard Kluger, "himself its impresario, of a volcanic despoiler of the stifling orthodoxy that America has become to him. He is, in short, a personality presumably pleased with his notoriety—one thinks only of Sinatra and Sonny Liston, among our other talented performers, as similarly notorious—and indifferent to his admirers' concern that he is burning up his talent in the headline act."

❦

While Mailer was fighting relentlessly to maintain his celebrity, his home life was once again in turmoil. By the time of his Carnegie Hall appearance he and Lady Jeanne had been separated for several months. The divorce would become final the following December, when Mailer flew to Juarez, Mexico, to obtain the decree on the grounds of incompatibility. Writer Frederick Christian saw Mailer in March, two months before the Carnegie Hall reading. "We've split," Mailer told him, referring to Lady Jeanne. "She's living in the Hotel Delmonico. I was crazy about her—she's a great girl. But the choice came down to this: Either she became a good wife and took care of my four children, or I became Mr. Lady Jeanne. Our two worlds were pretty far apart."

Managing Mailer's growing number of offspring would not be easy for any of his wives, but there were other domestic problems as well. Mailer's philandering was by now renowned. Though Adele had tolerated some of his more imaginative sexual escapades, Lady Jeanne would have none of it. Midge Decter remembers the accounts each gave after the marriage broke up. "They were really quite wonderful clues," she points out. "Norman said, 'Lady Jeanne gave up ten million dollars to marry me, but she would never make me breakfast.' " And Lady Jeanne complained that all they ever did was go to dinner with Mailer's mother.

Shortly after his separation from Lady Jeanne there was a pretty woman serving drinks at Mailer's Brooklyn home. When Frederick Christian asked him if this was his new girl friend, Mailer said she was not but added that he probably would get married again. "You never understand a woman until you marry her," he said. Then he grinned. "I fear I'm going to overtake Tommy Manville."

Mailer would be married again before 1963 was over; in fact, his future wife was with him at the Carnegie Hall reading. It was Mailer's friend Roger Donoghue who made the initial introductions. Mailer and Donoghue were sitting at the bar at P. J. Clarke's, a fashionable restaurant on Manhattan's East Side, one spring night shortly after Mailer separated from Lady Jeanne, when a pretty blond actress, Beverly Bentley, walked in, accompanied by former middleweight boxing champion Jake LaMotta. Donoghue had known Beverly slightly in the fifties, and he introduced her to Mailer. They began talking. "A couple of weeks later," recalls Donoghue, "I called Norman, since we were going out to dinner. He said he was bringing Beverly. I said, 'Beverly who?' And he said, 'The girl you introduced me to at the bar.' "

Beverly Bentley, born Beverly Rentz, was a southern girl, originally from Georgia, who spent most of her youth being shunted from one small town to another after her parents' marriage broke up. A drama student at Sarasota High School in Florida, she was forced to leave at sixteen to help support herself and her mother. Beverly was running a diner when she met Arthur Godfrey, who was appearing at the local naval air station. She contacted him in New York shortly afterward and became one of the Toni Twins on his CBS-TV show. It was Godfrey who changed her name to Bentley, because it sounded better than Rentz. "There was no affair," Beverly recalled, "but Godfrey was very kind to me."

In New York she was briefly married to an advertising executive and worked as a fashion commentator on TV game shows before landing her first film role in Mike Todd, Jr.'s ill-fated Smell-O-Vision movie, *Scent of Mystery*. While shooting in Spain she also met Ernest Hemingway, a fact that did not go unnoticed by Mailer.

In 1963 Beverly played her first lead on Broadway in *The Heroine*. The play closed after a four-week run. The night after, feeling lost at the age of thirty-three, she met Mailer. "I wanted a home and children desperately," she recollected. "I knew Norman was in trouble with his wives, but I was attracted to the vulnerability beneath his tough act. He walked me to my apartment. That night he was wonderful in bed." By the following fall, when she and Mailer were on their way back from a Las Vegas prizefight, Beverly told him she was pregnant. Mailer proposed, and they were married in the living room of his Brooklyn Heights home in December. In March 1964 his fifth child and first son, Michael Burks, was born.

The quick shift from a stormy marriage with the established Lady Jeanne to a new union with an uprooted southern girl who had never read one of his books seemed like reckless impetuosity. But

Mailer had an uncanny sense of what he needed from a wife at a given time, and Beverly reflected the American heartland, which was to become Mailer's new literary direction.

❦

The first book Mailer published in the sixties, other than a small volume of poetry, was *The Presidential Papers*, which he dedicated to both his recent wives: "Beverly Rentz Sugarfoot Bentley" and "Jeanne Louise Slugger Campbell." His four daughters, his secretary, Anne Barry, and his sister, Barbara, were also included in the dedication, as was his "adopted" daughter, Jeanne Johnson, a young woman he helped release from Bellevue after he got out. Johnson later married Paul Krassner, the editor of *The Realist*, in Mailer's Brooklyn Heights living room.

The Presidential Papers was published by G. P. Putnam's Sons in November 1963. Mailer originally had intended to call the book *Frankie and Johnny: The Presidential Papers of Norman Mailer*. The name Frankie was derived from the famous Franks who had been connected with the Democratic Party, including Franklin Delano Roosevelt, Frank Sinatra, and Frank Costello. But the title was simplified to *The Presidential Papers* and Mailer addressed himself in the book solely to the current Democratic president, John F. Kennedy.

The format was similar to that of *Advertisements*, but Mailer was no longer the angry young writer defiantly storming the walls of the literary establishment. Instead he consciously assumed the cheeky voice of an artist who is already taken seriously. The book contained all his work since 1959, including his "Superman" article on Kennedy, his profile of Jackie, his open letters about Cuba, some of his *Esquire* and *Commentary* columns, his debate with Buckley, and his Liston–Patterson piece.

Even though most of the reviews were written before Kennedy's assassination at the end of November, *Papers* drove many critics into a frenzy of analysis. Mailer's impudence in addressing his work to the President, combined with his intellectual earnestness and disarming honesty, even modesty, about his own grandiose intent, all served to undermine a simplistic view of the writer. What was new about *Papers* was a touch of irony that had been totally absent from *Advertisements*. In his introduction he boasted about the pieces: "Their subject matter is fit concern for a President." To soften the arrogant tone, he quickly added: "One is of course not throwing any disqualified devil's wishes into the ring for oneself, no, no, these are the Presidential papers of a court wit, an amateur advisor."

Mailer was taking a precarious new path by daring to look foolish and serious at the same time. "Mailer played it like a court jester, which was brilliant," recalls Doc Humes. "In a certain sense he played it for the ironies, something writers like Jack Kerouac or Scott Fitzgerald or J. D. Salinger weren't able to do. They were almost pure lovers, but Norman had a streak of the fighter in him."

Many of the reviewers realized that Mailer could no longer be pigeonholed and gave up insisting that he should return to the novel. What they began to see was that in his nonfiction Mailer was reflecting the sensibility of the country. In the February issue of *Commentary*, Midge Decter wrote, "No one is currently telling us more about the United States of America." Richard Kluger concurred in *Book Week:* "What Norman Mailer is doing, and doing more prolifically and more provocatively and occasionally more preposterously than any other literary figure we have, is to tell what life is like now in America."

Decter initially wrote her review of *Papers* for *The New York Review of Books* but they turned it down. She was finally told by editor Barbara Epstein that Robert Silvers, the editor-in-chief, felt the review just took Mailer too seriously. Decter today is convinced that she, and not *The New York Review of Books*, was right: *The Presidential Papers* marked the beginning of the change in the critical establishment's view of Mailer.

"There was a new generation of readers coming along," Decter says. "In retrospect you can see it now, that the old-brow divisions had effectively broken down, but it takes a long time for such processes to become evident. Mailer was one of the figures of the new wave of 'no brow'—not high or low or middle. The taking seriously of Norman Mailer was coextensive with that process. Norman's vision was also beginning to become established. He was no longer on the edges; he was at the center. What was in *The Presidential Papers* was Mailer the journalist, the reporter, and after all, if he didn't invent the New Journalism, he practiced it at its best."

The mass media were less intrigued. Although *Newsweek* hailed the "bold and original" voice of *The Presidential Papers*, *Time* was critical. "He is a fearless performer," wrote their critic in the November 29 issue, "a lively controversialist and handles heavy cultural names like King Lear, Dostoyevsky, Freud, Sartre like a demented, butter-fingered juggler."

But the most damning review was the one by John Kenneth Galbraith in *The New York Times Book Review*. It was published five days before Kennedy was shot. The economist made it clear that Mailer's attempts to be a political insider rather than a novelist were pathetically funny. "This book," he wrote, "is a definite forward step in the development of Norman Mailer's fiction, for it has a plot. The plot may be a trifle lacking in freshness; the story of the man who labors for another and then finds himself rejected in the moment of his friend's triumph has been used before. However, the novelist contrives a new twist by putting himself into the story—and giving significant supporting roles to the President of the United States and his wife."

The Kennedy establishment may not then have seen Mailer as a significant voice. But the events of November 22, 1963, in Dallas, would shake the country to its roots and give rise to a pervasive sense of alienation, even absurdism, which perfectly matched Mailer's new ironic tone of the sixties.

• XII •

AN AMERICAN DREAM

For almost a decade Mailer had been promising to return to fiction. Instead he had used his energies to regain a foothold in the literary establishment through his subjective nonfiction, his own brand of the New Journalism. Now, at the end of 1963, having decided he would no longer write his "Big Bite" column, he announced his return to the novel, the form that had made him famous. In his final column in the December 1963 issue of *Esquire*, Mailer stated that beginning the following month he would write a novel in the form of an eight-part serial for the magazine. Each installment would be written to deadline. The novel would be called, he said, *An American Dream*.

Some considered the project a literary stunt, but it would eventually force the critics, many of whom were still ignoring or patronizing him, to take a position on his talent. Mailer had also found a way of satisfying those readers who were skeptical about his ability as a novelist after the long hiatus since *The Deer Park*. At the same time he was sidestepping the big novel he was forever promising. The serialized novel would not have "the huge proportions and extreme ambition of the big book," he wrote in his *Esquire* column. "But it will be a good novel. I hope it will be a very good novel. If I fail, the first price to be paid is the large wound to one's professional vanity—If I succeed, well, we may all know more."

Two years later Mailer would confide that the real reason for doing a serialized novel was economic: "Since I'd been married four times, I was quite justifiably paying for my past. I had to earn a lot of money in a year. That meant I had to do a novel, and I knew the only way I could write a novel in a year was as a serial. Otherwise I'd work it over too much, never get it done."

The project was risky, but the public interest would be great. No modern American novelist had ever attempted it. As Mailer pointed out, one would have to go back to Dickens or, more significantly, to Dostoevsky for comparison. He modestly added that no direct comparison was intended, but he had cleverly entered the historical literary arena. Dostoevsky, in reality, would have more than a little influence on his *American Dream*.

"There was great, great interest in the suicidal nature of what he was doing," recalls Harold Hayes, who had become editor of *Esquire*. "The circumstances at best were tough. If everything had been done right, if he had no problems and if his work schedules allowed him to do everything that should be done, it still would have been tough. So there was a great deal of anticipation and excitement on the part of the editors. What the hell was going to happen?"

Though Mailer's game plan for the novel was provocative, his first installment, which appeared in the January 1964 issue, was even more so. The segment ended with the protagonist strangling his wife to death. Mailer purposely invited autobiographical comparison by creating a hero, Stephen Richards Rojack, with a history similar to his own and a wife displaying all the external trappings of Lady Jeanne. The author would also introduce a blond nightclub singer named Cherry, with whom Rojack would begin an affair shortly after the murder of his wife. Beverly concedes that the character is actually a composite of her and Carol Stevens, a nightclub performer whom Mailer had known previously. Carol would eventually become his fifth wife, if only briefly, and mother of his seventh child.

When he wrote the first installment of *An American Dream*, Norman and Beverly had just returned from a trip to Las Vegas to see the second Liston-Patterson fight. Mailer originally intended the novel to be about a similar journey. But once he started writing about his hero and the hero's wife, he impulsively ended the installment with the murder. "To have your hero kill his wife in the first installment of an eight-part serial is like taking your clothes off in Macy's window," he later said. "What do you do next? But I finally realized I was the one man in America who could do it. The clue to me is, I figure I've got as much physical courage as the next guy, but I'm profoundly afraid of being a moral coward."

The murder was in many ways a brilliant ploy. Invoking the stabbing of Adele, it would hook the sensationalists and carry them deeper into Rojack's mind, which brooded on the universal questions of modern dread and reflected Mailer's view of the violent nature of American power.

Rojack had returned from the war a hero with a Distinguished Service Cross and had become a congressman at the age of twenty-six. He was thus thrown into the public eye at a young age, just as Mailer had been. Horrified by the memory of German soldiers he had killed, and feeling like an "actor," Rojack committed political suicide by running for office in 1948 on the Progressive ticket, an echo of Mailer's involvement in the Wallace campaign.

As the story opens, Rojack is a middle-aged professor of existential psychology at a New York university who believes that "magic, dread and the perception of death were the roots of motivation." He has become a television personality and author of a popular book entitled *The Psychology of the Hangman*. Rojack is not immune to the fascinations of power, for he has married a wealthy heiress, Deborah Caughlin Mangaravidi Kelly, the daughter of a multimillionaire. As Rojack says of her, "She had been my entry into the big league. I had loved with the fury of my ego. . . . With her beside me I had leverage."

Deborah is also the quintessential "bitch goddess," a corrupt product of power. Rojack murders her to save his own soul from similar corruption. In some ways both Dreiser's *An American Tragedy* and Dostoevsky's *Crime and Punishment* would be reenacted in Mailer's novel but with significant moral differences. What Dreiser perceived as tragedy Mailer perceived as a dream of liberation. And Dostoevsky's punishment never comes, for Rojack is not prosecuted.

Mailer's first installment of *An American Dream* arrived at *Esquire* late, as would most of his chapters. Despite the rush of getting the segment into type, all the editors were enthusiastic about it—all except the aging publisher, Arnold Gingrich. Gingrich was becoming a passionate defender of "the New Puritanism," a movement being espoused by Charles de Gaulle in France to eradicate prostitution and pornography.

The New Puritanism was a return to older manners and morals

and stood in direct opposition to the attitudes of the younger *Esquire* editors who were trying to relax restrictions on language and obscenity. The early sixties were still something of a testing ground for censorship: The case of *Lady Chatterley's Lover* had recently gone to court, and magazines were still vulnerable to censorship threats. Mailer's two-decade battle with censorship was clearly not yet over.

"Mailer's first chapter presaged some pretty steamy stuff, and Gingrich was put off by it," Hayes recalls. "He was never that knocked out by Mailer to begin with. The rest of us were congratulating ourselves that we got it into type on deadline. We had announced this thing, and by God we were going to run with it. But the second installment was when the fun started."

In Mailer's second chapter Rojack, after strangling his wife, enacts a buggery scene with her maid. He then throws Deborah's body out a ten-story window onto the East River Drive to camouflage the murder. When the piece came in, Hayes sent it to Gingrich for his standard reading. Hayes received a perfunctory note back which said simply, "No." It looked as though *An American Dream* was over after only one installment. Hayes and *Esquire*'s literary editor, Rust Hills, who had been largely responsible for the magazine's literary inclinations in the early sixties, went in to see Gingrich in the hope of changing his mind. "We can't do this," Hayes told Gingrich. "We can't cancel this thing. We've announced it would go eight chapters, and we've only run one. We'd look foolish to our readers."

"Sure we can do it," Gingrich replied. "Just start something else."

"It was one of the few times I've known him to be absolutely unswervable in his conviction," Hayes reflects. "He felt it was unpublishable, and it was not going to run in a magazine he was associated with."

Hayes and Hills were fully aware of the problems. The installment contained a graphic depiction of buggery in which Rojack alternates between the maid's vagina and anus, a symbolic representation of the battle between good and evil. "It was as far as anyone had gone," recalls Rust Hills, "except for Norman himself in *The Time of Her Time*. That was quite shocking, but in a national commercial magazine such as *Esquire* it just couldn't be done."

Hills took the manuscript home to ponder the problem and came up with a solution that saved the novel from a premature death. "If I had an editorial thought there, it was to make the scene a little fuzzier," he says. "It became a choice—and this was implicit in Mailer's theme in the beginning—between good and evil. We just made it more metaphorical rather than physiological. Somehow Norman realized that if he wanted to go through with this project and not have it be an embarrassment to *Esquire* and himself, some moderation would have to be made. And he made it."

Gingrich was finally persuaded to accept the changes and reluctantly agreed to let the piece run. *An American Dream* continued on its course for six more monthly installments, all against grueling deadlines. Mailer's secretary, Anne Barry, remembers the long hours and the photo-finish sessions with Mailer working up to the last minute. "Sometimes he would even come back from a party and go to work," she says.

Mailer had continued to write in his third-floor studio or at the living-room table. But shortly after Beverly gave birth to Michael in March, Barry relinquished the second bedroom and began using the third-floor studio as her office. Mailer was forced to create a new work space. What he designed, above the living room, was an elaborate glass and wood gable which extends several levels up, like a mad, pyramid-shaped ship. Anne Barry recalls: "At the very top, one had to climb up a ship's ladder, then sidle across a wooden plank with a vast drop beneath, to reach a door. Inside was a small room with a skylight and a desk." This is where Mailer escaped to work as his family grew larger down below.

As Mailer continued to write his monthly installments of *An American Dream*, Barry remembers that she was generally not encouraged to make comments on the manuscript. She did, however, suggest small changes which Mailer subsequently incorporated. While he was working on the sixth installment, for instance, she mentioned that Rojack hadn't eaten anything in twenty-four hours. "Oh, I'll make up some scrambled eggs or something," Mailer replied. He did include a scene in which Cherry whips up steaks, spaghetti, and scrambled eggs for the now ravenous Rojack. "The novel was done in such haste," Barry says, "although I'm sure he had the framework of the plot in his mind. He has an extremely rational and orderly mind, and things naturally came up as he was writing it."

Barry also remembers that Mailer would scrawl brief notes on characterization on scraps of paper in longhand and then give them to her to type. She would return the neatly typed notes to him, and they would disappear for a time before they were filed. The technique, of course, was radically different from the carefully documented index-card system which Mailer had used for *The Naked and the Dead*.

Complications with the plot of *An American Dream* inevitably arose because of the haste with which Mailer had to conceive it and because nothing could be rewritten in the earlier segments. When Rojack threw his wife out of the window in the second installment, for instance, Mailer thought this would disguise the real cause of her death. By the fifth chapter, when Rojack is being grilled by police detective Roberts, Mailer asked Barry to double-check whether the time of death could be determined despite the long fall.

Barry called the coroner's office and discovered something called "dependent lividity." She was told that when someone dies, whatever, part of the body touches the floor becomes bruised. Rojack had turned his wife over before throwing her from the window, so she was bruised on both her front and back. Detective Roberts, however, had discovered her on the street faceup.

"Norman had several regrets over this one," Barry remembers, "but he took a deep breath and said, 'Well, I better get back to work.' He had this pixieish look in his eye, aware that he had written himself into a small corner. He couldn't change the fall scenario, since it was already in print, so he had narrowed the plot of the installment he was then working on." Mailer, however, successfully wrote himself out of the bind. When Detective Roberts asks Rojack how his wife could possibly have bruises on her front and her back since she was discovered lying in the street faceup, Rojack craftily replies that she was placed facedown on the stretcher which carried her away.

❦

While the *Esquire* serialization forced Mailer to finish his novel in eight months, the magazine certainly was not paying him the large amount of money which presumably was his reason for writing it. The money would come instead from a book publisher, and the deal would be one of the first of many orchestrated by Scott Meredith, Mailer's new literary agent. Meredith had a controversial reputation in New York publishing circles because he was one of the first agents to charge a fee for reading unsolicited manuscripts, which flood agents' offices. He was also one of the first agents to begin multiple submissions, in which a client's manuscript is sent to more than one publishing house at the same time. Although the practice was once frowned upon, it is now common in the publishing industry, and the Meredith agency is one of the largest in New York.

Meredith was also known as an agent who could get "top dollar" from publishers for his clients. Although he and Mailer had met casually several times over the years, it was not until 1963, when Mailer badly needed money, that he called Meredith. "I hear that you're the one who gets the money," Mailer said. Meredith answered, "I hear that, too. Let's talk."

Just before *An American Dream* began appearing in *Esquire*, Donald Fine, the vice-president of Dell and Delacorte, received a call from Meredith, who asked if he would be interested in publishing the novel in book form. Fine, who had once worked for Meredith and who is now president of Arbor House, was beginning to gain a reputation for wooing authors to Dell-Delacorte with large six-figure offers for joint hard- and soft-cover deals. Not only was the advance money substantial, but the authors were allowed to keep all their paperback royalties rather than split them 50-50 with the hard-cover house.

Fine was interested in adding Mailer to his list, but he eventually turned the project over to Richard Baron, the publisher of the Dial Press, a small, literary hard-cover house which is also a subsidiary of Dell.

Baron finally got the book after agreeing to a one hundred twenty-five thousand dollar advance for hard-cover rights alone. He then sold the paperback rights to Dell for a larger sum, although it was a standard deal in which Mailer would only keep half the paperback royalties. "A hundred thousand dollars in those days was a magic number," recalls Baron, "and we went even higher. Norman wanted to get into the big time, and he deserved to be there."

Mailer's move to Dell helped launch a publishing-industry revolution. Shortly after this, Fine was able to attract the two other famous World War II novelists, James Jones and Irwin Shaw. Both Jones and Shaw had been at their respective publishing houses, Scribner's and Random House, for more than a decade. Their moves foreshadowed a transformation in the publishing world from a gentlemen's business in which authors remained loyal to one house to a new system in which many writers signed with whoever paid the most money.

❦

In the seven months between the final installment of *An American Dream* in the August 1964 *Esquire* and the book's hard-cover publication in March 1965, Mailer worked on minor revisions with a succession of Dial editors. The first was Dial's editor-in-chief, Henry Robbins, who left Dial not long after Mailer arrived. The manuscript was then taken up by another Dial editor, Christopher Lehmann-Haupt, today a book reviewer for *The New York Times*.

Lehmann-Haupt remembers that the changes were not very significant. "Once the book was written, there wasn't a great deal of revising," he says. "It was part of Norman's pride in the whole project that he was going to do the Dickensian trick of a novel to deadline, and the manuscript was pretty clean. I did make about a dozen suggestions originally, having to do with language and imagery, and Norman, as always, was firm about what he disagreed with and gentlemanly about what he thought was a case in point."

Richard Baron, sensing that Mailer might want time to develop his first novel in ten years into a work of major scope, proposed delaying the book. "Everybody at Dell was hungry and wanted the book fast," Baron says, "but I knew what Norman's ambitions were, and I asked him if he wanted to take more time and extend it in depth. It really lent itself to that, and I thought it might fulfill his desire to do that big novel. He said the idea was intriguing but that I had to remember what his nut was, which was about a hundred thousand dollars a year, and he'd have to work a couple of years on it. I told him not to worry about it. He was quite touched by this and thought about it seriously, but he came back and said he wanted to do something else."

By the time E. L. Doctorow arrived at Dial to replace Robbins as editor-in-chief, Mailer's novel was already in galleys. Doctorow was then a virtually unknown thirty-three-year-old editor who had moved over from New American Library, where he had been managing editor. Mailer had always been one of his heroes. Despite Doctorow's hesitancy about making detailed editorial suggestions now that the book was in galleys, he did have one "crucial insight." He proposed to Mailer that the murder should take place at the end of the book rather than at the beginning.

"It seemed to me," Doctorow says today, "that by revealing Rojack was a killer at the beginning of the book, Mailer reduced its tension. The book was written with a sense of ambiguity and paradox and irony, so that it almost demanded we not know whether he in fact did the killing. Norman missed the bet there for a much stronger book, but he said a good thing for a young editor to hear. He said, 'Where were you six months ago when I needed you?' and then he indicated that it was too late for him to go back and rewrite the book at that point."

Doctorow also recalls a specific image Mailer used to explain why he did not want to revamp the book. "He had a good image, perhaps by way of defense, for not choosing to go ahead with an editorial decision he admitted was a good one. He said, 'A book that's written always stands between one on either side of the shelf that is not written.' The idea was that with a little shift in emphasis here or change there the book could become a different one—the one on either side of the shelf."

When *An American Dream* was published in book form in March 1965, Mailer and his new novel became the focus of a literary war. The debate over Mailer's talent had never reached such a pitch.

In the most vitriolic attack Elizabeth Hardwick called Mailer "a bombed-out talent, scraping in the ashes." "*An American Dream*," she wrote, "is a very dirty book—dirty and extremely ugly."

Joseph Epstein labeled the book "confused and silly," pointing up Mailer's excesses. Tom Wolfe, in his inimitable style, scoffed at Mailer's obvious imitation of Dostoevsky and compared him instead to suspense writer James M. Cain, saying, "I think Norman Mailer can climb into the same ring as James M. Cain. He's got to learn some fundamentals, such as how to come out of his corner faster. But that can be picked up."

Eliot Fremont-Smith added to the critical attack: "Mailer's vision," he wrote, "is so excessively romantic that it comes out a parody of itself, and of himself. It is a sad parody because Mailer shows no more awareness of it than of the hatred for women that vibrates off these pages—or indeed of the hopeless vacancies of his ideas."

Three days before Fremont-Smith's review ran in the daily *Times* of March 17, Conrad Knickerbocker in *The New York Times Book Review* predicted that Mailer was going to be in for a rough time of it with the critics: "They'll carve it to pieces as they have so much of Mailer's work not for what it is, but for what it is not. If only, they'll say, if only . . . Norman would behave. If only Rojack . . . had written a sweet Jewish letter to himself instead of killing his wife, we could forgive Mailer and give him our Mafia kiss."

John Aldridge was also encouraging in his review for *Life*. He pointed out that Mailer's detour into journalism had actually prepared him for a new novelistic style. *An American Dream*, he concluded, was Mailer's "major creative breakthrough."

Mailer saw Aldridge's review before it was printed in *Life*. Having heard that Elizabeth Hardwick was about to publish a negative critique of the book in *Partisan Review*, Mailer tried to offset it by asking William Phillips, the editor, to reprint Aldridge's review in full in the same issue as Hardwick's. When Phillips, understandably, refused, Mailer bought two full pages in the spring issue and reproduced Aldridge's review himself.

He prefaced this "Small Public Notice" with the following: "*An American Dream* has received the best and the worst reviews of any book I have ever written. Now it's rumored that Elizabeth Hardwick has written a bad review for *Partisan Review*. I hasten to shudder. She is such a good writer. I also hasten to furnish her for company a review by John Aldridge which appeared in *Life*. I cannot pretend I was displeased to see it there, but I'm nearly as satisfied to see it here, cut only to fit the space even if I pay for the pleasure."

John Aldridge hadn't seen any of the bad reviews when he wrote his own piece, but today he points out that the very thing that intrigued him about *An American Dream*—that Mailer had chosen himself as his own best fictional protagonist—was exactly what disturbed other critics. "Not long before *American Dream* was published," he says, "Norman had been a very bad boy in public, and that was very much on people's minds. There were a series of things he had done that made him a public figure, and the novel reinvoked that. Here's a man who kills his wife, etc., and some people pointed that out. *The Presidential Papers* didn't call to mind the public image of Mailer as much as *An American Dream* did."

Despite the conflicting opinions generated by Mailer's new novel, or perhaps because of them, *An American Dream* immediately sold almost fifty thousand copies and made the major best-seller lists. Mailer helped write the advertising copy, discussed the packaging of the book, and even worked on the dust-jacket design, which featured a small picture of Beverly imposed on a Day-Glo American flag. Norman "was quite articulate," says publisher Richard Baron. "His ideas were always constructive."

❦

The battle of critical opinion may have spurred sales of *An American Dream*, but it had also set off Mailer's combative mood, which he was to display at his publication party on Monday, March 15, 1965, at the Village Vanguard. Don Fine had persuaded a reluctant James Jones to attend, but as soon as Jones arrived Mailer engaged him in a sparring match. The other prize Delacorte author,

Irwin Shaw, also attended the event, but as Christopher Lehmann-Haupt says, "There was talk about other people not having shown up."

As Mailer continued to drink, he became increasingly pugnacious and depressed. Lehmann-Haupt recalls that at one point when he decided to help serve and got behind the bar, Mailer came up to him and angrily said, "Stop posturing." "I didn't have a clear enough image of myself then to know whether the comment was deserved," Lehmann-Haupt relates.

The young editor was slated to be on the receiving end of still more Mailer bellicosity that night. As the party wound down, Lehmann-Haupt came over to say good-bye to Mailer. "He was sitting alone behind a table," Lehmann-Haupt recollects. "He was fairly drunk and moody and deep in some funk. I've only seen him that one time in that degree of withdrawn moodiness." When Lehmann-Haupt reached over to shake Mailer's hand, the author, as if to ward off a punch, jerked his drink toward the editor, spilling its contents. Although Lehmann-Haupt still believes it was an accident, Richard Baron, who witnessed the event, thinks otherwise.

Boxer José Torres remembers that Mailer almost got into a fight with jazz musician Miles Davis at the party. Davis was flirting with Beverly, and Torres saw Mailer becoming tense. Torres himself was getting nervous because he knew if Mailer threw a punch, he would have to defend him. "I didn't want to hit Miles Davis," Torres says, "but I didn't want him to punch out Norman first. Luckily, Davis just walked away."

John Aldridge, who also attended the party, remembers Mailer's condition. "He was absolutely catatonic at that party at the end," he says. "I don't remember him being hostile, but I might have missed it because it was a very crowded affair. But about the time I was leaving, I went up to him, and he looked as though he was completely out on his feet. He was standing, but propped up against the wall, and he didn't seem to be focusing on anything at all. I think he was simply plastered."

The next day Aldridge had lunch with Mailer at his Brooklyn Heights home, and despite the night before, Mailer seemed in fine shape. Aldridge took notes of that meeting and today remembers the setting and the man vividly. "He had a large duplex with big windows," Aldridge recalls, "opening onto a spectacular view of Manhattan and the Brooklyn Bridge. The place was cluttered with every imaginable item, all projecting a great sense of vitality and disorder—gymnastic ropes and ladders and bars hanging from the roof and reaching down two stories into the living room. In a space next to one of the windows Mailer had built a huge model of the city out of plastic Lego blocks, a magnificent construction which I thought had real architectural elegance. It was his idea of the city that might rise after the 'shit' had inundated the present site of New York.

"On the walls were photographs of his two beautiful daughters by Adele, comic telegrams, mementos of parties, a pencil sketch of James Joyce dated 1917, a framed copy of the notorious ad for *The Deer Park* which was run in *The Village Voice*. In the bathroom there were various pornographic cartoons, mostly French, and more telegrams.

"The dining-room table had been set with just two plates, and he and I sat down. Members of the jazz group which had played at the party the night before were lounging in the living room listening to records but left soon after I arrived. His blond wife Beverly was present, as was his secretary, a small round girl with chubby cheeks and huge horn-rimmed glasses. There were also two black maids in white uniforms. It seemed distinctly a ménage and very much a Mailer ménage—crowded, busy, vital.

"Mailer himself seemed in better form than I had ever seen him, fatter by twenty pounds than five years before but very sharp and intense. He was no longer truculent and defensive as I last remembered him from Connecticut, where for a year we'd been neighbors with houses not far from the Styrons. He seemed to have undergone some obscure but remarkable inner change. He was putting out enormous psychic energy, reacting to everything, clowning, pacing back and forth, yet clearly a bit tense about our meeting, trying to project himself to me.

"He spoke about Styron, saying that Styron was having a larger social life than ever, his connections now running to the White House, to which Styron had been invited during the Kennedy period and again when Johnson was inaugurated. Mailer having *not* been. And that Styron's compulsion in the social direction, his need for it, was probably a bad thing for his writing. He had a choice, said Mailer, of either becoming a great writer and giving himself up to it or settling to be simply a very good writer. I said I thought during the Connecticut period Mailer had been more admiring of Styron than was quite called for, and Mailer replied that he'd been impressed by *Lie Down in*

Darkness and perhaps most by Styron's remarkable sense of family, which would probably impress him less now that he had had experience of family himself.

"He also spoke of the Bourjailys and said the death of their daughter had changed them both. Mailer felt that maybe if Vance went far enough in his suffering, he might yet write an important book. He then referred to our old trouble over *The Deer Park*, when I was called in by Rinehart to give a judgment of the book: negative. And Mailer said that we had a classic correspondence about it. I told him I had recently looked over those letters and decided I was partly wrong in the position I took. I said that I had sounded insufferably pompous. He said I was like Bill Buckley at that time: a tough man in an argument and full of the same oral severity.

"After lunch he walked me to the St. George Hotel, he wearing an old trench coat and looking like Harpo Marx. He shook my hand with real warmth and feeling, as if we had some affinity. I felt we had and felt sad to say good-bye to him. He's a very lovable and remarkable man, a genuine creative force, undoubtedly the very best we have."

Not everyone agreed, either then, or now. But by 1965 Norman Mailer was harnessing those creative forces for another attack on the national consciousness.

• XIII •

THE ABSURDIST AND THE MOVEMENT

During the early years of the sixties those in the radical movement, including Mailer, had been laying the basis for the cultural revolution that was to come. But outwardly the nation was relatively calm. The self-confidence that had characterized America for almost two decades had been shaken by the assassination of the young President near the close of 1963, but the sense of unease was not widespread, either among the youth or in the general media. Kennedy had sent only a small number of combat troops to Vietnam and the war in that torn Southeast Asian country was not uppermost in the national consciousness.

But from 1965 on, the unprecedented political and cultural changes that we now identify with the sixties started to assume dramatic proportions. Mailer had been shaping his radicalism for over a decade, and he was now ready to act as a philosophical mentor, role model, and activist in the upcoming foray against the establishment. He would encourage the younger leaders of the Movement, as the political protest of the sixties was called.

In the late fifties Mailer had been able to produce only two books, but in the fertile second half of the sixties he would publish still another novel, a new collection of pieces, a play, and two highly praised political nonfiction books, one of which would win him the

Pulitzer Prize, the George Polk Award, and a National Book Award. It was the beginning of the most prolific period of Mailer's life, a creative streak that would last until the end of the decade.

His prodigious productivity was impressive, but no less important was Mailer's emergence as an activist-performer, a role that was appropriate to the time. Each aspect of the sixties' cultural revolution would inspire Mailer: The theater of the absurd would lead to a new Mailer play; the emergence of camp and underground films to three Mailer movies; the struggle in Vietnam to his own political activism. By the end of the decade Mailer would become so involved that he would once again decide to run for mayor of New York City. In placing himself personally on the historical stage of this period, Mailer was also creating his own outrageous social theater, and the role he played both dismayed the critics and cemented his legend.

In July 1964, one month after he finished the last installment of *An American Dream* for *Esquire*, the magazine sent Mailer to cover his second political convention. This time it was the Republican convention in San Francisco, where Barry Goldwater was rallying his forces against the challenge of a moderate, Governor William Scranton of Pennsylvania. In Mailer's piece, "In the Red Light: A History of the Republican Convention of 1964," he characterized the convention as basically a war of "Main Street" versus "Wall Street."

Any Republican candidate would seem objectionable to Mailer, especially Goldwater, whose politics he had decried as early as his 1962 debate with William F. Buckley, Jr. But after weighing a Goldwater presidency against that of Lyndon Johnson, Mailer surprisingly opted for Goldwater. As an enemy, Mailer reasoned, Goldwater was more clearly defined. "For if Goldwater were President," he wrote, "a new opposition would form, an underground—the time for secret armies might be near again. And when in sanity I thought, Lord, give us twenty more years of Lyndon Johnson, nausea rose in some cellar of the throat . . . . Under Johnson we could move from the threat of total war to war itself with nothing to prevent it."

Mailer's article appeared in *Esquire* in November 1964, just before Johnson was overwhelmingly elected as President. His insights about the war were soon proven prophetic. One month after Johnson's inauguration the war in Vietnam was escalated, and by the following spring of 1965 Vietnam was becoming a fiercely debated national issue. A massive antiwar protest rally was staged in Berkeley, at which Mailer was asked to be a featured speaker.

Jerry Rubin, then a twenty-three-year-old activist, staged the protest, called Vietnam Day, in conjunction with the traditional Marxist-oriented left, who were then influential on college campuses. "The traditional left did not consider Norman to be a political person," says Rubin, "but I insisted on him because I thought he was a very important cultural statement of the reality of America at the time. Like a rock star, he interested a larger audience than the people who were just against the war."

Rubin had read Mailer's 1957 essay, "The White Negro," which had a profound effect on his emerging political attitudes. "I read that essay three or four times," he says. "I'm not saying that I fully understood it, but I read it many times. One of the major characteristics of the New Left was that white people admired and wanted to be like black people, a kind of reversal of the traditional American view. Norman advanced that idea in 'The White Negro' by saying that blacks were closer to their feelings than whites. He also broadened the definition of violence. Before, it would have been hard to imagine a plane dropping bombs as being violent. He was the first one who asked these questions and opened up the mind to these thoughts. Mailer combined an appeal to a wider public with an investigation of the unconscious."

Despite the traditional left's opposition to Mailer, Rubin prevailed. Months before the Berkeley rally he called the author at his Brooklyn Heights home and invited him to speak. Mailer was hesitant at first, but Rubin pointed out that there would be twenty thousand people in attendance; it would be the largest audience Mailer had ever faced. "Then Norman remembered that he was writing something on Johnson," Rubin recollects, "and thought it would be a good opportunity to test out the piece."

At the time Mailer was writing a review of Lyndon Johnson's new book, *My Hope for America*, for the *Herald Tribune Book Week* in which he excoriated the President for his "totalitarian" prose, adding that it was even possible that "*My Hope for America* is the worst book ever written by any political leader anywhere."

On May 2, 1965, Mailer spoke at Berkeley, where he employed some of the observations he had made about Johnson in his convention piece and in the *Tribune* review to indict the President. Mailer called Johnson a new "Caesar," claiming that his Great Society was moving from "Camp" toward "Shit." Johnson, Mailer went on, "is alienated from his own clear sanity."

If Johnson did not call off his air force in Vietnam, Mailer coyly warned, young people would persecute him by pasting L.B.J. pictures everywhere, upside down. "I do not advise it. I would tell these students not to do it to you, but they will . . . ," he told the crowd, speaking indirectly to the President. "Lyndon Baines Johnson will be coming up for air everywhere upside down."

"He got a standing ovation," recalls Jerry Rubin, "and people raved about the speech. He qualitatively changed the event. What he was really doing was giving us permission to insult a father figure, indicating it's okay to ridicule the President."

Another young radical, twenty-seven-year-old Abbie Hoffman, read Mailer's Berkeley speech when it was printed in Paul Krassner's satirical publication, *The Realist*, and was also influenced by the author. "The idea of turning L.B.J.'s picture upside down awakened in me dormant political ideas that had been brewing for a long, long time," Hoffman now says. "It helped lead us into the guerrilla theater that the counterculture became noted for in the late sixties." Writing about the incident, Hoffman added: "Mailer also showed how you can focus protest sentiment effectively by aiming not at the decisions but at the gut of those who make them."

Hoffman had become aware of Mailer when he read *The Naked and the Dead* while still in high school. "The image of a twenty-five-year-old Jewish writer who used words like *fug* and who told what army life was really about was very important to me," Hoffman says. "But if I had to pick out one essay by an American writer that was the most influential in my life, it was 'The White Negro.' That showed there was another way. It took everything that was being said culturally—what the beat generation was saying in poetry and what was being said in jazz—and added a political perspective to it. That essay opened me up to read Paul Goodman, Michael Harrington, and C. Wright Mills."

Hoffman had first encountered Mailer in person at a lecture the author gave at Brandeis University in 1959. Mailer looked like "some tousle-haired Hebraic James Dean," Hoffman recalled. He was "belting scotch from a bottle, and firing out insults and insights like body punches at a Brandeis audience. Wailing out at technology, craving for some primitive intellectual engagement, he lambasted the institutions of learning and culture. Exhorting the crowd to fan out from the hallowed grounds of academe, he predicted a New Age would be born in the gutters and back streets of America's bohemian underworld."

Hoffman had also witnessed Mailer's 1962 Chicago debate with

William Buckley, an event that strongly affected his growing radicalism. "There you felt on a gut level that William Buckley was representing everything you didn't like in your college experience," Hoffman says. "All the rah-rah baloney, the genteel and gentile power structure, the martini set and the Madison Avenue gray flannel suits. Buckley represented the empire, and Mailer was challenging the empire as a hip, ethnic street fighter. That was extremely appealing to me. There was no doubt emotionally about whose side I'd be on."

The Berkeley speech had strengthened Mailer's standing with the young radicals, for not only did he condone politics-by-disrespect, but his writing displayed none of the rigid conventions of some of the other anti-Vietnam intellectuals. Not long after Mailer even ridiculed a symbol of leftist intellectuality, the *Partisan Review.* The editors of the magazine, which then included Irving Howe, Alfred Kazin, Bernard Malamud, and Norman Podhoretz, had written an editorial objecting to American policies in Vietnam. Mailer was annoyed by the mild nature of the editorial's protest, and in a fall 1965 issue of the *Review* he replied in the absurdist tone that was gradually entering his work. "Three cheers lads. Your words read like they were written in milk and milk of magnesia," Mailer wrote. "Still your committee didn't close shop until after this extraordinary remark: 'The time has come for new thinking.' Cha cha cha."

Mailer then went on to castigate Johnson in his newfound jargon of ridicule: "If World War II was like *Catch-22*, this war will be like *Naked Lunch.* Lazy Dogs, and bombing raids from Guam. Marines with flame throwers. Jungle gotch in the gonorrhea and South Vietnamese girls doing the Frug. . . . Unless Vietnam is the happening. Could that be? . . . Cause if it is, Warbucks, couldn't we have the happening just with the Marines and skip all that indiscriminate roast tit and naked lunch, all those bombed-out civilian ovaries, Mr. J., Mr. L.B.J., Boss Man of Show Biz—I salute you in your White House Oval; I mean America will shoot all over the shithouse wall if this jazz goes on, Jim."

❦

At the same time that Mailer was assaulting the political and intellectual establishment, he was pursuing his interest in boxing as part of his belief in the mystique of personal violence—one that has always been in contrast to his condemnation of collective violence. On March 30, 1965, one month before his Berkeley speech, Mailer was sitting ringside at the light heavyweight championship fight in which his friend José Torres beat Willie Pastrano in the tenth round on a technical knockout.

Torres had been introduced to Mailer by Pete Hamill after the Liston-Patterson fight in 1962. As Torres recalls: "I didn't know who Mailer was. I asked Pete what this guy did, and Pete said, 'He's a writer.' I asked him what Mailer had written, and he said *The Naked and the Dead.* I still couldn't place him, but then Pete said, 'You know, the guy who stabbed his wife.' *Then* I knew who he was."

Mailer and Torres became friends, and by 1965, before Torres's championship fight, Mailer even offered to back the boxer when money problems arose with Torres's business manager. "Norman asked me how much I thought we could lose," remembers Torres, "and I said probably around sixty thousand dollars. He said, 'Well, I guess I can afford to lose sixty thousand dollars.' " As it turned out, relations were mended between Torres and his manager. "Norman wasn't that disappointed that he didn't have to put up the money," says Torres, "because it would have changed his life to become the manager of a champion."

At ringside Mailer showed little reaction as he watched his friend fight Pastrano. But when the technical knockout was declared in the tenth round, Mailer jumped into the ring with uncontrolled glee. Afterward he threw a large party for the new champion at his home in Brooklyn Heights. James Baldwin and Truman Capote were there, as were Reggie Jackson and Mitch Miller.

The following spring Jack Newfield explained in *The Village Voice* that the writer-fighter affinity was hardly new: Gene Tunney had been a traveling companion of Thornton Wilder; Sugar Ray Robinson and Chandler Brossard were friends; Budd Schulberg managed two heavyweights, Archie McBride and Alex Mitiff. And Papa Hemingway, of course, owned a gym and idolized former middleweight champion Stanley Ketchell. Now Mailer had his champion, José Torres.

During the summer of 1965 Mailer went to San Juan to watch Torres fight Tom McNeely. One of Torres's sparring partners there was Joe Shaw, a twenty-seven-year-old semiretired black boxer who was depressed because he had been unable to get an important fight for years despite some obvious talent. Torres had known Shaw since 1956, when they were both on the United States Olympic boxing team. In 1957 Shaw turned professional under the managership of

Cus D'Amato, who also managed Torres and Floyd Patterson. But Shaw was denied main fighting events by promoters and eventually ended up bitter and broke—forced to work as a merchant seaman. When Mailer met Shaw in San Juan, he decided to do something for him.

Mailer returned to New York in the fall and called a number of writers, including George Plimpton, novelist Harvey Breit, cartoonist Charles Addams, and Pete Hamill, who already knew Shaw. He also phoned his friends Roger Donoghue, Buzz Farbar, and stockbroker Tom Quinn. He eventually lined up ten people, each of whom agreed to put up six hundred dollars to form a syndicate to manage Joe Shaw.

When the syndicate was announced in the early spring of 1966, Shaw had not fought in over a year. He was eight hundred dollars in debt and was now working as a bouncer in the Dom on St. Marks Place in Manhattan. This did not discourage Mailer, who, in his new guise as manager, stormed into Madison Square Garden. Why, he demanded of promoter Harry Markson, was his boxer left out of important fights? Before Mailer left the Garden, Markson had assured him that when Shaw proved he still had something left the Garden would give him a main event.

For two years Mailer's syndicate tried unsuccessfully to edge Shaw toward the championship. "Shaw had the physical potential to be a champion," says Torres, "but he didn't have the complete interest, the head. When they put the money up to back him, it was a little late." Buzz Farbar agrees: "Unfortunately, we got him when he was on the way down. But we used to have a lot of meetings about Shaw. I remember I reserved a boardroom at CBS, where I was working, and at 5:30 P.M. we had our syndicate meetings."

George Plimpton recalls that whenever Shaw showed up at one of his parties, which he frequently did, he was quiet and soft-spoken. "If Norman could have given him a bit of his anger or his violent nature," Plimpton reflects, "he would have been the champion of the world. But Shaw didn't have that extra killer instinct."

❦

By the spring of 1966 Mailer's own violent instincts were more noticeable than those of his boxing protégé. This concerned his friends, who understood that Mailer's temper was continuously being tested by others. "Once he established a certain reputation, he was constantly provoked," says Mickey Knox. "It's like the champion who walks into a bar, and everyone wants to punch him. Those nobodies could then brag, 'Hey, I ran across Norman Mailer and flattened him.' I've seen it happen over and over. At parties people would constantly come up and give him that fish-eye look, and he would react. But he's avoided a lot of fights."

Being a fighter himself, José Torres understood the problem, but he also knew that Mailer did not like people to be too comfortable around him. This tendency in Mailer was acted out most blatantly with his wife Beverly.

When Mailer was drinking, the tension between the couple was tremendous. Torres remembers a trip he and his wife took to Provincetown shortly before Beverly gave birth to Mailer's sixth child, Stephen, in March 1966. It was the first time the boxer had been to Provincetown and the first time his wife had spoken with the Mailers. "Norman knew my wife was Puerto Rican," he says, "and although he was famous for cursing, he wouldn't do it in front of her." A considerable amount of wine was consumed at dinner. Mailer and Beverly became involved in a heated argument, but Mailer was respectful of Torres's wife and did not want to fight. "Wait a minute," Mailer told Beverly. "I don't want any punches." Beverly immediately answered that Mailer was hitting her in her private parts. Torres tensed as he noticed Mailer's embarrassment, but Beverly continued to provoke him, making a reference to Mailer's mother. White with fury, Mailer glared at his wife. "Beverly, I am going to get up and throw you out the window," he said. When Beverly repeated the line, says Torres, Mailer began to shake. Torres quickly took Mailer out and walked him around town. By the time they returned the atmosphere had calmed.

The battle between Mailer and his wife escalated during the summer of 1966, when the two of them founded an experimental coffeehouse theater, Act IV, in Provincetown. It was essentially Beverly's enterprise, providing her an opportunity to act, an ambition which had been deflected by motherhood.

Act IV seemed a good way for Beverly to have a creative life separate from her husband's, but this was not to happen. Instead the project stimulated Mailer's own theatrical interests, and he decided to stage a production of his play, *The Deer Park*. Beverly was not given the lead role of the dark, sensuous Elena but the subsidiary part of the blond starlet, Lulu. The situation grew worse the following January, when Mailer staged the play at the Theatre de Lys in New York, where Beverly was still cast in the role of Lulu. Although the casting may have been apt, Beverly considered it a professional put-down. Mailer rejected her, she later said, because "he doesn't want to share the limelight. He enjoys humiliating me—that's his problem."

Despite his matrimonial conflict, Mailer bought his first house in Provincetown that summer ostensibly as a gift for Beverly, although her name was never put on the deed. More than a decade later it became the subject of a bitter divorce dispute, but in 1966 both Mailers loved the house at 565 Commercial Street, which became the center of their family life. Set on the bay, the house, which had a large wood-paneled kitchen and a huge dormitory for Mailer's brood of six children, reflected Mailer's expansive life-style.

Vance Bourjaily remembers visiting the Mailers that summer with his wife, Tina. They found the house full of ropewalking equipment and special shoes in various sizes. "As soon as we entered the house," says Bourjaily, "I learned from Norman that there's a whole mystique about ropewalking. It's a feat of balancing that has religious import in some societies and is a circus act in others and a kids' show-off trick in still others. Norman has the capacity not only to get totally absorbed by something like that but also to communicate his enthusiasm for it to everybody else. We hadn't been there an hour before we were trying to find the right ropewalking shoes and Norman was showing us the basic technique. This remarkable enthusiasm for odd things seems to be an important part of his considerable magnetism."

❦

By that summer of 1966, Mailer's literary enthusiasms were becoming increasingly absurdist, and this was reflected in his third collection, *Cannibals and Christians*, which the Dial Press published in August.

"We live in a time which has created the art of the absurd," Mailer said in introducing the book. "It is our art. It contains happenings, Pop art, camp, a theatre of the absurd, a homosexual genius who spent thirty years as a thief; black humor is its wit, the dances are livid and solitary—they are orgiastic: orgy or masturbation—the first question posed by the art of the absurd. So the second: is the art rational or absurd?"

Mailer was about to make his own rational leap into the absurd. His continuing obsession with this era of "plague" had a central metaphor: "cancer." In such a world he saw only two types of people: Cannibals and Christians. The Cannibals are the right wing, those who "can save the world by killing off what is second rate." The Christians are the liberals or the Communists, who "are utterly opposed to the destruction of human life and succeed within themselves in starting all the wars of our own time."

The first part of the book, entitled "Lambs," includes Mailer's political pieces on the Republican Convention, his review of L.B.J.'s book, his Berkeley speech, and the *Partisan Review* reply. The book, in fact, is dedicated to Johnson, "whose name inspired young men to cheer for me in public."

Part two of the book, called "Lions," is primarily literary. It contains his "Goddess" piece, which is preceded by an essay on the decline of the American novel; a hostile review of Mary McCarthy's *The Group;* and reviews of a book about Hemingway, *That Summer in Paris*, and of *J.F.K.: The Man and the Myth.*

Part three, "Respites," includes an account of a television show on which Mailer appeared with Nelson Algren and during which a dispute arose over the worth of William Styron's work; Mailer's *Playboy* interviews on sex; a *Paris Review* interview; two pieces on architecture, one of which describes the 'Vertical City of the Future' that Mailer constructed from Lego blocks in 1965; and a story about a convict entitled "The Killer," which would later intrigue another criminal: Jack Henry Abbott.

The pieces in the fourth part of the book, entitled "Arena," were written before the others but advance the idea of absurdity most explicitly. Consisting, in part, of three self-interviews, the section explores abstract ideas about mood, scatology, and form and soul. It ends with a story about an American President who decides to blow up a plague-ridden earth so that enough force is generated to blast him and a handful of pioneering humans into the cosmos in a rocket ship.

Mailer's work was becoming more difficult to categorize. Some critics simply dismissed Mailer and his *Cannibals and Christians.* In its September 2, 1966 issue *Time* magazine commented: "Norman Mailer writes so obsessively and says so many silly things that the crowds he draws have learned to come with their pockets full of ripe eggs. . . ." *The New York Review of Books* would not print a critique of the book until the following year, perhaps because Mailer included a letter to editor Robert Silvers in *Cannibals*. The letter accused Silvers of not printing Midge Decter's review of *The Presidential Papers*.

But several other critics felt that in *Cannibals and Christians* Mailer was making a potent impact on contemporary consciousness. Eliot Fremont-Smith, who had panned Mailer's novel the previous year, even suggested that perhaps the author should receive the Nobel Prize for Literature. "What is odd is that the thought [of the Nobel] should shock," he wrote in the August 22 daily *New York Times*. "In terms of sustained courage, worthwhile provocation, original entertainment, wild but pertinent imaginativeness and sheer hard work, Norman Mailer has few, if any, peers writing today in the English language. . . . He gets inside of one, and churns things up. . . . The reward is the performance of a champion."

Wilfrid Sheed in *The New York Times Book Review* on August 21 theorized that the world Mailer created in *Cannibals* was very much like the new world of hallucinogenic drugs. It was, Sheed said, "a world in which the earth breathes and the body teems with separate identities . . . a guide to the new demonology—camp, frozen foods, bad architecture, polyethylene bags: all the malign or enfeebled spirits that war against our body-cells and are literally driving this country out of its mind. . . ."

When Sheed wrote this, he did not know that Mailer had already completed thirty thousand words of a new novel which was, in some ways, to reflect these ideas. Christopher Lehmann-Haupt, who was now at *The New York Times*, called Mailer in Provincetown that August to ask him about Sheed's notion that *Cannibals* was actually a guide to the new hallucinogenic vision. Mailer said it was possible, although he had never taken LSD. "I'm an old-fashioned pothead, you know, though marijuana probably provides similar experiences." Mailer added that he had started on a new novel in June, "but I can't tell what it is yet. . . . It's different from anything I've done." The novel was *Why Are We in Vietnam?*

Why Are We in Vietnam? took Mailer only four months to write. It was finished by September 1966, although it would be another year before the novel was published. Mailer was not exactly sure he *had* finished it, and he sat on the book for several months before deciding to release it. He had originally started out to write a story about two tough, mean rich boys who commit motiveless murders of massive brutality in Provincetown. "Yet because I could not thrust Provincetown into such literary horrors without preparation," Mailer later wrote, "I thought I would start with a chapter about hunting bear in Alaska. . . . The hunting might serve as a bridge to get them ready for more." After two hundred and eight pages of the bear hunt, however, Mailer realized he had written his novel.

Mailer's fifth novel sought out the voice of the LSD generation, added obscenity, and used it as an anti-Vietnam war statement. The first paragraph of the book gives a sense of the radically different style Mailer was employing:

> Hip hole and hupmobile, Braunschweiger, you didn't invite Geiger and his counter for nothing, here is D. J. the friendLee voice at your service—hold tight young America—introductions to come. Let go of my dong, Shakespeare, I have gone too long, it is too late to tell my tale, may Batman tell it, let him declare there's blood on my dick and D. J. Docktor Doc Dick and Jek has got the bloods, and has done animal murder, out out damn fart, and murder of the soldierest sort, cold was my hand and hot.

Divided into "Beeps" and "Chaps," the story is told by Ranald Jethroe, or D. J. (alternately Dr. Jekyll and Disk Jockey to America), an eighteen-year-old Texan from Dallas, land of assassinations.

Mailer's new absurdist style upset, even annoyed, some of the critics. Christopher Nichols wrote in *The National Review* that D.J. "gargles the current Zeitgeist like Cousin Brucie on an acid trip." Mailer used obscenities, puns, allusions, and black slang in D. J.'s frenzied "stream of conch," invoking a sense of William Burroughs and Henry Miller. As Anatole Broyard said in *The New York Times* about D. J., it was "as if he blew a fuse trying to tune in on Wilhelm Reich and Marshall McLuhan at the same time."

Mailer's novel only mentioned Vietnam twice on the very last page, but some critics thought Mailer had achieved a connection, even if it was tenuous. *Why Are We in Vietnam?* tells the story of two Texas teenagers, D. J. and Tex Hyde (Jekyll and Hyde), who go to Alaska on a bear hunt with D. J.'s father, Rutherford (Rusty) David Jethroe Jellicoe Jethroe, a corporate executive of a firm which manufactures plastic cigarette filters that cause cancer. In Alaska, using guerrilla tactics, an arsenal of weapons, and helicopters to hunt the terrorized grizzlies, D. J. bests his father in courage. Both he and Tex Hyde climb above the timberline, where the animals are still in communion with nature. There the two boys come to some understanding of their condition as human beings. On the last page Mailer reveals that D. J.

and Tex are on their way to Vietnam, and despite all indications that D. J. no longer needs the war to release his crazed aggressiveness, the novel ends with D. J. saying, "Vietnam, hot damn."

On the back cover were two absurdist pictures of Mailer: one in color showing him as a grinning rogue with a black eye, and the other a more contemplative black-and-white photo. Below the pictures was the caption: "Will the real Norman Mailer stand up?" Anatole Broyard took note of the strange cover in the opening paragraph of his *New York Times* review, then went on: "His career seems to be a brawl between his talent and his exhibitionism. Like Demosthenes, who exposed himself during his speeches in order to hold his audience, Mailer has made his life a blurb for his books. . . . *Why Are We In Vietnam?* may be a third-rate work of art, but it's a first-rate outrage to our sensibilities. Mailer, disk jockey to the world, gets the nod over Mailer, the novelist."

Charles Samuels was no kinder in *The Nation*. "Having discovered that one's own bafflement might be excused as mirroring the age's," he wrote, "Mailer was ready for the chaos that is *Why Are We In Vietnam?* The hero of *An American Dream* is obsessed with buggery, and many of the snippets in *Cannibals and Christians* conceptualize the anal. Though scores of people will agree that our government is engaged in unnatural acts with the Vietnamese, I doubt that this is what they have in mind."

But despite the expected backlash to what was possibly the most obscene book of American fiction ever published, many critics found *Vietnam* a powerful novel. In the daily *New York Times* Eliot Fremont-Smith wrote, "In this repulsive and also often painfully lyrical and moving book, Mr. Mailer has laid claim to his country." Eugene Glenn called the novel "a triumph" in *The Village Voice*.

Why Are We in Vietnam? was written to fulfill Mailer's three-year-old contract with Putnam's—though it was not the novel Walter Minton believed Mailer had promised. The contract was for a book tentatively entitled *The Devil Revisited* or *The Murder of Good Ideas*. The deal had been made just before Scott Meredith became Mailer's agent, and the advance, incredibly, was only a thousand dollars.

By the summer of 1966 Minton was putting pressure on Mailer to deliver the novel he owed Putnam's. Minton was concerned because Mailer was negotiating a million-dollar agreement for a novel with Dell-Dial. James Jones and Irwin Shaw were already receiving enormous advances, and Mailer wanted to join their privileged ranks.

"Norman wanted a million dollars. That was the magic number," recalls Richard Baron. "It was the start of the big buying days, and he wanted more money than he had been paid before. I was all for giving it to him. Ed [Doctorow] and I had come to the conclusion that Norman was at his most prolific period, but we had a lot of resistance from Dell because they considered Norman to be unstable. It was my job to convince them that he was stable and also to convince Norman that he really should sign up this big one with me."

Baron finally persuaded the powers at Dell, specifically Helen Meyer, who was then running the company, to agree to this huge advance for a specific number of words of fiction, which Baron recalls was about five hundred thousand. The deal would be for either one novel or more. But arguments over certain boiler-plate points in the contract began to erupt. According to Baron, Mailer and Scott Meredith insisted on getting rid of the standard publishing clause which states that the publisher has to find the manuscript "satisfactory in form and content."

Baron persuaded Mailer to compromise on leaving in either "form" or "content," but near the moment of final agreement Helen Meyer objected to the omission of either. "At that time," she says, "a million dollars was a lot of money. I don't think Dell objected to the sum, but they were worried about not having anything to show for it, not even an outline. Mailer had no idea what he was going to write about."

"That was Helen's way out of it," Baron believes. "She wanted to do what she could to shake me and shake Norman. It affected my career. From that moment on I had pretty well had it, and I sold the rest of the company shortly thereafter."

Even though the deal fell through, Dial's generous bid raised Mailer's stock among publishers, and shortly after, on July 23, 1966, Scott Meredith was able to sell the large-novel idea to New American Library for $450,000. The deal was significant not only because of its size but because it marked the beginning of Mailer's fascination with "lucky numbers," an enthusiasm once shared by Sigmund Freud.

Robert Gutwillig, the editor-in-chief of NAL, remembers the signing. "The deal was in round numbers," he says, "but Norman turned up at the signing and said he had been to either a numerologist or an astrologer, and he wanted the figure to end up with some lucky number. It was very bizarre. A lot of people were gathered together, and we had the contract and the check, and Norman had this number on a little slip of paper. We all looked at each other and said, 'Well, that's what happens when you deal with great people.' Norman's figure was for less money than the contract originally called for. It was very strange. I've never had an experience like that before."

"At that time Norman had lucky numbers and unlucky numbers," Scott Meredith explains. "He's dropped it by now, but then we had to change some of the figures in contracts around from round numbers to strange odd numbers. He was very serious about it."

To please Mailer, the deal was changed from $450,000 to $448,000. Mailer told Meredith he could afford to lose a couple of thousand dollars for certain lucky numbers. In September, in fact, a rider was added to the contract which stated: "The final change is the last of Norman's 'lucky' ones, and simply involves juggling some figures. In Paragraph 3(a), following the order of the advance as now listed, read $48,000 for $50,000, $24,000 for $25,000, $80,000 for $75,000, $124,000 for $125,000, $72,000 for $75,000 and $100,000 for $98,000."

Once again there was no outline, but the NAL contract did have a one-sentence description of the proposed novel: "It calls for a novel dealing with aspects of the whole Jewish experience, European and American, in the past 100 years." Scott Meredith believes the intention of the contract was somewhat different. "In all our discussions, from the very beginning, it was clear that Norman was going to go through thousands of years, from ancient Egypt to the future," Meredith says. "But I know Norman was very anxious not to get too specific. He said, 'The first thing people will say is that I'm competing with science-fiction writers or historical novelists' and so forth. So the NAL contract sounds like it was just limited to one hundred years, but that was never the intention."

Mailer insists that *Ancient Evenings*, the first volume of his new trilogy, is decidedly not about Jews, even though his NAL contract called for a novel about the "Jewish experience." But Scott Meredith maintains that the "Jewish experience" is what Mailer always had in mind. "When he first started this, he was going to follow a Jewish family like the Mailer family from ancient times to the future," Meredith says. "That has really not changed. He still considers it to be something like that, although it's autobiographical only in the broadest sense. Who knows where any of our roots were in that period? I think what bothered him is that when it was put that way, some press reports made it sound like he was turning into Chaim

Potok, which is not what he intended to do. I think that's why he makes such a strong point about the trilogy not being Jewish. But I think the genesis of it was the question of where the Mailer family, a Jewish family, started."

Mailer had been talking about his long novel for so many years that Walter Minton eventually began to think of it as the book Mailer had contracted for with Putnam's. Minton even recalls seeing some of it in a very early form. Putnam's president, Peter Israel, who was then a young editor at the same house, agrees that sometime after *Advertisements* was published, they read a portion of a fictional work by Mailer. However, he points out that the file indicates it was a three-generation autobiographical novel starting in Poland. Israel's report on the novel at the time stated: "I read a fragment of the new novel and thought it was the best work he has ever done."

Minton was not pleased when he learned that Mailer had signed with NAL for the novel; nor was he pleased when he received the short obscene novel *Why Are We In Vietnam?* as the fulfillment of his contract. "He wrote *Vietnam* to fulfill the contract, but I wouldn't accept it as that," Minton says. "I said it was a totally different book from the novel we discussed. I always thought he wrote *Vietnam* to bust that contract. And I think it's the one work of Norman's that would have been improved with a good editorial back and forth, but whether Norman would ever do that with anybody, and particularly at that time, I don't know. I also thought that he hung an absolutely impossible title on the book."

The wrangling with Minton was undoubtedly part of the reason *Vietnam* wasn't published until September 1967. The advance for it was not agreed to until March of that year. Instead of the one thousand dollars stipulated in the contract, Meredith was able to get twenty-five thousand dollars for the book. "Minton didn't consider it the novel under contract," says Meredith. "*Vietnam* was a small book, and Walter was saying, 'I expected a big book, and this isn't it. We'll do it, but it doesn't complete our commitment.' I said, 'Sure it does, but we'll see what happens in the future.' But there was never any contract with Walter for that specific big novel."

❦

The large sums of money being offered Mailer were proof that his career was on the rise, at least commercially. But during these negotiations Mailer's energies were being spent on everything except writing. While he was in Provincetown in the summer of 1966, Mailer was busy creating a new version of his old ten-act play. *The Deer Park*, for his playhouse, Act IV. A young director named Leo Garen started developing *The Deer Park* with Mailer in front of Provincetown audiences, improvising as they went along. By the end of the summer they had decided to coproduce the play and bring it to New York.

Casting began in the fall of 1966, when Mailer and Garen arrived in New York. Rip Torn was given the part of Marion Faye; Gene Lindsey would play Sergius O'Shaugnessey; Will Lee was cast as Herman Teppis, the head of Supreme Pictures; and Marsha Mason, now the wife of Neil Simon, would portray the call girl, Bobby. The role of Eitel went to Hugh Marlowe, and Mailer's actor friend Mickey Knox was cast as Teppis's son-in-law, Collie Munshin.

In addition to casting Knox as Collie Munshin, Mailer also cast his friend Buzz Farbar as the orgiast, Don Beda. Farbar had originally met Mailer in 1962 while Farbar was the senior editor of fiction at the *Saturday Evening Post*. He had gone to a Christmas party that year at the home of Rust Hills, and by the end of the evening he and Mailer were the only ones left. They became friends, and when Farbar moved to Simon & Schuster's hard-cover imprint, the Trident Press, in 1965, he tried to get Mailer to do a book for him. Nothing ever came of the offer, but then Farbar moved to CBS, where he headed the book division.

During the summer of 1966, while Mailer was staging *The Deer Park* at Act IV, Farbar visited Provincetown and signed Mailer up to write a book on bullfighting. A slick, ill-fated picture-book-and-record project was actually put together and released in 1967. Entitled *The Bullfight: A Footnote to Death in the Afternoon*, it featured an introduction by Mailer, followed by ninety-one photographs. The accompanying record included a poem by Federico Garcia Lorca which Mailer and his daughter Susan, then eighteen, had translated together. When Farbar arrived in Provincetown to sign up the book, Mailer took one look at his deep tan and white linen suit and said, "My God! It's Don Beda." That night Farbar acted for the first time as Beda.

Casting Elena was somewhat touchy since both Mailer's ex-wife Adele, on whom the character of Elena was loosely based, and his current wife, Beverly, read for the part. Rosemary Tory was eventually chosen as Elena but Adele was given the job of her understudy. Many were surprised by Mailer's ongoing relationship with Adele, especially after the stabbing. "Adele was obsessed with Norman after they split up," Rosalind Roose, an old friend of Adele's from Provincetown, points out. "She was totally preoccupied by him. She lived and talked Norman. I guess it was hard to follow up with anyone after him. She couldn't give it up, so she tried to remain as much in his life as she could."

For Mailer this was not unusual: At that point he maintained good relations with all three of his ex-wives and still considered divorce the beginning of a friendly rapport. "When you're divorced from a woman, the friendship can then start because one's sexual vanity is not in it any longer," he has said. "At least not in the same way. . . . A hint of tenderness returns."

Beverly Bentley is the only ex-wife who is no longer friendly with Mailer. The seeds of the discord were partially planted during the casting of *The Deer Park* in New York. Beverly was especially concerned about her acting career because her marriage was crumbling. Mailer brought much of this problem on himself, for as soon as Beverly had her first child, Mailer was reportedly off with other women. As Beverly told the press: "When I was pregnant, he had an airline stewardess. Three days after bringing home our baby, he began an affair."

Beverly was angry when Mailer cast her as Lulu rather than Elena because she felt he had done it on purpose to hold her back. But Mickey Knox thinks otherwise. "Norman never held her down," he says. "In fact, one of the reasons he did *Deer Park* was to put his wives into it." Mailer would be questioned about his use of friends and family in the production, but he replied straightforwardly, "Why not? Half the plays put on are put on with the playwright's friends, the director's friends."

Mailer had the liberty to cast the play as he chose because he was paying for the production. "He put all his own money into it," recalls Mickey Knox, "and he wouldn't have any backers, which is odd for the theater. I think he invested something like seventy-five thousand dollars, but as he said, 'It's my play, I wrote it, and I'll take complete responsibility.' " Mailer had become a financial gambler with his theatrical productions, and within a few years he would pay the price for complete control when he produced three movies. It would erode his financial security, which was already precarious because of his growing alimony and child-support payments.

Nonetheless Mailer was enjoying the role of impresario and

exercising his natural skills as a promoter. When the play opened at the Theatre de Lys in Greenwich Village on January 26, 1967, limousines pulled up in front of the marquee, which simply read: Norman Mailer's *The Deer Park*. No one was prepared for the theatrical spectacle. The play had been separated into two acts with forty scenes, or scenelets, in each. To dramatize the fast cuts between scenes, Mailer, with the help of designer Gerd Stern, had devised an electronic board, similar to the ones used in football stadiums, which ticked off a number as each scene ended. Flashing lights and bells augmented the visual effect of the board.

Mailer had not only infused his new *Deer Park* with absurdist and apocalyptic import but had also added humor to what had been a somber story. But he was not to be taken seriously as a dramatist; the play offended reviewers, who could easily perceive what ingredients had been added to the novel for sensational effect. "What Mailer has done," wrote Wilfrid Sheed in *Life*, "is to jazz up his old book with scraps of parody and philosophy, gags from back columns, references to the Viet war, atomic explosions, four letter words, anything he thinks might help. Total theater, baby. But alas—he is still stuck with that old book." Walter Kerr concurred in *The New York Times:* "What we are meant to look at is a kind of dramatic lasagna: a layer of metaphysics, a layer of stream-of-consciousness, a layer of almost anything to keep the ready-to-serve sausages apart."

But despite the critics' condescension, most felt that the evening was not dull. By the following May the play had run for a hundred performances and would go on for another thirty-two. Mailer had a hit which was partially kept alive, he confessed, by using an old Broadway ploy: extracting the few favorable adjectives in the notices and advertising them.

When Dial brought out the book version of the play, Mailer wrote an introduction which attacked the critics for misunderstanding *The Deer Park* while pumping up what Mailer considered mindless hits such as *The Odd Couple*, *Barefoot in the Park*, *Cactus Flower*, and *Don't Drink the Water*. These plays were the "Theatre of Plastic," Mailer said, adding that he had walked out on all of them after the first act. Even *Fiddler on the Roof* and *Man of La Mancha* reflected the worst sort of manipulation, Mailer said. The first manipulated the Jews while the second played upon the desire to be noble. *Hello, Dolly!* was one of five plays Mailer found worthwhile, mainly because the musical was too crude to be manipulative and was good "the way the ball club is good." The other plays that he liked had to do with madness, even psychosis: *Macbird*, *America Hurrah*, *The Mad Show*, and *The Homecoming*. "The future of the theatre," he wrote, "seemed most rich where the material was most insane."

The day that Dial published the play, April 31, 1967, the publishing company and Mailer hosted a crowded block party on Bedford Street in Greenwich Village to celebrate the book, as well as the one hundredth performance of the play. With the hundredth performance of his play, Mailer's ego was in fine form: As he sipped a colorless liquid from a milk container, his mood became buoyant, and the public Mailer assumed center stage.

"Now that they have taken the title away from Muhammad Ali, the greatest champion of them all," he joked to the crowd, "a little of it has fragmented to all of us. And now, I'm the greatest, by Mohammedan dispensation. . . . Things are fragmenting, and if you can fragment without acid, then you are three steps ahead of the rest, and you will not only be beautiful, but you'll be able to make children!"

High on his own pontifications, he went on: "And another thing! The mayor ain't here. And let me tell you I don't look lightly on that. There's gonna be a reckoning. Loooong John," he drawled, referring to Mayor Lindsay, "is gonna be saaad Tom." With that, the self-proclaimed champion stepped down. Mailer's personal social theater was now becoming more absurdist than his play.

❦

Mailer's *The Deer Park* was part of a growing experimental theater movement, which was mirrored in the movie world by a new wave of avant-garde films, specifically Andy Warhol's "camp" movies. The author now decided to turn his theatrical energies in this direction. His work in the film medium would prove to be time-consuming, personally expensive, and often painfully amateurish. Most critics were to mercilessly pan Mailer's filmmaking but some felt that his efforts broke through boundaries.

Dotson Rader, a young leftist writer who was a friend of Warhol's, remembers meeting Mailer for the first time that year at an antiwar rally at the Fillmore East, where Mailer was speaking. The speech itself was a disaster. Mailer opened it with a dirty joke, which he was compulsively to use over and over, even at his celebrated fiftieth birthday party in 1973. It has always produced the same negative, embarrassed effect. As Mailer tells it, "A man goes in a restaurant, an elegant place . . . and he sees his ex-wife across the room. They eye each other for a while, and finally he decides he must cross the room and speak with her. 'Darling, you're looking wonderful,' he says. 'And you're looking splendid,' says the wife, who was recently married to a much younger man. 'Darling, I have a question to ask. How does your young husband like sticking it up your worn-out old pussy?' 'He likes it just fine,' she replies, 'once he gets past the worn-out part.' "

"After that joke it was solid bedlam and boos," Dotson Rader recalls. "People were yelling, 'Don't give us your bullshit; give us your money.' " Following the performance, Rader went backstage and introduced himself to Mailer as a friend of Andy Warhol's. "Warhol is the most perceptive man in America," Mailer told him. When Rader asked what he meant, Mailer explained that Warhol was the only man in America who could, like himself, sense the shifts and trends in the culture six months to a year before anyone else. This made him a kind of genius, Mailer said.

Mailer's new interest in Warhol and underground movies was prompted by Jonas Mekas, then the guru of underground moviemakers. At Mekas's suggestion Mailer attended screenings at the Filmmakers' Cinematheque and saw Warhol's *The Kitchen* starring Edie Sedgwick, the subject of *Edie*, a popular 1982 biography. (Mailer had auditioned Sedgwick for *The Deer Park* but did not feel she was right for the part.) Mailer said about Warhol, "He made every director brave enough to make a slow scene without trying to speed it up." Slowness of action, unremitting concentration of the camera on just three actors, and the absence of a script would be the hallmarks of Mailer's first cinematic effort.

The idea for the film arose during the long, boozy early-morning hours when Mailer and the cast of *The Deer Park* retreated to the Charles IV in the Village after each performance to relax. Rather than sit with his stars or his wife, Mailer chose the company of his two drinking buddies, Knox and Farbar. Eventually an impromptu conversation began to take place among these three macho Brooklyn boys. They began to speak extemporaneously, like Mafia hoods. The trio even adopted street names: Twenty Years (Knox, for his twenty years of acting), Buzz Cameo (Farbar, for his cameo in *The Deer Park)*, and The Prince (Mailer).

The roles became so intriguing to Mailer that one night, as Knox recalls it, Mailer told the other two, "Hey, let's make a movie, the three of us. The things happening here are so funny and interesting, let's just shoot it. I've got an idea: We're three Mafia guys holed up in a loft." Knox and Farbar liked the idea. "Norman was very interested in film," Knox recollects. "It was something he had never done in his life, and something he felt he should do. In fact Norman feels he should do everything." Mailer offered to put up fifteen hundred dollars for the venture, and Farbar agreed to do the rest, which involved setting up a meeting with Donn Pennebaker, of Leacock and Pennebaker, the producers of the successful cinéma-vérité film about Bob Dylan, *Don't Look Back*.

"Originally when they came to me," recalls Pennebaker, "I thought they were going to do a semifictional thing about the Gallo brothers, a kind of historical rendering. As it turned out, that wasn't what they were going to do at all. They were going to produce a kind of burlesque, an enthusiastic literary version of Monty Python. When I realized that, I thought, *Terrific, why not?* It doesn't really matter what he does as long as he comes to grips with it in the editing room, because that's where a movie is truly made.

"So I kept saying, 'Let's shoot it and then stand back, and if it doesn't work, we'll try something else.' But I don't think Norman ever had that in mind. He was under some money constraints, or at least that's what I understood from his lawyer, Charles Rembar. Also, Norman didn't want to do any conceptual work on the film, partly because he didn't quite know how to do it, and partly because I don't think he wanted to spare the time to do it."

Mailer decided that there would be no script and no retakes. On four consecutive nights that March 1967, working in Pennebaker's non-soundproofed studio, from twelve at night until at late as five in the morning, Mailer, Farbar, and Knox tried to recreate their impromptu Mafia roles while Pennebaker recorded it on 16 millimeter film and magnetic sound tape, at a cost of about ten dollars a minute.

Two minutes into the action on the first night, the theme of the movie surfaced. Knox mentioned that they had been holed up for twenty-one days and Farbar responded, "Twenty-one days you been sucking my joint." After some hesitation director Mailer reasoned that Farbar's insult had some inherent logic: "If three Mafiosos were indeed holed up for twenty-one days in a loft, they might not have the use of metaphor available on happier evenings . . . so the obscenities continued . . . insults winged like darts, dignities rose, vanities fell—a style came out of it."

The final cast of thirteen included Beverly Mailer and José Torres, who played bit parts. When Torres arrived with Mailer's poodle, the dog prompted Mailer to a competitive barking match which was kept in the film. Three hours of film were eventually shot, then cut down to ninety minutes, the source of the movie's title, *Wild 90*. Much of these ninety minutes were composed of improvised dialogue, such as the following:

BUZZ CAMEO: Twenty years. Twenty years of shit, that's what you are. You're twenty years of nothin'. You're the prince of what?

TWENTY YEARS: Listen, big mouth . . .

BUZZ CAMEO: The prince of my pickle, that's what you're the prince of.

THE PRINCE: That's what I'm the prince of, your pickle—your pickle with its dirty little warts. French tickle, Buzz Cam.

As it turned out, Mailer did not edit the film by himself. A young film editor was hired who would eventually work with Mailer on two additional movies. "What I had imagined," says Donn Pennebaker, "was Norman sitting at the editing table himself all night long doing the conceptual work. But Norman figured he could tell an editor what to do and go back and look at it. I think it led him into some pitfalls. I didn't think the film was good enough for theatrical release, and I told him so, but Norman has a kind of arrogance. If he gets kicked in the ass, that's okay, he goes for that. People sort of like that spunkiness. He's not a person who's terrified of a big failure. So we released it theatrically, and we got really bashed."

In *The New Yorker*, Pauline Kael declared: " 'Wild 90' is the worst movie that I've stayed to see all the way through. . . . Mailer has not only found a painless fast way to make movies, but has invented the new celebrity-party-game movie. . . . People can pretend for a few nights what George Plimpton works at for long stretches. . . . It may, for a season, be the biggest thing around."

Mailer had yet to read Pauline Kael's review with its reference to George Plimpton, but his next movie, which was filmed shortly after *Wild 90*, not only had a number of celebrities acting the roles but featured Plimpton himself playing the part of Mayor Lindsay. The new movie, which was also shot in four nights without a script, was about one night in a fictitious Manhattan precinct station presided over by Lieutenant Francis Xavier Pope (Mailer), a hardheaded but lyrical Irish cop. Pope and his two equally cynical detectives, played by Mickey Knox and Buzz Farbar, work over an assortment of petty criminals, dramatizing the existential relationship between cop and crook. Among the crooks were Rip Torn and author Michael McClure, who played members of the Hells Angels, and author Jack Richardson, who was cast as a gambler. Beverly Mailer played Pope's wife.

Mailer's transformation from the Mafia gangster in *Wild 90* to the Irish lieutenant in the new film was marked by the emergence of a strong Irish brogue. Mailer's Celtic leanings are now legendary. When questioned about them, he explained to Vincent Canby: "I've always loved the Irish and felt very close to them. . . . The Irish have always had what the Jews didn't have. The Jews have this *funny knowledge* that if you respect life enough, it's going to respect you back. The Irish have never understood that. On the other hand, the Irish have this great *bravura, a style, an elegance*. . . . As an Irishman I can have moral conversations with my prisoners that I could never have if I were any other kind of detective."

Mailer's new film, originally entitled *Bust 80*, then *Beyond the Law*, was technically more complex than his first one. Mailer now used three cameras, filming scenes simultaneously. It was cinematically more advanced, but it was also chaotic. On the first night of filming, still photographers were colliding with the film crew. Mailer had wanted spontaneity, and he got it, but primarily because nothing was spelled out in advance. "Norman never said what he was going to do," Pennebaker recalls. "He never said, 'Watch me.' He just said, 'Okay, we'll start,' and assumed I could get anything he did."

George Plimpton remembers this spontaneous moviemaking with amusement. "Norman called me up and asked if I'd like to be in his film," he says. "I do everything Norman tells me to do, and I said sure. I went down to where he was shooting to discover it was sort of a parlor game."

"Where's the script?" Plimpton asked Mailer.

"There is no script," Mailer replied. "I will tell you the role you're to play, and then you walk through that door and do it."

"Do I have time," Plimpton countered, "to think about the role? Prepare?"

"No."

"Norman, come on . . ."

"No," Mailer responded. "It has to be spontaneous. Here's what you are: You're the mayor of New York. There's a prison through that door. You're checking up on reports of prison conditions. I'll give you four or five people who are on your staff."

"And with that," Plimpton says, "he shoved me through the door. The camera was turning on the other side. It was like playing charades. But I believe that was the way Norman made all his films; they were all spontaneous. Of course you can't make films that way. They had some striking individual character portraits, but they weren't held together by what a director or writer has to do, which is know how all these things fit."

Mailer was in no way discouraged by the chaos of the filming. By September 1967, just as his novel *Why Are We in Vietnam?* was appearing in bookstores, he was enthusiastically viewing the rushes of *Beyond the Law* and looking forward to editing the film. This, however, was not to happen for another six months. Late that September he received a call from an old acquaintance, Mitchell Goodman, who asked him if he would be willing to attend a march on the Pentagon in Washington during the weekend of October 21–22. After much consideration, Mailer reluctantly agreed to participate in an event that would lead him to his first Pulitzer Prize and to what many consider to be his greatest work since *The Naked and the Dead.*

· XIV ·

ARMIES OF THE NIGHT

On Thursday afternoon, October 19, 1967 Mailer stepped off a plane in Washington, D.C. He was met at the airport by Edward de Grazia, the lawyer for the Legal Defense Committee of the Mobilization Against the War in Vietnam, the group that was sponsoring the march on the Pentagon. De Grazia had first met Mailer in January 1965, during the Boston obscenity trial of William Burroughs's novel *Naked Lunch*. He had called on Mailer to testify on behalf of the book's morality, for as De Grazia points out: "I always saw Norman as essentially a moralist."

Like many of the younger radicals, De Grazia had been influenced by Mailer long before meeting him. A lawyer for a conservative law firm during the 1950s, De Grazia had eventually left for Paris to escape what he saw as the passivity of the Eisenhower era. It was not until he returned to America in the early sixties that De Grazia read *Advertisements for Myself* and "The White Negro."

"I still wasn't politicized," he recalls, "but Norman's writing had something to do with the change in me. He made you realize the possibilities of radical thinking and radical action. Some of the things in *Advertisements* gave me the idea that he was almost sponsoring a minorities' revolution in this country against the WASP's, especially by blacks, Jews, and Italians. Themes of that kind attracted me to him. Also there was his Berkeley speech in 1965, when he said we all ought to put L.B.J.'s picture upside down. I think for me Norman was one of the first people who said we've got to stop the war and somehow act. It seemed to be one of the first calls to action."

De Grazia had heard that Mailer, along with poet Robert Lowell, critic Dwight Macdonald, and author Paul Goodman, would be attending the march and decided that he would bring them together for a performance to raise money for bail bonds. It was to be staged that Thursday night at the Ambassador Theater in Washington. Not even Mailer could have predicted that with the imbibing of enough bourbon a "wild man in himself," or, as he would call it for the first time, "the slumbering Beast," would emerge with little advance warning that night.

At a dinner party scheduled before the performance there was little to distract Mailer from the alcohol except for Robert Lowell. Mailer latched onto this brooding, patrician WASP, who told him, "I really think you are the best journalist in America." Mailer quickly responded: "Well, Cal, there are days when I think of myself as being the best writer in America."

More bourbon was consumed by Mailer. When De Grazia and Mailer discussed who would be the master of ceremonies of the evening, De Grazia conceded the job to Mailer with some apprehension. "He's a wild man," says De Grazia, "even when he's not drunk. Who knows what he'll do, particularly when he's had as much to drink as he had that night. I was concerned. It was Norman trying to dominate things, and I wasn't sure his judgment was the best."

Mailer reached the Ambassador Theater clutching a full mug of bourbon. While thinking about the introduction he was to deliver, Mailer made his way to the men's room, which was pitch-dark. He missed the bowl and soggily realized that his error would have to be confessed to the audience. Otherwise the authorities would blame it on the demonstrators. He left the men's room, continuing to mentally prepare for his opening address. But when he reached the stage, he saw that De Grazia was already introducing Paul Goodman. *Traitor De Grazia! Sicilian De Grazia!* Mailer thought.

De Grazia admits he had almost forgotten about his Sicilian roots until he read Mailer's account of the night. "Norman," he says, "is very conscious of ethnicity." The attorney remembers a story Mailer told him about the time he worked in a mental hospital near Boston while he was a student at Harvard. "Being from Harvard was important to Norman at that time probably because he in some sense was trying to assimilate. When he went to work on his first day at the hospital, he walked in wearing a tweed jacket and his Harvard tie, but as soon as the patients saw him, one of them called out, 'Jew boy!' Norman figured they'd penetrated his disguise."

Mailer's sensitivity to ethnic roots would be confirmed in *Armies*, in which he sought to portray America's complex traditions through the young dissidents, the older liberals, the military, and his poignant portrayal of Robert Lowell as the New England WASP. Not surprisingly, that night on the Ambassador stage Mailer's own Brooklyn-Harvard identity was overwhelmed first by his Irishman alter ego, then by a bit of the black man, and finally by the mean southerner, all wrapped in bourbon-soaked obscenity.

As soon as Paul Goodman finished his speech, Mailer reclaimed the role of master of ceremonies to introduce Dwight Macdonald. The introduction was long in coming, for Mailer's "Beast" was beginning to surface. "What are you, dead-heads?" he shouted. "Or are you all . . . in the nature of becoming dead ahsses?" On Mailer went with his insults and obscenities, provoking the audience into catcalls and jeers. As De Grazia recollects, "I think there was a lot of hostility toward him. He's a person anyway who a lot of people have hostility toward, even when he's at his best or most peaceable. That night he was obviously aggressive and antagonistic."

Mailer was now roaring at the crowd: "We're going to try to stick it up the government's ass, right into the sphincter of the Pentagon." De Grazia and Dwight Macdonald were right behind Mailer, trying to get him off the stage. "He was so drunk," recalls Macdonald, "that I thought he was completely out of control. Also, he was holding up the whole thing. So I tugged on his coattails and said, 'Norman, sit down.' He was just going on and on. It's a miracle we ever got out of that place." After the event, Macdonald says, Mailer walked up to him, "with his most narrow-eyed Western bad-guy manner," and said, "Listen, don't *ever* do that to me again."

Mailer refused to relinquish his role as master of ceremonies, but he finally did introduce Macdonald and then Lowell. After Lowell read to a standing ovation, Mailer was back for his own show. This time the southern accent surfaced, punctuated by obscenities and his guilty admission that he had missed the urinal bowl. "But tomorrow, they will blame that puddle of water on the Communists which is the way we do things here in Amurrica . . . you know who I am, why it just came to me, ah'm so phony, I'm as full of shit as Lyndon Johnson. Why, man, I'm nothing but his little old alter ego."

The obscenities now started coming more furiously. "This yere dwarf alter ego has been telling you about his imbroglio with the p*ssarooney [sic] up on the top floor, and will all the reporters please note that I did not talk about defecation commonly known as sheee-it!. . . but to the contrary, speak of you-rye-nation . . ."

Mailer's bizarre performance was duly documented by the national press the next morning. In his uncanny way Mailer had focused more attention on the evening than it might have otherwise received. "Without him the evening would have been a flop," De Grazia concedes. "His excitement and his energy—however much it was fueled by the bourbon—but also this particular genius he has when he's drunk probably was the most important thing going on. The act he put on, however incorrigible he seemed, really tied the thing together. His behavior was outrageous enough and he was smart enough and politically directed enough to get the national press to publicize the whole event."

The "Beast" would stay relatively dormant for the rest of the weekend, but the jam Mailer had gotten himself into at the Ambassador would furnish the style of *Armies of the Night*. His candid analysis of his own psyche at the event led him into an analysis of the national psyche. As Mailer wrote of himself in *Armies*, "Mailer is a figure of monumental disproportions and so serves willy nilly as the bridge—many will say the *pons asinorum*—into the crazy house, the crazy mansion, of that historic moment when a mass of the citizenry—not much more than a mob—marched on a bastion which symbolized the military might of the Republic. . . . Such egotism being two headed, thrusting itself forward the better to study itself, finds itself therefore at home in a house of mirrors, since it has habits, even the talent, to regard itself. Once History inhabits a crazy house, egotism may be the last tool left to History."

On the day of the march, Saturday, October 21, 1967, Mailer made his way with Lowell and Macdonald and fifty thousand others to the Lincoln Memorial and from there crossed over the Arlington Memorial Bridge into Virginia and headed toward the Pentagon. In the parking lot of the Pentagon, Mailer witnessed Yippie Ed Sanders perform a mystical exorcism on the five-sided center of the military, shouting, "Out, demons, out," amidst Hari Krishna chants. "Yes the hippies had gone from Tibet to Christ to the Middle Ages, now they were Revolutionary Alchemists," Mailer reflected. "Well, thought Mailer, that was all right, he was a Left Conservative himself."

Mailer was no longer taking drugs, although he was consuming excessive amounts of alcohol, and he would decry the use of LSD in *Armies*. While Mailer felt he had an affinity with the hippies, by this time Abbie Hoffman saw Mailer—despite his prophetic writings on hipsterism—as a cultural conservative. Hoffman believes Mailer's antidrug stance put him at a distance from the young radicals who were then beginning to outstrip Mailer's own projections of them in "The White Negro."

"Norman could not understand the counterculture," Hoffman says. "Part of this was because he was a cultural conservative, and part of it was a traditional confrontation between those who chose alcohol as their chief stimulant and those who chose drugs. He was sort of a dabbler in pot by this time, but he really was a drinker. He had long bouts when he was really alcoholed-out. I've always noticed that the whole two-fisted, he-man drinker approach rejected the hippie philosophy and the unisex attitudes."

That Saturday afternoon Mailer was arrested at the Pentagon by the Military Police, but, as Hoffman might have predicted, his arrest was made in a manner befitting the author's social position. By contrast, Jerry Rubin and other hippies were clubbed and arrested in late-night assaults.

Before the arrest Mailer, Lowell, and Macdonald had all consulted with David Dellinger, the chief organizer of the march along with Rubin. Dellinger decided it would be useful for them to be arrested, so the threesome wandered around the Pentagon parking lot looking for an appropriate moment. Finally they found themselves facing a double line of MP's. A rope lay between the MP's and the demonstrators which was not to be crossed.

Dwight Macdonald recalls the dramatic moment: "Suddenly Mailer, saying, 'If we're going to be arrested, might as well do it now and get out sooner' . . . strode up to the nearest MP, made a neat end run around him, and was deep in enemy territory before two marshals grabbed him. He flung off their hands, wheeled around, and gave us a triumphant grin, then was grabbed again and hustled over the grassy slope until he disappeared from sight. Lowell and I looked at each other blankly. The man of action had taken the men of letters, as well as the enemy, completely by surprise."

But Abbie Hoffman believes that Mailer's arrest was more symbolic than actual. "The arrest at the Pentagon was ritualistic," he says. "It was not your average arrest, which took place at two in the morning and where people were clubbed to the ground and dragged to paddy wagons. It was a celebrity arrest."

Dotson Rader adds, "It hurt Norman's reputation amongst the youngsters that he wasn't beaten up, that he was protected in a certain way because of his celebrity. It's no reflection on Norman's bravery, but it was seen by a lot of the kids as grandstanding. I had heated arguments at that time with friends of mine in the movement about Mailer. Lowell, Macdonald, and Noam Chomsky were all in exactly the same position as he, but they weren't criticized for the fact that they were treated with kid gloves, only Mailer. It has to do with his celebrity. He was and is a celebrity to a degree that's totally beyond anyone else. He was a star. Although he couldn't help it, there was, by his very presence, a condescension that the kids in the movement felt."

Mailer was first taken to a temporary prison at a U.S. post office in Virginia. It was there that he called his wife Beverly, a call which reminded him of his fondness for her. On this peculiarly American march, he now realized that his wife was of a piece with the country he both loved and hated. "It was not inconceivable to him," Mailer wrote, "that if he finally came to believe that his wife was not nearly so magical as he would make her . . . why then he would finally lose some part of his love affair with America. . . ."

Mailer spent the night in jail. The following morning Edward de Grazia was called to help release him. Of the thousand people who had been arrested on "disorderly" charges, Mailer received one of the most severe sentences: thirty days in jail, with twenty-five suspended. De Grazia, with the help of lawyer Philip Hirschkop, managed to file a handwritten appeal and got Mailer released on five hundred dollars bail. Yet Mailer's benign attitude toward the U.S. commissioner who sat as his judge in the barrack-like building that also served as a jail and his subsequent portrait of him in *Armies* bothered De Grazia. "They were trying to sandbag Mailer to make him an example," he says. "They didn't like him, he was the enemy, yet Norman sort of eulogized his judge. He appreciates people who treat him royally even if their idea is to guillotine him for it. So he comes up against a man who had the power to put him in jail, and Norman sees this guy, who, incidentally, was wearing what Norman believed to be a Princeton tie, as someone he would enjoy to have a drink with, later on."

Whether it was the night spent in jail, or an understanding of his affection for America, or a Maileresque farce, his mood as he addressed the press outside the courtroom seemed almost a parody of a renegade sinner embracing Christ. "Today is Sunday and while I am not a Christian, I happen to be married to one," Mailer explained. "And there are times when I think the loveliest thing about my dear wife is her unspoken love for Jesus Christ." (Mailer would later add, "Unspoken it was, most certainly. She would wonder if he was mad when she read this. . . .") But he went on: "You see, dear fellow Americans, it is Sunday, and we are burning the body and blood of Christ in Vietnam. Yes, we are burning him there, and as we do we destroy the foundation of this Republic, which is love and trust in Christ."

Edward de Grazia could hardly believe the speech. "It was totally out of character," he says, "but sometimes Norman tries on a role like a new suit or jacket to see how it fits, both for himself and the public. Here he was playing a born-again Christian. Maybe the experience of jail had affected him or purified him in some way, so he was really thinking of those higher values of existence. Or maybe he was trying to communicate some message to Beverly. But Norman is essentially a moralist, and when he came out of jail that day, he was speaking as a moralist."

By moving from the drunken, obscene-talking revolutionary provocateur of Thursday night to the man of action stepping boldly across the police line on Saturday to the humble lover of Christ on Sunday, Mailer had managed to encompass the spectrum of American sensibility within himself. It was a sensibility that only the most expansive, sensitive—and egotistical—of American writers could claim to possess. All of it would be in *Armies of the Night*.

❦

Shortly after Mailer returned from Washington, Scott Meredith received a call from Cass Canfield, Sr., chairman of Harper & Row, asking if he would have dinner with him and Evan Thomas, also of Harper & Row. At dinner the editors told Meredith that they wanted to try to restore the prominence of *Harper's* magazine and were looking for important authors, to whom they would pay sizable sums. At the time *Harper's* best price for an article was about a thousand dollars.

"I said to them that there was something very interesting," says Meredith. "Norman Mailer had just come back from the Pentagon march in Washington and had told me all about it. I told them I thought it would make an absolutely marvelous article, but that we would never do it for a thousand dollars. They asked me what I wanted, and I told them ten thousand dollars, which was much more than they had ever paid. They both got very gloomy and changed the subject, but apparently they went home and thought about it. The next day Cass Canfield called me and said, 'Okay, you've got the ten thousand dollars."

Willie Morris, who had just taken over the editorship of *Harper's* at the age of thirty-two (he was the youngest editor in the magazine's history), was also in on the negotiations. Morris had wanted to publish Mailer in *Harper's* ever since he had become an associate editor on the magazine in 1963. He had first met Mailer in Austin, Texas, in the early sixties through Harold and Barbara Probst Solomon, while he was still the editor-in-chief of the *Texas Observer*. "Mailer and I hit it off," recalls Morris. "I always respected his writing and his courage as a human being. The night we met, we went out drinking, and I got him together with a girl." Morris laughs. "He later told me it was the worst night of his life."

After Morris joined *Harper's* in 1963, each time he met Mailer he asked him to contribute something to the magazine. Mailer finally sent him a fifteen-hundred-word section from *Cannibals and Christians* which Morris was forced to turn down. "Mailer was anathema to the group that was then running *Harper's*," Morris states. "They were scared to death of him. I think they expected some kind of naked Bolshevik."

Mailer was not pleased when Morris had to reject his piece, but the young editor told him that he would probably be taking over the magazine in a year, and things would change. "He wasn't rude," says Morris. "He just sort of chuckled. Norman and I always got along very well. There's an electricity between certain southerners and certain New York Jewish intellectuals. It's very real in this country, and Norman likes southerners. He keeps putting on that goddam southern drawl."

When Cass Canfield called Morris about Mailer's Pentagon story, the *Harper's* editor immediately tried to reach the writer in Brooklyn, but without success. Morris finally got in touch with Scott Meredith, and a deal was negotiated. Mailer would write twenty thousand words about his experience at the march in one month, and *Harper's* would pay him ten thousand dollars, which, as Morris points out, "was an astronomical figure for *Harper's* then."

Late that afternoon, with Meredith's verbal agreement confirmed, Morris left for the Algonquin Hotel to meet someone for drinks. Afterward he headed for the Sixth Avenue subway. "As I was walking up Sixth Avenue," Morris remembers, "who the hell did I run into but Norman with Buzz Farbar. I told Norman about the deal I had just made with Meredith, and he crouched like a boxer—he used to do that a lot in those days, like he was shadowboxing with me—and he said, 'I know you did; I've just talked to him. I'm going to Provincetown tomorrow, and I will have a great twenty thousand words in one month from today.' "

Midge Decter, who was by then literary editor of *Harper's*, recalls that immediately after the deal was made she and Morris tried to line up a book publisher for the project. "For a few days," Decter relates, "Willie was trying to put together a package with a book publisher, until Scott Meredith finally told him he would handle it himself. But for those few days Willie was asking around. We went to Macmillan, since I knew Jeremiah Kaplan, the president and publisher. We had a meeting and told him we were looking for a publisher who could add enough money as an advance. Kaplan said, 'What did Mailer's last book do? It was a dog, wasn't it?' He was going to pretend that this was not a valuable property and that he was doing us a big favor. But the minute he said that, Willie stood up and said, 'Well, thank you very much,' and out we marched."

Meredith then took the project to New American Library, where Mailer had been signed for his large historical novel. A separate deal was made for the book on the Pentagon march for approximately twenty-five thousand dollars on top of *Harper's* ten thousand dollars. "The advance wasn't very large," recalls NAL editor-in-chief Robert Gutwillig, "because we felt they didn't have the right to ask us for a lot of money. We had already laid out so much for the novel which wasn't being written. The deal for *Armies* was made before anything was seen, so nobody, including Norman, had any idea what kind of book it was going to be."

At the end of November, Morris, who was by now pressing to meet the deadline for the March issue in which Mailer's piece was scheduled to run, called the author in Provincetown. Mailer told him he was almost finished, and Morris proposed flying up with Midge

Decter to see the piece. When they got there, they were astounded. In one month Mailer had written not twenty thousand words but ninety thousand. Morris began reading the manuscript, some of which had been typed by Mailer's secretary and some of which was still in longhand on yellow legal paper. "I was stunned," Morris says. "He had gone up there and hadn't had anything to drink for a month, leading a Spartan life with Beverly, and he had turned out this incredible ninety thousand words. When I finished reading it, I remember, I embraced him. Then I got on the phone to our managing editor, Robert Kotlowitz."

"What's going on up there, Willie?" Kotlowitz asked.

"I've just finished reading a beautiful ninety thousand words," Morris replied. "One of the great works of American literature."

"That's great," Kotlowitz said. "I was just waiting to hear that. How many words do you think we should run?"

"Well," Morris told him, "I think we should run it all."

There was silence on the other end of the phone.

"Well, in how many installments?" Kotlowitz asked.

"Bob," Morris responded, "let's run 'em all at one time."

"This was a big editorial decision, and Willie made it in a minute," Decter adds. "Nobody had done it before that I knew of."

Mailer's piece for *Harper's*, which would be called "The Steps of the Pentagon," was then the longest work ever to run in a magazine. Although *The New Yorker* had devoted a full issue to John Hersey's *Hiroshima*, the length of that book did not compare to Mailer's.

"Norman and I celebrated that night," Morris says. "He hadn't had a drink in a month, but I had brought up a quart of Wild Turkey, and we opened that bottle and began cruising Provincetown in the snow, drinking straight from the bottle. We finally ended up at a bar of the VFW hut. Mailer was happy. He really felt he had written something that mattered, and I knew he had. After a while he said, 'God dammit, Morris, stop telling me how good it is. You're like every southern boy I ever knew. You're too effusive in your compliments."

If Mailer was content, it was evident to Midge Decter that Beverly was not. "Beverly was miserable for having spent this time up there isolated and bored," Decter says. "She wasn't very happy with that month she put in; that was very clear."

On the following day Mailer finished writing his conclusion in longhand, and his secretary typed it. Morris and Decter took the manuscript with them on a small plane back to New York to ready it for press. But as it turned out, Mailer was not yet finished with the project. He began to write a factual epilogue to the piece which would document everything about the march and the antiwar movement that he had not personally observed. After another month the epilogue had reached twenty-five thousand words in length. Jerry Rubin remembers that he spent about ten hours being interviewed by Mailer for this account. "He really described things exactly as they were. It's a fabulous journal," says Rubin.

Macdonald confirms Mailer's extraordinary reportorial skill. During the Pentagon weekend Macdonald recalled, Mailer took no notes, as far as he could see. "Yet he reproduces, with few errors or omissions I detected, the scenes and the dialogues of the weekend." Lowell noticed this as well after reading the *Harper's* piece. "Curious," he said to Macdonald, "when you're with X [another novelist], you think he's so sensitive and alert, and then you find later he wasn't taking in anything, while Norman seems not to pay much attention, but now it seems he didn't miss a trick—and what a memory!"

The twenty-five-thousand-word epilogue would appear in the April issue of *Commentary*, a month after the *Harper's* piece was published, with the title "Battle of the Pentagon." "I thought it was an anticlimax," says Morris, "and didn't want to run it." Norman Podhoretz pointed out that the unusual division of publishing Mailer's work in two magazines came about because the epilogue was impersonal whereas the article for *Harper's* was intensely personal.

Morris remembers that as "The Steps of the Pentagon" was being hurriedly readied for press by *Harper's*, the copy editor kept coming in and saying to him, "I don't understand these words; this sentence is too long; this is a word I've never read before." After about the tenth time Morris turned to her and said, "Honey, don't you understand, he's a great writer, he's creating the language, leave him alone."

But his language, and specifically the obscenities with which Mailer had faithfully reproduced his Ambassador performance, stimulated an onslaught of letters and some cancellations when the piece was published in March 1968. "Oddly enough," says Morris, "the cancellations we got were not over his stand on the Vietnam involvement but over the language. That piece broke new ground for American letters; it was a watershed issue because of the language. I knew when I read it that this was going to be a singular leap, but I also knew we'd have to go all the way and not compromise."

Midge Decter also remembers the raft of protest by loyal *Harper's* readers, but she points out, "Out there in town where talk was going on, there was a powerful response. It was very big stuff. This wasn't a breakthrough for Mailer—it was the culmination of a process for him which set the seal on the whole thing."

Mailer's new style, in which he portrayed himself as the protagonist in the third person, represented all he had been striving for since his "Superman" article: the imposition of his own ego directly on a piece of history, in this case, the march on the Pentagon. It was the emergence of Mailer—the "nice Jewish boy from Brooklyn"—as the universal American. In himself he had found his best, most integrated novelistic character.

On May 8, 1968, twenty years to the day after the publication of *The Naked and the Dead*, New American Library brought out a hardcover version of both the *Harper's* and the *Commentary* pieces under the title *Armies of the Night: History as a Novel, The Novel as History*. (Mailer had taken the *Armies* title from Matthew Arnold's "Dover Beach.") The critical response was exuberant. "Here, in this extraordinary book," wrote Eliot Fremont-Smith in the daily *New York Times*," . . . all the facets of Norman Mailer, man and artist, settle momentarily into place; and we sense, as he senses, perhaps for the first time (and unexpectedly, inconveniently, at 44) Mailer whole and in place."

A. Alvarez in *The New Statesman* added, "[The] earlier explorations of the imaginative reaches of politics which were the best things in *The Presidential Papers* and *Cannibals and Christians* now seem like so many training flights for this book." Alfred Kazin in *The New York Times Book Review* called the book "a work of personal and political reportage that brings to the inner and developing crises of the United States at this moment admirable sensibilities, candid intelligence, the most moving concern for America itself. Mailer's intuition in this book is that the times demand a new form. He has found it."

Finally, Richard Gilman wrote in *The New Republic*, "Mailer's embattled ego is seen to be the troubled, sacrificial, rash and unconquerable champion for all of ours."

About the time of the publication of *Armies*, Mailer was displaying both that embattled ego and his involvement in the political upheaval of the time. That May, Jack Newfield recorded Mailer's flurry of activity on a single day from 4:30 P.M. until midnight. Mailer, along with José Torres, Torres's brother and trainer, Pete Hamill, Hamill's brother, and Buzz Farbar, had joined Tom Hayden at a bar. Hayden extracted a promise from Mailer to speak to GI's at a coffeehouse in Columbia, South Carolina. In return Mailer asked Hayden to set up a meeting for him with Fidel Castro. "I want a guarantee," he said, "man to man, that I can see Fidel. Or else, fuck him. I'm not taking any chances of going there and not seeing him. My time is valuable, too."

At 6:30 P.M. Mailer and his entourage arrived at Dwight Macdonald's for a fund-raising party for the striking students at Columbia University. Mailer listened to Mark Rudd, head of Columbia's Students for a Democratic Society, describe police efforts to allegedly falsify evidence, and, on his fifth bourbon, the author told the student rebel, "I know that cops create evidence. They've done it to me. All cops are psychopathic liars. Your fight is to show that the people who run the country are full of shit."

Mailer was then off to the Merv Griffin show. Before appearing on stage, he had been throwing rights which had just missed Pete Hamill's face. "Not hitting you, Pete, takes something out of my character," he said to Hamill. Mailer went on stage with Griffin. He had faced a hostile Griffin audience before the Pentagon march, and was now to be equally provocative. When Griffin asked him how the mood of the nation had changed, Mailer replied to a stunned audience, "The instances of faggotry have gone up in the country."

At 9:30 that same evening Mailer was at Madison Square Garden for a heavyweight championship fight. After midnight he was climbing over a fence at Columbia University to talk to Mark Rudd.

It was typical Mailer.

❦

Mailer's energy was formidable. Not only was he involved with the protest movement, but he was editing *Beyond the Law*. His first film, *Wild 90*, had opened that January at the New Cinema Playhouse. "I thought it was going to get a very pleasant reception," he recalled. "Instead, I got cockamamied in the alley. *Bam! Boom! Boy*, those *mothers* [the critics]. I found out I was in a tough racket. So I thought, if it's a tough racket, get tough. Stop clowning around. Up to that moment I'd sort of enjoyed the fact that I was a little bit of a clown."

Directly after Mailer had finished editing *Beyond the Law* in the late spring of 1968, he was ready to try his third and most ambitious film, *Maidstone*. By this time Mailer had founded his own movie company, Supreme Mix, based on the name of the Hollywood studio in *The Deer Park*, Supreme Pictures. Buzz Farbar had quit his job at CBS to run the company, which would be short-lived and financially unprofitable.

"I think Norman was bitter about getting blasted in the first two movies," recalls Donn Pennebaker. "He never made any money off them. He felt he was doing all this hard work, and it was not being appreciated in the film world. Money means success. I'm sure he felt he needed to vindicate himself."

As with his two other films, *Maidstone* would be produced with Mailer's own money. In fact, Mailer had even subsidized the distribution of his second film, *Beyond the Law*. Mailer had sold the distribution rights to Barney Rosset of Grove Press for the relatively small sum of fifteen thousand dollars. It was already clear that the movie would not be a box-office smash, and eventually Mailer took the film back from Rosset and paid him all the money that had not been earned out. "At that time he wasn't rolling in money," recollects Rosset, "and it astounded me. It struck me as being crazy. He thought we hadn't done a good enough job in distributing, but, as far as I know, after he took it back it was never shown again."

The cost to Mailer would be even more staggering with *Maidstone*. The cast included more than sixty people; the film was shot in color instead of black and white; five camera crews were brought in; and fifty hours of sound and film would be used. To finance the film, which had start-up costs of seventy thousand dollars, Mailer was forced to sell ten of his fifteen shares of *Village Voice* stock, which brought him two hundred fifty thousand dollars. The film would take three years to edit, and some estimate that Mailer paid out more than one hundred and fifty thousand dollars for this venture, which brought back little in return. "He spent a lot of money, and he lost a lot of money," says his friend José Torres. "He has not been able to get out of financial trouble since then. He never recovered. When it came time to pay his taxes, he had no money."

Once again there was no script and little directorial control. Mailer had decided that various scenes would be shot simultaneously at different locations, so he assigned directorial powers to several of the actors. Mailer's lack of directorial control began to tell during the five days of shooting, producing tension and some shocking displays of egoism.

The theme of the movie—assassination—added to these tensions. Mailer had conceived the theme in the days directly after the murder of Robert Kennedy in early June 1968, and a surprise assassination by a secret police force, with Mailer as the target, was one of the key elements in the film.

On Thursday, July 18, Mailer assembled his huge cast on the East Hampton estate of Mr. and Mrs. David Brockman for "orientation." The shooting would all take place in the Hamptons, which added a resort, party atmosphere to the filming. Wearing a brown leather cap, tan suede shoes, and cut-off jeans, Mailer stood up before the group sprawled on the Brockman lawn to explain what the movie would be about.

In the crowd were Rip Torn; José Torres; Peter Rosoff, a children's book publisher who had also appeared in *Beyond the Law;* Noel Parmentel, a former *National Review* editor; actress Mara Lynn; poet Paul Carroll; Eddie Bonnetti, novelist and ex-light heavyweight prizefighter; poet Michael McClure, who had been in Mailer's second film; Leo Garen, the director of the play *The Deer Park;* Buzz Farbar; two of Mailer's ex-wives, Adele and Lady Jeanne; his then-current wife, Beverly; his future wife, Carol Stevens; and a host of press reporters who were covering the event.

"It's going to be a film about a notorious movie director—Norman T. Kingsley—who has come to the east end of Long Island—we'll call it Maidstone—ostensibly to look at sites for his new film," Mailer told the crowd. "He is a tasteful director, a maker of resonant, romantic films on sultry themes—sex and violence. He's a mystery even to those who know him best: some say he's the worst kind of monster imaginable; others call him a saint. Now this film within a film is going to be a sexual spoof on *Belle de Jour* called *Le Monsieur.* This time there will be a *male* house of assignation to which *women* come. In the house will be a bunch of male studs—the director's Rat Pack—which we're going to call the 'Cash Box.' "

Mailer proceeded to introduce members of the Cash Box: Farbar, Torres, McClure, Bonnetti, two black militants, and a friend from Provincetown, Tim Hickey. He also introduced Rip Torn, who would play Kingsley's half brother and closest ally in the guise of a character called Raoul Rey.

"Kingsley is also contemplating running for President," Mailer went on. "The movie takes place a year from now and we're assuming that all the present candidates—Rockefeller, Nixon, Humphrey—have been k-n-o-c-k-e-d off, a possibility which isn't so unlikely as it may seem. The men up for consideration in their place—about fifty—

are people like Sinatra, Baldwin, Buckley, and Brando, which is also in the realm of the possible. But Kingsley is not at all certain he wants to run. For one thing, he's scared. Assassination is in the air. He doesn't know whom he can trust. He lives on the edge of death. For another, politics bores him. In particular, he feels tormented by PACX—Protection Against Assassination Experiments—a combination of the C.I.A. and the F.B.I. and the Secret Service. PACX has sent a large contingent to watch him carefully; some are with him, want to protect him and see him President, others hate him and want to see him dead. . . . As soon as I finish all of you who haven't been assigned a part . . . will draw lots to find out first whether or not you are in PACX and second—assuming you are—whether or not you're in the assassination party. By the way, Kingsley will be played by me."

James Toback, a filmmaker and director who was covering the event for *Esquire* and also participating in the movie, later stated that Mailer's ego was at its zenith and that he had gone from "commoner to lord, from democrat to fascist, from neurotic to psychopath, from Marx to Nietzsche, from writer to hero."

For five days the action moved through the Hamptons, from the East Hampton estate of the Brockmans to the home of Barney Rosset to the wildly elaborate estate of sculptor Alfonso Ossorio to the venerable Robert David Lion Gardiner's house and finally to Gardiner's Island. It was an ongoing orgy of booze and sex along with heated ego battles with the director. "Anarchy was loose there," recalls Donn Pennebaker. "There were too many things Mailer couldn't control, too many diverse people, and by splintering everyone up we lost sight of each other. The only focus that the film could take was the pornographic one. Everybody felt that, and nobody knew what to do."

The explicit sexuality of the movie, which included close-ups of people making love, may have been influenced by the *I Am Curious Yellow* trial, which Mailer had attended two months before. He had volunteered to testify on the film's behalf, and Edward de Grazia, the attorney for the movie, remembers something significant Mailer told him during the trial. "He said he had felt that making a movie of people having sex was likely to be an invasion of their privacy, something he would morally disapprove of. But after seeing *Curious Yellow* he thought it was highly moral, not immoral."

Maidstone not only contained more sexual material than anyone had envisioned, it was also becoming a battleground of precariously poised egos. On the second afternoon Mailer wandered over to where the Cash Box was ready to shoot a scene. Rip Torn took Mailer aside and told him, "Go away, Norman, it will be looser without you." Mailer left, but paper cups and tin cans were thrown by the Cash Box cast with cries of "You're a little tyrant underneath" and "You never listen to anyone but yourself."

Norman T. Kingsley was eliciting hostile reactions which were clearly aimed at Norman Kingsley Mailer. Pennebaker felt the hostility was in part provoked by Mailer himself. "He had a lot of people out there, and they were stomped into a terrible emotional frenzy," he says. "They were like fish driven around and around and ready to jump out of the pond. I could feel the tension. The evenings at the Hilltop Acres Motel in Sag Harbor where everyone was staying were torturous: Who was in? Who was out? Who was a success? Who was a failure?"

By Sunday night, when a large party scene was scheduled to be shot at the estate of Alfonso Ossorio, the threat of emotional violence was evident. "Norman was really like a wild man that night," says Pennebaker. "He was suffering terrible paranoia about people in general, and about Rip and Beverly particularly."

The filming of the party scene did not begin until 2:00 A.M., and everyone was exhausted from having been up since early the previous morning. Tempers and the alcohol level were high. An argument began when a young Provincetown actor insisted on appearing in a scene that Mailer didn't want him to be in. As José Torres recalls it, "Norman told him, 'I'm the boss here, the director. You get out of this fucking scene.' The actor yelled back, 'You can take the camera and the crew and stuff it up your ass.' Norman gave him one shot right in the jaw. He was unconscious for about twenty seconds, and when he came to, he saw me and said I hit him." According to Torres, the actor's jaw was broken, and to protect his friend Torres, Mailer had to settle with the actor: Mailer would pay all the medical expenses if the actor signed a paper to the effect that Mailer, not Torres, had hit him. He signed it.

By the final day of filming, Tuesday, many of the actors had left and morale was low. Mailer made a closing speech to the remaining members of the cast, the crux of which was self-congratulatory. Even though much of what had gone on seemed chaotic, Mailer said, he knew what he was doing, and it would all work out in the editing room. "This was said when he had no film at all but didn't understand that," Pennebaker recalls. "The only person who understood that was Rip Torn."

Shortly after his speech Mailer decided to use up some extra film by making home movies. Pennebaker's camera was rolling as Mailer played with one of his children. Suddenly Rip Torn emerged with a hammer in his hand and shouted, "You're supposed to die, Mr. Kingsley. You must die, not Mailer." He then hit Mailer on the head three times, actually drawing blood. With Beverly and the children screaming in the background, Mailer wrestled Torn to the ground and bit open his ear.

"I was looking through the camera and watching Norman turn blue," Pennebaker says, "and I continued to film, thinking, *What am I doing?* Rip told me later that the movie was a sham. Norman hadn't thought it out. Norman should have known that if you're going to introduce the idea of assassination, that assassins don't do what they're supposed to do anyway. I finally understood that Rip had done something extraordinary without exactly understanding what it was, and he got very badly mauled with part of his ear torn away. But in fact he saved the movie."

Mailer was furious at Torn for assaulting him after the filming. He even left the "assassination" scene, in which Torn hit Mailer with the hammer, out of his first edited version. Pennebaker told him he was wrong. "That's the only part of the film that's real," he said to Mailer. "You've got to recut it, and whatever you do, you have to make that the focus, because that's all that happens. Everything else is just pretty pictures."

"He resisted for a long time," Pennebaker recalls, "but he finally realized he had so much money and so much pride in it that he was determined to give it his best shot. Nobody will ever make a film like it again. It's a particular kind of flawed jewel. It's as if Richard Nixon had made a film while in office."

Maidstone would not be released until September 1971, when it was shown at the Whitney Museum. Vincent Canby believed that it was actually worse than Mailer's second film. But the critic saw some value in it when taken in conjunction with an essay by Mailer entitled "A Course in Filmmaking" which had just been published in book form along with the screenplay. It was, Canby said in *The New York Times*, "an uproarious, would-be-uninhibited literary picnic in movieland." The critic then added about Mailer himself: "The introduction [to the book] quotes an onlooker at the *Maidstone* filming as saying that 'Mailer's ego is bigger than his ass,' which is, strictly speaking, true. But such egos, when they are also attached to what may be genius, are to be cherished and watched over and preserved as national resources."

❦

Mailer had come to a significant point in his career by the summer of 1968 despite his failure as a filmmaker. He had seen the fruition of his early writings, even his prophecy, in the cultural and political revolution that was engulfing the nation. His "White Negro" and other works had inspired such young radicals as Abbie Hoffman and Jerry Rubin to political action. He had even joined them—albeit as a protected celebrity—on the defiant march on the Pentagon to protest the Vietnam War, turning his participation into an award-winning personal journal.

The year 1968 had been a trying one for the nation. Lyndon Johnson had decided not to run again. Martin Luther King and Robert Kennedy had been assassinated. The hostility between the protesters and the "silent majority" was at a fevered pitch. Mailer had contributed to the conflict and had gloried in his achievement. But as the melee continued unabated, the author—always sensitive to the national mood—began to feel restive, even ambivalent, about the revolution he had helped spawn.

• XV •

THE LEFT CONSERVATIVE

Like millions of other Americans, Mailer was beginning to be affected by the excesses of the late 1960s, as perhaps he was by his own personal excesses. He was undergoing a subtle intellectual transformation, moving toward a less radical view of the country. In August 1968 a serious, bespectacled, blue-suited Mailer was in Miami Beach calmly taking notes about the Republican nomination of Richard M. Nixon and feeling a strange sympathy for the man. Two weeks after the Republican convention he was in Chicago observing Mayor Daley's troops teargas and beat Yippie demonstrators while Hubert Humphrey was being nominated on the Democratic ticket. Surprisingly, Mailer was less than sympathetic to these young leftists.

Willie Morris had commissioned Mailer to cover the conventions for *Harper's* but wanted to run the piece in the November issue. This meant that Mailer had exactly two weeks after the Democratic convention ended on August 29 to compose an article that was equivalent in length to "The Steps of the Pentagon." Mailer would write in the same participatory style he had developed in *Armies*, this time calling himself "The Reporter," but fewer of his observations would be filtered directly through his own ego. In this piece, "Miami and the Siege of Chicago," Mailer also voiced his first serious doubts about where his political loyalties now lay.

His new ambivalence had surfaced when he arrived in Miami

Beach. The prophet of hipsterism was now voicing respect for middle-American WASP's and their philosophy, and questioning the left, who, he said, "had not yet learned to talk across the rugged individualism of the more rugged in America. . . ." He added that the left was "still too full of kicks and pot and the freakings of sodium amytol and orgy, the howls of electronics and LSD."

Mailer surprised even himself by his feelings of empathy for Richard Nixon, a man who before had inspired nothing but "nausea" in him. Yet something in Nixon had changed, he felt. "The older Nixon before the press now—the *new* Nixon—had finally acquired some of the dignity of the old athlete and the old con—he had taken punishment, that was on his face now, he knew the detailed schedule of pain in a real loss, there was an attentiveness in his eyes which gave offer of some knowledge of the abyss, even the kind of gentleness which ex-drunkards attain after years in AA."

The author of "The White Negro" also felt new doubts about the black revolution as he waited impatiently at a press conference for Ralph Abernathy. Speaking of himself in the third person Mailer said: "He was getting tired of Negroes and their rights. It was a miserable recognition, and on many a count, for if he felt even a hint this way, then what immeasurable tides of rage must be loose in America itself?" Mailer even worried that he was "in some secret part of his flesh a closet Republican." He asked himself: "how else account for his inner, 'Yeah man, yeah, go!' when fat and flatulent old Republicans got up in Convention Hall to deliver platitudes on the need to return to individual human effort."

Mailer's criticism was saved for the liberal Democrats in Chicago—Hubert Humphrey, George McGovern, Eugene McCarthy—each of whom had some weakness which Mailer sniffed out. Humphrey was the subject of Mailer's most devastating portrait. "Humphrey had had a face which was as dependent upon cosmetics as the protagonist of a coffin. The results were about as dynamic. Make-up on Hubert's face somehow suggested that the flesh beneath was the color of putty—it gave him the shaky put-together look of a sales manager in a small corporation who takes a drink to get up in the morning. . . ."

The McGovern appraisal was less biting but no less disparaging: "A Christian sweetness came off him like a psychic aroma—he was a fine and pleasant candidate but for that sweetness. It was excessive. . . . Not artificial, but excessive."

McCarthy had remained enigmatic to Mailer until an encounter in a restaurant. Mailer and *Look* journalist Joseph Roddy went over to talk to the senator during his dinner. Roddy recalls the opening salvos which Mailer neglected to put in his piece. "Why, of course I know Norman Mailer," McCarthy said as he greeted them. He then went on to make a humorous allusion to Robert Lowell's comment regarding Mailer's talent as recorded in *Armies*. "You are the best journalist in America," McCarthy said. Mailer reached across the table to shake his hand, but McCarthy didn't stand up. "You'll notice, Norman, that I remain seated because we poets must observe our natural precedence over the prose crowd." McCarthy's sharp-witted comments endeared the candidate to Mailer, and as he later reflected: "McCarthy was the first who felt like a President. . . ."

❦

But the real drama in Chicago was to be found not on the convention floor but in Lincoln and Grant parks, where the SDS and the Yippies were resisting Mace and tear gas as Mayor Daley fought for control of the city. Mailer had learned about the Yippie plans as early as the previous December, when he was interviewing Jerry Rubin for his Pentagon book. He had been "overcome by the audacity of the idea" when Rubin proposed a demonstration to terrify the establishment and force Lyndon Johnson, who was then still in the running, to be nominated under the armed guard.

The march on the Pentagon had symbolic meaning to Mailer, but the Chicago demonstration and its Yippie outrage gave rise to fears which the author tried to reason out. He was under a tight deadline, and a beating by the police would set him back. But there was something else to ponder—a concern that his inner gyroscope, which had always kept him on a radical course, was now shifting. "With another fear, conservative was this fear, he looked into his reluctance to lose even the America he had had, that insane warmongering technology land with its smog, its superhighways, its experts and its profound dishonesty," Mailer wrote. "Yet, it had allowed him to write—it had even not deprived him entirely of honors, certainly not of income. . . . The Yippies might yet disrupt the land—or worse, since they would not really have the power to do that, might serve as a pretext to bring in totalitarian phalanxes of law and order."

Mailer the Left Conservative would, however, finally choose the side of the left and join with the radicals, who he felt were at least brave. Before leaving Chicago he would twice provoke the police to arrest him and also try unsuccessfully to round up a tenth of the Democratic delegates to march with the young. But despite his belated alliance with the protesters, Mailer's political loyalties were clearly changing and his radical friends sensed this. "I think the sixties surpassed him," says Jerry Rubin. "Norman pointed the way with 'The White Negro,' but then we started to practice what he wrote about. I don't think he ever believed in the disruption theory of changing history, and his ideas about violence were more symbolic than real."

The New Left had once taken Mailer's prophetic radicalism as its philosophical base, but they were now beginning to see his views as being at odds with their own. Mailer's witness in "Miami and the Siege of Chicago" was more in tune with the country at large than with the New Left. When New American Library issued a simultaneous paperback edition of the piece in conjunction with its publication in the November 1968 *Harper's*, the book was welcomed by the critics.

"Mailer does not have to try to keep up with the times," wrote Wilfrid Sheed in *The New York Times Book Review*. "He cannot help it. His early warning system, which he refers to as fear, is in fact an incredibly delicate power-gauge. In a large mixed congress of people, it flutters violently. Is there any future in this group? Can I safely march with that one?—fears that seem trifling, unless we realize that he is really checking out the accuracy of his instrument, of his responsiveness to America, which is the source of his talent."

Time magazine applauded Mailer's subtle political change. "Mailer—Eastern Seaboard exotic, alienated artist, New York practitioner of improvisational cinema—is strangely in touch with heartland America this election year," the newsmagazine stated. "His own surprisingly shifting views of civil rights and Negroes, of WASPs and Nixon, seem to reflect the national mood."

The literary establishment was not far behind the press. Four months later, on March 10, 1969, it was announced that Mailer had won the National Book Award in Arts and Letters for *Armies of the Night*. *Miami and the Siege of Chicago* had been nominated as well in the history and biography category but lost to *White Over Black* by Winthrop D. Jordan. Reached that day by Henry Raymont of *The New York Times* at Proferes Desmond Films on West Forty-fifth Street, where he was editing *Maidstone*, Mailer told the reporter, "I'm afraid there's something obscene about a middle-aged man winning a prize. Prizes are for the young and the old." When asked about persistent rumors that he intended to reject the award as a protest against the establishment, Mailer dismissed the idea with amusement, saying he always thought that Jean-Paul Sartre made a mistake when he turned down the Nobel Prize in 1964. Sartre, he told Raymont, did not want people to refer to him as "the perverted existentialist Nobel Prize winner."

Two days later, on March 12, Mailer accepted the National Book Award at Lincoln Center's Philharmonic Hall, where *Armies* was praised for "its marked originality of form and its radical energy." The award citation continued: "Out of political conflict, Mr. Mailer has created a work of literature that is brilliantly personal and sustained in perception and that constitutes something of an American epic."

Greeted by the loudest applause of the afternoon, Mailer evoked laughter when he opened his acceptance speech by retracting his earlier remark to the *Times* about the obscenity of accepting awards. "Your speaker is here to state," he said, "that he likes prizes, honors, and awards and will accept them. . . . They are measures of the degree to which an establishment brings itself to meet that talent it has hindered and helped. So it is a measure, an historic bench-mark, as each of us, one by one, gives up his grip on the old rail of established winning procedure and proceeds to whirl down the turns into that new future, airless, insane, existential and bright, which beats in the pulse on our neck. . . . So three cheers for good marks, that remonstrance of devoted parents and modest schools, and bless us all as we explore the night. Thank you."

Mailer's editor at New American Library, Robert Gutwillig, recalls that after the ceremony Mailer took his parents, his wife Beverly, and his children to a restaurant near Lincoln Center. Fanny had given Mailer a congratulatory kiss, and his mood was jubilant. "He was so pleased for his folks," Gutwillig says. "That's what it was all about. It was his first prize, and it meant a lot to him, being accepted. I know he has these ambivalent feelings about being antiestablishment, but it was so nice for his family."

Two months later in *Look*, Joseph Roddy would publish a humorous account of something Mailer had said about his mother in Miami during the Republican convention. While he was seated in a Miami bar, a female piano player told Mailer that his mother had just been in and told her how Norman got into Harvard when there was a quota on Jews. Mailer looked up at the piano player and said that he had written a poem which went something like the following: "The trouble with mothers is they give kisses of congratulations which make you feel like a battleship on which someone is breaking a bottle."

❦

Two weeks after his award speech at Lincoln Center, Mailer was standing in front of a large gathering of associates at his home in Brooklyn Heights, accepting the suggestion that he run for mayor of New York City in the upcoming Democratic primary. Rather than put his energies into further protest, Mailer was hoping to change the political status quo through the electoral process. The idea had first come up in mid-March 1969, when Jimmy Breslin, Jack Newfield, and Gloria Steinem met at Limericks, a bar near the offices of *New York* magazine. As Breslin recalls it, Jack Newfield mentioned that he had been on the Barry Gray radio program the previous night and said that Breslin and Mailer ought to run for office. "I had two drinks," says Breslin, "and then said, 'Get Norman on the phone. That's a good idea.' I called Norman in Brooklyn, and he said he had to go away and lose some weight; then he'd get ready to do it. I went back to the bar and said, 'The bum means it. The hell with it, we'll do it.' "

On March 31 an eclectic crew met at Mailer's Brooklyn Heights apartment. Peter Maas and Gloria Steinem came from *New York* magazine. From the *Voice* were Newfield and Mary Nichols. Speech writers Jeremy Larner and Paul Gorman were there, as was Pete Hamill. The New Left was represented by Jerry Rubin and the blacks by Flo Kennedy. On the right were Noel Parmentel and a criminal courts judge. The only political advisers present were Paul O'Dwyer and John Scanlon. Buzz Farbar and José Torres made up the Mailer entourage, and Breslin was there as Mailer's running mate. From the beginning the meeting was bedlam, but when Mailer announced his platform, "a hip coalition of the left and right," there were arguments from both sides. The only thing that was finally settled was that the ticket would be Mailer-Breslin.

"At that first meeting everybody was crazy," Breslin remembers. "Nobody knew what he was talking about. We had another meeting the next night which was just as crazy—ten thousand egos colliding and nobody had a clear idea of anything. Except Norman, who had the idea of New York City as the fifty-first state. He had it in his mind before we started, and I concurred. I thought it was excellent."

In addition to voicing the fifty-first state idea, which has also been attributed to both Clay Felker and Pete Hamill, Mailer began to work out theories about giving individual New York neighborhoods local political power. As Joe Flaherty, Mailer's campaign manager, recalls in *Managing Mailer*, "The idea of such a mind waging war on the Democratic Party was becoming an irresistible notion." But there was still the ticklish question of whether Mailer was eligible to run since he had stabbed his second wife and might be considered a convicted felon. Breslin fielded this question with grace, asking the group, "How many of you clowns got records?" A sea of hands went up. "What a fuckin' crew," he muttered.

Joe Ferris, a friend of Flaherty's who had given Mailer the idea of neighborhood control, reminded the group that they only had six weeks to obtain the necessary petition signatures to place Mailer and Breslin on the primary ballot. About fifteen thousand signatures were needed. Mailer, who was getting ready to go to Provincetown for two weeks to think the whole thing over, said, "Shit, if we can't get seventy-five thousand signatures in a couple of weeks, we have nothing going for us." Joe Flaherty recollected, "I began to get the feeling that he possessed a very conventional political trait—he wanted to be drafted by acclamation, or, as Richard Nixon was fond of saying, he would serve if destiny called."

Most of those involved in the original conception of the campaign realized that the assault on the Democratic Party was to be basically symbolic. Almost no one expected to win, except perhaps Mailer. The Mailer-Breslin campaign was designed to shake up the political establishment, especially since the candidates for the Democratic Party nomination that year—Controller Mario Procaccino, Bronx Congressman James Scheuer, and Bronx Borough President Herman Badillo—were unappealing to the liberal-left, except for Badillo. At that point former mayor Robert Wagner had not entered the race, but while Mailer was in Provincetown, Wagner's candidacy was announced. Joe Flaherty called Mailer to tell him the news about Wagner and urged him to openly declare himself as a candidate. Mailer suggested waiting. Flaherty felt again that Mailer "was hedging his ego against possible lack of interest in his candidacy."

By April 13 Mailer was back in town and agreed to begin drumming up a constituency by speaking at college campuses and Democratic Party clubs. Gloria Steinem found a headquarters on Fifty-eighth Street at Columbus Circle, and on April 22 Jimmy Breslin joined Mailer on the campaign trail. Mailer explained to the crowds that he was running on a left-right axis from "free Huey Newton to end fluoridation," while Breslin played the working-class hero, making students feel guilty about their middle-class comforts.

On April 25 James Wechsler published a piece in the *New York Post* entitled "The Odd Couple," expressing his astonishment that Mailer considered himself a serious candidate. "Suddenly, at a few moments after midnight yesterday," he wrote, "the truth was inescapable: Norman Mailer is taking himself seriously as a prospective candidate for mayor. Others may be putting *him* on, but he is viewing his incipient campaign with deadly solemnity, nay, even sobriety. The revelation came on Johnny Carson's show where, after a brief appearance by lovely Senta Berger, Mailer took the stage. But this was not the Mailer of local folklore, garrulous, disheveled, rambling, and profane. This was The Candidate, his demeanor sedately and sedatively reminiscent of Robert F. Wagner."

Despite his new professional political stance, Mailer's campaign would not be given credence by either the liberal or the conservative press. This would cause him much consternation. What he failed to realize was that his own team never believed they had a chance at victory. "I thought it was a terrific idea," Joe Flaherty recalls, "but not as a race to win. I thought it was a perfect time to blow some clean air into the body politic, especially when Wagner entered. But Norman was in it to win, and you could say that I and everyone in that room used him badly, because I don't think I was the only one. Pete Hamill certainly didn't think he could win; John Scanlon didn't. Maybe some on the far left did, but people on the ideological fringes don't know how to count."

❦

In early May 1969, at the Overseas Press Club, Mailer publicly announced his intention to run for mayor of New York City along with Breslin as the candidate for president of the City Council. The platform would be power to the neighborhoods and the creation of a fifty-first state. The campaign slogan would be, "No More Bullshit." After the announcement, Breslin began to recognize that he was no longer involved in a brief, perhaps humorous, exercise to discredit the regular politicians and their antique code. He realized that with a headquarters, a working staff, and hundreds of young people eager to offer their services, Mailer was totally dedicated to the race. Their speaking schedule was now a grueling sixteen hours a day. While Mailer followed through like an untiring political professional, Breslin began to want out. On May 6 he saw an opportunity: That day it was announced that Mailer had won the Pulitzer Prize for *Armies of the Night*.

"I was looking to get out of the race by then," Breslin recounts. "I figured this was a good excuse. Let him get all the publicity and run, and let me go home. I was just tired of it, and I figured he now had all the publicity, and what did he want me around for?"

That afternoon Breslin called Joe Flaherty to tell him he was going to hold a press conference to announce his withdrawal. Flaherty calmly asked Breslin to come to headquarters to talk it over. They reached Mailer, who was on the Upper West Side being interviewed by a high school underground newspaper. Breslin told him he wanted to quit, and Mailer said they would discuss it at dinner. Over dinner Breslin was eventually talked into staying in the race, and the ticket continued as it was.

Mailer had actually learned of his Pulitzer Prize award on the previous day, May 5. Three hours before the prize was confirmed, Bernard Weinraub of *The New York Times* was asking Mailer how he would feel if he won. "I can't tell what my reactions are to prizes anymore," Mailer said. "Years ago I used to be so bitter about not receiving any prizes. I covered myself with case-hard insulation. Now it's almost as if I don't react inside. I'm probably pleased, but I don't want to admit it."

Three hours later, while he was visiting Phoenix House, a rehabilitation center for narcotics addicts, a newsman told Mailer he had won the Pulitzer Prize. "Oh, yeah? Good," he replied. "You probably won't print this, but my fondest hope is that the prize will give Mr. Breslin and myself the same respectful press coverage on page one now accorded Mrs. Guggenheimer." Elinor Guggenheimer had just been named as a candidate for City Council. Mailer added that the thousand-dollar prize would be the first contribution to the Mailer-Breslin campaign fund.

On May 6 Mailer held a press conference ostensibly to accept the Pulitzer Prize but actually to discuss the inadequate coverage his candidacy was receiving. Speaking from his new position of strength as a Pulitzer-Prize winner, Mailer attacked the press, saying that if they continued to neglect his campaign, it would be a disgrace to their profession.

Mailer's Pulitzer had lent his candidacy the credibility it needed, but he was to undermine his new reputability two days later. On May 8 a fund-raising rally was held at the Village Gate. After more than enough liquor, Mailer tossed aside his new incarnation as the venerable author and serious mayoralty candidate and once again liberated his slumbering "Beast."

Joe Flaherty arrived at the Gate near midnight. The place was crowded, and the New York Rock and Roll Ensemble was blaring. Flaherty noticed with some displeasure that the hardworking volunteers had been shunted off to side tables with nothing to drink, while at Mailer's "booze laden" table sat his buddies Buzz Farbar and Bill Walker, longtime members of his entourage. Newfield, Breslin, Flaherty, and Mailer were all scheduled to speak, in that order, but Newfield's speech set a discordant tone for the rest of the evening. He first urged the audience to form a "guerrilla graffiti squad" to write the campaign slogan "No More Bullshit" all over the city, then went on to attack Dorothy Schiff, owner of the *New York Post*, who, he felt, was giving the Mailer-Breslin campaign unfair coverage.

"He really made that a bad scene," recalls Flaherty. "His vulgarity about Dorothy Schiff changed it to a brawlish evening." Breslin tried to salvage the event with some conviviality. Then Flaherty began his fund-raising pitch. As he was speaking a very drunk girl got up on the stage to ask for help in getting her job back. The evening was rapidly deteriorating as Mailer arrived on stage, white-faced. Flaherty noticed a change in his persona: "Mailer performed a Stanislavskian miracle—he grew fat and sweaty before our eyes. He also launched into his much-heralded southern accent." The "Beast" was loose upon the crowd, and as the lenses of the television cameras moved in closer, Mailer's sense of threat took over.

"You're all a bunch of spoiled pigs," he told the crowd. "You're more spoiled than the cops. I'll tell you that. I'll tell you that. You've been sittin' around jerkin' off, havin' your jokes for twenty-two years. Yeah. And more than that—more than that. . . . Don't come in there and help us, because 'we're gonna give Norm a little help.' Fuck you. . . . If you're gonna help me, then help me. But I don't want any of those dull mother tired ego trips. Work. . . . I thought I had a victory until I read in *The Village Voice* that the smell of political death was upon us. I know what the fellow was up to. He was saying—get out of this campaign. You're just a little Jewish fellow from Brooklyn and you don't know what's up. Well, let me tell you something. I know what's up because the greatest Jewish paper in New York, the despicable *New York Post*, won't print a word of what we're up to. And let me tell you what that means. Let me tell you this—I am proud of my people. Very few people understand the Jews, but I do, 'cause I'm one of them. [The crowd begins to clap.] Fuck you, let me talk. The Jews are an incredible people at their best. At their worst they are swine. Like every WASP I ever met at their worst. They are awful. All people are awful at their worst. Some are worse than others. But the Jews are sensational at their best, which is rare enough, given Miami and a fur coat. Don't laugh, because you don't know what you're laughing at. Okay, don't laugh. Think about it. Whenever a people loses its highest race, there's nothing funnier going on in the world." On and on Mailer went.

By the end of the Mailer tirade, Breslin was already headed for the exit. "I didn't know what the hell was going on," he states, "so I ran outside and grabbed a cabdriver who was having a hot dog and said, 'Forget the hot dog. Here's ten dollars. Drive me to Toots Shor's.' And I got stewed. I called Jack Newfield later that night and told him he had me running with a crazy man. 'Why didn't you tell me I was running with Ezra Pound?' "

Joe Flaherty was stunned after Mailer's speech, but in retrospect he understands what happened: "Of course it's another one of Mailer's tactics. When things are getting out of hand he thinks that maybe if he delivers the ultimate shock, he will draw everything back together. It's a little bit like Floyd Patterson knowing that Sonny Liston was going to beat him, so instead of bouncing around him for fourteen rounds he runs right into him. When I leaned on Norman the next day he was shocked and contrite. Tears came into his eyes when I told him how grievous his behavior was to the campaign. More so because of the kids, the troops I brought down to the Gate. It was their night to see their candidate shine, and they were crushed. Campaign headquarters the next day was a disaster. The attitude was, 'Well, we did this all for some guy to act like a boozed-out fool.' And then after that, of course, he was so dying to recoup the losses he perceived we took at the Gate, he started to play the ultra-straight candidate."

"His seriousness ruined him as a candidate," says Pete Hamill, "because everything you expected Norman to do as a candidate—where you'd say, 'God, this might really be fun'—he didn't do. He began to sound like Robert Wagner by the time it was over. He became very conventional, like a candidate playing a candidate."

The Village Gate fiasco was not helped by news stories five days later that Mailer had received close to 1 million dollars in advance royalties for a book about man's first landing on the moon, the upcoming Apollo 11 shot. Scott Meredith publicly claimed that payments for the total publishing rights would exceed that figure by the time the book was published. The amounts actually contracted for, however, came to considerably less than 1 million dollars: *Life* was paying $100,000 for magazine serialization; Little, Brown $150,000 for hard-cover American rights; and New American Library $150,000 for paperback rights. Meredith added that there was a fifty-thousand-dollar bid for German rights and that English and French rights had also been sold. All told, the advances had not exceeded a half-million dollars, but the million-dollar headline was emblazoned across *The New York Times* and the *New York Post*. Everyone now assumed Mailer was rich, and contributions to his mayoralty campaign dropped off.

❦

By early June the polls indicated that Mailer was not in good shape with the voters; morale among the workers was also low. Nothing seemed to be going right. On a June 6 trip to Washington to celebrate the first-anniversary Mass of Robert Kennedy's death, Mailer became involved, this time accidentally, in an unneeded fiasco. Mailer and Breslin had gone together to Arlington Cemetery, where Cardinal Cook was conducting the Mass. It was outdoors, and everyone was holding lighted candles. Breslin remembers the scene. "Norman, extremely curious, was moving his head to listen and to watch when the candle in his hand tipped forward into the long blond hair of a woman standing in front of him. It set her hair on fire. So I started swatting the woman and Norman started swatting her to stop the hair from completely going up. The whole crowd looked at us and said, 'They're drunk again.' It was the hand of the devil that got in the way all the time."

In those final weeks of the campaign drive, Mailer had also alienated his workers by surrounding himself in Brooklyn with his closest allies and seldom venturing into headquarters in Manhattan. "That's when the real animosity seeped into the campaign, and it was the saddest thing about it," says Flaherty.

Mailer was grouping his forces for the final push, but no one thought that he still believed he could win the election. "I had no idea how seriously he was taking it," says former campaign press secretary Peter Maas. "I thought if you pushed him to the wall, it was just another big ego trip." On the night of the returns, however, Maas discovered just how serious Mailer was.

Staff members had been invited to wait for the election returns in a suite in the Plaza Hotel. But before meeting the others Mailer invited Maas and his wife to join him and Beverly for dinner in another room at the Plaza. As the four were eating, Maas said, "You know, Norman, you did a hell of a job. I want you to know right now that I've already bet you're not going to come in last; you're going to beat Scheuer."

"He looked at me," Maas recalls, "as though I had hit him with a baseball bat. So I went on, 'We really turned in a respectable campaign that started out as a joke in a lot of people's eyes, and we are going to finish respectably.' "

"You mean I'm not going to win?" Mailer suddenly asked him. "You don't think I'm going to win?"

"He said this with enormous intensity," relates Maas, "and I realized, my God, he thinks he's going to win. So I told him he had nothing to be ashamed of. But then he disappeared into a closet—one of the large Plaza closets—and stayed there for about twenty minutes. He was just knocked out. I suddenly understood that during all those hours he spent going up to the Gaelic Society or this and that, he really thought he was going to win."

Mailer did beat Scheuer, coming in fourth out of the five candidates, with 41,136 votes, but it was Mario Procaccino who won. At Mailer headquarters at 11:00 that night, the author conceded. "If I'm right about this city being on the edge of doom, then heaven help this city, because there's not much to look forward to with the men they elected today." Breslin kept up his witty patter, saying, "I am mortified to have taken part in a process that required the bars to be closed." But as Breslin says in retrospect about their campaign, "Somewhere along the line you think it's real, there's no question. I have a better way of disguising it; maybe I'm a bigger fraud. But you inevitably get caught up in the thing, and the ideas were valid. As Norman now says looking back on it, we were both afraid. It takes a little guts to leave your house in the morning and go out and shake hands with virtual strangers and say you want their vote when they're laughing at you. It takes a little guts."

Joe Flaherty agrees. "You're talking about a guy who had early fame, came from Harvard, ran with the hip crowd that was into the arts, a special elite force. He never had this exposure before. But he went from theory to sweat. He was working on notions of what was wrong with America, many of them highly perceptive, and all of a sudden he moved down to the sweat of people who were living these kinds of things, and he learned from them. I think Norman has always had an idea of America as having absolute open-ended potential because of the diversity of people who come here, and I think he puts stock in that immigrant love of America."

Mailer, in the midst of the radical nihilism of the late 1960s, had exercised an American tradition by running for public office. He had fooled himself that he might become the next mayor of New York, but in the doing he had moved one step closer to integrating himself with a nation for which he had shown both an arrogant contempt and a naïve appreciation.

He had begun the decade in personal, emotional, and literary disarray. But during the sixties his work had both inspired and reflected the new radicalism of the time. He had examined the period at length; had participated in its protest; and had been honored for his insight. By the conclusion of the decade he had moved much closer to both tradition and personal stability. A year after the sixties were history, Wilfrid Sheed commented: "So goes Mailer, so goes the nation. This is the form his genius takes."

• XVI •

BEGINNING THE SEVENTIES: OF THE MOON

On July 1, 1969, two weeks after his unsuccessful mayoral primary bid, Mailer was in the heart of enemy territory, that bastion of American technology, the NASA Manned Spacecraft Center outside Houston, Texas. During his coverage of the Apollo 11 flight—the first time men walked on the moon—Mailer would be plagued by an unsettling ambivalence about the purpose of the space program. As Mailer wrote, he hardly knew "whether the Space Program was the noblest expression of the Twentieth Century or the quintessential statement of our fundamental insanity."

Mailer's radicalism would once have helped him settle such a question. But by the end of the sixties, Mailer's disenchantment with the "wild nihilism in his own army" had grown acute. Though Mailer had started the sixties as a cultural revolutionary, at the close of that pivotal decade he had achieved—despite his mayoralty defeat—new establishment recognition. He had won the Pulitzer Prize and the National Book Award, and he was now reevaluating both his own radicalism and that of the country. His first instinct was to protest; but his second, sometimes stronger, tendency was to reflect on what might be valuable in the culture.

As Mailer observed the extraordinary spectacle of technological heroism in Houston, he gradually came to understand that he would have to relinquish his old romantic radical visions. The era of Hemingwayesque heroism was over and in some ways, he felt, the new technology of the WASP's had triumphed.

❦

Assigning coverage of the moon landing to a writer who was notorious for his anti-technological attitudes was such an intriguing concept that two magazine editors had almost simultaneously approached Mailer with the idea during the spring of 1969. The first was Willie Morris of *Harper's* magazine, who was pleased by the success of Mailer's two previous pieces: his reports of the 1967 march on the Pentagon and the 1968 presidential conventions. Earlier that spring Morris was at a party given by Jean vanden Heuvel (now Jean Stein, author of *Edie*) when Mailer arrived late with Charles Rembar. Morris and Mailer began talking. Morris mentioned that NASA was going to send men to the moon that summer and suggested that Mailer should do a big piece on it for *Harper's*.

Charles Rembar told Morris that it was a terrible idea and would be a waste of Mailer's talent. Mailer did not dismiss it as rapidly. He thought for a minute and said, "No, it's a good idea; but these things I've been doing for *Harper's* have been participatory journalism. How can I participate in a landing on the moon?" Mailer then smiled and proposed a half-serious idea. "God dammit, I really would like to go to the moon," he told Morris. "I'd even get in shape. Willie, who do we know in Washington?"

Mailer's career as an astronaut was never launched, but soon after that he called Morris with some news. "Willie, this will be in the papers tomorrow and I want you to know it first," Mailer said to the editor. "I'm going to do the moon landing for *Life* because they offered me so much money." Morris said he was disappointed but that he understood; he appreciated Mailer's thoughtfulness in calling him.

It was Thomas Griffith, the editor of *Life*, who had sought out Mailer to write about the moon landing. *Life* had had an exclusive contract with NASA and the astronauts since the beginning of the space program, but by 1969 the contract had been rewritten and *Life*'s exclusivity now applied only to stories about the astronauts' families. "We were getting less and less journalistic freshness in the stories," recalls Griffith, "but our contract with NASA demanded that a large amount of space be devoted to the program, so we began reaching beyond the families." Science-fiction writer Arthur C. Clarke, author of *2001*, had been brought in to do a piece, as had poet James Dickey, but ideas for stories were rapidly dwindling.

"I thought that we hadn't really covered one part of the astronaut story," states Griffith. "It was the scruffy life around Cape Kennedy, and it occurred to me that we should get somebody with a more open, less Jack Armstrong type of attitude—someone like Norman Mailer—to do the piece. I think Norman was already committed to *Harper's* to do something like that, but we had more money to offer, and I felt that exclusive access to astronauts would really interest him."

Griffith called Mailer's agent, Scott Meredith, and a meeting was arranged. Meredith startled the *Life* editor by stating that negotiations would begin at $400,000. "Meredith told me," says Griffith, "that Norman had something like fourteen people on his payroll, and he started listing wives and children, and his parents. He said we had to take care of all of them if Norman was going to be taken away from the great novel he was writing. He also said Mailer had to get a book out of the article."

Life's parent company, Time, Inc., had recently bought the book publisher Little, Brown and Company, so it was decided that Little, Brown would do the hard-cover. This involved getting a release from New American Library who had first rights to anything Mailer wrote while he was under contract to them for the big novel. According to Griffith, NAL was annoyed about the Little, Brown contract until someone suggested they bid on the paperback rights to the moon book. The deal was finally set: Little, Brown would pay $150,000 for hard-cover rights; NAL $150,000 for paperback rights; and *Life* $100,000 for magazine serialization.

Mailer was concerned about his ambivalent attitude toward space exploration. While the financial arrangements were being worked out, Mailer met with Griffith several times, either on Griffith's turf, the Century Club, or at Mailer's usual meeting place, the Algonquin, for final discussions on whether Mailer should do the piece and whether there was actually a book in it. Griffith tried to convince Mailer that *Life*'s access to the astronauts would make the project feasible. He even offered to send Mailer to Houston before the shot so the author could do preliminary research. "I marveled at him when he turned this idea down," Griffith recollects. "He said he'd rather wing it at the actual event and have it happen only once."

Mailer finally agreed to do the story for *Life*. Contracts were made ready to sign, and *Life* notified the attorneys for the astronauts. "We thought there would be an instant ratification of Norman's name," says Griffith, "but we quickly began running into barriers. The lawyers wouldn't approve Mailer because they were afraid he would write harsh things about the astronauts. There was some concern that he'd regard them as silly fly boys and ridicule their language. They were quite worried about that."

When Griffith told Mailer of this problem, Mailer answered candidly: "Gee, why are they worried about that? I can be very tough on other writers, but I'm never tough on anybody who is doing something courageous. If I were writing about the Indianapolis speedway, I'd never make fun of the driver if he was ungrammatical. I admire guys who do things I can't do."

Griffith thought the answer was good and reported it back to the attorneys, but the reply was still negative: They wouldn't approve Mailer. "It gradually occurred to me," says Griffith, "that the astronauts themselves weren't worried that Mailer would say revealing things about them. I think they were afraid he'd be setting up their bosses, the NASA people, because of his antibureaucracy attitude. I believe that NASA itself was more worried than the astronauts about Norman's reporting."

Pleas were made to Houston, but the attorneys wouldn't budge. Griffith was finally forced to tell Mailer that *Life* could not make good on its promise of access to the astronauts which it had used to lure him away from *Harper's*. "Well, I'll do it without their damn access," Mailer told Griffith.

❦

That July 1 Mailer—now code-named "Aquarius" after his birth sign—was at the NASA Manned Spacecraft Center, which lay in a barren stretch of land twenty-five miles south of Houston. Neither the aridness of the location nor the people at NASA pleased him at first. The lower level NASA functionaries, he said, had "that absolute lack of surface provocation, or idiosyncrasy of personality," while the executives reminded him of the 112th Cavalry with which he had served during World War II. "They were, in short, Wasps," Mailer wrote, "and it was part of the folklore of New York that Wasps were without odor. . . . Wasps were, in the view of Aquarius, the most Faustian, barbaric, draconian, progress-oriented, and root-destroying people on earth. They had divorced themselves from odor in order to dominate time, and thereby see if they were able to deliver themselves from death."

The first person Mailer interviewed for the *Life* piece was Dr. Robert R. Gilruth, director of the Manned Spacecraft Center. As Mailer wrote of him, "He was remarkably gentle and determinedly undistinguished, as if his deepest private view suggested that good administration and public communication were best kept apart. In this sense, he was certainly no proper representative of the NASA style, much rather like a Chinese mandarin—completely pleasant, altogether remote—it occurred that Eisenhower had been a mandarin."

Mailer asked Gilruth the one question that would be the most difficult for a NASA executive to answer. "Are you ever worried, Dr. Gilruth," he said, "that landing on the moon may result in all sorts of psychic disturbances for us here on earth? I mean many people seem to react to the full moon, and there are tides of course." There was pain in Gilruth's eyes as he searched for an answer and then finally admitted that yes, there seemed to be a higher incidence of admission to mental hospitals during the full moon.

Today Dr. Gilruth is adamant in his disapproval of Mailer. "I was a Christian man until I met Mr. Mailer," he says. "He came in there and spent five minutes with me and then wrote some scathing things about me which I didn't appreciate. He asked me some question about the moon and I started telling him that the moon—even in modern times—has had a lot to do with insanity and mental patients and that men, particularly, are turned on by the phase of the moon.

"As I was talking about that, I suddenly thought, *My God, he's going to do something with this*, but I didn't really think he would because he's such a big name. Other people, who are less trusting than I, refused to talk to him. I really didn't even know who he was. I was so wrapped up in the program. Here was just another man coming to see me. I had a policy of talking to anybody, but I regret it in this case. He made no effort to find out my history or what I had done for the program and in my opinion he could not have cared less. He asked no questions about my background and probably figured he knew all he needed to know. After the book came out my friends said, 'Boy, Mr. Mailer sure made mincemeat out of you, didn't he? We should have told you not to talk to him.' The whole thing was very uncalled-for and cruel of him and I didn't appreciate it and still don't."

Mailer treated the astronauts themselves more kindly, for even though they were WASP's toiling in the bosom of technology, their heroism was implicit. He was admiring of Charles ("Pete") Conrad, Jr., the astronaut who would command Apollo 12 on the flight to the moon after Apollo 11. At a party at Conrad's house, Mailer heard the astronaut say, "For six years I've been dreaming of going to the moon." Mailer marveled: "The moon—as a real and tangible companion of the mind—was suddenly there before him."

Conrad, the only astronaut who agreed to meet Mailer personally, remembers how they came together. "*Life* magazine had a resident person in Houston named Dodie Hamlin," Conrad relates. "She called me up one day and said, 'Look, I've got to entertain this guy and I can't think of anybody else who will sit around and listen to him or get along with him, so maybe you'd do it.' She brought him to our house for dinner and together we managed to put away the good part of a bottle of scotch. It was a very polite evening. My job was to help Dodie entertain this guy, which I did. I wouldn't know a Norman Mailer book if I fell over it. The only thing I knew about him was what I read in *Time* and *People*, mainly that he had hit somebody else or divorced another girl.

"It was clear from the beginning," Conrad adds, "that we were either going to get along or get into violent arguments because his views and mine were quite opposite. People accuse me of flying right wing for Attila the Hun and he's rather on the liberal side. It was also a bad time period; we were in Vietnam. But I think he respected what I was doing and I respected his opinions so we got along very well. I didn't read the whole book all the way through when it came out, but he did have one of the better descriptions of the Saturn V lift-off. I thought he did a fantastic job with that."

Establishing a kinship with men like Dr. Gilruth and astronaut Pete Conrad was clearly not going to be easy for Mailer. To do the book he would have to modify his romantic view of heroism and accommodate it to the technological teamwork of NASA, the astronauts, and the purposes of the space program. As for the heroes of this mission, the WASP astronauts, Mailer had to question whether his own radical troops, who were debauching themselves with drugs and sex, were in fact equal: "The WASP's were quietly moving from command of the world to command of the moon . . . were they God's intended?"

Space travel had become a battle of *them* versus *us* for Mailer.

When he was later asked by *The Village Voice* if his perception of the failure of "his side" made him less inclined to embrace the space program, he replied, "Well, I think what I felt for the first time was a real feeling that the other side might win, which of course I felt all along . . . but I've always felt they were going to win because they were stronger. . . . After the moonshot, this was the first time I thought that maybe they were gonna win because they *deserved* to win, because they have been working harder at their end of the war than we have."

As Mailer shuttled from Houston to Cape Canaveral to watch the takeoff, then back to Houston for the moon landing that July of 1969, his depression was acute. He saw in astronauts Armstrong, Aldrin, and Collins the very contradictions that were troubling him. "It was a world half convinced of the future of death of our species yet half aroused by the apocalyptic notion that an exceptional future still lay before us," Mailer wrote.

The day before the astronauts returned to earth from the moon, Mailer left Houston for Provincetown, where he would watch the splashdown on a static-ridden television set. His first deadline for *Life* was three weeks off and he was desperate about starting to write, but the subject of space travel was troubling him deeply. "To write was to judge, and Aquarius may never have tried a subject which tormented him so," Mailer said. His usual discipline sustained him and on August 29 the first of Mailer's three pieces about the moon landing was published in *Life*.

Ralph Graves, who had become the managing editor just two months before, was startled when he looked at the size of the manuscript. Graves had just told his staff that one of the aims of his new administration would be to reduce the size of text pieces. When Mailer handed in the article, he told Graves, "I can't write anything in 5,000 words, and 10,000 words is just for poker money." Mailer's article, which was expected to be less than 10,000 words, came in at 30,000. Moreover, he had a contractual agreement with *Life* that no cuts could be made without his approval. "So," recalls Graves, "right after having announced we'd have to have shorter pieces, I wound up running the longest nonfiction piece in *Life*'s history—26,000 words.

"He was definitely nervous about the first piece," adds Graves. "How would this be treated and handled. How would he work in *Life* and with *Life*?" Mailer did agree to cut 4,000 words, but Graves remembers that he was very rigid about what *Life* could take out of the first installment. On the subsequent pieces, when Mailer realized the magazine would honor its commitment about cutting, he was more cooperative.

Mailer's manuscript contained a biting depiction of a dinner Time-Life held the night before the launch. Not only did Mailer ridicule *Life*'s publisher, but he was equally acerbic about the dinner guests, many of whom were major advertisers in Time, Inc. publications. When Graves saw the account, he told Mailer directly that he couldn't run it. Mailer then explained the reason for his bitterness. Since he was sitting at the dinner with author Cornelius Ryan, the publisher introduced them together as "the author of the longest day and the shortest campaign."

"This was after Norman's mayoralty campaign," says Graves, "and apparently it got a big laugh. Norman told me he was standing there with everybody laughing and said to himself, 'Okay, I'll get even.' So he wrote a scathing description of the dinner. We had a lot of discussion about it over a period of several days. Hedley Donovan, the editor-in-chief, said we just couldn't publish it. I told him that I knew we shouldn't publish it but that we had a no-cut contract with Mailer. While I didn't threaten to resign, I said to myself, 'If Norman doesn't agree to cut this and *Life* refuses to publish it, I'm going to quit.' But Norman finally said, 'Okay, I've got some of my spleen out,' and it was one of the things he agreed to cut. He didn't cut everything from the scene, but he did take out what we felt were its most offensive parts."

For the remainder of that fall and winter and into the spring of 1970, Mailer worked on his moon book, returning to Houston several times. He read exhaustive technical manuals on aeronautical physics, boning up on a subject he had not thought about since graduating in aeronautical engineering from Harvard. Although none of this would appear in the subsequent two installments in *Life*, in November 1969 and January 1970, half the finished book would be devoted to Mailer's detailed explanation of the technology of Apollo.

Mailer also described the physical condition of the astronauts. One of his roommates from the Harvard days, George Goethals, remembers talking to a professor at the Harvard Medical School after the book came out. The professor, who had been a consultant on the moon shots, told Goethals: "That classmate of yours astounds me. I was there in an official capacity to check these guys out medically. Mailer was peripheral and yet he was getting as good information as I was. I can't believe that someone with a nonmedical background could pull apart astronauts like that."

Of a Fire on the Moon was published by Little, Brown at the beginning of 1971. The book is divided into three parts. The first part, "Aquarius," records Mailer's observations of the Manned Spacecraft Center in Houston, where he initially confronts what he considers the technological WASP personality in the form of Dr. Gilruth, Charles Conrad, and the astronauts whom he sees at collective press conferences. Mailer then travels to Cape Canaveral to watch the launch of Apollo 11 after which he returns to Houston to cover the moon landing at the Manned Spacecraft Center. The second part of the book, "Apollo," which constitutes half the volume, is taken up by Mailer's detailed examination of the Apollo technology. "The Age of Aquarius," the third section of *Fire*, recounts Mailer's disaffection with "the wild nihilism in his own army" and his ultimate recognition that perhaps the American WASP had triumphed after all.

The reviews of the book were generally respectful but they were more negative than laudatory. The critics recognized that Mailer's personal philosophy would not easily accommodate this new technology. "This fundamental ambivalence about the role of technology in the future of human culture is the crux of Mailer's book," Hilton Kramer wrote in *Book World*. "At times he works very hard in *Of a Fire on the Moon* to endow this theme with a kind of Wagnerian resonance and mythos, but his heart isn't in it; he cannot make the subject his own. Mailer is neither a philosopher nor a poet; he is a novelist and a journalist, a connoisseur of experience deeply suspicious of anything that takes place beyond the boundaries of his own first-hand observation, and the closest he ever came to the moon was, as we all know, his television screen."

In *Newsweek*, Geoffrey Wolff wrote of Mailer's brilliance, but except for Mailer's extraordinary account of the lift-off, he was disappointed by the work. "Of course it was one of the world's great moments when the lunar module, Eagle, ('some boys dreams of a habitat') touched Tranquility Base. Mailer, for my money, is the most various and surprising and courageous and irreplaceable reporter alive," Wolff wrote. "And it must have seemed that he would be privileged to suggest the magnificence of the occasion, almost as though he were with Darwin on the *Beagle* or at Marx's elbow in the British Museum. But for all his labor to make something out of all those numbers and press releases, he cannot. He writes a magnificent prose poem to the rocket's ascent from its pad. The rest is anticipation, puzzlement, space."

Mailer later noted that by the time he wrote *Fire*, the technique he had employed to such brilliant effect in *Armies* and *Miami*—the use of himself as a third-person narrator—was wearing thin. "If you force an aspect of the imagination, it can come to the point where it ceases to return anything at all, and I think I probably got to that point by the time I wrote *Of a Fire on the Moon*," Mailer said. "I liked the book in a lot of ways, but I didn't like my own person in it—I felt I was highly unnecessary."

Fire had been a difficult assignment, but during the summer of 1969, Mailer's troubles were exacerbated by the rapid deterioration of his marriage to Beverly. "His wife and he were getting along abominably," Mailer wrote. "They had had hideous phone calls these last few weeks while he was away. Several times one or the other had hung up in the middle of a quarrel. It was impossible to believe, but they each knew—they were come to an end. . . . They had met on the night of the full moon, and would end in the summer of the moon."

• XVII •

MAILER AND THE FEMINISTS

Beverly had her first affair that summer, and on Labor Day Mailer suggested she travel for a while to think things out. While Beverly was away in Mexico, Mailer called his friend José Torres to ask his advice. "I said, 'You're asking me?' " recalls Torres. " 'I'm a Puerto Rican and a Catholic. If it were me, when she came back she would never see me again.' I have a double standard. If I caught my wife going around, I'd kill her. Norman has the same values. It was a very emotional thing."

When Beverly returned in the fall, she and Mailer were temporarily reunited in Brooklyn Heights, but they agreed to live on separate floors of the building. By the spring of 1970, with Mailer's moon book completed, they decided to spend their vacations apart. Beverly went to Nantucket, Mailer went to Maine, and the Provincetown house was turned over to their relatives for the summer. Mailer had agreed to take the children with him to Maine; he would see whether he could handle the domestic challenge. With him were his two daughters by Adele, Dandy, now thirteen, and Betsy, now ten; his daughter by Lady Jeanne, Kate, now seven; and his two sons by Beverly, Michael, aged six, and Stephen, four.

A local Maine woman helped with the laundry and cleaning, and

Mailer's sister, Barbara, came up for two weeks to assist. Finally Carol Stevens, whom Mailer called "his dearest old love," was invited up for the rest of the summer. In August, when Mailer learned that Carol had become pregnant, he felt compelled to tell Beverly about it. "That," says Beverly, "was the final split." By the following February, Beverly moved with her two sons to the house on Commercial Street in Provincetown, where she lived for years.

Carol would remain with Mailer for the next five years, giving birth to his seventh child, Maggie Alexandra, in March of 1971. They had initially met just after Mailer broke up with Adele in 1961, but Carol's career as a nightclub blues and jazz singer was going strong at the time, and it interfered with their relationship. As her friend Anne Edwards points out, "Norman just won't have anything to do with a woman who has a career."

Raised in a middle-class Jewish family in Philadelphia, Carol was a beautiful dark-haired woman with huge black eyes and almost biblical features. She had remained in love with Mailer throughout his marriages to Lady Jeanne and Beverly. "She always said to me that theirs was a true American love story, an historic love affair," Edwards recalls. "That no matter what happens or how many wives intervene, they would always come back together again. In her heart of hearts she still believes they will end up together."

Carol's arrival in Maine that summer of 1970 was fortuitous. Not only had Mailer realized that he couldn't live without a woman, but after six weeks of preparing menus and shopping lists and activities for the children, he had had enough. He claimed he could do it for years, if necessary, "but in no uncertainty that the most interesting part of his mind and heart was condemned to dry on the vine . . . So he could not know whether he would have found it endurable to be born a woman or if it would have driven him out onto the drear avenues of the insane."

It was while Mailer was contemplating this question of the woman's role in the family that his historic battle with the women's liberationists began. It would propel Mailer into a debate of magnitude, one which has not subsided to this day.

The call to confrontation with the feminists came from an editor at *Time* magazine. The editor called Mailer asking if he could send a reporter to Maine to do a cover story on his reaction to the extraordinary new surge of interest in feminism. Mailer immediately thought of his children and of Carol, and demurred. The editor assured him he had no intention of studying the author's private life; he simply wanted Mailer's views on Women's Liberation. As Mailer probably knew, he was the primary target of the feminists' attacks.

Mailer said he had no idea this was so.

"Well, you may as well face it," replied the editor. "They seem to think you're their major ideological opposition."

The *Time* editor was referring to a book called *Sexual Politics*, which was published that July. It was to become a bible of female liberation, but its author, Kate Millett, was then an unknown writer. Millett launched her attack on what she considered the anti-feminine, power-obsessed male patriarchy by quoting at length from three male novelists who, she felt, best represented the reactionary, "counterrevolutionary" sexual attitudes which had enjoyed a resurgence between 1930 and 1960. The novelists were Henry Miller, D. H. Lawrence, and Norman Mailer.

"Lawrence, Miller, and Mailer," Millett wrote in *Sexual Politics*, "identify women as an annoying minority force to be put down and are concerned with a social order in which the female would be perfectly controlled." Her strongest attack was reserved for Mailer, whom she branded an "archconservative," a "prisoner of the virility cult," who sees "sexual belligerence in terms of actual warfare." *An American Dream* was the target of her severest scorn: "Mailer's *An American Dream* is an exercise in how to kill your wife and be happy ever after. The reader is given to understand that by murdering one woman and buggering another, Rojack became a 'man'. . . . Mailer's *An American Dream* is a rallying cry for sexual politics in which diplomacy has failed and war is the last political resort of a ruling caste that feels its position in deadly peril."

Millett found Mailer the man almost as reprehensible as Mailer the author. In *Sexual Politics* she pointed out that during the fifties Mailer had the arrogance to put himself forward as a champion of the sexual revolution when his efforts amounted to nothing more than a crusade for greater explicitness in the description of sexual activity. And when the freedom of the sixties outstripped anything Mailer might have imagined, he began to call himself a Left Conservative, which, as Millett noted, is "a confusing hybrid whose stress falls with increasingly apoplectic emphasis upon the latter."

Mailer, she continued, had become "lyric" about chastity, "ferocious" about abortion, and "wildly opposed" to all birth control. Millett wrote, "Finally outstripping both the Victorians and the

Church, Mailer's line would sit well on a Nazi propagandist: 'The fact of the matter is that the prime responsibility of a woman probably is to be on earth long enough to find the best mate possible for herself and conceive children who will improve the species.' "

But a further irony which Millett noted is that Mailer does not want passive women as his heroines. Given his combative urges, there would be no challenge in subduing them. "His eagerness after a sparring partner causes the much-lamented 'bitchery' of American women to become a species of erotic currency."

Millett's final assault on Mailer involved his attitudes toward homosexuality. Considering his belief in virility and aggression, a renunciation of either, said Millett, is tantamount in Mailer's mind to renouncing masculinity or identity itself.

Today Millett explains why Mailer was her prime antagonist. "I felt he was the leading spokesman of that particular point of view for his generation and his voice was the most prevalent," she says. "You got it, for example, through his influence upon *The Village Voice* and the young men who wrote for that paper. He had many, many imitators. In the sixties one heard Mailer's point of view a great deal. It was the reigning attitude, the current, fashionable literary male chauvinism, and Mailer was its famous progenitor. At that point there wasn't any counter voice because the women's movement was just emerging. So Mailer's view had enormous power and was extremely oppressive to women with literary interests or ambitions."

Mailer was not in New York to hear firsthand the talk stimulated by *Sexual Politics*. Nor was he there to read the reviews of the book, few of which leapt to Mailer's defense. Most reviewers, in fact, seemed to be delicately separating themselves from Mailer so as not to risk similar assaults from the feminists. "Miller and Mailer are sitting ducks for the feminists," wrote psychoanalyst Ernest van den Haag in *The National Review*. "Their only flight is from castration fear into pseudo-virility. Some writers have not gone beyond the phallic stage of development and rationalize their failure in their writing." *The New Yorker* did not fully support Millett but it emphasized the weakness of Mailer's position: "The authors she [Millett] had chosen are in such psychological trouble themselves that it is hard to agree that they express typical attitudes toward women."

Millett received many letters about her book, but few supported Mailer. "When people took issue with me," she states, "it was chiefly over Lawrence, people who had been fond of his work and didn't want to see him in that light. But with Mailer and Miller there was a lot of agreement. By no means did it mean that they didn't like the rest of the authors' works. I did not attack these people as writers but for a specific attitude they had. I had a good deal of admiration as well. I think Mailer's journalism is super. I loved *Armies of the Night* and there's a good deal in *Why Are We in Vietnam?* that is superb. He has great insight into the whole American psyche. When he investigates male-chauvinist attitudes he seems to comprehend, and yet he is not able to remove himself from it. There's still an allegiance. It's as if one wrote about white supremacists and criticized them yet at the same time hankered after their view."

It was not until the call from the *Time* editor that Mailer realized he had been ignoring the early intimations of the Women's Liberation movement. He now remembered a lunch he had the previous year with Gloria Steinem, whom he calls the "never unattractive manifestation of Women's Rights." Steinem had probed him about the possibility of his running for mayor of New York City.

When he turned down the suggestion, Steinem said: "Well, at least I won't have to explain you to my friends at Women's Lib."

Mailer asked her what they could possibly have against him.

"Try reading your books someday," she replied.

Mailer recalled an interview he gave in which he had said, "Women at their worst are low, sloppy beasts." He told Steinem about it, then added: "I thought the next question would be, 'What are women at their best?' I would have replied that women at their best are goddesses."

"That," retorted Steinem, "is exactly what's wrong with your attitude."

Shortly following this conversation, after Mailer decided to enter the mayoral primaries in the spring of 1969, he ran into Congresswoman Bella Abzug at a campaign meeting in downtown New York. Abzug told him that she agreed with his views on the Vietnam War, but that his attitudes toward women were "full of shit." Mailer was amused, even spurred on, by her criticism.

"Listen, Bella," he said, "I can tell you that regardless of my views on women, as *you* think you know them, women in any administration I could run would have more voice, more respect, more real opportunity for real argument than any of the other candidates would offer you. What is our campaign promise of Power to the Neighborhoods but an offering to Women's Liberation?"

A year later Mailer saw an excerpt from *Sexual Politics* in *New American Review* but he did not bother to read the whole piece. When the favorable reviews of Millett's book began appearing late that summer, Mailer saw that the media were treating it as an honored tome. Six weeks after his conversation with the editor of *Time*, Kate Millett's face, not Mailer's, was on that magazine's cover. Mailer realized that he would have to think seriously about Millett and her argument. As he did, he began to feel that Millett's criticism was not only unfair but that it opened up the larger question of what women had done to him over the years and, conversely, what he had done to them. His scattered children were evidence of four marriages gone awry, and no matter who was to blame, Mailer recognized that his very life raised the issue of women's rights. He would once again have to play the devil in the fire.

The week before he left Maine that summer of 1970, Mailer found himself on a television talk show hosted by Orson Welles. The show was progressing well until Mailer suddenly uttered his now-notorious comment, "Women should be kept in cages." Welles responded quickly and prodded Mailer about his seeming misogyny.

"Orson," Mailer replied, "we respect lions in the zoo but we want them kept in cages, don't we?"

The dull response of the television audience troubled Mailer. He concluded that machines were moving in to replace humor, that dehumanizing technology was on the rise. "If that were so," he later wrote, "then the liberation of women might be a trap."

By the time Mailer finally left Maine, he knew that he would have to write something about women and their cause. Following a trip to Venice with Carol in September, Mailer returned to New York to find that he was not the only man under assault by the feminists. Willie Morris, the editor of *Harper's*, had become the unwitting target of feminist wrath one night at Elaine's. "Three or four ideological liberationists ganged up on me that night and tore me apart as a southern cracker who didn't care about women's rights," Morris relates. "They were brutal to me and it struck a chord because I wasn't that way. I felt bad about it. The next day I called up Norman in Brooklyn Heights. He was working on a book and he had holed himself away. I had deliberately not talked to him for a couple of months because I knew he was working on something."

Mailer was in fact writing his novel, and when Morris asked him to lunch, Mailer told him, "Dammit Willie, I'm working. I don't want to have lunch with you because I know you're going to have an idea for *Harper's.*" Finally Mailer gave in, saying, "I'm not going to write anything for you, but I'd like to see you."

They arranged to have lunch at a restaurant called Spats on Thirty- third Street. After three Bloody Marys before lunch Mailer told Morris, "Well, Willie, I know you have an idea and I know what your idea is. You want me to write a large piece of prose on women in America today."

"How did you know that?" Morris asked in astonishment.

"Because," Mailer replied, "I'm the one who will do it and furthermore I want to do it. I'm going to get us all in trouble. 'The Steps of the Pentagon' will be mild compared to this."

❦

In November Mailer left with Carol Stevens for Provincetown, where he rented a house, and during that bleak month he read what the leading feminists had to say. Most of them, such as Ti-Grace Atkinson, Valerie Solanis, Martha Shelly, Pati Trolander, and Mary Jane Sherfey, had published only in feminist journals, such as *Women's Liberation*, *Sisterhood Is Powerful* and *Off Our Backs*. Only a few had written books. Betty Friedan, of course, had published *The Feminine Mystique* in 1963, and Mailer now read the book in the Dell paperback edition. He also obtained a copy of *The Female Eunuch* by English feminist Germaine Greer, which had just been released in Britain. Greer's book, like Millett's, contained a substantial section attacking Mailer's heroines as either "great bitches" or "poison maidens." And of course Mailer read *Sexual Politics*, the book which had set off the Mailer-Feminist controversy.

Over the next month, in a fever of writing, Mailer produced nearly 50,000 words on the subject of women and sex. Millett had clearly aroused his wrath and Mailer's work, *The Prisoner of Sex*, was primarily a response to her claim that he was a "prisoner of the virility cult."

Mailer had divided the book into four parts: the Prizewinner, the Acolyte, the Advocate, and the Prisoner. Each had its own theme and each looked at another aspect of the relations between the sexes. The "Prizewinner" described his first awareness of the feminist attack and the realization that he would have to react. The title of the section refers to Mailer's musings on the possibility of his receiving the Nobel Prize and the conceptual polarities of the terms *Prizewinner* and *Prisoner*.

As the "Acolyte," Mailer examined the feminist programs and concluded that the concept of revolution had degenerated into nothing more than "scientific vanity, destroying every natural act of nature." The feminists' calls for contraception, extrauterine impregnation, test-tube babies, and abortion all bore witness to Mailer's favorite thesis, the dehumanization of society through technology.

Mailer's "Advocate" defended the other two writers who had been attacked by Kate Millett in *Sexual Politics*, Henry Miller and D. H. Lawrence. Their novelistic imagination, Mailer inferred, was necessarily supple, mysterious, and unrigid—or *feminine*—and not at all like the *masculine*, systematic thought of a feminist such as Millett. Miller, he said, was in awe of women and had to humiliate them so that he could dare enter them during sex. "It is the cry of an enlisted man whose ego needs equality to breathe," Mailer wrote, using an analogy from his own World War II experience. The case of D. H. Lawrence was more complex. Mailer believed that Lawrence, being a mama's boy, had to dominate women sexually in order to achieve transcendence.

In the "Prisoner," Mailer theorized that since Lawrence's death, the world had been twice technologized. Just as it is now more difficult for men to be heroes, it is harder for women to be feminine. For Mailer sex would have to be more than Miller's war or Lawrence's transcendence: It would have to be a direct and dimensional—or existential—confrontation with reality.

If conception remains a possibility, then the sexual act, Mailer feels, reflects back all that one is. "No thought was so painful as the idea that sex had meaning: for give meaning to sex and one was a prisoner of sex—the more meaning one gave it, the more it assumed, until every failure and misery, every evil of your life, spoke their lines in its light, and every fear of a mediocre death."

Millett was wrong and was an "enemy of sex," Mailer concluded. He claimed that she "saw the differences between men and women as nonessential—excesses of emotion to be conditioned out . . . she was the enemy of sex which might look for beauty at the edge of dread, she would never agree that was where love might go deepest . . . her ideas had been designed to leave spiritual pockets of vacuum which only technology could fill."

Mailer refused to retreat from the view that had caused such antagonism. He still believed that the prime responsibility of a woman was to find the best mate possible and have babies that would improve the species. He did, however, grant that liberation might help a woman find that mate. But his final plea was that women not "quit the womb," for then the dehumanizing inroads of technology would be sinister indeed and gravely affect both the sexes.

In late December, after Mailer had completed *Prisoner*, Willie Morris flew to Provincetown, just as he had done when Mailer had finished *Armies of the Night*. He was accompanied by his colleague Midge Decter and a friend, Muriel Murphy. Morris was pushing for his March deadline and wanted to see what Mailer had written; Mailer himself seemed anxious to have his observations. The three visitors began reading, and when Morris was three fourths of the way through, he remembers turning to Muriel Murphy and saying, "This is going to cost me my job, but we have to publish it."

"It was the whole explicit approach to sexuality in a national magazine," Morris now says. "I think Norman might have sensed that I was going to be in trouble, but I didn't tell him about my apprehension." That night Mailer and Carol, who was by now visibly pregnant, cooked dinner. The five of them ate by candlelight in quiet celebration of the finished work, but the controversy they knew would erupt over Mailer's article dampened the enthusiasm at the dinner table. As Morris recalls, "It was not as wonderfully wild as the night he finished *Armies*."

The next day Midge Decter took the manuscript back to New York, while Morris and Muriel Murphy stayed on. Morris remembers taking a wild ride over the rocky beaches in the land rover Mailer had bought the previous summer. Everyone had hangovers from drinking the night before but Mailer showed no appreciable wear as he careened over the beaches talking about how fine a boxer Ernest Hemingway had been.

When the March issue of *Harper's* reached the newsstands in late February, it became an instant media event. *Time* pointed out that Mailer's piece featured more four-letter words than *Harper's* had printed in its 121-year history, and added, "Mailer's 47,000 word exercise in sexual dialectic will probably blow brains not only among Lib ladies but a sizeable segment of the magazine's 359,000 circulation."

The magazine sold more copies on the newsstands than any other single issue of *Harper's* in history. But Mailer's piece, in Willie Morris's opinion, became the focal point of an ongoing dispute between Morris and the management of *Harper's*. Although Morris's problems with management were not new and although nothing was done to censor Mailer's article, Morris resigned under pressure on March 4. "The article in our current issue by Norman Mailer has deeply disturbed the magazine's owners," Morris told the press. Along with Morris went a good portion of the *Harper's* staff: David Halberstam, Midge Decter, Larry King, John Corry, Marshall Frady, and John Hollander. When Mailer learned of Morris's resignation, he immediately went to see him and even called the chairman of the board of the magazine, John Cowles, Jr., in Minneapolis, on Morris's behalf. Cowles told Mailer it was too late.

The exodus at *Harper's* only added to the interest in Mailer's piece. Mailer had stepped directly into the middle of perhaps the most pivotal battle of the decade and virtually everyone perceived his position from a different perspective. "I think when the woman question happened," says Abbie Hoffman, "he was seen as an enemy of the New Left. He actively sought that role, which is in keeping with his cultural conservatism, but it put him in a sticky-wicky camp with people who I don't think he's emotionally in tune with at all."

Midge Decter viewed Mailer's argument differently. "If you read *The Prisoner of Sex* carefully," she says, "you'll see that it is not antilib. In fact it leans toward the most radical of the lib statements and not the liberal ones. He was very hard on Millett, but he was also intrigued by all their theory and was not hostile."

Pete Hamill saw the argument from yet another perspective. "A lot of the people who hate him, particularly the feminists, get so literal," Hamill says. "A lot of what Norman is doing is like music. He's trying something new. Even if you disagree with the way his mind takes him, there's always some interesting weird place that he'll go that nobody has gone before. He might leave you stranded there but it's worth the price of admission."

Kate Millett was taken aback by what she considered the "personal animosity" in Mailer's *Harper's* article. "I was surprised by the ad hominem, below-the-belt attack that was really beneath critical argument," she now says. "He singled me out as the absolute worst and also said I was a terrible, terrible writer. I was a very new writer then and it was painful. It was unpleasant to have all one's friends reading Mailer tearing one apart. His very reputation alone made friends less persuaded of one's arguments than they had been before. But it was very sensational and sold a vast amount of copies and was talked about a great deal. It seemed to me to be a rearguard action, something beneath his talent: He was pushing his talent into the service of reactionary opinion."

❦

Before the *Harper's* piece was even published, Mailer was aware of the heated debate it would generate. Since he was setting himself up as the devil in the fire, he took full advantage of the controversy. The hard-cover book version of the *Harper's* article would be published by Little, Brown in late May of 1971, and Mailer decided to seek out the leading feminists for a highly visible public debate on March 31, just as *The Prisoner of Sex* would be reaching the bookstores. The forum was a public benefit at New York's Town Hall for the Theatre for Ideas. Mailer would be the moderator and Donn Pennebaker, who had produced *Maidstone* for Mailer, would film the debate.

When the feminists learned that a man, especially Mailer, was going to moderate the event, many of them, including Kate Millett, Ti-Grace Atkinson, Gloria Steinem, and Robin Morgan, refused to attend. In fact, Morgan said she would come only if she could shoot Mailer, adding that she had a license to carry a firearm. "I thought that the topic was really insulting," says Millett. "It was as if debating the rights of women was a debatable issue. That we had to say please and argue for it was deplorable."

Germaine Greer, however, was about to publish *The Female Eunuch* in America and a public debate with Norman Mailer provided an unparalleled opportunity to promote her book. She accepted Mailer's invitation, but soon after she heard that Kate Millett had refused to attend. It was not until Greer acquired a copy of *Harper's* and read *The Prisoner of Sex* that she began to see why. "There were legitimate and persuasive reasons for having nothing to do with the liberation of Norman Mailer," she stated. "For Mailer, Women's Liberation had become simply another battle of the books in a war in which he had been campaigning all his life."

Greer herself was no innocent when it came to playing the media game. In a number of press interviews before the debate, she mentioned that she wanted to seduce Norman Mailer in order to prove he was the "world's worst." She also announced that she wanted to "carry him like a wounded child across the wasted world."

Greer was concerned about the feminists' boycott of the event, but she had given her word; besides, critic Diana Trilling, *Village Voice* columnist Jill Johnston, and Jackie Ceballos, the president of the National Organization of Women, had also agreed to participate.

As the time for the debate approached, New Yorkers were being primed for an evening of enlightened entertainment provided by the leading masculine advocate and prominent feminists. Despite the competition of a major art opening by Andy Warhol across town, at 8:30 on March 31, 1971, the New York literary set streamed into Town Hall at West Forty-third Street. As *The New York Times* said: "The hall was filled with the elite of a thousand intellectual battles." *Harper's Bazaar* added: "Everybody came out . . . One could see in a single vision the entire Radical Chic corps—as well as some Conservative Chics, pseudo-radicals . . ."

The guests had to pay $25 for seats in the orchestra or $10 for the balcony. The audience was impressive: Arthur Schlesinger, Jr., Stephen Smith and Jean Kennedy Smith, Jules Feiffer, Betty Friedan, Susan Sontag, Stephen Spender, Elizabeth Hardwick, Philip Roth, Norman Podhoretz and Midge Decter, Richard Gilman, John Hollander, Cynthia Ozick, Jack Newfield, Anatole Broyard, Robert Brustein, and the editors of all the major magazines.

Germaine Greer and Norman Mailer, the media stars of the evening, had each brought along a retinue of photographers. When Greer arrived at the Town Hall's greenroom, Mailer was already there being photographed. Mailer introduced himself to Greer and added that she was better-looking than he thought she would be. He asked her to pose with him for the photographers, which she did. Greer had her own backup team, a BBC television crew, and Mailer posed with her, even holding up a copy of *The Female Eunuch* for the cameras. When Diana Trilling walked into this media spectacle, she was astounded that Greer, like Mailer, was using the occasion to forward her commercial ambitions. Later Trilling reconsidered and decided that by competing with Mailer directly in his promotional games Greer "had transcended traditional femininity and moved all of us up a notch in the scale of male-female equality."

The curtain went up on the four female panelists, who were seated around a table covered with notepaper and water glasses. Mailer, the moderator and fifth participant, was wearing a dark business suit and a white shirt stretched tightly over his thickening paunch; Greer wore a slinky black dress with a fur thrown over one shoulder; Jill Johnston was dressed in denim with a British flag sewn on her Eisenhower jacket; Diana Trilling looked sedate in a matronly dress and sensible shoes.

Jackie Ceballos of NOW, the first to speak, said: "What is important is that the world is changing and that women at last are awakening to the fact that they have a right and a duty to enter into the world and change it and work toward the society that governs them . . . ." At this point writer Gregory Corso got up from his orchestra seat and yelled, "For all the people, for all of them, not just for half of humanity." Ceballos replied that when women are emancipated, men will be, too, but Corso was already out the back door of the auditorium.

"Hey, Gregory," Mailer shouted after him, "you'll get bounced if you keep it up."

Someone then called out from the balcony that there was a woman outside who was too poor to get in.

"Knock it off," Mailer yelled up.

"But it's true, it's true," the heckler insisted.

"It'll always be true until it's not true," Mailer retorted.

Amidst this confusion Ceballos managed to finish her speech. After delivering an expanded compliment, Mailer asked her whether there was anything in NOW's program that would give men the notion that life might not continue to be as profoundly boring as it is today.

Germaine Greer was next. Her remarks centered, not surprisingly, on the ego of certain artists. "The creative artist in our society is more a killer than a creator," she said, "aiming his ego ahead of lesser talents, drawing the focus of all eyes to his achievements, being read now by millions and paid in millions. Is it possible that the way of the masculine artist in our society is strewn with the husks of people worn out and dried by this ego?"

Greer was thinking specifically of Mailer's last wife, Beverly, whom she had met a couple of weeks earlier in New York. As Greer recalls, Beverly was "gallant, a little wry and regretful, mildly astonished that Mailer had been so careless of her actress's talent when he had so much opportunity to indulge it."

Greer finished her remarks and sat down to thunderous applause. Mailer then defied the audience and criticized the speech for failing to provide the means to the end. He called Greer's comments "diaper

Marxism," and suggested that a woman can be "a goddess and a slob at different moments."

"I think Mailer's performance at Town Hall was distinctly crummy," Greer says in retrospect. "It just wasn't distinguished in any way. It wasn't bad-assed, it wasn't articulate, and it was loaded with cheap shots which the audience let him get away with—careless dismissals of arguments he couldn't confront. Every time he said anything, he looked his audience right in the eye and gave them a sort of complicit grin as the insider. And New York is immensely parochial. My overriding impression of him was of someone who had been shamefully indulged in that New York way. He was just one of theirs and they adored him and anything he did was okay. I think it's because he's part of New York history and they had all grown old together."

Jill Johnston's turn was next.

"I think Germaine was born in Australia and I was born in England," she said. "I can't help it, that's just the first thing I thought of."

"You may use your time like the flight of birds," Mailer told her, "but I'll have to call you in ten minutes."

Johnston then discussed lesbianism, claiming that "all women are lesbians except those that don't know it yet." When she had continued to speak for fifteen minutes, Mailer tried to stop her by asking her to "be a lady." Still unable to dissuade her, Mailer had to ask for a show of hands from the audience, then took a voice vote. The nays were louder, but at that moment two of Johnston's girl friends got up on the stage and the threesome embraced wildly, then rolled together on the floor. This spectacle hardly shocked the sophisticated New York audience, and an annoyed Mailer was eventually able to break it up. Johnston subsequently left the hall.

Later in the evening Mailer made a statement about lesbianism which was a direct response to Johnston's comment. "Women's Liberation is two things: It is a profoundly sexual movement which quite naturally takes on huge lesbian overtones," he told the Town Hall audience. "It does not mean at all that every woman who's interested in Women's Liberation is a lesbian, obviously not, and anyone who'd go ahead and say I said that is a fool. But what I am saying is that it's quite natural for lesbians to center on Women's Liberation because there's a peculiar difficulty with lesbianism which homosexuals, although they are much cursed, would, I suspect, not have. Which is why every man is vulnerable to homosexuality, because he cannot have it with a woman. He must go to a man to fundamentally feel like a woman. He must go to a man to have something up his anus or in his mouth."

At this juncture a man in the audience shouted, "Up your anus!"

"Not up mine, buddy," Mailer replied. The audience burst into laughter. Mailer finished his point: "However, with women the difficulty is that any man who is a really superb lover can be about 90 percent as good to a woman as a lesbian. Just give me the things that a lesbian does, and he's got all the other stuff. . . . So the question I want to ask Jill Johnston is, 'What is she going to do about all us 90 percenters?' " Since Johnston had left the hall, she could not respond.

It was Diana Trilling's turn to speak next. She gracefully moved her way to the podium to offer some enlightened comments on Mailer's professed biological determinism in *The Prisoner of Sex*. While she was speaking, she noticed, out of the corner of her eye, that Germaine Greer kept passing notes to Mailer. He became so absorbed in these missives from Greer that he cut Trilling off while she was paying him one of the few compliments of the evening. Mailer had, she said, "a splendid imagination of women . . . the imagination of women in love."

Greer disagrees with Trilling's opinion that she was seeking to upstage her. "Norman wrote on the corner of his program, 'Would you like a drink?'—meaning would I go out with him after the show," Greer explains. "I wrote back on my program, 'Of what, hemlock?' So we really weren't passing notes back and forth. Scribbling a few words twice hardly amounts to an attention-getting ploy. Apart from anything else, Norman is afraid of Diana because she is Lionel's widow."

Mailer had not missed a word of Trilling's speech and he began his own remarks that night by responding to hers. "What I was trying to say in my usual incoherent fashion in *The Prisoner of Sex* was that biology, or physiology, if you will, is not destiny, but it is half of it and that if you try to ignore the fact you then get, at least as far as I can see any prospectus of the future, you then get into the most awful totalitarianism of all, the left totalitarianism."

Mailer went on to say: "And there is an element in Women's Liberation that terrifies us. . . . I'm not here to say that every woman must have a child, that every woman must have a vaginal orgasm, or that every woman must conceive in any way that I lay down. . . . What I'm trying to say is let's get hip to this little matter and recognize that the whole question of Women's Liberation is the deepest question that faces us, and we're gonna go right into the very elements of existence and eternity before we're through."

When Mailer concluded, the feminists in the audience assailed him, but not without some humor, even affection. Cynthia Ozick spoke of her "fantasies" about Mailer's testicles, anointing him a "transcendent sacerdotal priest." Elizabeth Hardwick wanted to know whether he did any housework, and Susan Sontag took him to task about his use of the word *lady*.

But to Germaine Greer the opposition was excessively mild; she was shocked by the leniency with which they dealt with Mailer. "I was surprised," she says, "because even a person like Susan Sontag was indulgent with him. She didn't bring the full power of her brain to bear on him. They all treated him as if he were a little boy." Mailer, however, felt less than indulged. As he stood there, he felt like a "Danton" besieged by witches. And he later added, "That night ended my political career. My hair turned white."

Midge Decter now believes that the whole evening was something of an intellectual put-on. "The ladies were after him, but everyone was having fun," she says. "Germaine Greer was totally flirtatious and provocative with Mailer and he with her. It was a big show, but nothing serious. He's not really the focus of feminist wrath because he's always very special."

Donn Pennebaker, whose film of the evening's proceedings was named *Town Bloody Hall*, agrees. "Whenever feminists walked out of the film," he recounts "they would say, 'Boy, it sure shows what a shit he is,' but they loved him. The meanest lesbians who like to denigrate Norman love him in that film."

Greer agrees with Decter that Mailer hardly represented the archetypal male-chauvinist opposition. "I thought one of the funniest things," Greer says, "is that he sort of collared the argument so that it appeared to relate to him. He set himself up as a kind of burlesque ringmaster of the feminist circus, and I'm still mystified why he did it. I think he was desperate for money, and anyone dealing with him should realize that the man is an alimony slave."

After the debate Mailer and Greer did not slip out for a drink. Rather, they went to the large postdebate party in the West Village, where Greer was introduced to Mailer's parents. "It was neat meeting them," she recalls. "I mean, considering he pretended to be an Irishman for so long. I loved it. I thought, 'He's really slipping into the right slot after all this time.' The parents themselves were very simple people. His mother didn't act anything out; she was very shy and reserved and obviously very proud. I like him better for his mother."

Meeting Fanny Mailer undoubtedly influenced Greer when she wrote a long piece for *Esquire*, published in September 1971, entitled "My Mailer Problem." She stated: "The concept of the worshipped feminine which holds the Prisoner of Sex in thrall is the Omnipotent Mother. To this day Mailer's relationship with his mother is important: When he confesses that he has never been able to live without a woman, it is not just sex and company that he needs but nurture."

❦

Two months after the Town Hall debate, *The Prisoner of Sex* was published to predictably mixed reviews. The critics seemed to divide along simple lines: men for the book, women reviewers against it. In *Harper's*, V. S. Pritchett wrote that "Norman Mailer comes in with *The Prisoner of Sex* and steals the show from the blue-stockings. He is what it lacked: a go-getting whistle-stop clown . . . a paranoiac with a good boyish punch, a gentle eye, a sentimentalist—four wives, clearly not interested in women but in something they had got—yet with sensible flashes in his rage and savage laughter."

Joyce Carol Oates, in the same issue of *Harper's*, expressed a contradictory view: "It is appropriate that Norman Mailer has become the central target of the fiercest and cruelest of women's liberation attacks, not because Mailer is prejudiced against women, or bullying about them, not even because he claims to know much about them but because he is so dangerous a visionary, a poet, a mystic—he is shameless in his passion for women, and one is led to believe anything he says because he says it so well."

It was on the front page of *The New York Times Book Review* that Mailer received his most scathing critique. Brigid Brophy said of Mailer: "No knight has adventured out to restore justice and reason. All that's happened is that a minor victim of the book's [Millett's] injustice has issued a rejoinder. This consists of an appreciative meditation by Norman Mailer on Norman Mailer. It establishes merely that if Kate Millett could put him down with bad logic and bad prose, he can puff himself up with more and worse of both."

S. K. Oberbeck came to Mailer's defense in *Newsweek*. "Mailer has written a brilliant broadside," he said. In the daily *New York Times* Anatole Broyard called *Prisoner* "Mailer's best book." He went on to say: "What Mailer has tried to do here is write a love poem. Let us hope that women never become so liberated that it is impossible to write love poems to them."

Today, Germaine Greer believes that Mailer pushed himself into the feminist debate because it actually made him feel more masculine, more heroic. "There was a lot of feminist wrath around," she says, "and he bought it. I mean he laid in his chin. He wanted to be the subject of that rage and he courted it because it made him feel more masculine. It's the same reason he goes to dockside cafés and gets beaten up. The only difference is the feminists never land a punch because they punch so wildly all the time. Mailer wants a woman who is stronger than him. In fact, at a party at Marion Javits's house a few weeks after the debate, Norman accused me of not being tough enough. He thought I was going to be some sort of archetypical rocky female. But I'm not tough. I'm ruthless, but not tough in the way that would excite him."

At the Javitses' party Mailer's masculine ego was on curious display all evening. Greer had brought along Dick Fontaine, the BBC producer who had filmed Mailer during the Pentagon march. As Greer recollects, "Mailer was showing off and talking about what a great actor he would have made and how he would have transformed the act of picking up a cup just by the way he did it. I don't know if he mentioned Brando, but he was obviously thinking of himself as a Brando figure. I think he was showing off for Dick, the unspoken theme being his film *Maidstone*, but the whole thing was tedious."

Dotson Rader was at the same party. If Mailer was testing Greer's toughness as a feminist, he was also testing Rader's toughness as a macho homosexual. Rader wanted Mailer to go along with him to one of two bars Truman Capote had told him about. One was a necrophiliac bar which Capote claimed always had a dead body about. The other was an all-black bar which only allowed whites in on Thursday nights. Capote claimed he was the only white male who could go to the bar whenever he desired. Rader wanted to see whether Mailer had the courage to go there on this night, which was not a Thursday.

Mailer agreed to try the black bar, and Greer, according to Rader, invited herself along. Rader believes that Greer had designs on

Mailer. "In the cab she started coming on to him, and he started getting hostile." Greer denies this, but at Sixtieth and Park, Mailer told the cab to stop, and Greer got out.

Mailer then told Rader he did not want to go to the black bar first. He went to another bar and phoned Carol, who arrived shortly afterward. "When she came," says Rader, "I knew we wouldn't go to the black bar. I also thought he invited her so we wouldn't go." By the time Carol walked in, Mailer and Rader, who had been drinking heavily, were in the middle of a complex wager. In the course of making the bet, Mailer consistently challenged Rader. "I made a remark that was mildly critical," Rader continues, "and Norman hit the table and said, 'Strike one.' I did it again, and he hit the table and said, 'Strike three and we go out and fight.' I think it had to do with Norman's ambivalence about homosexuals. To the best of my knowledge, I'm the only homosexual who has become a close friend of his. Because of my nature, Norman has never felt threatened or attracted sexually to me. We can admire women, and I can have the same sexual appreciation in kind that he does. So I'm a homosexual that Norman doesn't perceive as homosexual. When he's with me, he puts it out of his mind. He doesn't like talking about it. He even acts like it's not there.

"But I think Norman is attracted to difference, to what is most unlike himself. He senses that what is most unlike himself may be most truly what he is. That's why he's attracted to violence and a whole spectrum of sexual and social deviances. He is a kind, loving, decent, ethical man, but I think that's an act of will. Norman is an auto-voyeur. He's solipsistic to the degree that he looks at the world in order to find a mirror that reflects some part of himself that he can't see within himself. I think his most magnificent creation is himself. He created himself out of whole cloth."

The wager that they were involved in that night had to do with Rader's getting Mailer an introduction to Billy Graham. Rader had also drunkenly boasted that he could arrange a meeting with Richard Nixon as well. "Norman was keenly interested in meeting Graham because of his spiritual prestige and because that prestige was connected with real and great political power," Rader adds. "Norman is a deeply religious man in a profoundly secular age, and therefore he is essentially uncomfortable in the period in which he lives. He can talk at great length about the nature of God, soul, eternity, sin, things that are by definition theological. There's a curiosity that isn't fulfilled by his secular friends, who are all agnostics or renegade Jews."

That night Rader began a three-year writing campaign to Billy Graham, but he was never able to arrange the meeting. The last letter he got from Graham simply said, "I am praying for you."

At the height of Mailer's conflict with the feminists, he had become good friends with Dotson Rader, but he was about to lose an old friend, Gore Vidal. Mailer had entered the feminist revolution as a self-proclaimed opponent, but Vidal was already a staunch defender. Vidal had, Mailer said derisively, "an impeccable nose for ripe liberal issues." Vidal had read *The Prisoner of Sex* and now recalls that he thought Mailer's views on women were "fascistic," an opinion he still holds. The two were clearly at opposite ideological poles of the issue. The growing antagonism between them was not helped by Vidal's quips to the media about Mailer's machismo, nor by Mailer's letter to *Women's Wear Daily* earlier that year which pointed out that Vidal had never married or fathered any children.

Vidal had wanted to review *The Prisoner of Sex* for *Harper's*, but the book had already been assigned by the magazine to someone else. Instead, Vidal decided to air his views about Mailer and women in a critique of a book by Eva Figes in *The New York Review of Books* on July 22, 1971, only four months after Mailer's Town Hall debate. "There has been from Henry Miller to Norman Mailer to Charles Manson a logical progression," Vidal wrote. "The Miller-Mailer-Manson man (or M3 for short) has been conditioned to think of women as, at best, breeders of sons; at worst, objects to be poked, humiliated, killed. . . ."

The fuse of controversy had been ignited and Mailer ached to confront his old friend. The opportunity came five months later when Dick Cavett asked Mailer to appear on his show with Vidal and *New Yorker* writer Janet Flanner. Years later, Mailer would chronicle the event in an *Esquire* piece entitled "Of a Small and Modest Malignancy, Wicked and Bristling With Dots."

Mailer arrived at the studio after having stopped off at the publication party for Pete Hamill's new novel, *The Gift*, where, Hamill says, "Norman just drank." Mailer later stated that he "had enjoyed three or four drinks to the hilt. Mailer had the operative definition of 'to the hilt': it was the state where a carelessly lit match sent you up in flames."

While Mailer was waiting in the backstage greenroom before the show, he felt a touch at the back of his neck which he characterized as "caressing" and which Vidal calls "friendly." When Mailer turned and saw Vidal, he gave him a light slap across his cheek. Vidal slapped him back, and the war was on. Mailer then gave Vidal a stiff butt in the head with his head, a fighting technique he had adopted and for which he has since become notorious. This would set the stage for Vidal's remarks about Mailer's love of violence.

Vidal went on first, followed by Janet Flanner. Their witty, civilized repartee, especially Vidal's fond and intimate comments about Eleanor Roosevelt, only served to fire the rage in Mailer. The "slumbering Beast" was wakening.

When Mailer walked on stage, he refused to shake hands with Vidal. Cavett asked him why and Mailer answered that Vidal was "shameless in intellectual argument." The audience, which had warmed to Vidal, bristled at this. When Mailer added that he thought the contents of Vidal's stomach were "no more interesting than the contents of the stomach of an intellectual cow," the audience booed him. Mailer realized that he had to get to the subject of Vidal's review of *Prisoner of Sex* quickly. He had brought the page from *The New York Review of Books* with him, and he asked Cavett to give it to Vidal to read aloud. When Vidal refused, Mailer stepped up his attack.

MAILER: You seem to have figured out that the next reincarnation for me is going to be Charles Manson.

VIDAL: Well, you left yourself—

MAILER: Why don't you read what you wrote?

VIDAL: You let yourself in for it, and I will tell you—I'll give you a little background here—that Mailer has—

MAILER: We all know that I stabbed my wife years ago, we do know that, Gore. You were playing on that.

VIDAL: Let's just forget about it.

MAILER: You're a liar and a hypocrite. You were playing on it.

VIDAL: But that wasn't a lie or a hypocrisy.

MAILER: The fact of the matter is that the people who read *The New York Review of Books* know perfectly well—they know all about it, and it's your subtle little way of doing it . . .

VIDAL: Oh, I'm beginning to see what bothers you now. Okay, I'm getting the point.

MAILER: Are you ready to apologize?

VIDAL: I would apologize—if it hurts your feelings, of course I would.

MAILER: No, it hurts my sense of intellectual pollution.

VIDAL: Well, I must say, as an expert you should know about such things. [Laughter]

MAILER: Yes, well, I've had to smell your works from time to time, and that has helped me to become an expert on intellectual pollution, yes.

The audience now began heckling Mailer, calling out, "You're rude."

To counter, Mailer launched into a remarkably candid defense, one so resonating with wounded pride that the audience actually applauded him at the end. "I've been so bold as to pretend to be the presumptive literary champ, you know, whether I deserve to be or not," Mailer told them. "The reason people always talk about me in relation to Hemingway is that Hemingway at a certain point said to himself with his huge paranoia, 'They're going to kill me for this, but I'm going to be the champ—it's all I care about.' And he shifted the course of American letters because up to that point people who wrote books were men of letters, they were gentlemen, they wrote books, and Hemingway said, in effect, 'No people who write books take as much punishment as prizefighters, and one of them has to be champion.' . . . I have presumed, with all my extraordinary arrogance and loutishness and crudeness to step forth and say, 'I'm going to be the champ until one of you knocks me off.' Well, fine, but you know, they don't knock you off because they're too damned simply yellow, and they kick me in the nuts, and I don't like it."

Mailer intended to go on and talk about Women's Liberation but a commercial intervened. During the pause it was decided that Vidal would have time to respond but only if he read from his review. "Well, I'll begin to answer Norman's charge about what a bad person I am," Vidal said. "The attack on him, really, if you want to know, Norman, is simply what I detest in you—and I like many things in you, you know. I'm a constant friend despite this—but your violence, your love of murder, your celebration of rage, of hate . . . *An American Dream*—what was the dream? A man murders his wife and then buggers this woman afterward to celebrate an American man's dream. This violence, this knocking people down, this carrying on, is a terrible thing. Now, it may make you a great artist . . . but to the extent that one is interested in the way society is going, there is quite enough of this stress, quite enough of this violence, without what I think are your celebrations of it, your attitude toward women in this thing, which I thought really horrible, and you said I compared you to Charles Manson. I said Henry Miller in his way, Norman in his, and Manson in his far-out, mad way are each reflecting a hatred of women and a hatred of place."

At this point Mailer got up, went to where Vidal was sitting, and snatched the review away from him as Vidal flinched. Mailer then began reading the review aloud himself, after which he and Vidal started a biting debate about whether murder was nonsexual. In his anger, Mailer attempted to defend the buggery scene in *An American Dream*. "The character I have there is a particularly complex character, and, in fact, he did not simply bugger a woman, he entered her the other way as well, and there was a particularly complicated . . ."

Just then Janet Flanner exclaimed, "Oh, goodness' sake," provoking laughter. It prompted Mailer on to higher defenses. "I know you've lived in France for many years," he told her, "but believe me, Janet, it's possible to enter a woman another way."

"So I've heard," she replied to more laughter.

"On that classy note . . ." Cavett said, and the show came to its conclusion.

When Mailer chronicled the entire talk-show exchange six years later in *Esquire*, he pointed out that after the debate he received hundreds of letters, mostly positive, just as Vidal probably received hundreds which commended him.

But the reaction among some of Mailer's friends was more pained than positive. His old war buddy Francis Irby Gwaltney watched the show in Arkansas with his wife. As Mrs. Gwaltney recalls, "Norman's trouble comes when he's backed into a corner and says foolish things. But people do bait him. I could see both sides of the Cavett show. I could see how he thought the audience was full of idiots and how they thought he was a boor. When he said he was the gentlest one there it seemed totally ludicrous, but I knew what he meant and in many ways he was. Also, Norman can be funny, but he doesn't have a quick wit. I think he would love to have that, but he's basically a Jewish aesthetic."

José Torres was watching the show from the rented house in Vermont where Mailer and Carol Stevens were then living. "It was the first time I saw Norman do poorly on television," Torres said. "When he came back and saw me, I wouldn't tell him how bad it was. But then he told me what he had done in the greenroom, and when he got up to snatch the review away from Vidal, it was clear how Norman had intimidated him. He intimidates in a profound way. When Vidal saw Norman coming, he was sure he was going to be hit."

❦

The animosity between Mailer and the feminists—and their defenders—has not disappeared over the years. But despite his machismo, his patriarchal stance as father of eight, and his intellectual assaults on the technology of sex, Mailer is not seen by everyone in the feminist or radical communities as the champion of male chauvinism.

Germaine Greer herself sees Mailer's perspective as peculiarly that of a writer and somehow different from typical male chauvinism. "Mailer set himself up at the Town Hall debate as a kind of stereotypic male, which as a writer of course he isn't," Greer now says. "Writers are a curious bunch."

Abbie Hoffman views Mailer's public antifeminist stance as being inconsistent with his true personality. "His attitude about feminism is strange," says Hoffman, "because he is one of the few people who remembers the name of the wife of every famous person he meets. Others who pride themselves on conquering their male chauvinism only want to talk to the famous men and ignore the wives. Mailer talks to women. He is a strange contradiction. He sees feminism as the decline of civilization. Technology is taking over and women are leaving the kitchen to go and press buttons along with the men."

Hoffman's attitude might reflect certain truths about Mailer, but to the Women's Liberation movement of the 1970s, and to many today, Mailer's *Prisoner of Sex* was the antibible of feminism.

• XVIII •

EGO AT THE HALF CENTURY

The story of Norman Mailer is one of an ego of large, sometimes outrageous, proportions. Mailer had exercised that ego in his conflicts with the political and literary establishments, in his work, and in his relations with women. The symbols of masculinity—drinking, womanizing, and the combative sports—were especially appealing to him. Now as Mailer approached the half-century mark, he decided to add the skill of being a trained boxer to his masculine repertoire. The opportunity came when his friend, ex-light heavyweight champion José Torres, proposed that he teach Mailer to box in exchange for editorial help.

The two men had rented houses a mile apart from each other in Vermont, where they were both writing books. Mailer also had a small studio nearby, and it was here that Torres worked on his book about Muhammad Ali, *Sting Like a Bee.* The boxer would get up at 7:00 A.M., write for two hours, then box with Mailer at his house for an hour before lunch. He'd then go back to work in the studio, returning to Mailer's house at five in the afternoon. At night Mailer would go over what Torres had written.

"He's a very strange editor," Torres says. "He would ask, 'What are you trying to say here?' and I would tell him. Then he'd say, 'I want you to write it the way you just explained it to me.' But sometimes he would just say, 'This is no good.' I'd ask him why, and he would tell me to figure it out. So I would go and rewrite the page and come back, and he'd say, 'No good.' On the third day of this I told him if he didn't go into detail, I was going to have trouble. 'I can't think for you,' he told me. 'It's no good, but I can't tell you why it's no good.' The next day I came in with something new, and he said, '*This* is what I wanted.'

"I didn't know consciously the basic difference between the first three days and this day, but Norman had told me to go to bed, and while I was asleep, I would be working on the book. He was teaching me not how to think or what to think but to think."

In exchange for that help, over a period of three months Torres taught Mailer how to box. "I knew this would be the best thing that could happen to Norman," Torres says. "Once he knew how to box, he wouldn't get into fights, because he would feel superior to the other guy, and deep down he always wants to have a fair fight. He never punches first; he always waits for the other guy—with the exception of the young actor during the filming of *Maidstone*." By the time Torres finished coaching his pupil, he felt that Mailer was as good a fighter as a top Golden Gloves contender. "He could even be a champion of the Golden Gloves," Torres asserts.

Mailer's interest in boxing as an expression of ego soon led him to attempt an article on the sport. In the same month that *Harper's* published *The Prisoner of Sex*, March 1971, Mailer was covering the Muhammad Ali-Joe Frazier championship fight for *Life*. He had only two days after the Monday night fight at Madison Square Garden to meet the Wednesday evening deadline for the March 19 issue. Despite the grueling schedule, he wrote 9,000 words of copy examining not only the fight—in which Ali was knocked to the floor in the fifteenth round yet managed to finish the losing battle—but Ali's ego as well.

Ego, Mailer's own Excalibur and his Achilles' heel, became the title of the piece. Identifying with Ali as a champion, Mailer said that ego was "that extraordinary state of the psyche which gives us authority to declare we are sure of ourselves when we are not." And Ali has America's greatest ego, Mailer assured us.

Life managing editor Ralph Graves was astounded by Mailer's professionalism in getting the piece in so rapidly. "He was out in Brooklyn sending it in by sections," Graves remembers. "He wrote it out in longhand, his secretary typed it, and then we'd get it messengered to the office, where we would put it into the works. Every time he finished a take, he'd call and say, 'Another take is ready and how much more time do I really have?' He's an incredible writer under deadline. It was remarkable how fine the copy was when it came in. When I told him how marvelous it was, he said, 'Well, I felt I owed you a really good one.' He realized that some of the astronaut pieces were long and in many ways philosophical, without a strong narrative like this one."

The now-proficient boxer had observed the Ali-Frazier match with sophisticated eyes, and his *Life* article on the fight, "Ego," would become the opening piece of Mailer's new collection which Little, Brown published in the spring of 1972. It set the theme for the book, which was a testament to Mailer's own extraordinary ego, or, by his definition, his authority to declare himself sure of himself when he was not. The collection, entitled *Existential Errands*, contained none of the personal narrative of the three previous compendiums, but it had its own unity. It contained pieces Mailer had written over the past few years: an essay on theater which was the preface to his play *The Deer Park;* his *Esquire* article on the making of *Wild 90* and his preface to the screenplay of *Maidstone;* a one-act play of *Why Are We in Vietnam?;* his National Book Award acceptance speech; an open letter to Richard Nixon; and two mayoralty campaign speeches, including the transcript of his disastrous performance at the Village Gate.

One of the pieces in *Errands*, his review of Norman Podhoretz's book *Making It*, which Mailer had written in the spring of 1968 for *Partisan Review*, was to embroil the author in another controversy with a friend. *Making It* had caused a furor when it was published. Podhoretz had tried to expose the establishment's embarrassment about wanting success, what he called their "dirty little secret," and his literary peers were dragged into this autobiographical confession. Mailer, in fact, had been the inspiration for the book. Podhoretz wrote: "For several years I toyed with the idea of doing a book about Mailer that would focus on the problem of success, but in the end I decided that if I ever did work up the nerve to write about this problem, I would have to do it without hiding behind him or anyone else."

The backlash to Podhoretz's book within the literary establishment was so severe that Mailer tried to reason out the cause. He concluded that Podhoretz had endangered the fine art of the put-on, which was, Mailer felt, all that the literary establishment was. It had started out in the forties as a coterie of left-wing intellectuals interested in literary criticism. By the sixties, under Kennedy, it had become powerful. By the late sixties it had developed its own chic ultra-left ideology. "They will play the shell game, do the dance of the veils," Mailer wrote, "adore the put-on, elevate Camp, praise Pop, rush to install plastic fashions, and avoid like demons and witches confrontation upon a point. Can that be why *Making It* was so abominable to them? Because Podhoretz was blind to the defenses of the put-on and had the idiocy or the suicidal strength to move to the center of the stage, open his box, exhibit his tricks?" Mailer ended his review by pointing out that the tragedy of Podhoretz's book was that it laid itself open to the charge that it was a put-on itself: "Is this noble act the work of a whack or the superbest put-on of all?"

Despite Mailer's seeming defense of his friend, Podhoretz was not pleased by the review. Podhoretz felt that Mailer had fallen into the grips of the establishment. "When confronted with the full force of the opposition to *Making It*," Podhoretz later said, "and realizing that in defending it he would in all probability unleash the 'terror' against himself as well, he simply lost his nerve."

Mailer and Podhoretz would drift apart after the *Making It* dispute, but it was not until the publication of Podhoretz's book *Breaking Ranks* in 1979 that their friendship was cleanly severed. In that book Podhoretz described the ostracism that he had been subjected to after 1968, and spoke of Mailer's review as the inevitable product of a man who had become part of the establishment. Podhoretz wrote: "Mailer himself would not have done it that 'plastic' way ten years earlier, but that is how he would have done it in the climate of the late sixties, with a newly solidified popularity to protect."

"He was offended by what I said about him and told a lot of people that," Podhoretz now says. "But from the time the establishment started going left in the late sixties, I didn't regard Mailer as a rebel at all anymore. He became for all practical purposes a conformist and remains so. Nevertheless, he continued pretending to himself and others that he was a bad boy and a rebel, so in some sense he was not aware that he had been taken over by the establishment."

Mailer had perceived his new connection to the establishment, especially after winning the Pulitzer Prize, but in *Errands* he subtly denied the link. He pointed out that his pursuits were of a more profound, existential nature than the "put on" of the establishment. He set the tone for many of his reviewers who were tempted to see him as an establishment figure, yet still could not do so.

"Lesser literati look hopefully for signs of Norman Mailer becoming at least something of a cultural institution," wrote S. K. Oberbeck in *Book World*. "But seventeen books and a lot of action later, it is still just as hard to pin down that inspired, inspiring hustler as ever."

"He is as permanent as Andy Warhol or Jackie Onassis," wrote Cynthia Buchanan in *The New York Times Book Review*, but she added that he is also a "man of his own inner scruple."

❦

In the summer of 1972 Mailer decided to cover his fourth presidential nominating convention. Mailer had wanted to write about both the Democratic and Republican conventions for *Life*, but the magazine felt that the Republican convention didn't present enough of a challenge. "Everyone knew that Nixon would get it," recalls *Life* managing editor Ralph Graves, "so we didn't want to do that one, although Norman went to it as well."

Life would publish Mailer's account of the Democratic convention, which was held in Miami, in their July 28 issue, shortly after it was over. A revised version of this piece as well as Mailer's coverage of the Republican convention, which was also held in Miami in August, would be published by the paperback division of New American Library that fall under the title *St. George and the Godfather*.

According to political writer Gary Wills, Mailer told everyone he met at the Democratic convention that he was afraid of imitating himself. In fact, for the *Life* piece and in the book that followed, Mailer would adopt the old name he had used in *Of a Fire on the Moon*, Aquarius. Political conventions had become something akin to a comfortable marriage for Mailer, and while he would observe the goings-on with his usual sharp perceptions, there were fewer themes for him to capitalize on. Watergate, which would shock the nation the following summer, was only alluded to by Mailer in these early days after the break-in. Yet Mailer intimated his new concern with the idea of conspiracy, specifically by the CIA and FBI.

The Democratic convention of July 1972 held none of the drama of the 1968 battle and Mailer was forced to admit that "deaths are more interesting than births." With the nomination of George

McGovern, Mailer felt a certain nostalgia for the old political wheeling and dealing. He concluded his *Life* piece, entitled "Some Evil in the Room," by stating: "One had to be partial to a man whose delegates had the fair and average and open faces of an army of citizenry, as opposed to an army of the pols, and Aquarius knew then why the convention was obliged to be boring. There was insufficient evil in the room."

For the first time, Mailer may have failed to spot chicanery. As Gary Wills would point out, Mailer had missed all the "off-stage manipulation that had put McGovern over the top." Wills was amused to note that once Mailer had learned of all the double crosses going on, he changed the conclusion in the book to the following: "Aquarius knew then why the convention was bound to be boring. There was insufficient evil in the room. With all the evil he had seen, all the lies and deals and evasions and cracks of the open door, with the betrayals of planks and the voids of promises, still there had been so little of real evil in the room."

Mailer's article ran in *Life* before the controversy erupted over McGovern's choice of a vice-presidential running mate, Senator Thomas F. Eagleton, who, it was disclosed, had undergone shock treatment a number of times. Mailer interviewed Eagleton in Washington on the day of his resignation and later reflected, "Aquarius . . . sometimes thought it was his life's ambition to come up with evidence that the CIA was tripping on American elections. . . ." Speaking to Warren Beatty outside McGovern's office, Mailer asked him when he had first found out about Eagleton. Beatty told him he had received a call from a couple of reporters, who had in turn been told via an anonymous call from Rochester, New York."Why bother to look for the CIA," Mailer wrote, "when there was always the FBI." Mailer's new fascination with conspiracy would intensify five months later at his fiftieth birthday party.

The Watergate conspiracy is first mentioned in Mailer's book when he describes an interview with Henry Kissinger in the Sans Souci restaurant. As Mailer and Kissinger passed the table of Larry O'Brien, the former Democratic Party chairman, O'Brien joked with Kissinger, who had just returned from Paris, about Watergate. "That was good luck, Henry, to get away just before it hit the fan," O'Brien said.

Mailer was more interested in talking to the secretary of state about Vietnam than about Watergate, but he sensed that Kissinger and Nixon were in greater accord on China and Russia than on Vietnam and this made for some hesitancy. Mailer left the meeting liking Kissinger and questioning his own instincts.

In speaking to Kissinger, Mailer had called Nixon a genius, and back in Miami in August for the Republican convention, he began to see the President not only as a genius but as an artist. "Nixon was the artist who had discovered the laws of vibration in all the frozen congelations of the mediocre," he wrote. "The major work of Nixon's intellectual life [was] to chart the undiscovered laws of movement in the unobserved glop of the wad. . . ." But if Mailer had a certain respect for Nixon's political acumen, he also realized that the war he loathed was a consequence of that shrewdness: "Yes, it was Nixon's genius to know that every bomb dropped somehow extinguished another dangerous hippie in the mind of the wad. . . ."

Most reviews of the book pointed out that Mailer had done his best with two relatively dull conventions, but several critics felt that Mailer was repeating his form, something he had avoided before. As Gary Wills wrote in *The New York Times Book Review*, "Mailer is our literary Rojack; he can get away with murder. And it seems on the face of it, a journalistic crime for him to circle back, doing Miami-and-Miami, after his *Miami and the Siege of Chicago*."

Mailer was aware of the self-parodying style that Hemingway had adopted before his suicide. He had no intention of being ensnared in the same literary trap. If his own third-person hero was becoming stale, he would find a new hero, or heroine.

❦

In September 1972, a month before *St. George and the Godfather* was published, Mailer, Carol Stevens, and their infant daughter Maggie Alexandra, moved into the Wyndcote estate on Yale Hill in Stockbridge, Massachusetts, which Mailer had purchased for seventy-five thousand dollars with a sixty-thousand-dollar mortgage from the Lenox Savings Bank. The huge fifteen-room brown-shingled house was surrounded by several outbuildings and five acres of land, making it one of the most impressive residences Mailer had yet owned.

The Stockbridge house would be Mailer's main residence until 1975. Although he still kept the Brooklyn Heights apartment, it was rarely used. The Stockbridge estate was in constant flux: There were visiting guests, visiting children, including Carol's twenty-two-year-old son David, and ex-wives. Fanny Mailer, who became even closer to her son after Barney Mailer's death that year, was also a regular visitor.

Carol had all but given up her career while she managed this household, but it was to start up again that winter after she met author Anne Edwards at a Stockbridge dance exercise class, which they called "Over-Thirty-fives." Edwards was then living with her future husband, Stephen Citron, a nightclub entertainer, who had opened an inn and cabaret in Stockbridge. Edwards suggested to the dance group that after their class on Sunday afternoons they retreat to his inn, Orpheus Rising, for drinks. It soon became something of a salon, with husbands and friends joining what was now called "Le Club Dimanche." Carol began singing again at these sessions, and one evening as Edwards and Citron were sitting with Mailer and Carol over a bottle of rum, it was decided that Carol would perform at the inn on Friday nights.

On her opening night Carol appeared in a bright green chiffon gown with rhinestone clips at her shoulders, her dark hair piled atop her head. She looked rather stunning in that provincial setting. Mailer was sitting at a window banquette which offered the best view of the stage; next to him were two men who had been drinking heavily and become quite loud. In her book *The Inn and Us*, Anne Edwards recounted what happened next. "Carol began her first number," she recalled. "Norman leaned over and politely asked the man seated closest to him to be quiet. The man ignored him. Norman bristled, drew back, but all the while Carol was singing it was obvious the strangers were straining his tolerance level. Halfway through Carol's third number, the man nearest Norman turned away from his companion and called out, 'Is that broad stacked!'

"Be quiet," Norman ordered.

"Sex-y!" the man continued.

"With that Norman turned to face the stranger, grabbed him by the ears and in a split moment had butted his own head so hard against the man's head that there was a resounding craaaaack! The stranger was holding his head and moaning. Norman had turned back to watch Carol. She was a ghostly sight, unable to conceal the fear in her eyes as she raised the decibel level of her voice.

"That old man nearly cracked my skull," shouted the stranger, pointing to Norman's tousled gray head.

"Norman rose to his feet and pushed the table back. 'I challenge you to a re-butt,' he said."

Carol stopped singing, and both Edwards and Citron rushed to break up the fight. As Edwards recollected, "Carol was behind me. 'If you do this, Norman,' she said over my shoulder, 'I'll never forgive you.' She began to cry and I turned and held her against my shoulder." Mailer suggested that he and the stranger go outside. As Edwards took Carol upstairs, Carol cried, "Someday someone will have a knife. Maybe that crazy man he challenged has one."

But when Edwards went back downstairs she discovered Mailer and the stranger "bear-hugging and toasting each other." She added that "the man had met Norman in a re-butt and had been able to remain on his feet, thereby gaining Norman's sincere respect."

Mailer's respect for worthy combatants extended to the women in his life as well. It was part of his twenty-year-old pattern. "There's a violent thing that happens between Norman and his women and it was true of Carol," Anne Edwards says. "He was trying to toughen her up through provocation." If this introduced difficulties, so did Mailer's philandering. José Torres recalls that at the Miami conventions the previous summer, Mailer had already become involved with a new woman, who was then acting as his assistant.

With three fond ex-wives, an angry separated wife in Provincetown, a loving mistress and the mother of one of his children in Stockbridge, and a new mistress in the wings, Mailer must have felt as though he were an expert on the emotions and motivations of complex women. He was also an expert on alimony debt and once more he was in dire economic straits. But with all his difficulties—financial, professional, and personal—Norman Mailer could hardly begrudge life for what it had handed him as he neared his half-century mark.

❦

On January 31, 1973 Mailer would be celebrating his fiftieth birthday. His third wife, Lady Jeanne Campbell, and Frank Crowther, an old friend who was a *Paris Review* editor, wanted to throw a large party for him. When Crowther first suggested the idea to Mailer, he declined, saying, "Another ego trip? Who needs it?" Later, however, he decided to use the party to introduce a grandiose idea that had been gestating in his mind: It was a mysterious concept called the Fifth Estate.

In early December, invitations printed in purple were sent

out to five thousand people announcing Mailer's birthday and stating: "He will make an announcement of national importance (major)." Tickets for the event, which was to be held at the elegant Four Seasons restaurant in Manhattan on February 5, would be fifty dollars per couple. Even the press was required to pay for the birthday party. This was unprecedented, but it was noted that the proceeds were to benefit the enigmatic Fifth Estate. While Mailer was working in Stockbridge, Lady Jeanne and Frank Crowther set up an office in the Algonquin Hotel, where the money was to be sent, and they made all the arrangements for the party.

Curiosity about the event grew as February 5 drew closer. People were telephoning until the last moment for tickets and to inquire how to dress. The invitation had only noted "finery." When Mailer and Carol arrived from Stockbridge on February 5 and checked into the Algonquin at noon to rest up for the party, people were still calling in for tickets.

More than five hundred people showed up at the Four Seasons that night shortly after 10:00 P.M. A glittering cross section of Manhattan's elite had come to hear what their culture hero had to say. Shirley MacLaine brought Jack Lemmon; Lily Tomlin announced on her way in, "I've come to study macho"; Jessica Mitford and Jean vanden Heuvel arrived with Senator Jacob Javits; Marion Javits brought Andy Warhol; Bernardo Bertolucci caused a stir—his critically acclaimed *Last Tango in Paris* had just opened in New York. The guest roster also included Paul O'Dwyer, George Plimpton, Bobby Short, Charlie Mingus, Senator Eugene McCarthy, Princess Diane Von Furstenberg, Jules Feiffer, Arthur Schlesinger, Jr., and his wife Alexandra.

The press was out in force: Dorothy Schiff, publisher of the *New York Post* came, as did the managing editor of *Time*, Henry Grunwald. The editors of *Newsweek*, *New York* magazine, and *The Village Voice* were all there, as were Pete Hamill, Murray Kempton, and Jack Newfield. In addition to Lady Jeanne and Carol Stevens, Adele Mailer attended the party, as did four of Mailer's seven children and his mother, Fanny. It was all a remarkable reflection of the expansive power base Mailer possessed at fifty years of age. Fanny Mailer was beaming over her genius son. "Norman was not an ordinary child," she told Sally Quinn. "Other children always had that sameness about them, but not Norman. He was just different."

Only Mailer could have attracted such a formidable crowd and asked them to pay for their pleasure. But only Mailer could also have alienated just about everyone in the room before the night was over. The guests had been anxiously anticipating his announcement of the Fifth Estate when Jimmy Breslin mounted a red plush platform in the Four Seasons' Pool Room at midnight and introduced his former running mate as "one of the half dozen original thinkers in this century."

By this time Mailer had consumed a substantial amount of liquor. Dressed in his tuxedo and blue shirt, with a bourbon on the rocks in one hand, he ascended the podium. "Can everyone hear?" he asked the crowd, grinning. "Then I know if I hear people talking, they are simply not interested in what I have to say. All right. Must size up the opposition. I want to say I've discovered tonight why Richard Nixon is President. I've been pondering it for many years, you know, and having written a book on the subject, I've given it some deep thought. But I realized tonight that I found myself being photographed more times than I can count, and I couldn't see. You see green after a while, you see red, you see your own mortality. I know why he is President. Richard Nixon has gristle behind his retina."

There was medium laughter and some restlessness. The crowd wasn't completely with him. Sensing this, Mailer launched into his oft-used dirty joke about the ex-wife and the young lover and getting past "the worn-out part." When he finished there were boos, some nervous laughter, and much embarrassment. "Christ, he's done it again," Judith Freed of the New York public television station whispered to Patricia Bosworth. "Norman's antagonized everybody before getting to the heart of the matter." In the bar, journalist Linda Francke saw Joe Flaherty, Mailer's old campaign manager, drop his head into his hands at this repeat of the Village Gate disaster. "Oh, sweet Jesus," Flaherty moaned. "Here we go again."

About a quarter of the guests made their way to the exit with Mailer yelling, "Get their names at the door." Mailer then told the crowd that he had asked Frank Crowther to give him examples of the terrible things people were saying about the evening. The worst apparently was, "Mailer is throwing this party in order to pay for his vasectomy."

By the time Mailer got around to his Fifth Estate idea, the people who had not already walked out had all but tuned out. Those who were listening heard Mailer propose an incredible theory of American governmental conspiracy—that the CIA and the FBI were manipulating the American public. He warned that they needed to be curtailed. "I wanna start a foundation," said Mailer, as Lucian Truscott watched his left arm pumping "defiantly" at his side, "with a few people who would be willing to explore this notion. I want a people's FBI and a people's CIA to investigate those two. . . . If we have a democratic secret police keeping tabs on Washington's secret police, which is not democratic but bureaucratic, we will see how far paranoia is justified. . . . What happened in Dallas? What about Martin Luther King? The real story behind Watergate? How many plots are there in America? Two? Three? None?"

At the time, most people in the room considered the idea outlandish. When Mailer asked for serious questions, someone yelled out, "What *about* paranoia, Norman?" Mailer shouted back angrily, "*What about it?*" There was laughter, and people started talking and milling about. Mailer was losing control, and his next few thoughts about America veering toward totalitarianism seemed confused to those few who were still listening. After announcing that he would form a steering committee in the next few days, Mailer told the group he would be back for serious questions in thirty minutes and stepped off the podium to no applause.

The kitchen was opened for omelets, and as Mailer continued to mingle among the crowd, reporters were gathering reactions. "I didn't know a thing about it," Jack Lemmon said to Linda Francke. "I didn't even know it was his birthday. I don't even know him." Pete Hamill looked discouraged. "Why couldn't he just give a party and have everyone throw balloons?" Murray Kempton was off to counsel Mailer. "Mailer has just been Spike Jones," he said, "and I must go and reassure him he's still Toscanini." Neither Adele Mailer nor Carol Stevens would comment, but Sally Quinn overheard Adele saying to friends, "I didn't understand what the whole thing was about. I think he blew it."

Frank Crowther and Lady Jeanne discouraged Mailer from taking any more questions, and by 2:30 A.M., with most of the guests gone, Mailer was pacing in the Pool Room, saying to himself, "I blew it. It was a great party and I blew it. I have a demon inside me."

At about three o'clock in the morning, a gray-haired lady in a brown leather motorcycle jacket confronted Mailer. "I'm not gonna be your gumshoe," she said defiantly.

"I didn't ask you to, angel," Mailer told her.

"Why don't you talk sense, Norman?" she cried, after having

flung her arms around his neck only to be patiently disengaged by Mailer. "Why? Why? Why? Why don't you *think* about what you're saying—why didn't you prepare?"

"I've thought years about the manipulation of history. Leggo," Mailer told her as a small crowd gathered around them.

"You think you can pull this off—this counterespionage," the woman sneered at him. "Throw out a dangerous idea like that—at a party? It was—perverted. Fund raising—phony baloney! Oh, you defiant, silly bastard, why can't you let other people be center stage and lead?"

Murray Kempton finally broke up this embarrassing tête-à-tête, and by 3:30 Mailer was sparring and butting heads with his old boxing protégé Joe Shaw as José Torres looked on. "This time I'll be Frazier and Ali," Mailer instructed Shaw, "and you be yourself." Both Sally Quinn and Patricia Bosworth approached Fanny Mailer, who was one of the last guests there, to get her reactions to this remarkable evening. She beamed at Quinn. "I think it's all wonderful." Fanny then told Bosworth, "This was the best party for Norman. The second best was his bar mitzvah in 1936."

The next day a hung-over Mailer held a press conference at the Algonquin to salvage what was left of his idea. He would also write a piece, "The Morning After," for *The New York Times Book Review* explaining his true intent. His Four Seasons speech, he admitted, "was a disgrace." He then added: "It had neither wit nor life—it was perhaps the worst speech on a real occasion that the orator had ever made." At the press conference he also said he regretted calling the counterespionage organization "a people's police" and explained that its structures and goals would be open-ended, determined by a steering committee that would be set up. "What I'm proposing literally is that we face up to the possibility that this country may be sliding toward totalitarianism. . . . We live in a land riddled with moral absurdity. I propose we start something equivalent to Nader's Raiders or the American Civil Liberties Union." He added that he would definitely not head the group but that he would like to have "an umbilical relationship" with it. Suggesting several potential areas for investigation, he mentioned the assassination of John F. Kennedy, the Warren Commission report on that murder, possible Republican involvement in the Eagleton affair, and Watergate.

At least some of Mailer's "paranoia" proved to be prophetic. A little over a month later, Woodward and Bernstein broke the Watergate cover-up story. "Mailer was right," Frank Crowther said. Jimmy

Breslin agrees: "Look at what happened with Watergate and the investigation afterward. He was right. If he says something it's not lunacy. He's a thoughtful man and there's always a chance he's right. What he says most certainly should be listened to and examined carefully before you reject it."

Mailer would be intensely interested in Watergate by the following summer, as would the nation. In June he would spend a week in Washington at the Watergate hearings. But at the first meeting of the Fifth Estate in February, his concerns were focused more on his CIA and FBI assassination conspiracy theories. He had indeed sensed the conspiratorial climate that would force Nixon out of office, but his concentration on the FBI and CIA still seems obsessive to some of his friends.

"I had great sympathy and sadness for him," recalls Arthur Schlesinger, Jr. "I thought he was crazy. The FBI and CIA are both rather sinister agencies, but I think it was excessively conspiratorial the way he presented it that night at the Four Seasons. It was the novelist's imagination at work. Ever since Dallas, conspiracy theories had been going strong and it was already well known that the FBI and CIA had withheld from the Warren Commission facts which were very relevant to the investigation. So there was a general recognition that secret agencies are a dangerous thing to have. Also, Watergate was at an early stage, but there was still a lot of concern about it."

"The Fifth Estate seemed to me part of the paranoia of the time," adds Pete Hamill. "I just tended to be skeptical of all that stuff. But I did admire Norman for the risk he took: that he was willing to look like a fool to promote something he believed in with passion."

Dotson Rader recollects that there were only two meetings of the Fifth Estate held at the Algonquin that February and that Mailer was mainly interested in investigating both Kennedy assassinations, which he suspected were ordered by the CIA. He was less interested in the Martin Luther King killing. Rader had managed to set up a meeting between Mailer and Episcopal bishop Paul Moore, who was involved in civil rights issues, in order to gain Moore's support for the Fifth Estate. As Rader and Mailer headed up to the Cathedral of St. John the Divine to meet the bishop, Rader briefed Mailer and told him he should avoid stressing the conspiratorial nature of the Kennedy assassinations and instead emphasize Martin Luther King's assassination. Above all, Rader warned him, he should not discuss his satanic theories with the bishop.

Rader, a Baptist, was aware of Mailer's interest in theologians.

Rader was also one of the few fellow writers to whom Mailer could talk about theology. "He's not altogether sure he believes in God," Rader says. "But he does believe in Satan, not simply as a force but as a being."

Rader had done his best to coach Mailer for the meeting with the liberal Bishop Moore but it was to no avail. "When we got there," Rader recalls, "Norman brought up Martin Luther King and his conspiracy theories, which was fine. But he then went on to bring up the Kennedy killings and the CIA, which took him blithely into a rather convoluted monologue on the nature of evil, the existence of Satan, and the general impotence of the church to do any good about anything. I was sitting there groaning, and Moore's reaction was like a bird to a snake: He was appalled and yet riveted. When we left, Norman was as happy as Orphan Annie meeting Daddy Warbucks. He thought he had been absolutely brilliant and had totally captured the bishop."

Over the next year Mailer would speak about his counterintelligence Fifth Estate plan on more than twenty campuses and would compile a list of several hundred people interested in watching the CIA and FBI. Mailer's group finally merged with a Washington-based organization called the Committee for Action Research, renamed the Organizing Committee for a Fifth Estate. Mailer's work on what he described as "the best political idea in my entire life" then wound down as he turned his attention to new projects.

• XIX •

NORMAN AND MARILYN

The fall before Mailer's fiftieth birthday party, he was offered an intriguing literary project, one that would dominate the next year of his life and develop into a powerful obsession. It would be a fantasy love for the movie queen Marilyn Monroe, whom Mailer was to call a woman with "the basic stuff out of which Brooklyn dream girls are made." He would write two books about Marilyn, a woman he had never met: one a biography, the other a pseudo-autobiography. In 1981, he would even write a play about her called *Strawhead.* His attraction to Marilyn was to become an imaginary affair of the heart and mind.

It all began when Mailer's agent called to say that Grosset & Dunlap wanted him to do a twenty-five-thousand-word preface to a picture book and would pay him fifty thousand dollars for the work. The subject was Marilyn Monroe. While Mailer was covering the Republican convention in late August, Lawrence Schiller, a former *Life* photographer who was now a creator of books, movies, and special magazine projects (Schiller had interviewed Jack Ruby on his deathbed and Susan Atkins during the Manson trial), had approached Harold Roth, the president of Grosset & Dunlap, with a proposal. Schiller wanted to do a picture book of a photographic exhibit he had recently produced in Los Angeles, "Marilyn Monroe, The Legend and the Truth." The exhibit, which Schiller took to five foreign countries and thirty American cities, featured six hundred photographs of Monroe by such photographers as Henri Cartier-Bresson, Milton Greene, Philippe Halsman, Eve Arnold, and Schiller himself.

Harold Roth talked the suggestion over with Robert Markel, his editor-in-chief. At the time Markel thought it was a poor idea and said he wouldn't be at all interested unless someone important wrote the accompanying text. After returning from the Frankfurt Book Fair in early October 1972, Schiller approached Markel and informed him that he had lined up a *Life* writer who would do a twenty-five-thousand-word text. When Schiller told him who it was, Markel did not think the name was important enough. Schiller then suggested Gloria Steinem, whom Markel also turned down.

Markel and Roth had a meeting over the weekend. "Harold kept saying we should do something with the book," recalls Markel, "and I said he was wrong. Then spontaneously I said the only thing that would make a difference is if we could get someone like Norman Mailer. Roth looked at me and said, 'That's a terrific idea.' I said, 'Yeah, but why would he do this?' I dismissed it."

Nevertheless, two days later Markel went to see Scott Meredith. Markel was surprised when the agent told him that he thought Mailer would indeed be interested. Mailer was then in Texas on a lecture tour, but Meredith assured Markel that he would call him the following evening. In the meantime Markel discovered that Schiller was negotiating the Marilyn book with Random House. "I immediately called Schiller," Markel remembers, "and told him not to sign anything because I thought I could get Norman Mailer. Schiller said, '*What?* I won't do anything until I hear back from you.' As it turned out, Mailer was interested. He needed the money and I think the idea intrigued him."

In November the two deals with Schiller and Mailer were put together. Mailer would receive a fifty-thousand-dollar advance for the text while Schiller and the various photographers would split another fifty thousand dollars. The royalties would be divided three ways: a third each for Mailer, Schiller, and the photographers. A week after signing the contract, Markel made an appointment for Mailer to come to his office, where he had laid out a large box of pictures from Schiller's exhibition. "Norman came to my office," Markel recalls, "and before he sat down he looked all around at the pictures. The first one he looked at was the famous Kelley calendar picture of Marilyn in the nude. 'My God,' he said, 'that's what caused all that trouble.'

"He wasn't just looking at the pictures," Markel adds. "He was looking at Marilyn and thinking about her right there. He was meeting her, in a sense, for the first time. My bet then was that Norman would not be able to hold to twenty-five thousand words. I was sure he'd do more. I just felt the faucet would continue to flow."

After admiring the pictures, Mailer asked Markel, "Okay, what are we going to do about Bobby Kennedy?" "By 1972," says Markel, "nothing seemed bizarre. We had a brief conversation about it and I told him it was something we'd have to talk about. But it was at that point that I realized that he was really interested in the project." Mailer's interest in Bobby Kennedy would later be expanded into a controversial conspiracy theory.

Mailer and Carol Stevens took a nine-day cruise in the Caribbean aboard the S.S. *Statendam*, and on December 13 Mailer returned to Stockbridge, where he began to work on the *Marilyn* book. The twenty-five-thousand-word piece was due in two months. This was a difficult deadline under any circumstances, but the situation was further complicated when Mailer read Fred Guiles's book *Norma Jean*. Mailer became intrigued with Marilyn and suddenly decided that he wanted to write more than a preface; he had to write a biography. "I wanted to say to everyone that I know how to write about a woman," Mailer later told *Time* magazine. "When I read the other biographies of Marilyn, I said to myself, 'I've found her; I know who I want to write about.' "

Mailer was determined to complete the book in the time allotted by the contract, but as he worked, the piece grew first to forty, then fifty, then one hundred and five thousand words. Robert Markel recalls that after they had agreed on extending the text to fifty thousand words, Mailer called him one night and said, "Well, I've just completed the first sixty-seven thousand words of the fifty thousand, and I haven't gotten to Arthur Miller yet." As the text increased in size, the book's original single-column design was changed to a double-column format. Grosset was aiming for an early fall 1973 publication, but by March all they had in hand was a rough first draft of Mailer's text.

The Book of the Month Club was by now pressing to see fall books, and Robert Markel realized that if he didn't show them something, it would be too late. "I was faced with the dilemma," he says, "of whether to give the manuscript to the Book of the Month Club in such a messy state: Pages were crossed out with arrows, and it was really in a rough first-draft stage. I decided to make Xeroxes of this mess, and I wrote a cover letter explaining. I then took the whole photographic collection and the dummy and made a formal presentation to the BOMC executives. They caught the excitement of the whole thing and the judges took it as a full selection, but for midsummer. That meant we had to have books no later than June."

More complications arose as the text—now cut to 90,000 words—was rushed into galleys. Mailer insisted that photographs of Marilyn as a child as well as pictures of the people she knew in her early life be added to the book. He indicated that they should be run as small photos in the margin so that readers could see what he was talking about in the text. "Schiller argued against it vehemently," Markel recalls. "He felt that it was destroying the whole concept. The book was not a documentary and the pictures weren't meant to illustrate Norman's text. We even had a meeting in the VIP lounge at Kennedy Airport. There was a monumental stalking around and slamming of doors, and I had to go out with each of them for individual walks and cooling-off periods. It was Schiller's book in the beginning and now Norman had come in and taken over.

"Schiller felt that Norman was overshadowing everything else and that he was not going to be able to hold up his end because he had promised the photographers this book," Markel adds. "Now it was Norman Mailer's book and, incidentally, there were pictures. I kept telling Schiller that he was making a fool of himself because it *was* Norman's book. In the end Schiller felt a compromise had been arrived at which was artistically unfortunate—because we did throw in those small pictures as a sop to Norman."

Finished books were expected in early June, just in time for the American Booksellers Association convention in Los Angeles. Mailer had agreed to attend the convention, but when he arrived at the Beverly Hills Hotel, he had not yet seen the printed version. Robert Markel arrived in Los Angeles twenty-four hours after the first book was off the press on June 6. Mailer immediately called him and asked to see it. "I walked to his bungalow," Markel recalls, "and he was walking to meet me. It was right there that I gave him the book. Norman didn't know until he saw it that we were not putting his name or the title on the front of the jacket. All we had was that wonderful Bert Stern photograph of Marilyn. I had not told him because I couldn't figure out a way to do it on the phone. He looked at the book and smiled at me, and I thought, 'Thank God, he's not going to do something dreadful.' Then we walked together and talked about the decision. He didn't love it."

Mailer's *Marilyn*, which he would call "a novel ready to play by the rules of biography," was in many ways a love letter to the actress and to the myth she left behind. She was "every man's love affair with America," he wrote. "She was our angel, the sweet angel of sex . . . a very Stradivarius of sex." Since the 1950s, after her marriage to Arthur Miller, Marilyn had haunted Mailer's own sexual fantasies. For like Miller, Mailer was an intellectual Jew from Brooklyn. "The secret ambition, after all, had been to steal Marilyn," Mailer confessed. "In all his vanity he thought no one was so well-suited to bring out the best in her as himself. . . . It was only after a few marriages (which is to say a few failures) later that he could recognize how he would have done no better than Miller and probably have been damaged further in the process."

The lure of fantasy was there, but it was also Marilyn's contradictions that attracted Mailer. In them he could see himself and his entire generation: "In her ambition, so Faustian, and in her ignorance of culture's dimensions, in her liberation and her tyrannical desires, her noble democratic longings intimately contradicted by the widening pool of her narcissism . . . we can see the magnified mirror of ourselves, our exaggerated and now all but defeated generation."

After chronicling her illegitimate birth and the line of insanity that had passed down from her grandfather, her grandmother, and her mother, Mailer would theorize that the famed actress who emerged from this unstable background must have had a double soul: Perhaps she was the karmic reincarnation of no less a person than Napoleon. The words *karma* and *reincarnation* had lately been slipping into much of Mailer's work. Even his book on the 1972 convention, *St. George and the Godfather*, opened with the line, "Greeting to Charles Dickens across vales of Karma: it was the best and worst of conventions."

In 1975 Laura Adams would question Mailer about his use of *karma* and *reincarnation*, pointing out that they had not been part of his vocabulary before. Mailer told her it was actually James Jones who had introduced him to the concepts in 1953. "He gave me the standard explanation, which is that we are not only reincarnated, but the way in which we are is the reflection, the judgment, the truth, of how we lived our previous life. . . . Jones went on about it and I said, 'You *believe* in that?' Because I was an atheist and a socialist in those days. He said, 'Oh, sure. That's the only thing that makes sense. . . .' I thought about it over and over and in the last three or four years I began to think, 'Yes, that does make sense.' Jones was right."

At the age of fifty Mailer was beginning to reevaluate the idea of mortality, particularly his own. The concept of reincarnation would steadily grow as a Mailer theme throughout the decade, leading not only to his second Pulitzer Prize-winning book, *The Executioner's Song*, but to his massive novel, *Ancient Evenings*.

Mailer would be criticized by some reviewers for his introduction of the idea of reincarnation in *Marilyn*. But it is clear that in trying to unravel the enigmatic reality of Monroe, Mailer was experiencing an overwhelming empathy for her. As he later told *Time*, he "felt some sort of existential similarities with Marilyn Monroe." In 1980, after the publication of his second book on Marilyn, *Of Women and Their Elegance*, Mailer confessed: "I always thought that if I had been a woman, then I would have been a little bit like Marilyn Monroe." In fact, in *Elegance*, Mailer tried to enter her mind and assume her voice, as if it were her autobiography.

Mailer's feelings for the actress became obvious as he described her lonely years in an orphan asylum and her early struggle in Hollywood. Although many of his facts were taken from two previous biographies by Fred Guiles and Maurice Zolotow, his interpretations were uniquely Mailer's own. "Since the orphan's presence in the world is obliged to turn drab, the life of fantasy, in compensation can become extreme," he wrote in *Marilyn*. "We are all steeped in the notion that lonely withdrawn people have a large inner fantasy. What may be ignored is the tendency to become locked into a lifelong rapture with one's fantasy, to become a narcissist."

Her narcissism, Mailer believed, was the cause of Marilyn's difficult love life. She had "the incapacity to love anyone else, except as a servant to one's dream of glamor." Joe DiMaggio, her second husband, played this servant role until Marilyn realized that the well-publicized mating of two magnificent physical specimens was not enough. "She needs a double soul more like her own," Mailer guessed, "a computer with circuits larger than her own, and a devil with charm in the guise of an angel, something of that sort she certainly needs, but *wholly* devoted to her." DiMaggio's insistence that she stop acting was harmful, Mailer was convinced. Marilyn needed "someone who will bring her *out*!"

Playwright Arthur Miller, who became her next husband, was not the one to do it, Mailer concluded. It was in his depiction of Miller that Mailer's jealousy for Marilyn's love began to show as he engaged in intellectual one-upmanship with the playwright. "Miller had only a workmanlike style, limited lyrical gifts, no capacity for intellectual shock, and only one major play to this credit. . . ," Mailer said. "His verbal ideas were banal, his processes of reasoning while not disagreeable were nonetheless not remarkable. . . . Yet this blond heaven wants him."

Mailer became snide. He claimed that Miller was living off Marilyn's money and that she had acquired "the most talented slave in the world." Near the end of their marriage, Mailer says, Marilyn "came to suspect that her own mind was more interesting than his." By the filming of *The Misfits* their marriage had fallen apart, but Marilyn was united in this film with Clark Gable, the man whom she had always thought of as a father figure.

Gable's death after the filming and her breakup with Miller catapulted Marilyn into a deep depression which culminated in her death. But Mailer was not able to concede that it was suicide. His Marilyn must be a victim of larger, more sinister forces, especially since there were rumors that she was having an affair with Bobby Kennedy. "Who is the first to be certain that it was of no interest to the CIA, or to the FBI, or to the Mafia, and half of the secret police of the world, that the brother of the President was reputed to be having an affair with a movie star who had once been married to a playwright denied a passport for 'supporting Communist movements,' " Mailer wrote. Mailer was ready to offer even more mystical theories about Marilyn. She may even have been the First Lady of American ghosts, Mailer suggests. "Why then not also see her in these endlessly facile connections of the occult as giving a witches turn to the wheel at Chappaquiddick?"

❦

The official publication of *Marilyn* was set for August 1, 1973; a huge 285,000 first American printing was scheduled. The book was expected to provoke interest but no one predicted the controversies it would generate.

On June 22 it was announced that the British publishers of the book, Hodder & Stoughton, would halt their release of *Marilyn*, scheduled for October 8, due to an allegation that large sections of the work were plagiarized by Mailer from two earlier biographies of Monroe. The allegation came from Mark Goulden, chairman of W. H. Allen, the British publisher of *Norma Jean* by Frederick Guiles and *Marilyn Monroe* by Maurice Zolotow. He claimed that sections of Mailer's book were taken from these two previous biographies without permission. He added that Mailer had written to Guiles requesting permission to reproduce 28 specific quotes. "Guiles," said Goulden, "although he had no legal right to do so, said 'yes' and asked for a set of proofs of the book. When the proofs arrived, Guiles counted no less than 255 sections of his book lifted by Mailer, ranging from sentences to half pages."

After several transatlantic calls were made, Harold Roth announced on June 23 that both Grosset & Dunlap and Hodder & Stoughton planned to go ahead with their respective publication dates. "There is one truth that does not alter worldwide," Roth told *The New York Times*, "and that is that we have written permission to use the material."

Three days later Mailer issued an angry statement through his agent, Scott Meredith. "No one is going to call me a plagiarist and get away with it," Mailer said. "I do not need other writers' words or thoughts to make myself a book. I made it clear on many a page of *Marilyn* that I looked to [the other two works] for a great number of my facts. I quoted from them copiously and the authors were paid more than the customary rate for permission to do so. *Marilyn*, however, in its style, spirit, and interpretation does not rest at all on these gentlemen or other authors. In fact, it goes very much in other directions, as anyone will be able to tell who compares the text."

Reached that day by the *Times*, Mark Goulden of W. H. Allen reiterated his allegation. "Mailer does not want anyone to call him a plagiarist: I will," Goulden declared. "He is an author of great experience and he knows damn well that you do not apply to an author to quote from his books; you apply to the publishers who hold the rights. No one knows this better than Mr. Mailer."

Grosset & Dunlap was disquieted by Goulden's attitude because it was holding up a serialization deal with *The London Times* which was the cornerstone of their international sales campaign. It was obviously also threatening their deal with Hodder & Stoughton. "I think we all felt," reflects Robert Markel, "that Mark Goulden was simply blocking us. Anyone else in that position would have said this is unfortunate, give us credit and pay us a certain amount of money, but would not have held us back the way he did."

While Grosset was working out a financial arrangement with Goulden, even more controversy began to surround Mailer's *Marilyn*. On July 13, *60 Minutes* broadcast a Mike Wallace interview with Mailer which focused on the book's concluding chapter in which Mailer theorized that Monroe might have been murdered. "All Hollywood was gossiping about Marilyn having an affair with Bobby Kennedy," Mailer told Wallace, "which I believe in fact she was not having, although they were dear and close friends. So, if she could be murdered in such a way that it would look like a suicide, for unrequited love of Bobby Kennedy, it would be a huge embarrassment for the Kennedys."

When Mailer went on to say that no one was talking about what actually happened that night, Wallace cut to another interview, prefacing it with the remark: "Someone is talking about that night, the one person, in fact, who could invalidate all of Mailer's tortured theorizing about the Monroe murder plot." Wallace then interviewed Eunice Murray, Monroe's housekeeper, who was with the actress the night she died. Murray insisted they were alone that night and murder would have been "impossible."

Asked by Wallace why he never attempted to get in touch with Murray, Mailer replied, "I hate telephone interviews. . . . I hate that way of getting the facts." Wallace started to question him about his extensive use of other books, and Mailer explained, "I don't pretend to the reader that I'm discovering new facts. I tell the reader ten times over that I'm depending on other books, that this is a secondary work." Mailer then asked Wallace if he thought *Marilyn* was a good biography and Wallace responded, "I've got to say no . . . because you acknowledge that you have taken most of your chronological material from a couple of other people, and you don't know if it's accurate or not. And in the crucial last chapter you have failed to do the necessary research that would have made it a good biography."

Mailer defended himself by pointing out his time pressures to get the book done, then made an unusual confession. "I was doing something that you don't normally do with a book," he told Wallace, "which is I was getting into the end of the book with a half-finished exploration, and I decided it was important enough to get out there half finished rather than not to get into it at all." Wallace concluded,

"The best criticism of the book we've heard so far is Norman Mailer's own: It got out there half finished."

The plagiarism suit and the Wallace interview only added to the huge publicity that attended *Marilyn*. Three days after Mailer was interviewed on *60 Minutes*, a cover story about the book appeared in *Time* magazine. As *Time* pointed out, "An industry is under way, triggered by this irresistible shotgun wedding of talents."

Mailer's theories in *Marilyn* were destined to attract attention, and the media cooperated; his belief in Marilyn Monroe's reincarnation only added to the controversy. On July 16, Christopher Lehmann-Haupt criticized Mailer in a *New York Times* book review for this karmic interpretation of the actress. "I doubt he has taken this line because he literally believes in Karma and reincarnation (whether he does or not is really beside the point); or, for that matter, that he seriously disdains conventional psychology," wrote Lehmann-Haupt. "Rather, I think he concocts this rather bizarre theory as a device for getting free from testable interpretations—as a way of erecting a self-contained mythology that is impregnable to argument." Lehmann-Haupt concluded by saying that the book did not succeed on these terms and that Mailer had "not really justified the liberties he [had] taken with the literal truth."

Two days after that review appeared, Mailer held a press conference at the Algonquin to respond to the plagiarism charges as well as to criticisms of the book's conspiracy theory. Maurice Zolotow had already publicly declared Mailer to be a plagiarist, and Mailer told the press that he would sue Zolotow for libel unless Zolotow retracted the charge and offered an apology. Fred Guiles was no longer a problem. On July 16 he had issued a statement through Scott Meredith that "no dispute existed." This was due to the quick action of Grosset & Dunlap, who had reached a settlement with Guiles's American publisher, McGraw-Hill.

"Harold Roth and I went to see Harold McGraw," recalls Robert Markel, "and we told him, 'Look, Norman has done this thing and he is a major literary figure, so it's a complicated question. He's perfectly willing to give appropriate credit and we would be happy to pay far beyond normal permissions.' We felt we had to settle with McGraw in a hurry because we wanted to eliminate the domestic problem and confine it to England. McGraw threatened our timing and the Book of the Month Club and the *Time* magazine cover we had in the works."

On the day of Mailer's Algonquin press conference, Zolotow announced his intention to sue Mailer, not for plagiarism or copyright infringement but for libel. A six-million-dollar libel suit would shortly be filed for the "defamations" of Zolotow's book in *Marilyn*. The passage Zolotow found most scurrilous was the following: "His [Zolotow's] material is reamed with overstressed and hollow anecdotes untrustworthy by the very style of their prose, a feature writer heating up the old dishes of other feature writers." The Zolotow libel suit, which was actually filed on August 3, included no charges of plagiarism or copyright infringement, but on August 6 Mailer told *The New York Times* that if Zolotow did not apologize for calling him a plagiarist, he would sue. As to the libel suit Mailer said, "Of course, if Mr. Zolotow were ever to win his suit, a literary critic could no longer afford to expose a piece of writing as meretricious and no author could ever be described as less than talented."

The Zolotow libel suit was eventually dropped, but at his July 18 press conference at the Algonquin Mailer was also challenged about his conjecture that Marilyn Monroe's death was the result of murder and not suicide. Mailer said he had conducted further interviews and investigations after the book was printed, then read a press release he had prepared. It stated that no residue of sleeping pills was found in Marilyn's stomach and that when the Los Angeles coroner, Dr. Thomas Noguchi, was questioned about this, he said the pills could have passed into her small intestines. The small intestines, however, were not examined, Mailer claimed. Nor, he said, had Noguchi found any evidence that a stomach pump had been used; nor was there any evidence of a lethal injection.

"The facts are moot," Mailer concluded. "The explanations are without explanation. In summary, she could not have died from a simple overdose since no remains were found in her stomach, yet by the evidence no stomach pump could have been employed, and there are by the coroner's statement no marks of a lethal injection, a set of such mutually prohibitive hypotheses that by medical logic one cannot discover how she ever died at all. . . . So an invitation is offered to the press. Let them call for a coroner's inquest."

Although many scoffed at Mailer's conspiracy theory at the time, nine years later, during the spring of 1982, the coroner's report on Marilyn's death was publicly challenged.

❦

Mailer's theories and the allegations of plagiarism had by now attracted considerable publicity. But four days after his Algonquin press conference, Pauline Kael commented on another provocative aspect of *Marilyn:* Mailer's fit of jealousy over Marilyn's relationship with Arthur Miller. In her front-page critique in *The New York Times Book Review*, Kael said that Mailer "has made us more aware than we may want to be of his titles and campaigns, his aspiration to be more than a writer, to conquer the media and be monarch of American arts—a straight Jean Cocteau who'd meet anybody at high noon." Kael continued: "Something has been withheld from Norman Mailer: his crown lacks a few jewels, a star. He has never triumphed in the theater, never been looked up to as a Jewish Lincoln, and never been married to a famous movie queen—a sex symbol . . . Mailer's waddle and crouch may look like a put-on but he means it when he butts heads. *Marilyn* is his whammy to Arthur Miller. . . . Miller and Mailer try for the same things: he's catching Miller's hand in the gentile cookie jar."

Mailer's assault on Arthur Miller almost caused Mailer to lose a prestigious award, the MacDowell Colony Medal, which was scheduled to be presented to him on August 19. John Leonard, who was on the awards committee and who finally did present the medal to Mailer, remembers what happened. "Arthur Miller had been a benefactor of the MacDowell Colony for many years and he was quite disturbed by *Marilyn*. When the book came out we began to get a lot of unhappy feedback about whether Mailer was an appropriate choice for a medal winner. Also, the medal is usually given to people who are about to die and who are already considered to be in the pantheon. The notion of giving it to someone who had just turned fifty was a little bizarre, and also someone who was as controversial."

A further problem arose when Elizabeth Hardwick, who had agreed to give the presenting speech, received a grant which took her off to Italy. "When Elizabeth couldn't make the speech," says Leonard, "I said okay, let me take the heat and I will make the case—which was essentially a brief for the defense of Norman Mailer in what I assumed was a very hostile situation. But of course we couldn't rescind the medal."

Leonard had asked Mailer to come up the night before the award ceremony and stay at his cottage, which was on the estate of his wife's parents, the Elting Morrisons, near Peterborough, New Hampshire, the site of the MacDowell Colony. Mailer agreed and Leonard arranged a large picnic at the Morrisons' family pond, inviting a number of MacDowell Colony writers. On Saturday afternoon Mailer arrived with Carol in their sports car. Mailer was perfectly genial at the party, and afterward he and Leonard went for a walk. "As we were wandering around," says Leonard, "Mailer suddenly began telling me that he knew I was out to get him. But everything I had ever written about him was favorable except for a radio review of his book of poems for Pacifica Radio, which he remembered. I think it was more a sense that he was going to get a medal and he wanted an enemy. But how do you talk to people in a mood like that? I said, 'Look, I would not invite somebody up here and have them under my own roof if I intended to subvert them. That's not my idea of civilization.' I'm not sure if he believed me.

"But the next day when he was accepting the medal, he was the Mailer who is the most astonishing of all, the person who decides this is a wonderful day and I want to make your day wonderful, too. He got up and extemporized and he had all of those people—who might have felt he was weird and radical and unfair to poor old Arthur Miller—eating out of his hand. He stayed for hours afterward, talking to anybody who wanted to come up and talk. He was splendid. It's hard to describe that change from the wary boxer stance to the stance of 'Oh my God, they like me after all, therefore I will be a good boy.' "

By December, with most of the reviews of *Marilyn* in, Mailer added a fillip to his promotional campaign for the book. It was reminiscent of the *The Deer Park* advertisement he had composed for *The Village Voice* eighteen years before. Mailer's own double-spread advertisement in *The New York Times Book Review* opened with the large headline, WHY, NORMAN MAILER NEVER EVEN MET MARILYN MONROE! Under the first subhead, which read, "No, Norman Mailer never met Marilyn Monroe," he quoted a glowing review of the book by Ingrid Bengis from *Ms.* magazine, the feminist bible. Beneath the next subhead, "No, Norman Mailer never met Marilyn Monroe and he wrote his book for money," he attacked Mike Wallace for stating on his show that *American Dream*, *Vietnam*, *Armies*, *Miami*, and *Prisoner* were all written for money, as was *Marilyn*. Mailer himself had pointed out in the *Time* cover story that he had written *Marilyn* for money since he was badly in debt, especially to the IRS, and needed $200,000 a year just to live. Now he wanted to make it clear that his royalty on *Marilyn* was not the usual 15 percent but only 4 percent. He had not asked to change the contract when the preface turned into a biography.

The next subhead stated, "No, Norman Mailer never met Marilyn Monroe and maybe he didn't do the book for money (although he may even make some now) nor did he commit plagiarism." Mailer then printed retractions of the allegations from Zolotow, Guiles, and Goulden. The fourth subhead featured more of the Mailer wit. It read, "What makes you so bitter about Mailer?" and went on to excerpt an interview Pauline Kael had given after her review of *Marilyn*. She had said, "I think he's our greatest writer. And what is unfortunate is our greatest writer should be a bum. . . ."

Mailer then listed some negative comments from reviews: "The decade's coffee table freak," "Supercolossal exploitation," etc. The good reviews came next, under the subhead "*Marilyn* is a literary phenomenon, a mine of comment with ore at every strata. Too grand eloquent? It is also a giant banana split. *Marilyn* is yummy. See below!" Mailer also made it clear that the book had sold ninety-eight thousand hard-cover copies in the stores and that three hundred thousand had been distributed by the Book of the Month and other book clubs.

The ad was pure Mailer. As Robert Markel relates, "Norman wrote the ad and insisted on our running it. We didn't want to run it, we thought it was a waste of money, but Norman insisted, saying, 'You're going to have to because of all the controversy and things that have happened.' It ultimately came down to doing him a favor."

The ad appeared just after Mailer had been named winner of the "Sour Apple" award by the Hollywood Women's Press Club. The facetious award had not been given since 1967, when it went to Jane Fonda; now it was pointedly being directed at Mailer for his biography of Marilyn Monroe. He was cited for "cashing in on the tragedy of a star with a cruelly unauthentic version of her life story." Within a matter of months Mailer had been sued for libel and plagiarism, awarded the MacDowell Medal, a coveted honor of the literary world, and had been insulted by the women journalists. It was all part of the routine mayhem that surrounds Norman Mailer.

❦

A few months after *Marilyn* was published, Markel asked Mailer what he was doing about his long-awaited novel. "There was some controversy at that point with his contract for Little, Brown," says Markel. "He wasn't happy, so I said, 'Why don't you park your novel here?' He said, 'Terrific, that's a great idea; talk to Scott Meredith.' The upshot was that Meredith told us he wanted a million dollars. Harold Roth and I discussed it and decided it wasn't wise. We didn't know if Norman would ever deliver, and we didn't want to make that kind of investment. It was to be paid out over a number of years, there was to be no evidence of satisfactory progress, and we were to give him $250,000 a year."

Three years before, Mailer had signed a million-dollar contract with Little, Brown for his new novel but he was now interested in talking to Grosset because of dissatisfaction with the terms. In December of 1970 Meredith had secured a completely new contract for Mailer's novel with Little, Brown. The contract called for one million dollars to be paid out as Mailer delivered 500,000 to 700,000 words, with the stipulation that Little, Brown was not allowed to read the material while it was being written. The reason for this move to Little, Brown, in addition to the money, was that a number of editors had left the hard-cover division of his old publisher, New American Library, by the time Mailer had delivered *Fire*. Little, Brown had the attraction of editor Larned Bradford, who had worked with Mailer on the moon book and who admired the author. Bradford would remain Mailer's editor for ten more years. He died in May 1979, just before *The Executioner's Song* was published.

The million-dollar Little, Brown deal was a substantial increase over NAL's $450,000, but by then Mailer had won the Pulitzer and National Book Award and his currency among publishers was at a new high. NAL was annoyed about relinquishing a star author they had signed up relatively cheaply. "We went to NAL," recalls Scott Meredith, "and said, in effect, 'Let my people go.' We paid quite a penalty for that. They didn't just say give us back our money. We had to give them a substantial amount to get a release—more than Norman was paid and more than the interest accrued. Some of the first money we got from Little, Brown went to NAL and it was more than they had paid out."

The *Marilyn* book had helped Mailer financially but by November 1973, a few months after its publication, Mailer was still pressed for funds. Scott Meredith renegotiated the Little, Brown contract that month, which brought Mailer some financial relief. Then, shortly after this, in an attempt to get more money for Mailer, Meredith approached Sidney Kewitt at Warner Brothers and sold him the film rights to the unwritten novel for a minimum of $250,000. By April 1974, when this story found its way to the press, there was speculation that with escalators the movie deal could exceed one million dollars.

After all the accusations of commercial exploitation leveled at

Mailer for *Marilyn*, these stories about his large advance for the novel did not please him. When *People* called the author in March 1974 after a *Times* story was released about his million-dollar deal, Mailer snapped at a reporter: "There are a lot of writers making money. Why is it only news when I do?" He added, "I always start a book for money. If you've been married five times, you have to." He told *People* that he needed $250,000 a year to cover expenses and back taxes, a $50,000 increase over what he had told *Time* the previous year.

❦

Mailer had never denied that money was the original stimulus for the *Marilyn* book. But in the writing, Mailer had found himself drawn to the project and to Marilyn herself. *Marilyn* proved to be a successful book, obviously flawed, partially derivative, but with a touch of magic that came from Mailer's strange affinity for the beautiful waif of a star.

• XX •

THE CELEBRITY WRITER

In the seventies, thus far, Mailer had not written a work as masterful as *The Naked and the Dead*, "The White Negro," or *Armies of the Night*. His reputation had been maintained somewhat by *Of a Fire on the Moon*, *The Prisoner of Sex*, and *Marilyn* but his career was being sustained more by controversy and promotion than by solid accomplishment. The decade itself lacked a coherent theme and this vacuity was being reflected in Mailer's own failure to interpret the time.

Mailer may not have been producing seminal works but the cumulative effect of his life and writing career had brought him to the height of his fame. In her review of *Marilyn*, Pauline Kael had written what Mailer had hoped a leading critic would someday say—that he had equaled his hero-image, Hemingway. "Hemingway wasn't the monarch of American arts but our official literary celebrity—our big writer—and by the end of the sixties, after *An American Dream* and *Cannibals and Christians* and *Armies of the Night* and *Miami and the Siege of Chicago*, the title had passed to Mailer," Kael stated.

That summer of 1974 Mailer, Carol, and the children went to Maine, where the author relaxed and worked on his novel. While he was in Maine, Mailer learned that not everyone considered his status as a celebrity writer to be positive or of any benefit to him as an artist. In fact, *The New York Times Magazine* published a rather searing indictment of several celebrities—and specifically Mailer—by Robert Brustein, director of the Yale Repertory Theater. A new phenomenon was beginning to shape the cultural and political events of our time, Brustein said. It was what he called "news theatre," an arena in which certain celebrities exploited by the media and were in turn exploited by it.

Mailer, Brustein felt, was the prime example of such a celebrity. "Mailer personifies most dramatically the kind of havoc that the news theatre can visit on a creative personality. . . . Mailer seems to me almost preternaturally preoccupied with his cultural image, as if his overarching impulse were to dominate the Celebrity Register, to superimpose the star system on literature." Mailer's interest in himself, Brustein went on to say, had begun to overshadow his interest in external events. The only significant thing about his promised novel, he said, was an "unprecedented advance of $1 million."

Mailer was in danger of losing his soul, Brustein claimed. "We must conclude that the conscious pursuit of success does indeed cripple a man spiritually in this country, regardless of the degree of his self-consciousness—or, to put the problem into the language of a previous time, one can gain the whole world and still lose one's soul. Mailer has shown us that it is impossible to work through the corruptions inherent in the pursuit of success—in that sense only can we call his career exemplary."

Not surprisingly, Mailer's next book, *The Fight*, written late in the fall of 1974, was the last in which he spoke of himself in the third person, and in this case, it was a modest "Norman." In *The Fight*, Mailer faced the criticism of his egotism head-on. "Now, our man of wisdom had a vice," Mailer stated. "He wrote about himself. Not only would he describe events he saw, but his own small effect on events. This irritated critics. They spoke of ego trips and unattractive dimensions of his narcissism. Such criticism did not hurt too much. He had already had a love affair with himself, and it used up a good deal of love. He was no longer so pleased with his presence."

Mailer had gone to Kinshasa, Zaire, to cover the heavyweight title fight between Muhammad Ali and George Foreman. In Zaire, Mailer had an experience which became the subject of intense fascination to George Plimpton, who was also covering the same event. Mailer had agreed to go running with Ali one morning shortly before the fight. Though Mailer had not jogged since the summer, he kept up with Ali for a mile and a half as they ran in the predawn countryside upriver from Ali's compound at Nsele. Finally Mailer had to stop, but Ali and his sparring partners kept going.

As Mailer was walking back to the compound, he suddenly envisioned a heroic scenario for his own death: In the African woods he heard the unmistakable sound of a lion roaring. His mind flashed back to a moment in Provincetown, when, sailing in a small sailfish, he had passed a whale. "What a perfect way to go," Mailer wrote in *The Fight*. "His place in American literature would be forever secure. They would seat him at Melville's feet. Melville and Mailer, ah, the consanguinity of the M's and L's—how critics would love Mailer's now discovered preoccupations (see Croft on the mountain in *The Naked and the Dead*) with Ahab's Moby Dick. Something of this tonic sangfroid was with him now. To be eaten by a lion on the banks of the Congo—who could fail to notice that it was Hemingway's own lion waiting down these years for the flesh of Ernest until an appropriate substitute had at last arrived?"

Plimpton recalls that Mailer told him about the lion and the whale that night at dinner. The subject of how authors see themselves dying began to haunt Plimpton, and back in the States he began checking biographies and politely informing dinner guests, "Ahem . . . I'm collecting deaths." He started corresponding with all the writers he knew, telling them about Mailer and the lion and asking them about their own fantasies of death. By the end of his research he had amassed a fascinating and funny series of profiles, which he included in his book *Shadow Box*.

Mailer's preoccupation with his own death in *The Fight* was tied to his increasing interest in the ideas of karma and reincarnation. While in Zaire he began reading *Bantu Philosophy* and discovered that "the instinctive philosophy of African tribesmen happened to be close to his own. Bantu philosophy, he soon learned, saw humans as forces, not beings . . . a man was not only himself, but the karma of all the generations past that still lived in him." Mailer's existential theology was taking a perceptible turn toward the idea of immortality.

Plimpton observed something surprising about Mailer in Zaire, which the critics would make note of as well when *The Fight* was published by Little, Brown the following July. As Plimpton recalled, "In Africa I had never seen Mailer in such a relaxed mood and at ease with himself, which always meant that he was splendid company. I remember being slightly surprised because he had spoken of the country as Hemingway's territory, which was going to require him to be on his mettle."

It was the absence of his usual pugnacious ego in *The Fight* that the critics noticed. All the old Mailer signposts were duly pointed out—his self-involvement, excesses, confessions without apology, clowning, bravado, and mysticism, but Christopher Lehmann-Haupt still concluded that the book was a "sensitive portrait." Michael Wood in his front-page review for *The New York Times Book Review* pointed to Mailer's "odd compassion."

Sensitive and *compassion* were not words often used to describe Mailer's work, just as *relaxed* and *at ease* were not terms usually applied to his demeanor. Something seemed to be quieting in the fifty-two-year-old writer. As Michael Wood noted, he was now "seeing the humor of his own perfect seriousness. . . . A rare gift." The flamboyant author appeared to be turning toward middle age with less defensiveness and more humor about his excesses.

❦

A twenty-six-year-old Arkansas art teacher, Barbara Norris, would find Mailer's new ease particularly seductive when she met him in March 1975, three months after he returned from Zaire. Mailer had gone to Loyola University in New Orleans to give one of his innumerable lucrative lectures and had promised to pass through Russellville, Arkansas, afterward to see his old friend Francis Irby Gwaltney. Gwaltney, who was then teaching a creative writing class at Arkansas Polytechnic College, picked Mailer up at the airport at Little Rock and asked him if he would speak to his students. Mailer agreed.

Mrs. Gwaltney also taught English at the college, and that afternoon, after Mailer spoke, she invited about twenty faculty members to their house for tea. During the tea, as Mrs. Gwaltney recalls, Barbara Norris, a tall, stunning auburn-haired woman who taught art at the local Russellville High School and who had illustrated Gwaltney's book, *Idols of Ecstasy*, phoned the house. "I understand Norman Mailer is there. Could I crash?" she asked. The Gwaltneys asked her to come over.

Norris remembered that first meeting with Mailer. "I walked in and had on blue jeans and a shirt tied at the waist and tall wedgie shoes, and I was about six feet two. Well, Norman is five feet eight. I walked up and said, 'How are you, Mr. Mailer?' and he turned around and walked out of the room."

Jan Olympitis, then Jan Cushing, who would meet Norris for the first time the following year, relates the story as it was told to her by Norris. "Norris was astounded that he turned his back on her, but shortly after the tea, Mr. Gwaltney called her and asked if she would like to join them and Mailer for dinner. Norris then said, 'Well, I don't think he wants to have dinner with me, he turned his back on me.' But Mr. Gwaltney said, 'On the contrary, he was so attracted to you he was riveted. He's the one who wants you to come.' " Olympitis says that Norman confirmed the story to her. "He was so attracted to her he couldn't bear to look at her anymore, that she was so beautiful he just turned away."

Mrs. Gwaltney describes that first evening in Russellville in much the same way. "Apparently," she says, "he was quite taken with her. We had been invited by a friend who lives way out in the woods to eat pizza and we asked Norman to go, and he said sure. But he then spoke to Fig [Francis Gwaltney] and said, 'Why don't you ask her,' meaning Barbara, 'to come along?' Which we did. It was obvious they had eyes for no one else that night. He was certainly struck, and it was obvious to everyone how much he enjoyed her that night."

Norris has recalled that Mailer seemed fascinated that evening by her humble Baptist upbringing in Atkins, Arkansas, a town which had a population of two thousand. An only child, she worked summers in a pickle factory. Her father was a heavy-equipment instructor for a Job Corps center and her mother ran a beauty salon. Norris had attended Atkins High School and then Arkansas Polytechnic College and had married the first boy she dated, Larry Norris, who had the same small-town roots as she. They had a child, Matthew, who was only three when she first met Mailer. Larry Norris was a Vietnam veteran, and as Mrs. Gwaltney says, "from the time he came back, they didn't get along. Like so many vets, he just couldn't get himself together when he came back. I felt sort of sorry for him." By the time Barbara Norris met Mailer, she was divorced and on her own, supporting herself and her son on a $7200 salary as an art teacher at Russellville High School. She had also taught at the Benedictine Order Boys School in the mountains.

Mrs. Gwaltney recalls that before Barbara was introduced to Mailer, she had read *Marilyn*, which was one of the reasons she wanted to meet him. "I don't think she had read any of his other books," Mrs. Gwaltney says, "but she was pretty young then, only twenty-six, almost the same age as Norman's oldest daughter, Susan. But she was certainly aware of who he was. She had a good education, but was not particularly literary because she was an art major."

Mailer was no less attracted to Norris because she was not literary: he has always felt comfortable with nonliterary women. In 1981 he commented on this to Jeffrey Michelson and Sarah Stone: "I've usually been drawn to women who aren't necessarily that interested in my work. My present wife [Norris] had read one book of mine before we met. She hardly knew anything about me. It's probably analogous to the poor young rich girl, who wants to be loved for herself and not her money . . . you definitely don't want to be loved for your literary fame because you know more about it than anyone else and you know literary fame has very little to do with your daily habits. I mean, finally you're an animal who lives in a den and goes around, and finally, you know, has to be liked or disliked as an animal first."

That night in Arkansas Norris found Mailer "charming, funny and witty—and very sexy. He has this way of talking to you that makes you feel like no one else is in the room." Mailer had to leave the next morning, but they stayed up very late talking to each other, just as he and Adele had at their first meeting twenty-five years before. The next morning Gwaltney drove Mailer to the airport, but two weeks later he flew back to visit Norris. By the summer she had quit her job, sold her house, and moved to Brooklyn Heights with her three-year-old son over the objections of her parents. As Mrs. Gwaltney recollects, "She really went about it once she made her mind up, and didn't turn back."

Norris's arrival further complicated an already complex domestic situation. Carol, who had been living with Mailer in Stockbridge, was waiting for him to return. Beverly was still legally married to him, and his current girl friend had begun to put pressure on Mailer to get married. "Norman had worked out a deal with her, saying, 'Give me six months.' But during that time he met Norris," José Torres reveals.

Norris was unconcerned about the competition for Mailer's affection. When she came to New York, she received his full attention. Mailer even suggested she change her name from Barbara Norris to Norris Church because he thought that it sounded better professionally. She soon began to model for the Wilhelmina Agency for seventy-five dollars an hour and before long her face was appearing in *Vogue* and other magazines in advertisements for Clairol, Ben Kahn furs, and Gloria Vanderbilt sunglasses. Her modeling career would continue until she became pregnant with their son, John Buffalo, in the summer of 1977.

The competitiveness of Mailer's previous wives seemed absent in Norris. José Torres says that Norris is "a nice lady" and the best of his women. Mrs. Gwaltney has observed Mailer's marital relationships ever since Beatrice Silverman and agrees with Torres. "It seems to me Barbara [Norris] is wiser about how to get along with Norman than some of the other ones," she says. "For some time Fig and I had noticed a feeling of competition that women had with Norman. Barbara doesn't do that at all. Adele wanted to be a painter, Beverly wanted to be an actress, and Bea was just very, very smart. It seemed to me that at times their ambition gave rise to a little bit of challenge. But Barbara is able to be very supportive."

Grove Press publisher Barney Rosset, who met Norris shortly after she arrived in New York, noticed a remarkable change in Mailer's demeanor. The violence he had witnessed during the filming of *Maidstone* seemed to have disappeared. He remembers that he and his wife and Mailer and Norris all went to Rao's, a small Italian restaurant in Spanish Harlem that Mailer had been going to for twenty years. "Norris was very shy," Rosset recalls. "They had just met in Arkansas and this was like the second night she was in New York. Norman was so different that night. He seemed very mellowed. Maybe if he hadn't changed, he never would have met Norris, but he really was a changed person."

❦

About the time that Norris came to New York, Rosset developed an idea for a new Mailer book, one which also involved Mailer's friend, Buzz Farbar. Farbar and Rosset had gotten to know each other well when Farbar was running Mailer's movie company, Supreme Mix, and Rosset was distributing *Beyond the Law*. The film company was then defunct and Rosset tried to think of a project Farbar could edit. "I puzzled over it," Rosset says, "and then remembered that Mailer had always expressed an admiration for Henry Miller. I thought that might be a good idea for both Mailer and Buzz."

The book was to be a select anthology of Miller's work with comment by Mailer, entitled *Genius and Lust: A Journey Through the Major Writings of Henry Miller*. Bantam Books agreed to put up the advance money of fifty thousand dollars, which was to be split among

Mailer, Miller, and Farbar. Mailer's advance was to be higher than Miller's, but he would have the same royalty. Grove would print the hard-cover and Bantam the paperback.

Mailer spent about three months that fall reading through Miller's work. He then chose the most powerful and least sanitized prose by Miller, who he felt had "the largest stylistic influence of any twentieth century American author" with the exception of Hemingway. After that Mailer sat down to write his narrative. As with *Marilyn*, he would inadvertently plumb his own contradictions to arrive at an understanding of Miller's motivations. Miller looked at the paradoxes of the great artists and concluded that "the greater they are, the more they fail to fulfill their own idea of themselves." Mailer also presented Miller as a man who was different from himself, one with an unloving Germanic mother and an inability to have sex with love.

Most of the critics agreed that Mailer's analysis of Miller was excellent, but the book sold only 10,000 hard-cover copies when it was published in November 1976. With higher expectations of sales, Grove had printed a good deal more. Mailer had used a few of the most controversial passages on Miller from *The Prisoner of Sex* in *Genius and Lust* and once again certain feminists were up in arms against him. In the December 6, 1976 issue of *The Village Voice*, a month after *Genius and Lust* was published, Vivian Gornick tore into Mailer, attacking Miller, Philip Roth, and Saul Bellow as well. In a long piece entitled "Why Do These Men Hate Women?" she accused these writers of misogyny and arrested development, citing Mailer's book to prove her case. Mailer, she said, was the worst of the lot: "Mailer has remained fixed in this literary mode of sexual antagonism which, even as the life within it evaporates decade by decade, he coldly, somewhat hysterically insists on raising to the level of religious ceremony. . . . It is in his misogyny that Mailer is most regressive, most at a distance from the creation of live literature."

Mailer, seemingly at peace in his sexual and love life at long last, could not escape confrontation with his feminist enemies—and their defenders. The following fall *Esquire* would publish a piece by Mailer which recounted several of his television appearances, including the 1972 Dick Cavett show on which he fought with his longtime profeminist foe, Gore Vidal. After the *Esquire* article was published, Mailer attended a party at Lally Weymouth's during which his feud with Vidal re-erupted.

Vidal had unexpectedly arrived in town on the day of Weymouth's party. Jason Epstein, Vidal's editor at Random House, called Weymouth to ask if he could bring the author along. Weymouth, who is friends with both Mailer and Vidal, agreed. As Vidal describes it, when he got to the party and passed by Mailer, Mailer said to him, "You look like a dirty old Jew." Vidal answered, "Well *you* look like a dirty old Jew." Needing no furthur provocation, Mailer threw his drink in Vidal's face and Vidal says that he bit Mailer's finger.

Vidal today claims he is not feuding with Norman Mailer. But he is still somewhat passionate in his dislike of his old verbal sparring partner. "He has no new ideas, either political or intellectual," says Vidal. "His much-acclaimed radicalism is based purely on self-promotion. I'm a public writer, I'm in politics, but I don't make public spectacles of myself drinking and engaging in fights. I used to think he was nice; he's not nice, he's foolish."

Shortly after the Weymouth party, Norris Church attended a dinner without Mailer, who was off researching a book. Norris was confident enough to defend her lover's honor while he was gone. During the meal someone stood to toast Mailer, but immediately after, Ahmet Ertegun, the head of Atlantic Records, who was seated next to Norris, rose for another toast. "Instead of drinking to the absent writer Norman Mailer," he said, "I think we should drink to another absent writer who is also a genius, Gore Vidal." As one of the dinner guests recalls, "Norris stood up and doused him with a whole glass of wine right in his face. Ahmet's wife was there and they both laughed. I was surprised, honestly, because if someone other than Norris had done it, they wouldn't have stood for it."

The quarrel between Mailer and Vidal was becoming more bitter than even Mailer's long-term feud with William Styron. On January 2, 1978 Mailer and Vidal had a rematch debate on the Dick Cavett show. Vidal, no longer speaking metaphorically, pointed out that Mailer's knife had actually gone into Adele's back as well as her front. Mailer was visibly upset. Cavett tried to soothe him, but Mailer would not be mollified. "I can't just be called anything all the time," he responded. The press judged that Mailer had failed to rebut.

❦

Norris Church is quick to defend her husband against all attackers, including the feminists. "I get really angry when people call him a chauvinist," she has said. "It was twenty years ago that he made those jokey remarks to Orson Welles about women needing to be kept in cages, and no one's ever forgotten it. . . . He's been supportive of my career while he gets on with his own. He's not the least bit chauvinist."

One indication of his support was Mailer's request that Norris draw the sketch of Henry Miller which was printed on the cover of *Genius and Lust*. Jan Olympitis remembers Mailer asking her about Norris's sketch when she met the couple for the first time at a dinner party at Pat Lawford's in the fall of 1976. It was the beginning of a close and enduring friendship. "When we were introduced," she recalls, "Norman said to me, 'Have you seen the sketch on the cover of my book about Henry Miller?' I said yes, and he asked me what I thought of it. Thinking it was a sketch of Mailer and not Miller, I told him I thought it was terrible. He said, 'Don't tell that to my girl friend because she did it.' "

Olympitis spent an hour before dinner talking to Norris, who, she says, was very honest and open about living with Mailer. At dinner Mailer asked Olympitis what she thought of Norris. "I didn't really know him," she relates, "but he obviously wanted a woman's opinion. So I told him I thought Norris was a good egg. Norris later told me that when they got home that night, Norman said to her, 'I think Jan is going to be a good friend of yours because she said you were a good egg and that means more for a woman to say than all the other bullshit I've been getting.' Apparently, all these other people had said she was beautiful, a knockout, that kind of thing."

Norris had told Olympitis that she did not know a soul in New York. Olympitis, who is well known in New York social circles, decided to take Norris under her wing. She invited her to lunch with Alexandra Schlesinger and gave a dinner for Norris and Mailer to which she invited the Schlesingers and Pat Lawford, among others. "I felt it was important, living with a famous writer like Norman, that she have her own identity and meet her own friends," Olympitis says. "If she met them all through Norman, it would be thanks to Norman, and therefore she would be dependent on him. With her own friends I thought Norman would respect her more. She fit in immediately. The only thing she changed, in addition to her name, was her accent. She had an Arkansas accent at the beginning, a bit of a hickier accent, which she has since lost."

❦

Fitting in with the Schlesingers and Pat Lawford in 1976 was not exactly a move in the direction of independence for Norris; Mailer himself was by now a good friend of the Kennedy clan. They had perceived him as a radical and an unstable outsider in 1960, but by 1968 both his new stature and his backing of Robert Kennedy's campaign had made him welcome. Schlesinger, who had been an RFK supporter as early as his 1964 senatorial campaign, was impressed that Mailer was one of the very few on the left who had also seen RFK's qualities that soon. Mailer had written a piece on Kennedy for *The Village Voice* in 1964 entitled "A Vote for Bobby K.—Possibility of a Hero," which Schlesinger had found very perceptive.

"Norman sensed in 1964 what Robert Kennedy was really like," Schlesinger says, "and sensed what part of Kennedy was emerging. That was early in his career. RFK had been counsel to a congressional committee, then later attorney general under his brother, but it wasn't until he started running for President in 1968 that most people saw his political side. In 1964 he was viewed mainly as an FBI man even though he was trying to impose controls over J. Edgar Hoover during John Kennedy's administration. I'm sorry that Norman and RFK never knew each other better because they would have liked each other. I guess the Jews and the Irish are alike anyway and Norman has an Irish temperament."

Schlesinger, who characterizes Mailer as "a Roosevelt-Kennedy Democrat," was surprised in 1976 when Mailer showed unusual zeal for Jimmy Carter, who was then running for President. In fact, two months before *Genius and Lust* was published in November 1976, Mailer wrote a Carter profile for the September issue of *The New York Times Magazine*. Some thought that his interest in the man was connected with the fact that Mailer was living with Norris who, like Carter, had a small-town southern Baptist background. But in his *Times* piece Mailer made it clear that his interest in Carter had a more profound source. He was "excited by Carter's theological convictions."

When Mailer went to Plains, Georgia, in the late spring of 1976 to interview Carter, he was determined to discuss religion with the presidential candidate. In his zeal he forgot, or ignored, the fact that presidential candidates do not feel free to discuss religion candidly. Mailer used up almost the entire first hour expounding on his own religious theories, including his views of Satan. Incredibly he asked Carter "if he had any belief in reincarnation, in the reincarnation of karma as our purgatory here on earth." Increasingly, Mailer's existential religious beliefs were being replaced by the concept of reincarnation. The aging Mailer did not want his profoundly interesting life to end in a simple death.

Just as Bishop Moore had been stunned by Mailer's irrepressible theological opinions, Carter could only smile wanly. He answered that he thought we had just one life, then tried to turn the conversation to more solid political ground. Mailer realized he had gone too far and in no way blamed Carter, whom he likened to an astronaut. "He had that silvery reserve only the most confident astronauts ever showed," Mailer later said.

When Mailer continued the interview the next day, the author spoke only of politics. Mailer was taken by the Plains peanut farmer and wrote that "he would find himself on Election Day happy to vote for him: after all, it was not every day that you could pull the lever for a man whose favorite song was 'Amazing Grace, how sweet the sound that saved a wretch like me—I once was lost, but now I'm found, was blind but now I see.' "

Arthur Schlesinger remembers that he and Mailer had dinner together the night Carter gave his acceptance speech. "I was surprised," Schlesinger recalls, "to see how pro-Carter Norman was at that point. He thought Carter was an honest, radical populist. Quite soon after, while Carter was still in office, he regretted it."

Mailer's interest in Carter did not alienate the Kennedy clan. Only a month after the elections they were out in force at a party Mailer gave in his Brooklyn Heights home to celebrate the first wedding anniversary of Doris Kearns and Richard Goodwin, the Kennedy speech writer who sixteen years before had sent *Esquire* a parody of Mailer's less-than-complimentary piece on Jackie Kennedy. It was a testament to Mailer's long successful journey from the angry radical of the early sixties that Jackie Kennedy herself attended the party. As Charlotte Curtis wrote about the former First Lady on the society pages of *The New York Times:* "In the old days, she went to nothing but exquisite little dinners and big, glamorous galas. Today, she goes almost anywhere, including Brooklyn. But it helps if Norman Mailer is the host."

Mailer had become a writer of true celebrity. As Pauline Kael had said, he had matched Hemingway in fame. His place in the American establishment finally seemed secure, but time was passing in the decade and there were rumblings within the literary community that he had not produced a work of great value since *Armies of the Night*. If anything characterized his writing in the seventies, it was a shift away from autobiographic narrative toward biography. Mailer had written about Marilyn Monroe, Muhammad Ali, and Henry Miller, and his new interest in people mirrored the era's disinterest in abstract ideas. But his recent work was not considered powerful enough to maintain his literary reputation. Mailer needed a new, heroic piece of work, one that would bring him sufficient accolades to refute the growing criticism.

• XXI •

THE REINCARNATION OF NORMAN MAILER

The project that would enable Mailer to end the seventies in triumph came unexpectedly. It would tie together many of the approaches to contemporary literature and journalism that he had been experimenting with over the last two decades. On January 17, 1977, Mailer read in the morning newspaper that a convict, Gary Gilmore, had been executed by a firing squad in the state of Utah. The case was unusual not only because it was the first time that capital punishment had been used in America in over a decade but also because the convict himself had refused to participate in continued appeals to the governor, asking instead to be executed.

"I felt I might just understand what Gilmore was doing," Mailer later said. "But I didn't think about it any more than that." On the evening news Mailer watched his old partner in the *Marilyn* project Lawrence Schiller, who had obtained exclusive rights to the Gilmore story. Mailer noticed that Schiller seemed to be moved. Not long after, Schiller called Mailer and asked him to read an interview with Gilmore that he and Barry Farrell had done for *Playboy.* Mailer thought the interview was superb and even suggested directing a two-character off-Broadway play based on the dialogue. Schiller told him, "You can, but first you have to write the book."

Mailer had been working well on his novel and did not want to stop, but there was once again the pressing need for money.

Although Scott Meredith had renegotiated his contract for a novel with Little, Brown in 1976, insuring Mailer a monthly payment of $12,500 which was not conditional upon delivery of material, a yearly income of $150,000 was hardly enough to cover alimony expenses, school tuition payments for his children, and taxes. In fact, in February 1977, Mailer sold his Stockbridge house, where Carol had been living, for $100,000 to the founder of *Screw* magazine. Even then Mailer was not able to pay his 1977 taxes.

A lucrative deal with Schiller was attractive, but there had to be a more profound pull if Mailer were to drop his novel and write another book. Schiller sent him more material on Gilmore, including his prison letters to his girl friend Nicole and Mailer began to recognize that he had a certain kinship with the convict. One reason for this kinship was the convict's apparently firm belief in reincarnation, a subject to which Mailer had increasingly been drawn.

"He appealed to me," Mailer later told John Aldridge, "because he embodied many of the themes I've been living with all my life long before I even thought of doing a book on him. . . . I felt here's a perfect example of what I've been talking about all my life—we have profound choices to make in life, and one of them may be the deep and terrible choice most of us avoid between dying now and 'saving one's soul'—or at the least, safeguarding one's soul—in order, conceivably, to be reincarnated. Maybe there is such a thing as living out a life too long, and having the soul expire before the body. And here's Gilmore with his profound belief in Karma, wishing to die, declaring that he wants to save his soul. I thought, here, finally, is the perfect character for me. So I was excited about the book."

Both Mailer and Schiller were looking for substantial advance money but Little, Brown did not want to put up additional funds, especially since Mailer was already receiving so much for his unfinished novel. Schiller had dealt with Howard Kaminsky, the president of Warner Books, in 1973, when Kaminsky bought the mass-market paperback rights to *Marilyn* for a hundred thousand dollars. Warner was one of the publishers they now attempted to interest in what was to become the eminently successful "true life novel," *The Executioner's Song*.

"Schiller and Norman came to see me," recalls Kaminsky. "Norman was under an outstanding contract with Little, Brown for the novel, so in order for me to buy *Executioner's Song*, it was understood that Little, Brown would get to do the hard-cover for a nominal advance of twenty-five thousand dollars. I paid Mailer and Schiller a five-hundred-thousand-dollar advance for the paperback rights. I was not all that interested in the subject until Norman became attached to it. Once I met him and talked about it, I thought it had the potential to be a very big book."

The contract called for a hundred twenty-five thousand words from Mailer and it was agreed that Schiller and Mailer would split the money equally since much of the material would be based on the sixty interviews Schiller had already done as well as the forty or fifty he would yet do with the people who knew Gilmore. It was also agreed that Mailer himself would go out and talk to many of the people involved, but no one foresaw that he would conduct about a hundred interviews himself. Nor was it anticipated that his book, which he estimated would take six months to write, would take two and a half years and end up being more than five times longer than originally agreed upon.

Mailer began his work in May 1977 and spent the next six months simply sorting out all the players. He then devoted the next year and a half to reading the voluminous transcripts Schiller had acquired, flying to Utah for follow-up interviews with the friends and family of the executed convict. Mailer rented an apartment in Provo for two months and drove around the state, getting the feel of the spartan, dry landscape, just as twenty-five years before he had driven to Palm Springs to absorb the setting for what had become his third novel, *The Deer Park*. He slept in Gary Gilmore's hotel room and met Nicole Baker, Gilmore's girl friend, with whom the convict had corresponded at length about his wish for death and his belief in reincarnation. An aborted suicide pact between Gilmore and Nicole became a subject of fascination for Mailer, who later said, "I thought these elements of tragic love were so operative for the modern temper that they're almost unbelievable." Mailer was so taken with Nicole that he later invited her to New York and taught her to play chess.

The mass of material that had to be synthesized by Mailer—documents and records of court proceedings plus fifteen thousand pages of transcripts from the combined interviews of Schiller, Mailer, his researchers and his secretary—was overwhelming. Finding a style that could encompass that material as well as portray the inherent drama of the story was not easy for a writer whose tendency had been to impose his own ego on the events he was describing.

Ever since his 1974 book on Ali, *The Fight*, Mailer had begun to sense that his autobiographical style, so lauded in the sixties, was no longer working. The self-involved pieces he had written on his television battles and on Carter were received with increased dismay by the critics, who seemed weary of Mailer's absorption with himself. Mailer instinctively gauged that he would have to change his style if this book was to be read by a large audience.

Mailer had initially conceived a complex story within a story, nothing like the simple, potent narrative he ended up with. "Originally, I was going to write the book in a totally different way," he explains. "I had a wonderful scheme. I was going to write a book about a man, a sad middle-aged writer, whose name was Staunchman. He was writing a movie about the life of Gary Gilmore for someone like Francis Ford Coppola, who had said to him, 'Listen, Larry Schiller has gotten hold of the rights to the Gilmore story and he's gotten Norman Mailer to write the book. You have got to come in first with this movie.' That was going to be the pretext for it. Coppola would tell him, 'Just keep writing these long letters about Gilmore. I'm not interested in the screenplay; I only want to understand what Gilmore is like, what his insides are like. You just keep telling me about Gilmore.' And in the course of it Staunchman writes these long endless letters to Coppola about Gilmore and they would get into the discussion of what kind of book Mailer was probably writing.

"That book appealed to me, but then I realized it would add another three hundred pages and would probably violate the material, because the material was so strong and simple. It would have been like putting ribbons on a prize bull. So I didn't do it. But writing *The Executioner's Song* wasn't automatic. In the beginning I went through the bends writing in that simple style, but then I began to enjoy it. I'd go back tomorrow to the other autobiographical style if it worked. It works for certain kinds of experiences, but I think something in the seventies burned out a lot of the possibility for that kind of style.

"The seventies was a period in which we became tremendously fed up with personality. Personality became one of the artifacts of the media. And you were just asking to go into the meat grinder if you kept trying to inflict your own pesonality on to the consciousness of the seventies. At a certain moment I just threw up my hands and said, 'Admit it, you're licked. The seventies is never going to accept the way you are writing, they hate it. And you're not going to be able to reach anybody you want to reach if you keep writing that way.' It was a military decision—you've got to get your troops out of the ravine. Then this Gilmore book came along and it was the perfect book with which to make the move. I wish I had invented it because it would have been an extraordinary piece of invention. The Literary Gods were good to me; they finally gave me a book that was asking to be written."

❦

In October 1978, while Mailer was working on *The Executioner's Song*, often for twelve hours a day, Beverly Mailer finally sued him for divorce. Although she had been living in the Provincetown house since 1971, with Mailer making the mortgage payments, she now wanted to return to New York to resume her acting career. The four hundred dollars a week Beverly was receiving from Mailer was, she said, not enough. The divorce proceedings were strung out until the following spring, just as Mailer was completing the Gilmore book. Throughout the ten full days of testimony, Mailer's difficult financial position was laid bare before the public.

The divorce trial was held at the Barnstable Probate Court in Massachusetts, where Beverly accused Mailer of cruel and abusive treatment, pointing to his many affairs with other women since they had separated, specifically with Carol Stevens and Norris Church, both of whom had given birth to a child of Mailer's. Beverly sued for one thousand dollars a week support and also wanted custody of her two sons, all school and medical bills paid by Mailer, and possession of the Provincetown house, which was then estimated to be worth $135,000.

During the course of the trial Mailer told the court that he simply couldn't afford Beverly's financial demands. In addition to the four hundred dollars a week he was giving her, he was paying four hundred dollars to Carol, four hundred dollars to Adele, and six hundred dollars a week to Norris, a total of $93,600 a year. Mailer added that he was $500,000 in debt, including the $185,000 he owed to his agent, Scott Meredith. Moreover, the IRS had placed a $100,000 lien on his Provincetown house for his failure to pay $80,500 in back taxes for 1976 and 1977.

In February, just after *People* magazine had published a revealing interview with Beverly, Mailer told the court: "We all know I'm not a man with an excellent reputation to begin with but what little reputation I have is being slaughtered." He charged that Beverly and her attorneys had been going over his financial statements for five years and that she had delayed divorce in hopes that he would suddenly receive a large sum from his work. "At a certain point," Mailer said, "she decided that there would never be any real money and she set out to gather publicity. What Beverly is doing is looking for publicity that will advance her career."

In the midst of the trial, on April 20, Mailer's much-loved Provincetown house was auctioned by the IRS for only $65,000 to Cape Cod See of San Jose, California. Although Mailer had 120 days to buy back the property, Norris, who was then handling all the bills and alimony payments, told reporters it was unlikely that Mailer would be able to reclaim the house. "Norman has no money and nowhere to get any," she said. Beverly was also reached for comment. "I feel extremely helpless," she said. "My heart is just breaking. Norman gave me this house in 1966, but my name was not on the deed. We laughed at the time and he said it would be taken care of."

On May 2, 1979, soon after the Provincetown house was lost, the final arguments were presented in the divorce trial. "We have here a marriage which by any admission was hell from the beginning," Mailer's lawyer, Monroe L. Inker, told the court. He called Beverly's suit "economic blackmail," while Beverly's lawyer, Ruth Budd, countered, "I think she simply wants a little security."

Edward L. Lucci, Mailer's New York accountant, testified that the author had only survived financially in the past few years by selling off assets, delaying payment of taxes, and borrowing money. He added that in 1977, a good year for Mailer, the author received $347,000 in gross income but had less than $60,000 in disposable income after business expenses, taxes, and interest on loans were deducted. By 1979 Mailer's financial position was so precarious that he was forced to sell the bottom two floors of his Brooklyn Heights house, keeping only the top floor and the third-floor office-studio.

When the divorce was finally granted in September, Beverly received a lump sum of $7,500 as well as $575 a week in alimony and an additional $100 a week in child support. But her battle for security was far from over; Beverly immediately filed an appeal. It was denied, but her lawyer approached the Supreme Court of Massachusetts for the right to file another appeal on the grounds that the couple were not legally divorced. In November 1980, Mailer underwent whirlwind marriages to both Carol Stevens and Norris, but Beverly's right to appeal was finally granted in September 1982. This means, Beverly now says, "technically, we're still married."

Beverly also carried on a long court fight to regain the Provincetown house after it was auctioned off by the IRS. This battle was less successful; on September 30, 1981 she was evicted and charged with owing $13,650 in back rent.

❦

A few months before the final divorce arguments were being presented, Mailer had handed in his manuscript of *The Executioner's Song* to Little, Brown. Howard Kaminsky of Warner Books, the paperback publisher of the book, clearly remembers receiving a copy of the massive work. "Norman came in and handed me four black looseleaf binders, each one containing five hundred pages of manuscript triple-spaced," Kaminsky says. "I brought it home that night with great trepidation and started reading. Within half an hour all the weight of anxiety lifted off me and I knew we were home. It was fabulous. I was surprised at the voice. He had told me that this was going to be totally different, like nothing else he'd ever done. But of course until one sees it themselves, one never believes writers. The architect is really not the one to tell you how the house will turn out."

Mailer's editor at Little, Brown, Larned Bradford, died before the book was published, but he had worked with Mailer on cutting the book down to manageable length. The final version, which was published in October 1979, came to a thousand seventy-two pages. The sparse, anonymous third person narrative, which Larned Bradford admiringly called "straight jailhouse prose," was totally devoid of the Mailer ego or the circuitous, sometimes baroque, mental flights which had become characteristic of his work. As Mailer later told John Aldridge, "I wish a few critics could see that I may feel a legitimate kinship to Picasso's need to keep changing his style. Preserving one's artistic identity is not nearly so important to me as finding a new attack on the elusive nature of reality. I've always been amused by people who say, 'Oh, well, Norman Mailer can't write a simple sentence.' There's nothing easier than to come full circle and write a book with prose even simpler than *The Naked and the Dead*."

Only a few weeks before the book's publication, Mailer asked his publishers to classify it as a novel, which they did. The book was labeled "A True Life Novel," a new literary genre which would give rise to much controversy, and much praise. As novelist Tim O'Brien pointed out in his review of *The Executioner's Song* in *New York* magazine, "The heart of nonfiction . . . is to dispel mystery. But the heart—and art—of fiction is both to generate and to celebrate human mystery, to allow ambiguities and contradictions to resonate, to explain little of a character's inner drives operating in a dramatic context. This is Mailer's strategy. . . . By not explaining him away, Mailer maintains the essential human mystery that keeps Gilmore alive in the reader's imagination."

Others would see *The Executioner's Song* as a subtle vehicle for Mailer's own subjective concerns. "Mailer's docility is itself highly deceptive," Earl Rovit remarked in *The Nation*. "The impersonality of the author is also an effective mask for a special kind of artistic arrogance. After all, it is not Gilmore qua Gilmore, but *Mailer's* Gilmore who is presented to us; and all the strategies of distancing, interpolating lifelike irrelevancies, and practicing the devices of *cinéma vérité* fail to conceal the fact that Gilmore of *The Executioner's Song* is Mailer's golem."

James Wolcott also noticed that Gilmore's life comfortably accommodated all the aspects of Mailer's evolving philosophy. "Karma, reincarnation, occult reckonings, psychopathic rage—all Mailer's obsessions are in Book One of *The Executioner's Song*," he wrote in *The Village Voice*, "and he's dramatized them in a slangy, unadorned style that carries a lethal chill."

But still other reviewers, such as Joan Didion, who called it "an absolutely astonishing book," found the narrative open to different interpretations. In *The New York Times Book Review* Didion said that it "was to be a novel of the West, and the strongest voices in it, as in the place itself, would be those of women. Men tend to shoot, get shot, push off, move on. Women pass down stories." Frank McConnell noted in *The New Republic* that the book could be read from two perspectives, that it "reflects equally the reality of [Mailer's] own time and the reality of his own imagination: so much so that we do not know whether to be more dazzled by the reflection outward or the one inward. The novel is mythology constructed to catch the moral ambiguity of its age."

In 1969 Mailer had won the Pulitzer Prize for *Armies of the Night* by filtering events directly through his ego. In 1980 he would be awarded the same prize for the subtle submersion of that ego in *The Executioner's Song*. In both cases, however, he was presenting a portrait of America at the time. Mailer's entire body of work has been a reflection of the changing reality of postwar America as he himself experienced that change. Gilmore was in many ways an archetype of the displaced American soul of the 1970s.

Perhaps more important to Mailer was the fact that Gilmore wished to die so he could save his soul and be reincarnated.

❦

By the time *The Executioner's Song* was published in the fall of 1979, Mailer had finished approximately 1,000 pages of his Egyptian novel, and his contract had been renegotiated, according to his agent, Scott Meredith, so that he would receive $30,000 a month. By the following fall he had already been paid $1.4 million for the book and the contract was again renegotiated. The novel would be considered the first volume of a trilogy, and he would be paid a total of $4 million for *Ancient Evenings* and the two additional volumes plus one small novel. To maintain his enormous family, Mailer would continue to receive his monthly payments.

Scott Meredith confirms that as a result of this new contract and the success of *The Executioner's Song*, Mailer was out of financial trouble by the beginning of 1982. He had even repaid his agent the loans which by then had reached a total of $250,000. Mailer finally had the financial freedom to focus exclusively on the writing of his Egyptian novel.

If *The Executioner's Song* could be seen as a reflection of the contemporary American psyche, *Ancient Evenings* hinges solely on Mailer's imagination. For the first time in his work there is no American reality to penetrate. The historical setting of Egypt in 1130 B.C. is not meant to provide a distant mirror of current times, and unlike his nonfiction work, there are no determined facts of another person's life to harness his imagination. It is pure Mailer, obsessions and all.

Critic John Leonard made an observation about Mailer's personality at a luncheon shortly after *The Executioner's Song* was published—a comment which proved to be prophetic about *Ancient Evenings*. "He [Mailer] was genial, but suspicious," Leonard said. "It was as if, behind the skull plate, his brain were an amniotic sac, inside of which [was] a very little boy and a very old man. . . ." A very little boy and a very old man are the two main protagonists and narrators of *Ancient Evenings*, each of whom is in a different stage of reincarnation.

Mailer's obsession with reincarnation is at the core of *Ancient Evenings*. Ever since Mailer planned the eight-novel scheme which evolved into *The Deer Park*, he has been concerned with the conundrum of time, and in *Ancient Evenings* the concept of reincarnation allows him to experiment with time through the lives of his two main characters, Menenhetet I and his great-grandson, Menenhetet II. The reincarnations of Menenhetet I had been achieved through a secret method divulged by an old Jew: dying at the moment of ejaculation into a woman.

As the novel opens, the Ka's—or doubles in death—of the two Menenhetets meet each other in their joint tomb. The twenty-one-year-old Ka of Menenhetet II tries to remember his past, and as he does, he flashes back to when he was a six-year old-boy. This device allows Mailer to use the young boy's unfolding memory of one night at the palace of Ramses IX in 1130 B.C. as a way of telling the story of the four lives of Menenhetet I.

In the boy's flashback his great-grandfather is in his fourth life at the age of sixty—Mailer's age as the novel is published—even though he is actually one hundred and eighty years old. Menenhetet I recounts his four lives to the Pharoah in the hope of dispelling rumors that he is a mad eccentric and because he wants to become the Pharoah's vizier. Through the depiction of Menenhetet's first life, which occupies more than half the book, Mailer's fantasies and obsessions emerge against the historical backdrop of ancient Egypt. Fantasies of royal birth, heroism and bravery, success and power, and sex with the beautiful Egyptian queen Nefertiri are integrated with Mailer's well-known theories about scatology, buggery, magic, violence, incest, and the world of taboo.

Ancient Evenings is a self-contained cocoon of Mailer's imagination, a testament to his obsessions. Probably no other American writer has demonstrated his personal compulsions so consistently in his work; it is clearly Mailer's great strength as well as his weakness.

❦

Mailer's formidable ego has enabled him to continually recover from failure by creating radically new styles for his next work. Just as critics begin to observe a staleness in his writing, perhaps even a decline into self-parody, Mailer returns with a triumphant breakthrough. "The devil in me loves the idea of being just that much of a changeling," Mailer says. "You can never understand a writer until you find his private little vanity and mine has always been that I will frustrate expectations. People think they've found a way of dismissing me, but, like the mad butler, I'll be back serving the meal."

Mailer's entire career has been like an elusive comet, shaking literary traditions and conventional mores in a blast of brilliance which has yet to settle into historical perspective. It is a career with time still to run and with works to be written. Whether Mailer is ultimately perceived as a strange, aberrational flash in the postwar American night or as one of the most seminal and enduring voices in contemporary literary history remains to be determined.

But one thing is certain: Norman Mailer is an individual of enormous imagination, courage, and energy in an age that too often seems devoid of such traits. He is admired, hated, castigated, and honored. Often he seems the very embodiment of the time, a reflection of our growing moral paradoxes. For that alone his life and work will be remembered.

Notes

I: THE PARADOX OF NORMAN MAILER

In addition to sources cited below, information in this chapter is drawn from the author's personal interviews with: Paul Montgomery of *The New York Times*, Thomas Hanrahan of the New York *Daily News*, Mike Pearl of the *New York Post*, Cynthia Fagen of the *New York Post*, Jean Malaquais, Jack Henry Abbott, John Leonard, Shelley Mason of the YMHA, Jason Epstein, Scott Meredith, Jonathan Silverman, Roger Donald, José Torres, Buzz Farbar, Mrs. Francis Irby Gwaltney, Jan Olympitis, Pete Hamill, Abbie Hoffman, Arthur Schlesinger, Jr., Manoli Olympitis, Elaine Kauffman, Norman Podhoretz, Beatrice Silverman, Midge Decter, Peter Maas, Milton Greene, George Plimpton, Jimmy Breslin, Dotson Rader.

Mailer entering courtroom and physical description: From interviews with Mike Pearl, Cynthia Fagen, Thomas Hanrahan, Paul Montgomery.

No longer jogging and boxing: Interview with José Torres.

Just started drinking: Interviews with Arthur Schlesinger, Jr., and Jan Olympitis.

Entourage: Interviews with Jean Malaquais, Mike Pearl, Cynthia Fagen, Thomas Hanrahan, Paul Montgomery.

Mailer-Abbott relationship: Interview with Jack Henry Abbott; accounts in *The New York Times*.

"out of nowhere . . .": *The New York Times Book Review*, July 18, 1981.

"It's a tragedy all around." *The New York Times*, January 15, 1982.

"You scum, Abbott . . .": *The New York Times*, January 16, 1982.

Leaving for lunch: Interviews with Jean Malaquais and Paul Montgomery.

Testimony: From court transcript.

Press conference: Interviews with Jean Malaquais, Paul Montgomery, Mike Pearl, Cynthia Fagen, Thomas Hanrahan; accounts in the New York *Daily News*, *The New York Times*, and the *New York Post* (all January 19, 1982); the *Soho News*, January 26, 1982.

Suit against *Post:* From deposition to the Supreme Court of the State of New York, obtained through Slade Metcalf, attorney for the *New York Post*.

YMHA reading: Interviews with Shelley Mason and John Leonard; YMHA tape of the event.

"Dostoyevsky and Marx; Joyce and Freud . . .": Norman Mailer, *Advertisements For Myself* (New York: G. P. Putnam's Sons, 1959), p. 477.

"I have given up the Egyptian novel . . .": Personal interview with Norman Mailer.

"If his candles had been burning low . . .": Norman Mailer, *The Fight* (Boston: Little, Brown, 1975), p. 34.

Warner Brothers deal: *The New York Times*, April 16, 1974; interview with Scott Meredith.

Foreign rights deals: Interview with Jonathan Silverman.

Meeting Norris Church: Interview with Mrs. Francis Irby Gwaltney.

Another young woman: Interview with José Torres.

"It's sort of interesting not drinking . . .": Norman Mailer, *Pieces and Pontifications* (Boston: Little, Brown and Company, 1982), p. 173. (As the two parts of this book are paginated separately, henceforth sources will be identified as either *Pieces* or *Pontifications*.)
Butting heads with Breslin: Interview with Jimmy Breslin.
Butting heads with Gregory Hemingway: Interview with George Plimpton.
Birthday party: Interviews with Arthur Schlesinger, Jr., Pete Hamill, Dotson Rader.
Fourth Most Outstanding Celebrity: *The New York Times*, January 6, 1981.
"If I have any entree at all . . .": Mailer, *Pontifications*, p. 135.
Kennedy inner circle: Interview with Arthur Schlesinger, Jr.
"I don't socialize much . . .": Personal interview with Norman Mailer.
"Other people, meeting me . . .": Mailer, *Advertisements*, p. 92.
"As you get older . . .": *The New York Times Book Review*, June 6, 1982.
Description of children: Interviews with Buzz Farbar, José Torres, Jan Olympitis.
"Call. . . to a Hebraic world . . .": Diana Trilling, "The Moral Radicalism of Norman Mailer" in *Norman Mailer: The Man and His Work*, edited by Robert Lucid (Boston: Little, Brown, 1971), p. 136.
"He had a fatal taint . . ." Norman Mailer, *Armies of the Night* (New York: New American Library, 1968), p. 153.
Breakfast with Fanny: Interview with Jan Olympitis.
"His mother is the *only* Mrs. Norman Mailer": *People*, February 26, 1979.
Completing *Ancient Evenings:* Interview with Roger Donald.
"It's probably helped my mind . . .": Personal interview with Norman Mailer.
"For Mailer, it has always been the criminal . . ." James Atlas, "The Literary Life of Crime," *The New Republic*, September 9, 1981.
Trapnell letter: Interview with Jack Henry Abbott.
"To be a punk . . ." Jack Henry Abbott, *In the Belly of the Beast*, (New York: Random House, 1981), p. 80.

II: YOUNG MAILER AT HARVARD

In addition to sources cited below, information in this chapter is drawn from the author's personal interviews with: Bowden Broadwater, Richard Weinberg, Seymour Breslow, Harold Katz, John Crockett, Robert Gorham Davis, Hope Hale Davis, Beatrice Silverman, Larry Weiss, George Goethals, Hallie Burnett, Marvin Barrett, John Blum, Larry Alson, Theodore Morrison, Theodore Amussen, John Marquand, Jr.

Physical description: Interviews with Beatrice Silverman, Seymour Breslow, George Goethals, Larry Weiss, John Crockett, Bowden Broadwater.
Accent: Interview with Richard Weinberg.
Model airplanes: Philip H. Bufithis, *Norman Mailer* (New York: Frederick Unger Publishing Company, 1978).
Acceptance by M.I.T.: Brock Brower, "Always the Challenger, Never the Champion" *Life*, September 24, 1965.
"I thought I would go to Harvard . . .": Frederick Christian, "The Talent and the Torment," *Cosmopolitan*, August 1963.
Pinup girls: Interview with Richard Weinberg.
Financial situation: Interviews with Beatrice Silverman, Larry Alson, George Goethals.
Quota system: Interviews with Richard Weinberg and John Blum.
Roommates: Interviews with Seymour Breslow and Harold Katz.

"Your class has a prototype . . .": MacLeish's speech reported in 1943 Harvard Yearbook.
"We were going through a barbed wire fence . . ." Mailer, *Advertisements*, p. 391.
"We must convince ourselves . . .": 1943 Harvard Yearbook.
Campus politics: Interviews with Robert Gorham Davis, John Crockett; 1943 Harvard Yearbook.
Fake bibliography: Interview with Mailer in *The Washington Post Book World*, July 11, 1971.
English A: Interview with Richard Weinberg.
Roster of teachers: Norman Mailer, preface to *The Fiction Writers Handbook*, edited by Hallie Burnett (New York: Harper & Row, 1975).
Mailer's Freshman reading: Mailer, *Advertisements*, p. 27; Christian, *Cosmopolitan*.
"Farrell demonstrated to me . . .": *Washington Post Book World*, July 11, 1971.
Proletarian novel: Interview with Larry Weiss.
American Studies Program: Interview with Robert Gorham Davis.
First short stories: Laura Adams, *Norman Mailer: A Comprehensive Bibliography* (Metuchen, N.J.: The Scarecrow Press, 1974).
Final Freshman English Exam: Interview with Richard Weinberg.
Remaining in Physics: Interviews with Beatrice Silverman and George Goethals.
Claverly Hall: Interviews with Seymour Breslow and Larry Weiss.
Description of roommates: Interview with Larry Weiss.
Cambridge "townie": Interview with Larry Weiss.
Weekend amusement: Interviews with Seymour Breslow and Larry Weiss.
"Novice in the Golden Gloves": Preface to *The Fiction Writers Handbook*.
Emulating Hemingway: Interviews with Seymour Breslow and Larry Weiss.
Football antics: Interview with Larry Weiss.
Mailer's generosity: Interviews with Larry Weiss and George Goethals.
"*Story* was its own legend . . .": Preface to *The Fiction Writers Handbook*.
Advocate: Interviews with George Goethals, Marvin Barrett, Bowden Broadwater, John Crockett.
Final Clubs: Interview with George Goethals; 1943 Harvard Yearbook.
Signet lunches: John Crockett, George Goethals, John Blum.
First brothel escapade: Interviews with Larry Weiss and Seymour Breslow.
No Percentage about a rich boy: Christian, *Cosmopolitan*.
Fanny and Barney Mailer's backgrounds: Interviews with Beatrice Silverman and Larry Alson; Bufithis, *Norman Mailer*.
Young reading: *Washington Post Book World*, July 11, 1971.
P.S. 161 and musical instruments; Bar mitzvah speech: Raymond Sokolov, "The World of Norman Mailer," *Newsweek*, December 9, 1968.
Bowery incident: Interviews with Beatrice Silverman and Larry Alson.
"Norman always had the highest marks." Sokolov, *Newsweek*.
High School achievements: 1939 Boys High School Yearbook.
Fanny as economic backbone: Interviews with Beatrice Silverman and Larry Alson.
Writing notebooks: Brower, *Life*.
"From his maternal grandfather . . .": Ibid.
Political mood on campus: 1943 Harvard Yearbook.
"Either we must believe that Hitler . . .": Ibid.
"the goal of all persons . . .": Ibid.
"Scylla the Dean . . .": Ibid.
Theodore Morrison's class: Interview with Theodore Morrison.
Derivative of Faulkner: Mailer, *Advertisements*, p. 84.
Lunch with Burnett: Preface to *The Fiction Writers Handbook*.

Larsen no longer reading Mailer: Christian, *Cosmopolitan.*
"Though Secretary of Hull's stand . . ." 1943 Harvard Yearbook.
Mailer playing football on Harvard lot: William Manchester, *The Glory and the Dream* (Boston: Little, Brown, 1973), p. 251.
Writing Burnett: *Story* correspondence file in Princeton University Library.
Mailer's version of the *Advocate* contretemps: Norman Mailer, *Pieces,* pp. 1-5.
Meeting Bea at the concert: Interviews with Beatrice Silverman and Larry Weiss.
David Kessler: Interviews with Larry Alson and Beatrice Silverman.
Convertible: Interviews with Seymour Breslow and George Goethals.
"I was assigned to the most violent ward . . ." Brower, *Life.*
Writing *Transit:* Mailer, *Advertisements,* p. 27.
Politicized campus: 1943 Harvard Yearbook.
"I have often thought . . .": *Twentieth Century Authors* (New York: Wilson, 1955), p. 628.

III: THE NAKED AND THE DEAD

In addition to sources cited below, information in this chapter is drawn from the author's personal interviews with: Beatrice Silverman, Mrs. Francis Irby Gwaltney, Larry Alson, Norman Rosten, Adeline Lubell, Arthur Miller, Stanley Geist, Jean Malaquais, Theodore Amussen, Norman A. Hall.

Living quarters and studio: Interview with Beatrice Silverman.
"romantic, morbid . . .": *Twentieth Century Authors,* p. 628.
"The only explanation I can find for such a delay . . .": Norman Mailer, introduction to *A Transit to Narcissus,* printed in *The New York Times Book Review,* December 4, 1977.
Edwin Seaver and *Cross Section:* Edwin Seaver, *Cross Section* (Toronto: McClelland & Stewart, 1944), introduction; Mailer, *Advertisements,* p. 28.
Elopement, Fanny's objection, and wedding ceremony: Interview with Beatrice Silverman.
Information about *Transit to Narcissus:* Mailer, introduction to *A Transit to Narcissus.*
Pacific picture: Manchester, *The Glory and the Dream,* pp. 343-344.
Mailer sent to Leyte then Luzon to join 112th Armored Cavalry: *New York Star,* August 22, 1948.
War jobs: Ibid.
War reading: Interview with Beatrice Silverman; *The Washington Post Book World,* July 11, 1971.
"A couple of fire fights . . ." *New York Star.*
"I kept my war diary . . ." Ibid.
"We can't all be poets . . .": James Atlas, "Life With Mailer," *The New York Times Magazine,* September 9, 1979.
Texas accent: Interview with Larry Alson.
"I spent the first day griping . . .": Interview with Francis Irby Gwaltney by W. G. Rogers, A.P. News Features, July 8, 1955.
"We stayed up all night . . ." and subsequent Gwaltney quotes: Brower, *Life.*
"At a certain point you get awfully tired as an infantryman . . .": Atlas, *New York Times Magazine.*
Patrol behind enemy lines: *New York Star.*
Embarking for Japan: Divisional History of the 112th Armored Cavalry Regiment.
"The Captain ordered me to apologize . . .": Brower, *Life.*
"The next morning . . .": Ibid.
"magic day": Harvard Class of 1943 Tenth Anniversary Report.
Beginning *The Naked and the Dead* in Provincetown: Interviews with Beatrice Silverman and Larry Alson.

Three-by-five cards: Interview with Beatrice Silverman.
"This is going to be the reactionary's century": Norman Mailer, *The Naked and the Dead* (New York: Rinehart and Company, 1948).
"Some characters, he didn't even bother to change their names": Brower, *Life*.
"Oh, you always get to know them . . .": *New York Star*.
"force is the only thing the Russians understand . . .": Manchester, *The Glory and the Dream*, p. 411.
Wallace, U.S.-Soviet Friendship rally: Norman D. Markowitz, *The Rise and Fall of the People's Century: Henry A. Wallace and American Liberalism* (San Francisco: The Free Press, 1973).
"I never thought of its being an anti-war book . . .": *New York Star*.
"They were just a bunch of Anti-Semiten . . .": Mailer, *The Naked and the Dead*, p. 206.
Two-room Brooklyn apartment and description: Interview with Beatrice Silverman.
Interest in aerial photography and baking: Interview with Beatrice Silverman.
Garret and financial situation: Interview with Beatrice Silverman.
"I doubt if ever again I will have a book . . .": Mailer, *Advertisements*, p. 92.
"But, Norman! The language! . . .": Brower, *Life*.
Description of Charles Devlin: Interviews with Norman Rosten, Larry Alson, Beatrice Silverman.
"It's a better book than I thought it would be . . .": Mailer, *Pontifications*, p. 165.
Little, Brown contretemps over *The Naked and the Dead:* Interview with Adeline Lubell.
"Oh, Lord, don't write a war novel! . . .": *New York Star*.
The Naked and the Dead to Rinehart: Interviews with Norman Rosten and Theodore Amussen.
Rinehart acceptance: Interview with Theodore Amussen.
"We agreed that I would cut it . . .": *New York Star*.
Invention of *fug:* Interview with Theodore Amussen.
"a way of getting two hundred dollars . . .": Christian, *Cosmopolitan*.
Paris apartment and bathing: Interview with Beatrice Silverman.
Mark Lindenthal: Interview with Beatrice Silverman.
Sorbonne course: Interview with Beatrice Silverman.
Café des Deux Magots: Interview with Beatrice Silverman.
"first of the existentialist novels in America": Mailer, *Advertisements*, p. 106.
Paul and Odet: Interview with Beatrice Silverman.
Malaquais' teachings: Interview with Jean Malaquais.
Rinehart ad campaign for *The Naked and the Dead:* Interview with Adeline Lubell.
Advance paperback editions: Interview with Norman A. Hall.
"the hot breath of the future . . ." Trilling in *Norman Mailer: The Man and His Work*, p. 116.
The arrival of Fanny, Barney, and Barbara; European trip: Interview with Beatrice Silverman.
American Express office: Atlas, *The New York Times Magazine*.
"We got more and more hysterical . . .": Brower, *Life*.
"That was the last time . . .": Atlas, *The New York Times Magazine*.

IV: FROM SUCCESS TO THE SHORES OF FAILURE

In addition to sources cited below, information in this chapter is drawn from the author's personal interviews with: Beatrice Silverman, Calder Willingham, Robert Loomis, Horace Sutton, Lillian Hellman, William Sladen, Jean Malaquais, Gene Kelly, Irwin Shaw, Hannah Weinstein, Dwight Macdonald, Irving Howe, Saul Chaplin, Mickey Knox, Robert Gorham Davis, Norman A. Hall.

Royalties: Lillian Ross, "Talk of the Town," *The New Yorker*, October 23, 1948.
First royalty check: Interview with Robert Loomis.
"It gives you fantastic security . . . ": Horace Sutton, *Cue*, August 21, 1948.
"He looked as if he had just run over from a stickball game . . ." Sutton, *Cue* and personal interview.
"We'd heard rumors . . ." Ross, *The New Yorker*.
"Norman Mailer, Harvard degree or no . . ." Rochelle Girson, "48's Nine," *The Saturday Review*, February 12, 1949.
"Whenever I make an appearance . . .": Ross, *The New Yorker*.
"a node in a new electronic landscape . . ." Mailer, *Advertisements*, p. 92.
"My first reaction . . .": Sutton, *Cue*.
"I don't think the book is at all a documentary . . .": *New York Star*, August 22, 1948.
"I was painfully aware . . ." Atlas, *The New York Times Magazine*.
Troubled by the cold war: Interview with Beatrice Silverman.
"Italy is pretty bad right now . . .": *New York Star*.
"He on the platform . . .": Norman Podhoretz, *Breaking Ranks*, (New York: Harper & Row, 1979), p. 44.
"Nearly all the townspeople . . .": Norman Mailer, *New York Post*, October 8, 1948.
"He must always work everything out for himself . . .": Norman Podhoretz, "Norman Mailer: The Embattled Vision," in *Norman Mailer: The Man and His Work*, p. 68.
Wallace's showing: Markowitz, *The Rise and Fall of the People's Century*.
Waldorf Conference: Interviews with Beatrice Silverman, Jean Malaquais, Irving Howe, Dwight Macdonald; *The New York Times*, March 27, 1949; *Facts on File*, March 20-26, 1949.
"prominent and empty . . .": Mailer, *Advertisements*, p. 92.
"After *The Naked and the Dead* . . .": Personal interview with Norman Mailer.
"It was like a Chekhov comedy . . .": Sutton, *Cue*.
"with the integration of the worker . . ." Norman Mailer, *Barbary Shore* (New York: Rinehart and Company, 1951), p. 223.
Fifty-dollar surrealist movie: Girson, *Saturday Review*.
Laurel Canyon house: Interviews with Beatrice Silverman and Jean Malaquais.
Goldwyn script and contretemps: Interviews with Beatrice Silverman, Jean Malaquais, Mickey Knox.
"Out there in Hollywood . . ." Norman Mailer, *Existential Errands* (Boston: Little, Brown, 1972), p. 103.
Approaching Clift and Boyer: Interview with Jean Malaquais.
Dorothy Parker meeting and Lillian Hellman's quote: Mailer, *Pieces*, p. 34.
Farmhouse in Vermont: Interviews with Beatrice Silverman, Jean Malaquais, Larry Alson.
"I became successful so suddenly . . .": Mailer, *Pontifications*, p. 123.
"I was two personalities . . .": Christian, *Cosmopolitan*.

V: BREAKING OUT

In addition to sources cited below, information in this chapter is drawn from the author's personal interviews with: Calder Willingham, Daniel Wolf, Mickey Knox, Tobias Schneebaum, Vance Bourjaily, Tina Bourjaily, John Aldridge, Lewis Allen, Larry Alson, Louis Auchincloss, Hortense Calisher, Frederic Morton, William Styron, Judy Feiffer, Chandler Brossard.

Depression and stylistic reversion: Mailer, *Advertisements*, pp. 107-108.
"Here he had this nice, big white house . . ." Brower, *Life*.

Wolf's background: Interview with Daniel Wolf; Kevin McAuliffe, *The Great American Newspaper* (New York: Charles Scribner's Sons, 1978), p. 10.
Adele with Fancher and Kerouac: Interviews with Ed Fancher, Dan Wolf, Vance Bourjaily.
Adele meeting Mailer: Brower, *Life*.
"Adele's an Indian . . .": Atlas, *The New York Times Magazine*.
"That early period . . .": Brower, *Life*.
East village apartment: Interviews with Dan Wolf, Tobias Schneebaum, Vance Bourjaily, Mickey Knox.
Mailer's parties: Interviews with Vance Bourjaily, Tina Bourjaily, Lewis Allen, Tobias Schneebaum, Larry Alson, Mickey Knox, Calder Willingham, Louis Auchincloss, Judy Feiffer.
Village Bars: Susan Edmiston and Linda Cirino, *Literary New York: A History and Guide* (Boston: Houghton Mifflin, 1976).
"Norman found that if you invited people . . .": Ibid., p. 99-100.
"Word had been passed around . . .": Hortense Calisher, *Herself* (New York: Arbor House, 1972), p. 93.
Relationship with Willingham and accent: Interview with Chandler Brossard.
Literary groups: Interview with Vance Bourjaily.
"The fact that I was a Wall Street lawyer . . .": Louis Auchincloss, *A Writer's Capital* (Boston: Houghton Mifflin, 1979), p. 121.
Meeting Styron: Interview with William Styron.
"Mechanical" novel about Hollywood and war stories: Mailer, *Advertisements*, pp. 106-108.
Meeting with magazine editor: Ibid., p. 154.

VI: THE DEER PARK: A NEW PERCEPTION

In addition to sources cited below, information in this chapter is drawn from the author's personal interviews with: Mickey Knox, Robert Loomis, John Aldridge, Vance Bourjaily, Lewis Allen, Tina Bourjaily, Henrique Lopez, Anthony Tuttle, Theodore Amussen, Rose Styron, Walter Minton, William Koshland, Charles Scribner, Jr., Gloria Jones, Peter Israel.

Prologue and eight-part scheme: Mailer, *Advertisements*, p. 154.
"which tickles at the heart of their desire": Mailer, "The Man Who Studied Yoga," *Advertisements*, p. 176.
"a man who seeks to live in such a way . . .": Ibid., p. 185.
Ovington Studios: Edmiston, *Literary New York*.
Fellatio scene: Norman Mailer, *The Deer Park* (New York: G. P. Putnam's Sons, 1955), p. 364.
Rinehart editors not pleased: Interview with Robert Loomis.
Aldridge-Rinehart correspondence and report; Aldridge-Mailer correspondence: Interview with John Aldridge.
"The book needed something . . .": Mailer, *Pontifications*, p. 20.
Rinehart's reception: Interview with Robert Loomis.
Terms of Rinehart contract: Mailer, *Advertisements*, p. 228.
Ten-thousand-dollar advance: Interviews with Walter Minton, Theodore Amussen.
Bad liver: Mailer, *Advertisements*, p. 228.
Marriage to Adele: Interviews with Tina Bourjaily and Tobias Schneebaum.
Mexican house: Interview with Lewis Allen.
"Down in my deep depression . . .": Mailer, *Advertisements*, p. 232.
Idiosyncratic way of walking: Interview with Henrique Lopez.

Interest in bullfighting: Interviews with Lewis Allen, Vance Bourjaily, Henrique Lopez.
Phone conversation about bullfight: Interview with Henrique Lopez.
Description of duplex: Interview with Judy Feiffer.
The Deer Park's progression and Rinehart's demand: Mailer, *Advertisements*, p. 229.
Calling Amussen: Interview with Theodore Amussen; Mailer, *Advertisements*, p. 229.
"I don't like *The Deer Park* . . .": Mailer, *Advertisements*, p. 230.
Bennett Cerf's reaction: Interviews with William Koshland and Walter Minton.
Knopf sequence: Interview with William Koshland.
"I think your book was turned down . . .": Letter from James Jones courtesy of Gloria Jones.
Putnam sequence: Interviews with Peter Israel and Walter Minton.
Rinehart's reneging on contract: Mailer, *Advertisements*, p. 232.
"I was out of fashion . . .": Ibid., p. 234.
"Mary Jane . . .": Ibid., p. 278.
John Maloney: Interview with Rose Styron.
Journal of ideas: Mailer, *Advertisements*, p. 235.
"a timid, inhibited book": Ibid., p. 222.
Drugs: Ibid., p. 243.
Reviewers: Ibid., p. 240.
Deadline and mescaline: Ibid., pp. 244-245.
"*The Deer Park* in the last analysis . . .": Orville Prescott, *The New York Times*, October 14, 1955.
"Though it is not wholly successful . . .": John Brooks, *The New York Times Book Review*, October 16, 1955.
"Subpoena envy": *Time* October 17, 1955.
Gill, Cowley, and Hutchens reviews: Mailer, *Advertisements*, p. 246.
Letter to Hemingway: Ibid., p. 266.
Letter from Hemingway: *The Collected Letters of Ernest Hemingway*, edited by Carlos Baker (New York: Charles Scribner's Sons, 1981).

VII: THE VOICE

In addition to sources cited below, information in this chapter is drawn from the author's personal interviews with: Ed Fancher, Jerry Tallmer, John Wilcock, Lyle Stuart.

"I said, 'My God, we are not inferior . . .' ": Sokolov, *Newsweek*.
Wolf's approach to Mailer and stock division: Interview with Ed Fancher; McAuliffe, *The Great American Newspaper*.
"Up until that point . . .": Atlas, *The New York Times Magazine*.
Voice ad: Mailer, *Advertisements*, p. 249.
Circulation manager: Interview with Ed Fancher.
"Someday I'm going to tell my children . . .": McAuliffe, *The Great American Newspaper*, p. 31.
Ideological differences: Interviews with Ed Fancher, Jerry Tallmer, John Wilcock; McAuliffe, *The Great American Newspaper*.
Stock redivision: Interview with Ed Fancher.
"the declaration of my private war . . .": Mailer, *Advertisements*, p. 278.
"What he wanted at the time . . .": Brower, *Life*.
Rosten letter: McAuliffe, *The Great American Newspaper*, p. 27.
Mailer's columns and readers' letters: Mailer, *Advertisements*, pp. 279-234.

"As his moods got blacker . . ." McAuliffe, *The Great American Newspaper*, p. 29.
"Norman, for a socialist . . .": Interview with Jerry Tallmer.
Hemingway clue: Interview with John Wilcock; Mailer, *Advertisements*.
"Well, we may be dead tomorrow . . .": Mailer, *Pieces*, p. 30.
Letter from James Jones: Courtesy of Gloria Jones.
"Nuisance" typo: Interviews with Jerry Tallmer and Ed Fancher; McAuliffe, *The Great American Newspaper;* Mailer, *Advertisements*.
Final stock agreement: Interview with Ed Fancher.
Mailer's father as accountant: Interview with Ed Fancher.
Kicking Seconal and Benzedrine: Mailer, *Advertisements*, p. 331.
Signature "so dim in its fashion that year": Norman Mailer, *The Presidential Papers* (New York: G. P. Putnam's Sons, 1963), Appendix C.
Malaquais's reaction to *The Deer Park:* Interview with Jean Malaquais.
Baldwin's state: James Baldwin, "The Black Boy Looks At the White Boy," *Esquire*, May 1961.
"So it did not seem worthwhile . . .": Ibid.
"I'm willing to bet . . .": Mailer, *Papers*, p. 146.
Algerian bar: Ibid., Appendix C.
"Spanish Lady . . .": Ibid.

VIII: A WHITE NEGRO IN CONNECTICUT

In addition to sources cited below, information in this chapter is drawn from the author's personal interviews with: Lewis Allen, Jay Presson Allen, Chandler Brossard, Leslie Aldridge Westoff, John Aldridge, Rose Styron, Robert Loomis, Lyle Stuart, Irving Howe, Norman Podhoretz, Robert Gorham Davis, Vance Bourjaily, Seymour Krim, Larry Alson, Gloria Jones.

Move to Connecticut: Interview with Lewis Allen.
Getting into shape: Mailer, *Advertisements*, p. 331.
Punching bags: Christian, *Cosmopolitan*.
Bennett Cerf incident: Interviews with Lewis Allen, Jay Presson Allen, Rose Styron.
"When our conversation . . .": Christian, *Cosmopolitan*.
"There always seemed to be tension . . .": Ibid.
Gwaltney letter: Courtesy of Mrs. Francis Irby Gwaltney.
Lyle Stuart visit: Interview with Lyle Stuart.
"the idea of Negroes . . .": Mailer, *Advertisements*, p. 332.
Faulkner exchange and Eleanor Roosevelt reply: Ibid., pp. 333-34.
Quotes from "The White Negro": Ibid., pp. 337-358.
Reaction to "The White Negro": Interviews with Irving Howe and Norman Podhoretz.
"one of the most morally gruesome ideas . . ." Norman Podhoretz, *Doings and Undoings* (New York: Farrar, Straus & Giroux, 1959), p. 157.
"Bored with my own sensibly moderate liberal ideas . . .": Podhoretz, *Breaking Ranks*, p. 47.
"It is the doctrine which . . ." Trilling in *Norman Mailer: The Man and His Work*, p. 122.
"Your whole life is a lie . . .": Mailer, *Advertisements*, p. 503.
Difference between beats and hipsters: Ibid., p. 373.
Jones–Styron–Mailer triangle: Interviews with Rose Styron, Larry Alson, Lewis Allen, Jay Presson Allen, Gloria Jones, Chandler Brossard.

IX: THE MESSIAH AND THE NEW JOURNALIST

In addition to sources cited below, information in this chapter is drawn from the author's personal interviews with: Walter Minton, Bill Ward, Harriet Sohmers, Seymour Krim, Calder Willingham, Mickey Knox, John Marquand, Jr., Jean Malaquais, George Plimpton, Harold Hayes, Clay Felker, Peter Maas, Pete Hamill.

73 Perry Street: Interview with Lyle Stuart.
Borrowing style: Mailer, *Pieces*, pp. 6-8.
"I think if I discovered . . .": Personal interview with Norman Mailer.
"I have been running for President . . .": Mailer, *Advertisements*, p. 17.
Mailer's entourage: Interviews with Seymour Krim, Norman Podhoretz, Pete Hamill, Midge Decter.
Provincetown entourage: Interviews with Seymour Krim, Bill Ward, Harriet Sohmers.
"Mailer arm-wrestled, shadow-boxed . . ." Seymour Krim, "Norman Mailer Get Out of My Head," *New York Magazine*, April 21, 1969.
Sohmers's fight with Adele: Interview with Harriet Sohmers.
"Calder Willingham in a clown . . .": Mailer, *Advertisements*, p. 470.
"Jones has sold out badly . . .": Ibid., p. 463.
Jones's copy of *Advertisements:* Interview with Gloria Jones.
"I wonder if anyone who gets to know [Styron] well . . .": Mailer, *Advertisements*, p. 463.
"Any feud which exists . . .": Myrick Land, *The Fine Art of Literary Mayhem* (New York: Holt, Rinehart & Winston, 1963).
"His judgement of myself seemed so wide of the mark . . .": James Baldwin, "The Black Boy Looks at the White Boy."
"You're the only one I kind of regret hitting . . .": Ibid.
"His moral imagination . . .": Trilling in *Norman Mailer: The Man and His Work*, p. 136.
"ragtag assembly . . .": *The Collected Letters of Ernest Hemingway.*
Move to *Esquire:* Interviews with Harold Hayes and Clay Felker.
At convention: Interview with Clay Felker.
"So, finally, would come a choice . . ." Mailer, "Superman Comes to the Supermarket," *Papers*, p. 59.
"I felt like a drunk marine . . .": Mailer, "An Evening with Jackie Kennedy," *Papers*, p. 84.
Kennedy scenario: Interview with Peter Mass; Mailer, *Papers*, p. 47.
Esquire contretemps: Interviews with Harold Hayes and Clay Felker.
"This piece had more effect . . .": Mailer, *Papers*, p. 60.
"Napoleonic mood . . .": Ibid., p. 87.

X: THE STABBING

In addition to sources cited below, information in this chapter is drawn from the author's personal interviews with: Dwight Macdonald, George Plimpton, H. L. Humes, Anna Lou Aldrich, Seymour Krim, Larry Alson, Jason Epstein, Norman Podhoretz, Barney Rosset, Lewis Allen, Jay Presson Allen, Harriet Sohmers.

Air raid drill: Christian, *Cosmopolitan*.
Taxi incident: Interview with Dwight Macdonald; Macdonald, "Massachusetts vs. Mailer," *The New Yorker*, October 8, 1960.
Birdland incident; "The guy thought I was rude . . .": *The New York Times*, November 15, 1960.

Mayoral campaign: Interviews with George Plimpton, H. L. Humes, Seymour Krim.
Castro letter: Mailer, *Papers*, pp. 67-75.
Mailer's constituency: Interviews with George Plimpton and H. L. Humes.
"fights quickly broken up . . .": Richard Gilman, *The Confusion Of Realms* (New York: Random House, 1963), p. 90.
Dividing guests into lines: Ibid., p. 91.
Adele's comment: Interviews with George Plimpton, Anna Lou Aldrich, H. L. Humes, Larry Alson.
"a thrust near the heart": Benjamin DeMott, "Docket No. 15883," *American Scholar*, Spring 1961.
Adele's state after the stabbing: Interviews with H. L. Humes and Anna Lou Aldrich.
Adele taken to hospital: Interview with H. L. Humes; *The New York Times*, November 22, 1960.
Fallen on glass: Ibid.
"He was depressed. He just came at me . . .": *Time*, December 5, 1960.
"I don't want to see him . . .": *New York Mirror*, November 23, 1960.
"The knife to a juvenile delinquent . . .": *Time*, December 5, 1960.
"I got into quite a scrape": Ibid.
"Let me say that what I did . . .": Brower, *Life*.
Outside Adele's room; "always carried a knife": DeMott, *American Scholar*.
Denies stabbing: Ibid.
"In my opinion Norman Mailer is having an acute paranoid breakdown . . ." *The New York Times*, November 23, 1960.
"Naturally I have been a little upset . . .": Ibid.
"Your recent history . . .": Ibid.
"It is hard to see the purpose of the showing . . .": *The New York Times*, November 23, 1960.
"The guts to let me out . . .": Brower, *Life*.
Bail: Ibid.
Adele "feeling fine": *The New York Times*, December 21, 1960.
"I have no complaint . . .": *The New York Times*, December 22, 1960.
"cheek to cheek, Norman": DeMott, *American Scholar*.
January 12th hearing: Ibid.
Grand Jury indictment: *The New York Times*, January 31, 1961.
Plea of not guilty: *The New York Times*, February 3, 1961.
Agreed to speak at YMHA: YMHA contract files.
Size of audience: *The New York Times*, February 6, 1961.
Background of poems: Mailer, *Existential Errands*, pp. 198-204.
"So long as you use a knife . . .": Norman Mailer, *Deaths for the Ladies and Other Disasters* (New York: G. P. Putnam's Sons, 1962).
Very bad poems: *New York Herald Tribune*, February 8, 1961.
Show of hands: Ibid.
"Dear Kike . . .": Mailer, *Deaths for the Ladies*.
Ginsberg joins him on stage: *Star Ledger*, February 8, 1961.
Ginsberg's letter: YMHA files.
Mailer pleads guilty: *The New York Times*, March 10, 1961.
Sentence postponed: *The New York Times*, May 11, 1961.
"explosive temper . . .": Ibid.
"The man wasn't good enough . . .": Mailer, *Papers*, p. 64.
Suspended sentence: *The New York Times*, May 11, 1961.
"A decade's anger made me do it . . .": Atlas, *The New York Times Magazine*.

XI: ENTERING THE SIXTIES

In addition to sources cited below, information in this chapter is drawn from the author's personal interviews with: Jack Newfield, Lyle Stuart, Midge Decter, Seymour Krim, Larry Alson, Clay Felker, E. L. Doctorow, Harold Hayes, Pete Hamill, Norman Podhoretz, Anne Barry, Roger Donoghue, Calder Willingham, James Baldwin, Gore Vidal, Robert Gorham Davis, Beverly Bentley, H. L. Humes, Beatrice Silverman.

"At periodic moments in our history . . .": Arthur Schlesinger, "The New Mood in Politics," in Jack Newfield, *A Prophetic Minority* (New York: New American Library, 1966), p. 48.
Background on New Left: Ibid.
"an indifference to ideology . . .": Ibid.
"How could they not dig Mailer . . .": Jack Newfield, "On the Steps of a Zeitgeist," *The Village Voice,* May 30, 1968.
Fair Play for Cuba ad: Interview with Lyle Stuart.
"If Nixon had won in 1960 . . .": Newfield, *Prophetic Minority,* p. 40.
Mailer's JFK letter: Mailer, *Papers,* pp. 65-79.
"At least I can say I went two rounds . . .": Brower, *Life.*
"We managed to empty a room . . .": Atlas, *The New York Times Magazine.*
"The night I met him . . .": Ibid.
Lord Beaverbrook disapproved: Interview with Midge Decter.
Living quarters: Interview with Anne Barry.
"It had the specific density . . .": Norman Mailer, *An American Dream* (New York: The Dial Press, 1965), p. 21.
"Their courtship, their marriage . . .": Tom Wolfe, *The Washington Post Book Week,* March 14, 1965.
"There's been a change in the minds of most men . . .": Norman Mailer, *Cannibals and Christians* (New York: The Dial Press, 1966), p. 199.
Jacqueline Kennedy letter and Mailer's reply: Mailer, *Papers,* p. 87.
"The vanity was no doubt outsize . . .": Ibid., p. 92.
"a quiet parody . . .": Ibid., p. 93.
"If anyone is a leftist, or a radical . . .": Ibid., p. 135.
"Your columnist would warn you . . .": Mailer, "The Big Bite," *Esquire,* November 1962.
Chicago speech: Mailer, *Papers,* pp. 161-174.
Chicago debate: *The New York Times,* September 24, 1962.
"Something pent up for years . . .": Mailer, *Papers,* p. 258.
Liston press conference: Ibid., pp. 264-265; interview with Pete Hamill.
"Who knew any longer where Right was Left . . .": Mailer, *Papers,* p. 267.
Commentary columns: From interviews with Norman Podhoretz and Midge Decter; Mailer, *Papers.*
"Everyone I knew at Harvard read *Esquire* . . .": James Toback, "At Play in the Fields of the Bored," *Esquire,* December 1968.
"Gore, admit it . . .": Mailer, *Cannibals,* p. 104.
All quotes from "Some Children of the Goddess" in: Mailer, *Cannibals,* pp. 104-130.
Vidal's help after Bellevue: Interview with Gore Vidal.
"These statistics of course prove nothing . . .": Mailer, *Pieces,* p. 55.
"Carnegie Hall has a grand tradition . . .": Millicent Brower, "The Novelist Comes to Carnegie Hall," *The Village Voice,* May 30, 1963.
Carnegie Hall reading: Interviews with Norman Podhoretz, Midge Decter, Robert Gorham Davis; Richard Kluger, *Washington Post Book Week,* November 10, 1963.

"We've split . . .": Christian, *Cosmopolitan*.
"You never understand a woman . . .": Ibid.
Beverly Bentley's background: Interview with Beverly Bentley; *People*, February 26, 1979.
Original title on *Papers:* Brower, *The Village Voice*.
"Their subject matter . . .": Mailer, *Papers*, p. 1.
"bold and original voice . . .": *Newsweek*, November 11, 1963.
"He is a fearless performer . . .": *Time*, November 29, 1963.
Galbraith review: *The New York Times Book Review*, November 17, 1963.

XII: AN AMERICAN DREAM

In addition to sources cited below, information in this chapter is drawn from the author's personal interviews with: Harold Hayes, Rust Hills, Anne Barry, Scott Meredith, Donald Fine, Richard Baron, Walter Minton, Christopher Lehmann-Haupt, E. L. Doctorow, John Aldridge, José Torres, Beverly Bentley.

"Since I'd been married four times . . .": Brower, *Life*.
"To have your hero . . .": Ibid.
"She had been my entry into the big league . . .": Mailer, *An American Dream*, p. 17.
Gingrich and the New Puritanism: Interview with Harold Hayes.
"Let a stranger take a bath": *The New York Times Book Review*, March 14, 1965.
Hardwick review: *Partisan Review*, Spring 1965.
Rahv review: *The New York Review of Books*, March 25, 1965.
Epstein review: *The New Republic*, April 17, 1965.
Wolfe review: *Washington Post Book Week*, March 14, 1965.
Fremont-Smith review: *The New York Times*, March 17, 1965.
Aldridge review: *Life*, March 19, 1965.
Aldridge notes: Interview with John Aldridge.

XIII: THE ABSURDIST AND THE MOVEMENT

In addition to sources cited below, information in this chapter is drawn from the author's personal interviews with: Jerry Rubin, Abbie Hoffman, José Torres, George Plimpton, Buzz Farbar, Mickey Knox, Beverly Bentley, Vance Bourjaily, Scott Meredith, Richard Baron, Walter Minton, Helen Meyer, Robert Gutwillig, Anne Edwards, Dotson Rader, D. A. Pennebaker.

"For if Goldwater were President . . .": Mailer, *Cannibals*, p. 41.
Description of Berkeley rally: Interview with Jerry Rubin.
"*My Hope For America* is the worst book . . .": Mailer, *Cannibals*, p. 48.
Berkeley speech: Ibid., pp. 68-82.
"Mailer also showed how you can focus protest . . .": Abbie Hoffman, *Soon To Be A Major Motion Picture* (New York: Berkley Books, 1980), p. 83.
Brandeis lecture: Ibid., p. 83; interview with Abbie Hoffman.
"Three cheers lads . . .": Mailer, *Cannibals*, pp. 84-90.
Backing Torres: Interview with José Torres.
Torres party: Interview with José Torres.
Joe Shaw background and anecdotes: Interviews with George Plimpton, Buzz Farbar, José Torres; Jack Newfield, *The Village Voice*, May 19, 1966.
Fight between Mailer and Beverly: Interview with José Torres.
"he doesn't want to share the limelight . . .": *People*, February 26, 1979.
Provincetown house as gift: Interview with Beverly Bentley.
Description of house: Interviews with Buzz Farbar and Beverly Bentley.

"We live in a time . . .": Mailer, *Cannibals*, p. 2.
Cannibals and Christians: Ibid., p. 4.
"I'm an old-fashioned pot head . . .": *The New York Times Book Review*, August 21, 1966.
"Yet because I could not thrust Provincetown . . .": Mailer, *Pieces*, pp. 9-12.
"Hip hole and hupmobile . . .": Norman Mailer, *Why Are We In Vietnam?* (New York: G. P. Putnam's Sons, 1967), p. 7.
Nichols review: *The National Review*, October 31, 1967.
Broyard review: *The New York Times Book Review*, September 17, 1967.
Aldridge review: *Harper's*, February, 1968.
Samuels review: *The Nation*, October 23, 1967.
Fremont-Smith review: *The New York Times*, September 8, 1967.
Glenn review: *The Village Voice*, September 28, 1967.
Putnam contract: Interviews with Walter Minton and Scott Meredith.
Dell-Dial deal: Interviews with Richard Baron, Scott Meredith, Helen Meyer.
NAL deal: Interviews with Robert Gutwillig and Scott Meredith.
Mailer's lucky numbers: Interview with Scott Meredith.
NAL contract: Interview with Scott Meredith.
Israel's report: Interview with Peter Israel.
Farbar's background: Interview with Buzz Farbar.
"When you're divorced from a woman . . .": Mailer, *Pontifications*, p. 97.
"When I was pregnant . . .": *People*, February 26, 1979; interview with Beverly Bentley.
Description of *The Deer Park* play: Michael Smith, *The Village Voice*, February 9, 1967.
Sheed's review: *Life*, February 24, 1967.
Kerr's review: *The New York Times*, February 1, 1967.
Mailer's introduction to play: Mailer, *Existential Errands*, pp. 61-88.
Block party: Stephanie Harrington, *The Village Voice*, May 4, 1967.
Mailer's dirty joke: Interview with Dotson Rader; Lucian Truscott, *The Village Voice*, February 8, 1973.
Interest in Warhol: Vincent Canby, "When Irish Eyes Are Smiling," *The New York Times*, October 27, 1968.
Origins of *Wild 90:* Interviews with Mickey Knox and Buzz Farbar; Mailer, *Errands*, pp. 94-97.
Shooting *Wild 90:* Interviews with D. A. Pennebaker, Buzz Farbar, José Torres, Mickey Knox; Mailer, *Errands*, pp. 89-122.
"the worst movie that I've stayed to see . . .": Pauline Kael, *The New Yorker*, January 20, 1968.
Shooting of *Beyond the Law:* Interviews with George Plimpton, Buzz Farbar, Mickey Knox, José Torres, D. A. Pennebaker.
"I've always loved the Irish . . .": Canby, *The New York Times*.
Call from Mitchell Goodman: Norman Mailer, *Armies of the Night*, (New York: New American Library, 1968), p. 16.

XIV: ARMIES OF THE NIGHT

In addition to sources cited below, information in this chapter is drawn from the author's personal interviews with: Edward de Grazia, Dwight Macdonald, Abbie Hoffman, Jerry Rubin, Dotson Rader, Scott Meredith, Willie Morris, Midge Decter, D. A. Pennebaker, Buzz Farbar, José Torres, Barney Rosset.

"a piece of yard goods . . .": Canby, *The New York Times*, October 27, 1968.
De Grazia's background: Interview with Edward de Grazia.

Account of the Ambassador speech: Interviews with Edward de Grazia, Dwight Macdonald; Mailer, *Armies*, pp. 24-65.
"Mailer is a figure of monumental disproportions . . .": Mailer, *Armies*, p. 68.
"Yes the hippies had gone . . .": Mailer, *Armies*, p. 143.
Mailer's arrest: Dwight Macdonald, "Politics," *Esquire*, May 1968; interviews with Abbie Hoffman and Dotson Rader.
"It was not inconceivable to him . . .": Mailer, *Armies*, p. 193.
Christ speech: Mailer, *Armies*, p. 240.
Harper's deal: Interviews with Scott Meredith and Willie Morris.
NAL deal: Interviews with Scott Meredith and Robert Gutwillig.
"He reproduces with few errors or omissions . . .": Dwight Macdonald, *Esquire*.
Title from *Dover Beach:* Interview with Willie Morris.
Fremont-Smith review: *The New York Times*, April 26, 1968.
Alvarez review: *The New Statesman*, September 20, 1968.
Kazin review: *The New York Times Book Review*, May 5, 1968.
Gilman review: *The New Republic*, June 8, 1968.
Newfield's recollection of Mailer's one day: Newfield, *The Village Voice*, May 30, 1968.
"I thought it was going to get a very pleasant reception . . .": Canby, *The New York Times*.
Supreme Mix: Interview with Buzz Farbar.
Maidstone costs: Interviews with José Torres and D. A. Pennebaker.
Mailer's orientation speech: James Toback, *Esquire*, December 1968.
Curious Yellow trial: Interview with Edward de Grazia.
Cash Box scenario: Toback, *Esquire*.
Lane Smith scenario: Interview with José Torres.
Rip Torn scenario: Interview with D. A. Pennebaker.
Torn's comment: *Time*, November 15, 1971.
Canby review: *The New York Times*, September 26, 1971.

XV: THE LEFT CONSERVATIVE

In addition to sources cited below, information in this chapter is drawn from the author's personal interviews with: Willie Morris, Jerry Rubin, Robert Gutwillig, Jimmy Breslin, Jack Newfield, Pete Hamill, Joe Flaherty, Peter Maas.

"had not yet learned to talk . . .": Norman Mailer, *Miami and the Siege of Chicago* (New York: New American Library, 1968), p. 63.
"The older Nixon . . .": Ibid., p. 44.
"He was getting tired of Negroes . . .": Ibid., p. 51.
"How else account . . .": Ibid., p. 51.
"Humphrey had had a face . . .": Ibid., p. 208.
"A Christian sweetness . . .": Ibid., p. 122.
"Why of course I know Norman Mailer . . .": Joseph Roddy, *Look*, May 27, 1969.
"McCarthy was the first who felt like a President.": Mailer, *Miami*, p. 131.
"Overcome by the audacity . . .": *The New York Times*, January 28, 1970.
"With another fear, conservative was this fear . . .": Mailer, *Miami*, p. 186-87.
Sheed review: *The New York Times*, December 8, 1968.
Time review: October 11, 1968.
"I'm afraid there's something obscene . . .": *The New York Times*, March 11, 1969.
National Book Award acceptance speech: *Story* archives, Princeton Library.
Poem to his mother: Roddy, *Look*.
Original idea for mayoralty race: Interviews with Jimmy Breslin and Jack Newfield.

Original meeting at Mailer's: Interviews with Jimmy Breslin and Joe Flaherty; Joe Flaherty, *Managing Mailer* (New York: Berkley Books, 1969).
"a hip coalition of the left and right": Flaherty, *Managing Mailer*, p. 15.
"The idea of such a mind . . .": Ibid., p. 22.
"How many of you clowns . . .": Ibid., p. 19.
"Shit, if we can't get seventy-five thousand . . .": Ibid., p. 23.
Breslin wanting out: Interview with Jimmy Breslin; Flaherty, *Managing Mailer*.
"I can't tell what my reactions are to prizes anymore . . .": *The New York Times*, May 6, 1969.
Village Gate scenario: Interviews with Jimmy Breslin, Joe Flaherty, Jack Newfield.
Mailer's speech at The Village Gate: Flaherty, *Managing Mailer*, pp. 99-102.
Million-dollar deal: *The New York Times*, May 13, 1969.
Kennedy mass: Interview with Jimmy Breslin.
Plaza dinner: Interview with Peter Maas.
Mailer-Breslin concession speeches: Flaherty, *Managing Mailer*, p. 188.

XVI: BEGINNING THE SEVENTIES: OF THE MOON

In addition to sources cited below, information in this chapter is drawn from the author's personal interviews with: Willie Morris, Thomas Griffith, Dr. Robert Gilruth, Charles Conrad, Jr., Ralph Graves, George Goethals, Beverly Bentley, Anne Edwards.

Idea of moon shot piece: Interviews with Willie Morris and Thomas Griffith.
Life's exclusive contract with NASA: Interview with Thomas Griffith.
"They were, in short, Wasps . . .": Norman Mailer, *Of A Fire on the Moon* (New York: New American Library, 1970), p. 15.
"He was remarkably gentle . . .": Ibid., p. 20.
"Are you ever worried . . .": Ibid., p. 21.
"The moon—as a real and tangible companion . . .": Ibid., p. 20.
"I think what I felt for the first time . . .": Ron Rosenbaum, "The Siege of Mailer: Hero to Historian," *The Village Voice*, January 21, 1971.
"It was a world half convinced . . .": Mailer, *Fire*, p. 48.
"It could be very well that the Lord would . . .": Ibid., p. 75.
"To write is to judge . . .": Ibid., p. 382.
"I can't write anything in 5,000 words . . .": "Letter from the Editor," *Life*, August 29, 1969.
Time-Life dinner scenario: Interview with Ralph Graves.
Hilton Kramer review: *The Washington Post Book World*, January 10, 1971.
Geoffrey Wolfe review: *Newsweek*, January 4, 1971.
"If you force an aspect of the imagination . . .": *The New York Times Book Review*, June 6, 1982.
"His wife and he . . .": Mailer, *Fire*, p. 382.

XVII: MAILER AND THE FEMINISTS

In addition to the sources cited below, information in this chapter is drawn from the author's personal interviews with: Willie Morris, Kate Millett, Abbie Hoffman, Midge Decter, Pete Hamill, Germaine Greer, D. A. Pennebaker, Dotson Rader, Gore Vidal, Mrs. Francis Irby Gwaltney, José Torres, Beverly Bentley.

Beverly's affair: Interview with Beverly Bentley.
Living on separate floors: Interview with Beverly Bentley.
"His dearest old love . . .": Norman Mailer, *The Prisoner of Sex* (Boston: Little, Brown, 1971), p. 10.

"That was the final split.": Interview with Beverly Bentley.

"But in no uncertainty that the most interesting part of his mind . . .": Mailer, *Prisoner*, p. 12.

Call from *Time* editor: Mailer, *Prisoner*, p. 16.

"Mailer's *An American Dream* is an exercise . . .": Kate Millett, *Sexual Politics* (New York: Ballantine Books, 1970), p. 20.

"a confusing hybrid . . .": Ibid., p. 451.

"Finally outstripping both the Victorians . . .": Ibid., p. 452.

"His eagerness after a sparring partner . . .": Ibid., p. 457.

Gloria Steinem scenario: Mailer, *Prisoner*, p. 19.

Bella Abzug scenario: Ibid., p. 21.

Orson Welles scenario: Ibid., p. 29.

Lunch with Morris: Interview with Willie Morris.

"scientific vanity . . .": Mailer, *Prisoner*, p. 56.

"It is the cry of an enlisted man . . .": Ibid., p. 116.

"No thought was so painful . . .": Ibid., p. 213.

"she saw the differences between men and women . . .": Ibid., p. 224.

Morris's resignation: Interview with Willie Morris and Midge Decter.

Reactions to Mailer's view of feminism: Interviews with Abbie Hoffman, Midge Decter, Pete Hamill, Kate Millett.

Town Hall Debate: Interviews with Germaine Greer, Midge Decter, D. A. Pennebaker; *The New York Times*, May 1, 1971; Natalie Gittleson, *Harpers Bazaar*, July 1971; Rosalyn Drexler and Frederic Morton in *The Village Voice*, May 6, 1971; Germaine Greer, "My Mailer Problem," *Esquire*, September 1971; Diana Trilling, *We Must March My Darlings* (New York: Harcourt Brace, 1977).

V. S. Pritchett review: *Atlantic Monthly*, July 1971.

Joyce Carol Oates review: Ibid.

Brigid Brophy review: *The New York Times Book Review*, May 23, 1971.

S. K. Oberbeck review: *Newsweek*, February 22, 1971.

Anatole Broyard review: *The New York Times*, May 27, 1971.

Vidal-Mailer debate on Cavett show: Interview with Gore Vidal; Mailer, *Pieces*, pp. 55-73.

XVIII: EGO AT THE HALF CENTURY

In addition to the sources cited below, information in this chapter is drawn from the author's personal interviews with: José Torres, Norman Podhoretz, Ralph Graves, Anne Edwards, Pete Hamill, Arthur Schlesinger, Jr., Jimmy Breslin, Dotson Rader.

Torres's boxing training: Interview with José Torres.

"that extraordinary state of the psyche . . .": Mailer, *Existential Errands*, p. 3.

"For several years I toyed with the idea . . .": Norman Podhoretz, *Making It* (New York: Harper & Row, 1980).

"They will play the shell game . . .": Mailer, *Errands*, p. 196.

"When confronted with the full force of *Making It* . . .": Podhoretz, *Breaking Ranks*, p. 264.

S. K. Oberbeck review: *The Washington Post Book World*, April 30, 1972.

Cynthia Buchanan review: *The New York Times Book Review*, April 16, 1972.

"One had to be partial to a man . . .": Norman Mailer, "Some Evil in the Room," *Life*, July 28, 1972.

"Aquarius knew then why . . .": Norman Mailer, *St. George and The Godfather* (New York: New American Library, 1972), p. 86.

"Aquarius . . . sometimes thought . . .": Ibid., p. 102.

"Why bother to look for the CIA . . .": Ibid., p. 104.

"Nixon was the artist . . .": Ibid., p. 138.
"Yes, it was Nixon's genius . . .": Ibid., p. 154.
Gary Wills review: *The New York Times*, October 15, 1972.
Anne Edwards scenario: Anne Edwards and Stephen Citron, *The Inn and Us* (New York: Random House, 1976), pp. 76-79.
Fiftieth birthday party: Interviews with Jimmy Breslin, Arthur Schlesinger, Jr., Dotson Rader, Pete Hamill, Jack Newfield, José Torres; Patricia Bosworth, *The Saturday Review*, March 1973; Sally Quinn, *The Washington Post*, February 7, 1973; Lucian K. Truscott IV, *The Village Voice*, February 8, 1973; Linda Francke, *Newsweek*, February 19, 1973; Mel Gussow, *The New York Times*, February 6 and 7, 1973.

XIX: NORMAN AND MARILYN

In addition to the sources cited below, information in this chapter is drawn from the author's personal interviews with: Robert Markel, John Leonard, Scott Meredith.

Schiller background on Marilyn: Interview with Robert Markel.
Grosset deal: Interview with Robert Markel.
"I wanted to say to everyone . . .": *Time*, July 16, 1973.
"every man's love affair . . .": Norman Mailer, *Marilyn* (New York: Grosset & Dunlap, 1973), p. 15.
"The secret ambition . . .": Ibid., p. 19.
"In her ambition so Faustian . . .": Ibid., p. 17.
Laura Adams interview: Mailer, *Pontifications*, p. 89.
"Since the orphan's presence in the world . . .": Mailer, *Marilyn*, p. 37.
"She needs a double soul . . .": Ibid., p. 100.
"Miller had only a workmanlike style . . .": Ibid., pp. 142-43.
"For who is the first to be certain . . .": Ibid., p. 242.
"witch's turn to the wheel at Chappaquiddick . . .": Ibid., p. 242.
W. H. Allen's allegations: *The New York Times*, June 22, 1973.
Mailer's rebuttal: *The New York Times*, June 27, 1973.
60 Minutes broadcast: *The New York Times*, July 13, 1973.
Lehmann-Haupt review: *The New York Times*, July 16, 1973.
Mailer press conference: *The New York Times*, July 19, 1973; press release printed in *The Village Voice*, August 9, 1973.
Zolotow's suit and Mailer's reaction: *The New York Times*, August 4 and 7, 1973.
Pauline Kael review: *The New York Times Book Review*, July 22, 1973.
MacDowell Medal award scenario: Interview with John Leonard.
Mailer's ad: *The New York Times*, December 9, 1973.
Sour Apple award: *The Berkshire Eagle*, December 18, 1973.
The million-dollar deal: Interview with Scott Meredith.

XX: THE CELEBRITY WRITER

In addition to the sources cited below, information in this chapter is drawn from the author's personal interviews with: Mrs. Francis Irby Gwaltney, Jan Olympitis, Dotson Rader, José Torres, Barney Rosset, Gore Vidal, Jason Epstein, Arthur Schlesinger, Jr., Scott Meredith.

Pauline Kael review: *The New York Times Book Review*, July 22, 1973.
Brustein article: Robert Brustein, *The New York Times Magazine*, June 6, 1974.
"Now our man of wisdom had a vice. . . .": Mailer, *The Fight*, p. 31.
"This man has to be the literary champ . . .": Ibid., p. 35.
"What a perfect way to go . . .": Mailer, *The Fight*, p. 92.
"the instinctive philosophy of African tribesmen . . .": Ibid., p. 38.

"In Africa I had never seen Mailer in such a relaxed mood . . .": George Plimpton, *Shadow Box* (New York: G. P. Putnam's Sons, 1977), p. 259.
Lehmann-Haupt review: *The New York Times*, July 14, 1975.
Michael Wood review: *The New York Times Book Review*, July 27, 1975.
Mailer to Arkansas: Interview with Mrs. Francis Irby Gwaltney.
"I walked in and had on blue jeans . . .": Judy Klemesrud, *The New York Times*, April 16, 1979.
Norris Church's background: Interview with Mrs. Francis Irby Gwaltney; *The New York Times*, April 16, 1979.
"I've usually been drawn to women . . .": Mailer, *Pontifications*, p. 126.
"Charming, funny, witty and very sexy . . .": *The New York Times*, April 16, 1979.
Modeling career: Ibid.
"the greater they are . . .": Norman Mailer, *Genius and Lust: A Journey Through the Major Writings of Henry Miller* (New York: Grove Press, Inc., 1976), p. xii.
Weymouth party: Interviews with Gore Vidal, Jason Epstein.
"I just can't be called anything . . .": Eliot Fremont-Smith, *The Village Voice*, February 6, 1978.
"I really get angry when people call him a chauvinist . . .": *The London Daily Express*, September 16, 1981.
"any belief in reincarnation . . .": Norman Mailer, "The Search For Carter," *The New York Times Magazine*, September 26, 1976.
"He had the silvery reserve . . .": Ibid.
Goodwin party: Charlotte Curtis, *The New York Times*, December 20, 1976.
Monthly payments on novel: Interview with Scott Meredith.

XXI: THE REINCARNATION OF NORMAN MAILER

In addition to sources cited below, information in this chapter is drawn from the author's personal interviews with: Scott Meredith, Howard Kaminsky, Beverly Bentley.

"I felt I might just understand . . .": John Aldridge, "An Interview With Norman Mailer," *Partisan Review*, Spring 1980.
"You can, but first you have to write the book.": Ibid.
"because he embodied many of the themes . . .": Ibid.
Warner deal: Interview with Howard Kaminsky.
Activities in Utah: Atlas, *The New York Times Magazine*.
"I thought these elements of tragic love . . .": Aldridge, *Partisan Review*.
"I was going to write the book in a totally different way . . .": Personal interview with Norman Mailer.
Divorce trail: Interview with Beverly Bentley; *The Boston Globe*, February 2, 1979; April 21, 1979; May 3, 1979; June 24, 1979.
Beverly's appeal granted: Interview with Beverly Bentley.
"I wish a few critics . . .": John Aldridge, *Partisan Review*.
Tim O'Brien review: *New York Magazine*, October 15, 1979.
Earl Rovit review: *The Nation*, October 20, 1979.
James Wolcott review: *The Village Voice*, October 1, 1979.
Joan Didion review: *The New York Times Book Review*, October 7, 1979.
Frank McConnell review: *The New Republic*, October 27, 1979.
Renegotiated contract on novel: Interview with Scott Meredith.
"He was genial but suspicious . . .": John Leonard, "Private Lives," *The New York Times*, November 7, 1979.
"You can never understand a writer . . .": Personal interview with Norman Mailer.

Permissions

Quotation from *Herself* © 1977 by Hortense Calisher is reprinted by permission of Arbor House Publishing Company.

Material from *The Great American Newspaper* © 1978 Kevin McAuliffe (Charles Scribner's Sons) is used with the permission of the author.

Material from "At Play in the Fields of the Bored" © James Toback (*Esquire*, December 1968) is used with the permission of the author.

Quotations from Richard Kluger's review of *The Presidential Papers* in *The Washington Post Book Week*, November 10, 1963, are reprinted by permission of *The Washington Post*.

Material from "Massachusetts vs. Mailer" © Dwight Macdonald (*The New Yorker*, October 10, 1960) is used with the permission of the author.

Material from *Managing Mailer* by Joe Flaherty is reprinted by permission of Coward, McCann & Geoghegan, Inc. Copyright © 1970 by Joe Flaherty.

Material on Beverly Bentley from *People* used by permission of Martha Smilgis/*People Weekly*. © 1979 Time Inc.

Material from "Always the Challenger, Never the Champion" by Brock Brower (*Life*, September 24, 1965) is reprinted by permission of Candida Donadio & Associates, Inc. Copyright © 1965 by Brock Brower.

Material from *The Inn and Us* © 1976 Anne Edwards is reprinted by permission of Random House, Inc.

Material from "The Talent and the Torment" by Frederick Christian © *Cosmopolitan*, August 1963 is used by permission of *Cosmopolitan*.

Photo Credits

Bruce Barton, Mailer at *Advocate:* Courtesy Harvard Club of New York
Portrait of Norman Mailer: Wide World Photos.
Mailer and Beatrice Silverman: Culver Pictures, Inc.
Peace Conference, 1949: Wide World Photos
Styron and Mailer: By permission of Henry Carlisle.
Mailer and Adele with Joneses: By permission of Gloria Jones.
Mailer being led from cell: Wide World Photos.
Mailer and Adele after hearing: Wide World Photos.
Mailer and Wolf at *Voice:* © Fred W. McDarrah 1982.
Mailer being ejected from press conference: United Press International.
Mailer and Muhammad Ali: Wide World Photos.
Mailer at Convention: © Fred W. McDarrah 1982.
Pentagon March: © Fred W. McDarrah 1982.

Mailer, Beverly, and sons: Wide World Photos.
Lego-block model: © Fred W. McDarrah 1982.
Mailer and Breslin press conference: Wide World Photos.
Mailer in Brooklyn Heights home: Wide World Photos.
Mailer boxing with Torres: Ken Regan/Camera 5.
Mailer and Germaine Greer: © Fred W. McDarrah 1982.
Mailer and mother at Four Seasons: Wide World Photos.
Mailer at Algonquin press conference: Barton Silverman/NYT Pictures.
Mailer and Norris Church in Americus: Wide World Photos.
Mailer and Jacqueline Onassis: United Press International.
Mailer with Capote and Rader: Wide World Photos.
Mailer and *Post* headline: Wide World Photos.
Mailer with Norris Church and son: © Gianfranco Gorgoni 1979/Contact.
Mailer, Norris Church, and Lady Jeanne Campbell: Gianfranco Gorgoni 1979/Contact.
Mailer and children: © Gianfranco Gorgoni 1979/Contact.
Mailer and Norris Church at Valentino show: © Bettina Cirone 1982.

Index